Asian Christian Theology

Asian Christian Theology
Emerging Themes

Edited by Douglas J. Elwood

Revised Edition
of
What Asian Christians Are Thinking

The Westminster Press
Philadelphia

Originally published under the title *What Asian Christians Are Thinking* by New Day Publishers, Quezon City, Philippines. Philippine Copyright, 1976, by New Day Publishers.

Revised Edition copyright © 1980 The Westminster Press

Published by The Westminster Press®
Philadelphia, Pennsylvania

PRINTED IN THE UNITED STATES OF AMERICA

9 8 7 6 5 4 3 2 1

Library of Congress Cataloging in Publication Data

Main entry under title:

Asian Christian theology.

   Bibliography: p.
   Includes index.
   1. Theology—Addresses, essays, lectures.
2. Christianity—Asia—Addresses, essays, lectures.
I. Elwood, Douglas J. II. What Asian Christians are thinking.
BR50.W48 1980   230'.095   80–21228
ISBN 0–664–24354–1

For My Former Students
at Four Asian Seminaries
Who Awakened Me to the Asian Context
and Thereby Inspired This Undertaking

Saint Andrew's Theological Seminary, Manila, Philippines
Silliman University Divinity School, Dumaguete City, Philippines
Tainan Theological College, Tainan, Taiwan
Union Theological Seminary, Manila, Philippines

Contents

Foreword
By a Western Theologian

The tremendous value of this book for Christians everywhere in the world is the picture it gives of the creativity, vitality, and variety of Christian thought in the Asian churches today. In this it continues, in somewhat abridged but updated form, the work begun by the first edition, published in the Philippines four years ago. To read these essays, in the earlier volume and in this, is, for the Westerner, to enter a world in which the familiar themes of faith take on quite new meanings against new backgrounds and in which strange themes from other cultures start to shine with Christian meaning. Here, new theology and new social ethics are being formulated which take seriously the orthodoxies of the West—both Christian and at times Marxist—but do not let them become the final arbiters. Here churches are thinking in their own original ways about their mission, their relation to cultures which have not been Christian, and their participation in the struggle for development, justice, and liberation.

The key to all these essays is the contextuality of the Christian message. Shoki Coe describes it as "that critical assessment of what makes the context really significant in the light of the *Missio Dei.*" What happens here is not just the indigenization of a "foreign" message; nor is it only the revolutionizing of an old society. Contextuality means rather the continuing transformation of every society and every human life by the gospel of God's work within it. To discern this and make it known is the aim of all these writers.

They do it very differently. There are unresolved conflicts and even contradictions within the volume that cry out for further work. One seems to see different authors going in quite opposite directions—toward recovery of an ancient cultural and religious tradition in harmony with Christian faith, toward social struggle for a new society inspired by biblical example and liberation theology, or toward a new definition of nationhood informed by Christian substance. In this edition, as distinct from the first, even the careful synthetic theological work of the Christian Conference of Asia no longer comes through as the voice that pulls these diverse directions together. But it would be wrong to ask for synthesis too soon. The cultures of Asia are, thank God, widely varied and so are their approaches to modernization and the human future. What we have here is Christian reflection on many different experiences of what it means to be Christian reaching for a common insight that God will give in his time.

Meanwhile the theological work we read here has nevertheless a certain focus. It differs with different Asian societies, for it is always concrete. The struggle of Indian theology with the religious and the secular dimensions of that society is well reflected. So is the effort of the Japanese church to find the word of God for a nation caught in the tension between an old culture and powerful modernization. The Philippine, Korean, and Taiwanese contributions are windows into the same problematic in their countries. The focus is sharpest, however, in the final section of the book, new to this edition, where churches themselves confess their faith—in Korea, Taiwan, and the Philippines—as a part of their political witness. Here is theology in action, guiding Christians whose freedom and lives are on the line. Here the church speaks as it lives, in mission.

What, then, does the Westerner have to learn from all this? First of all, repentance for the narrowness of his own vision of Christian faith and life, steeped as it is in at least a thousand years of Christianized culture and at least two hundred years of capitalist technology. Second, new and liberating insights into the way of Christ with culture and society also in our own countries. We have had our fill, in the Western world in recent years, of pseudo salvations from the East—whether Maoist, Taoist, Hare Krishna, or Zen. We may have in this book the beginnings of a real word of God to us from the Asian experience.

CHARLES C. WEST

Foreword
By an Asian Theologian

There is a quiet determination among Asian Christians that their commitment to Jesus Christ and their words about Jesus Christ must be responsible to the life they live in Asia today. Such theology is called a living theology. "Which of these three do you think proved neighbor to the man who fell among the robbers?" Jesus asks the lawyer in the parable of the good Samaritan (Luke 11:36). Theology that "passed by on the other side" denies the neighbor himself, Jesus Christ. Asian theology seeks to take the encounter between life in Asia and the Word of God seriously. This is the primary reality. In this encounter the location of theology is found. Faithfulness in mentioning the name of Jesus Christ in any particular locality is the basis for ecumenical theology. Such theology can make its own contribution to the church universal.

Let me illustrate this briefly. The Confession of Faith of the Presbyterian Church in Taiwan has this line: "We believe God gives the human person dignity, ability, responsibility, and a homeland, so that he/she may participate in God's creation and manage the world together with him" (May 1979). An editorial in the *Taiwan Church News* (Aug. 19, 1979) addresses this powerful paragraph to the government:

> For the past 30 years the people have only heard slogans from the government saying "Love the Country" and "Work Together." However, they have never heard or seen any evidence or action on the part of the government wanting to identify with Taiwan as its Homeland. For example, the old men in the Legislative Yuan have not identified with the people of Taiwan. Consequently, they continuously and singlemindedly take the will of the officials to be the will of the people and make laws on this basis. They make laws on the basis of the government's wishes rather than the people's. Is it really possible to make laws for the welfare of the people of Taiwan in this way?

Since for Taiwan the subject of "homeland" is a critical national issue, theology there must reflect on the meaning of "homeland" and its people within the historical context of Taiwan. This is the question people are asking. Why should theology work on a subject which is distant from the people?

Twenty-six Christians came together in July 1978 in Mindanao, Philippines, when tension and misunderstanding between Muslims and Christians was high. The letter written by this group has two sections, addressing Muslims and Christians respectively:

> We ask of you, our Muslim brothers, that our presence among you will be welcomed. We are humbled by much that has marked our past history and we ask your forgiveness for our large share of the blame for the tragic past. Now we wish to come with nothing but ourselves—stripped of pretensions and with no ready-made answers to the problems that hinder a fruitful relationship.
>
> We seek a dialogue of life with you. With God's help we sincerely desire to achieve a more comprehensive viewpoint of his plan that includes all of us as brothers. . . .
>
> To you, our fellow Christians, we wish to point out that the history of this region where we are at work—Mindanao and Sulu—and the prevailing atmosphere in Christian-Muslim relations here, press us to weigh carefully the implications of our presence among our Muslim brothers. From a Christian perspective a dialogue of life implies at least the following: Christians need to take seriously and treat respectfully the Islamic religion and culture of Filipino Muslims. We need to understand and celebrate the fact that the Philippines is a multifaceted and plural society religiously and culturally rich in its diversity. . . .

Here is an expression of the mission of reconciliation in the context of the Philippines.

Theology responsible to a particular locality of culture, history, and people focuses itself upon the question posed by Jesus: "Who do men say that the Son of man is? . . . But who do you say that I am?" (Matt. 16:13, 15). This question comes to Asian Christians, who live in a world of great religious traditions, modernization impacts, ideologies of left and right, international conflicts, hunger, poverty, militarism, and racism. Within these confusing and brutal realities of history the question comes to them. Here the depth of soul of the East is challenged to engage in a serious dialogue with the Word of God. Jesus refuses to be treated superficially.

Students of theology who take seriously Jesus' question will find a genuine fascination in the discovery of theologies developed in cultural zones other than their own. The identity of Jesus Christ is interwoven in a discussion of responsible life in the homeland and of interreligious reconciliation. The theology of the West is as culturally conditioned as the theology of the East. The ecumenical movements throughout centuries show the limitation and promise of this situation. No theology can exhaust "the immeasurable riches of his grace in kindness toward us in Christ Jesus" (Eph. 2:7). But such locally rooted theologies will assume ecumenical dimensions when they are placed together under the light of God in Jesus Christ. "For with thee is the fountain of life; in thy light do we see light" (Ps. 36:9).

In July 1979, Christians in the Federal Republic of Germany wrote a paper titled "Ecumenical Freedom and Responsibility—Plea for an Ecumenical Future." Toward the end of that paper we find this paragraph:

> A church and theology which in this way will expose themselves to concrete situations of temptation, suffering, and obduracy can no longer limit themselves solely to abstract questions of principle, but will train and qualify people for responsible, free action for future generations as well. Perhaps we shall discover a new grasp of reality where our theology is too cerebral, new charisma where we trust too much in bureaucracy, new spirituality where our piety has become banal. We need the ecumenical movement to be freed from Babylon.

This plea is addressed to all of us. The study of the theologies of Asia by Westerners and the study of theologies of the West by Asians may lead to Christianity's emancipation from its Babylonian captivity. Our commitment to the ecumenical movement gives us the inspiration to study the following pages.

KOSUKE KOYAMA

Notes on Contributors

Abesamis, Carlos H., S.J.

A teacher of Scripture and theology at the Loyola School of Theology, Ateneo de Manila University, Fr. Abesamis has been a participant in the Ecumenical Association of Third World Theologians from its inception. He is a contributor to a symposium, with fellow Jesuits, titled *Towards "Doing" Theology in the Philippine Context* (Loyola Papers, No. 9), published by the Loyola School of Theology, Manila, in 1977.

Arevalo, Catalino G., S.J.

Another Filipino Jesuit, professor of ecclesiology and theology of atonement at the Loyola School of Theology, Ateneo de Manila University, Fr. Arevalo is the only Asian member of the Pontifical International Theological Commission. He has lectured widely on missiology and the theology of development and liberation, and has contributed to a variety of journals and symposia, Catholic and Protestant, including the abovementioned Jesuit symposium.

Athyal, Saphir P.

Principal of Union Biblical Seminary in Yeotmal, Maharashtra, India, Dr. Athyal has served as General Coordinator for the Asia Theological Association, related to the World Evangelical Fellowship, and is a member of the Planning Committee for the Consultation on World Evangelization to be held in Thailand, June 1980, sponsored by the Lausanne Continuation Committee.

Cho, Kiyoko Takeda

A Japanese lay woman theologian, Dr. Cho served as one of the presidents of the World Council of Churches from 1971 to 1975. She is a leading historian of modern Japanese thought and teaches in that field at Tokyo's International Christian University. In addition to numerous articles and edited works in Japanese, she has published the following important books on modern Japanese thought: *Ningenkan no sokoku* ("Competing Concepts of Man"), *Dochaku to haikyo* ("Indigenization and Apostasy"), and *Seito to itan no Aida* ("Between Orthodoxy and Heterodoxy"). Her main concern has been with the dynamic and complex relationships between Christianity and Japanese culture.

Coe, Shoki

Dr. Coe served for seventeen years as principal of Tainan Theological College in Taiwan, and more recently as director of the Theological Education Fund, an agency of the World Council of Churches which has existed for the "advancement of theological education in the Third World." In both these roles he pioneered in the renewal of theological education in Asian Protestant seminaries. In 1972, while he was director of the TEF, he and his staff developed the widely influential "Working Policy Statement" on contextualization for the implementation of TEF's Third Mandate. The TEF has since been reorganized as the Programme of Theological Education.

De Silva, Lynn A.

A Sinhalese Methodist clergyman in dialogue with Buddhists, Dr. De Silva is Director of the Ecumenical Institute for Study and Dialogue, Colombo, Sri Lanka, and editor of its journal, *Dialogue*. He has been a member of the Central Committee of the World Council of Churches, and is the author of a number of books on Christianity and Theravada Buddhism, including *The Problem of the Self in Buddhism and Christianity, Reincarnation in Buddhist and Christian Thought, Why Believe in God?* and *The Christian Answer in Relation to Buddhism.*

Fung, Raymond

The Rev. Raymond Fung has been Director of the Hong Kong Christian Industrial Committee, a group active in urban industrial mission in Hong Kong. He is also Executive Secretary of the Division of Mission of the Hong Kong Christian Council. Mr. Fung was one of the speakers at a Workshop on Evangelism sponsored by the World Council of Churches Commission on World Mission and Evangelism, at Bossey in Switzerland, June 1979.

Kappen, Sebastian, S.J.

One of the younger Roman Catholic theologians of India, Fr. Kappen is among the first to have attempted to develop an Asian theology of liberation for India in a systematic way. He is the author of *Jesus and Freedom,* an Orbis publication, and contributed a paper to the seminar on "Theologizing in India Today," held at Pune in 1978. He is Director of the Centre for Social Reconstruction in Madras.

Kim, Yong Bock

Dr. Kim is an associate director in charge of study and research at the Institute for Development and Mission, in Seoul. According to a recent report he was arrested in December 1979, and after being cruelly tortured, has since been released. He is one of a number of Christians in South Korea who have suffered for their stand on human rights.

Koyama, Kosuke

Professor of ecumenics and world Christianity at Union Theological Seminary, New York, and formerly Executive Director of the Association of Theological Schools in Southeast Asia and editor of the *Southeast Asia Journal of Theology,* Dr. Koyama is well known for his *Water-buffalo Theology,* which grew out of his experience as a Japanese missionary-teacher in Thailand from 1960 to 1968. His latest books are titled *No Handle on the Cross* and *Three Mile an Hour God.*

Lee, Jung Young

Associate professor of religious studies and humanities at the University of North Dakota, Dr. Lee is a North Korean by birth. He earned his Th.D. from Boston University and is the author of many volumes, including *The I: A Christian Concept of Man, Theology of Change: A Christian Concept of God from an Eastern Perspective,* and other works linking theology, philosophy, and history of religions.

Nacpil, Emerito P.

Executive Director of the Association of Theological Schools in Southeast Asia and editor of the *Southeast Asia Journal of Theology,* Emerito Nacpil was formerly president of Union Theological Seminary in Manila, and has been a member of the Faith and Order Commission as well as the Central Committee of the World Council of Churches. He is author of the book *Mission and Change,* coeditor of *The Human and the Holy: Asian Perspectives in Christian Theology,* and contributor to a number of symposia.

Ohki, Hideo

Professor of social ethics and president of Tokyo Union Theological Seminary, Hideo Ohki was Visiting Professor of Social Ethics at Lexington Theological Seminary in Lexington, Kentucky, in 1972. His first book in Japanese was on the theology of Emil Brunner (1962). In this book he criticized "Japanese Barthians" and called for the liberation of the Japanese church and theology from "Germanic captivity." He is also senior minister of Takinogawa Church (Kyodan).

Pieris, Aloysius, S.J.

Founder and Director of the Centre for Research and Encounter, between Buddhists and Christians, at Kelaniya, Sri Lanka, Fr. Pieris is also coeditor of *Dialogue,* journal of the Ecumenical Institute for Study and Dialogue, in Colombo. He is a specialist in Buddhist philosophy and was a resource person at the Asian Theological Conference of Third World Theologians held in Wennappuwa, Sri Lanka, in January 1979.

Rayan, Samuel, S.J.

Professor and Dean of Theology at the Vidyajyoti Institute in Delhi, Fr. Rayan is one of the Roman Catholic members of the Faith and Order Commission of the World Council of Churches. He has lectured widely on the theme of "Justice and the Bible" in India, Malaysia, Thailand, Italy, and the United States, and was Visiting Professor at Maryknoll Seminary, Maryknoll, New York, in 1977. He earned his doctorate in theology from the Gregorian University in Rome. He is author of *The Holy Spirit: Heart of the Gospel and Christian Hope,* an Orbis publication.

Samartha, Stanley J.

A former principal of Serampore College, Calcutta, Dr. Samartha now directs the World Council of Churches' study unit on Dialogue with People of Other Living Faiths and Ideologies. He is author of *The Hindu Response to the Unbound Christ, The Hindu View of History,* and *The Courage for Dialogue,* and editor of a whole series of volumes emerging from interfaith dialogues sponsored by the WCC. These include *Living Faiths and Ultimate Goals* and *Faith in the Midst of Faiths: Reflections on Dialogue in Community.*

Song, Choan-seng

Dr. Song is Associate Director of the Department of Faith and Order of the World Council of Churches, and was formerly principal of Tainan Theological College, in Taiwan. He is author of *Christian Mission in Reconstruction: An Asian Attempt* and *Third-Eye Theology: Theology in Formation in Asian Settings,* and coauthor of *Asians and Blacks: Theological Challenges.* He has edited a volume on *Doing Theology Today,* as well as other volumes for the Faith and Order Department.

Takenaka, Masao

Professor of Christian ethics at Doshisha University, Kyoto, Japan, Dr. Takenaka has been chairman of the Advisory Group on Urban and

Industrial Mission of the World Council of Churches. He is the author or editor of *Reconciliation and Renewal in Japan* (1957), *Creation and Redemption Through Japanese Art* (1966), and *Christian Art in Asia* (1975). He was Visiting Professor at Union Theological Seminary, New York, in 1962, and at Yale Divinity School in 1973.

Thomas, M. M.
  Director emeritus of the Christian Institute for the Study of Religion and Society, Bangalore, and editor of its journal, *Religion and Society,* Dr. Thomas remains Senior Research Fellow of the Institute. He is a lay churchman of the Mar Thoma Church of South India and past chairman of the Central Committee of the World Council of Churches. He is the author of many volumes, including *The Christian Response to the Asian Revolution, The Acknowledged Christ of the Indian Renaissance, Secular Ideologies of India and the Secular Meaning of Christ, Man and the Universe of Faiths, Salvation and Humanization,* and *Towards an Evangelical Social Gospel.*

Ting, Kuang-hsun
  Currently Director of the Centre for Religious Studies, Nanking University, and Vice-President of the University, he was formerly president of Nanking Theological College, and bishop of the Chekiang Diocese of the Sheng Kung Hui—Anglican Church in China. In August 1979 he visited the United States as deputy leader of the Chinese delegation to the World Conference on Religion and Peace held at Princeton Theological Seminary.

West, Charles C.
  Stephen Colwell Professor of Christian Ethics and Academic Dean of Princeton Theological Seminary, Dr. West has been a missionary in China and a fraternal worker in Germany. Before going to Princeton he was Associate Director of the Ecumenical Institute at Bossey, Switzerland. He is the author of *Communism and the Theologians, The Power to Be Human,* and other important volumes. He has written a Foreword to the volume in hand.

Asian Christian Theology in the Making: An Introduction

Douglas J. Elwood

That Asian Christians are thinking, no one doubts! This fact is well documented.[1] Not only are they thinking; more and more they are speaking out, as titles within the last few years indicate: *Southeast Asians Speak Out; Voice of the Church in Asia;* and *Asian Voices in Christian Theology.*[2] Furthermore, the whole church is beginning to listen to what they are saying. What Charles W. Forman saw already happening in the 1960's is now evident. Here I quote from the conclusion to his book *Christianity in the Non-Western World.*

> Christianity has been breaking with the idea that it depends on a Western base and has been asserting its Eastern identity. . . . From now on the topics for discussion will be centered as much on the implications of Eastern-based Christianity for Western patterns of life as on the older questions. . . . Its new freedom and indigenous nature, however, should enable non-Western Christianity to speak to both the Western and Eastern elements of its environment on its own initiative and terms and not as an echo of Western Christendom. . . . Non-Western Christianity has come of age.[3]

It is not always easy to discover exactly what Asian Christians are thinking. This is especially true, of course, of some of the Communist parts of Asia. To a lesser extent it is true also of the Asian church as a whole, characterized as it is by the widest cultural diversity. Asia is not one but many! To add to the complexity, all of Asia is caught in the vortex of social revolution, and Asian man is searching for a new identity and a fuller human life. The role of Christian theology must be seen in relation both to the cultural past and to the changing cultures of the present.

This volume attempts to bring together from a wide variety of scattered sources a select number of theological essays and statements representing the major cultural strands, Christian communions, and themes under discussion over the past ten years.[4] It is hoped that this collection will help to better acquaint Western churches, as well as other Third World churches, with contemporary Asian Christian thought. Asia's cultural diversity should keep us from expecting to find an easily identifiable "Asian Christian Theology," as we have grown to expect of European, Latin American, and North American theologies, or even as we might anticipate from Africa. What is actually emerging in the Asian church is a variety of Asian approaches to Christian theology, ranging from Indian and Indonesian in the south to Japanese and Korean in the north. When I speak of Asia in general I do not presuppose that Asia is a unity either in culture, social structure, or politics but that, to paraphrase M. M. Thomas, "in spite of its plurality of cultures, political ideologies, and social structures, we can discern certain common features in what Asian peoples are revolting against and are struggling for," which justifies the use of the phrase "Asian theology" in the singular.[5] When Asian Christians theologize as part of the universal church responding to its situation in Asia, there is a contribution to Christian theology which may rightly be called *Asian* theology.

The major development of Asian Christian theology, taken as a whole, has been in the past decade. Many of the earlier attempts, especially in India, had foundered on the rocks of a syncretism which was in vogue in the 1920's and 1930's.[6] An Indian Christian, G. V. Job, writing in 1938, said, "The Christian movement in India has no theology, not even an indigenous heresy to show that serious thoughts . . . are simmering in its mind."[7] Some of the Asian church leaders at the Bangkok Assembly of the East Asia Christian Conference, in 1950, expressed suspicion of all attempts to express the Christian gospel in the thought forms of Asian cultures. American theologian Walter Horton, writing in 1955, predicted that it would be "at least another generation" before Asian theological writings would "begin to influence the thought of Christendom at large."[8] Winburn Thomas, writing about the same time, agreed, saying that "thus far, most of the theological contributions of Asian Christian scholars have been mere rewrites of Western theology."[9] To the extent that this was true in the 1950's, it was due in part to the fear of syncretism and to the sheer youthfulness of most of the Asian churches.

That Asian theology is now recognized as coming into its own, less than a generation after Horton and Thomas wrote their comments, is due in part to the fact that the Western church has begun to transcend its "Western parochialism."[10] Robin Boyd, in his assessment of Indian theology, concludes by saying: "Indian Christian theology has arrived! It is far from negligible in volume, is marked by a lively concern to grapple with the problems of witnessing to the gospel in the Indian cultural environment, and represents a wide variety of traditions and viewpoints."[11] Charles Germany, in his treatment of Protestant theologies in Japan from 1920 to 1960, says, "The time has now come . . . for a mature church and a mature theology to enter into a painful and dangerous process of incarnation in Japanese society."[12] Paul Schilling, writing about theologians in Southeast Asia, says that "with creative power and openness to new insights they are now beginning to develop their distinctive contributions. . . . They can be expected to enrich Christian thought, East and West, with new understandings and illuminating ways of expressing God's truth for our time."[13] Here, then, are three positive assessments by Western theologians of theological achievements in the three principal regions of Asia—South, Southeast, and Northeast Asia.

While Western theologians are beginning to recognize the maturity of Asian Christian thought and welcome its contribution to the *oikoumenē,* they may not all sense the urgency of learning from the experience of the Asian church, a point expressed in different ways by leading Asian churchmen. T. K. Thomas, who is Literature Secretary for the Christian Conference of Asia, in a recent talk he gave in the United States, observed that "the credibility of Western Christianity is at a low ebb." Lynn de Silva of Sri Lanka, a Methodist minister and student of Buddhism, has said that "Christianity in the West is desperately in need of help, and it is the Third World that may provide this help."[14] Bishop Paulos Gregorios of the Indian Orthodox Church—Asia's oldest church —boldly declares that Western Christian theology is bankrupt and doomed to collapse.[15] The Nairobi Assembly of the World Council of Churches, in the Section Report on "What Unity Requires," spoke about new conflicts concerning the shape of theology "as the churches of Asia, Africa, and Latin America challenge the long dominance of Greek and Latin forms of thought."[16] In India the cry for liberation from Western thought came early with the "Rethinking Group," led by lay theologian P. Chenchiah.[17] Although it came somewhat later in Japan, a similar note was struck by one of the younger theologians, Prof. Hideo Ohki, when he pleaded, "Deliver Japanese theology from Germanic captivity!"[18] The Catholic novelist Shusaku Endo has been saying the same thing in a number of novels in which he expresses his uneasiness about the "Western dress" of Japanese Christianity.[19]

It has been well said by an editor of *The Christian Century* that "systematic theology, by and large, remains in a state of Teutonic captivity. The Aryan bias of Christian doctrine is perhaps the most serious intellectual obstacle to full ecumenical fellowship with the younger churches, to their own theological creativity, and to Christian evangelism in Asia, Africa, and Latin America."[20] Setting aside their earlier reluctance to "do theology" contextually, Asian Christian leaders reached a consensus at a consultation sponsored by the Christian Conference of Asia, in 1965, where they frankly acknowledged that "the Asian churches so far, and in large measure, have not taken their theological task seriously enough, for they have been largely content to accept the ready-made answers of Western theology or confessions." But today, the statement continues, "we can look for the development of authentic living theology in Asia," a theology that will "speak to the actual questions men in Asia are asking in the midst of their dilemmas; their hopes, aspirations, and achievements; their doubts, despair, and suffering." For "we believe that Christ has more of his truth to reveal to us as we seek to understand his work among men in their several Asian cultures, their different Asian religions, and their involvement in the contemporary Asian revolution."[21]

CONTEXTUAL THEOLOGY IN ASIA

Contextualization, as defined by the Theological Education Fund Committee (now the Programme of Theological Education), is "the capacity to respond meaningfully to the gospel within the framework of one's own situation."[22] The historic TEF statement, implementing the Fund's Third Mandate, points out that the basic truth in the older concept of "indigenization" is retained in the newer concept, that is, the idea of making Christ "at home" in a particular place and time, of letting the gospel "take root" in the environment. But contextualization moves beyond the limitation of indigenization, partly because the latter usually suggests mere adaptation of a Western interpretation of the gospel. Here I quote directly from the TEF statement:

> Contextualization has to do with how we assess the peculiarity of Third World contexts. Indigenization tends to be used in the sense of responding to the Gospel in terms of a *traditional culture*. Contextualization, while not ignoring this, takes into account the process of secularity, technology, and the struggle for human justice, which characterize the *historical moment* of nations in the Third World.[23] (Italics added)

In other words, a new concept is needed because a new situation demands it. The old concept is too static, too provincial. Contextualization is a dynamic concept focusing not only on cultural and social aspects of the environment but also on economic, political, and ecological aspects. Roman Catholics and Protestants—mainline and conservative—

are now united in a common concern for the contextualization of the gospel.

A process of decontextualizing appears to be necessary before the recontextualizing can properly begin. All of us have received the Christian message in some already-contextualized form. Philippine Christianity, for example, is largely an accommodation to Hispanic and/or American cultural forms. The temptation of the Asian Christian is to try to contextualize a secondhand expression of the faith. D. T. Niles once expressed this concern in a brilliant image. Christianity in Asia, he said, is like a "potted plant" which has been transported without being transplanted. In his words, "the Gospel is a seed sown in the soil of culture. The plant bears the mark both of the seed and the soil. There is one Gospel; there are many 'Christianities.' In Asian countries, Christianity is a potted plant which needs to be rooted in the cultural soil of the East."[24] Kosuke Koyama, using a similar figure, points out that in contextualizing the Christian faith we do not begin with "adjustments to a transplantation"—like the transplanting of a grown tree from Amsterdam to Djakarta, or from New York to Manila—but with "locating the *living seed* of faith in what was received," then guarding, watering, and nurturing it as it roots itself in the native soil.[25]

There is an important difference, of course, between "contextual" theology and "nativistic" theology. Paul Devanandan of India once spoke pointedly of this distinction in saying that the task of Christian theology in Asia is not to work out a Christian expression of, say, Hinduism or Buddhism, but to effect an Asian expression of Christianity. "We seek neither to Hinduize Christianity nor to Christianize Hinduism," he says. "Our goal is not a Christian expression of Hinduism but an Indian expression of Christianity."[26] In other words, theology's responsibility is not so much to restate Asian traditions in terms of Christian faith as to restate the Christian faith in terms of Asian traditions. The same is true of Asian sociopolitical realities today. The TEF statement on contextualization, already quoted, carefully distinguishes between authentic and false forms of contextualizing:

> False contextualization yields to *uncritical* accommodation, a form of culture faith. Authentic contextualization is always *prophetic,* arising out of a genuine encounter between God's Word and His world, and moves toward the purpose of challenging and changing the situation through rootedness in and commitment to a given historical moment.[27]

Authentic contextualizing, therefore, never implies an easy accommodation, for it challenges the very context by the power of the gospel. On the personal level the mandate for contextualization calls each of us to fuller obedience to Christ in our own context—to be "not conformed to this world but transformed by the renewal of our minds," to quote St. Paul. Contextualization in its genuine expression is the cultural and political perspective of discipleship.

There are risks involved. One is the danger in an exaggerated emphasis on a particular cultural experience that leads to exclusivism in relation to the church ecumenical. Contextual relevance, while necessary, should not be for its own sake but always for the sake of the mission and task of the church in the world and in history. A contextual theology must be ecumenically oriented. Mutual correction and mutual enrichment are the great values of an ecumenical approach. As Dr. Visser 't Hooft once said, "Every historical form in which Christianity has expressed itself needs to be challenged by other forms of expression in order that it may not become frozen, that it may remember its own limitations."[28] It is especially true today that Western forms of Christianity need to be questioned from the point of view of an Asian Christianity. While allowing the gospel to speak meaningfully to particular cultures, we must at the same time seek to avoid the kind of captivity to particular cultures or class interests which blunts the church's faithfulness as a messenger of the gospel. Warning of the danger of exclusivism, M. M. Thomas, Asia's foremost lay theologian, says that although ecumenism should not be confused with foreign imposition, on the other hand "isolation is impossible, and undesirable even if it were possible."[29] "We need each other," says the Nairobi Assembly report on "Confessing Christ Today"—we need each other "to regain the lost dimensions of confessing Christ and even to discover dimensions unknown to us before."[30]

There is likewise a danger that in our preoccupation with the "context," we may lose sight of the "text"—the "Word that became flesh." Shoki Coe has given us a useful guideline for balancing the need for both relevance and faithfulness, in the formula, "Faithful to the text, relevant to the context." By the "text" he refers to all that gives authority and authenticity to the Christian message and the Christian life. By the "context" he means the total situation in a particular place and time. He insists that faithfulness and relevance are equally necessary to any responsible handling of the "text" in its total context.[31]

There is the further danger of allowing the gospel to become an ideological tool. To take an obvious example, we may use Marxist theory as a tool of social analysis, but as Christians we cannot embrace the Marxist philosophy and world view. When we do so we run the risk of making the Christian faith an instrument of Marxist ideology. As Filipino theologian Antonio Lambino puts it, "Christianity is not fully compatible with any ideology of which a 'this-worldly utopia' is an essential part, whether that ideology be capitalist or socialist."[32]

The mandate is clear and the risks are ever present. But they are risks that have to be taken. Dangerous or not, the theological task of contextualizing Christian faith and life must be accepted as part of our calling and commitment to Jesus Christ. Contextualization is not just a fad. In the language of the TEF statement, it is "a theological necessity demanded by the incarnational nature of the Word."[33] Theology is always a human effort to grasp and express the meaning of the revelation. There is a "changing" element and a "changeless" element in Christian faith. This distinction reminds us that the forms and structures—including the conceptual forms—in which the Christian message has come to Asia, for example, are not in themselves sacred. In St. Paul's language, they are only "earthen vessels"—clay pots in which the "treasure" we call the gospel is carried. "We have this treasure in clay pots," he writes to the Corinthian Christians (II Cor. 4:7), "to show that the transcendent power belongs to God and not to us." Part of our theological task is to replace the clay pots, where necessary, with more suitable ones so that the treasured message may speak more meaningfully to Asians in terms of their own cultural and historical experience. It is the revelatory message that is to be contextualized, and not just a Western interpretation of it. What is clearly called for, then, is a more direct contact between the biblical faith and Asian experience.

No reader who is conscious of the ecumenical character of the church will look in this volume only for esoteric or exotic themes never before treated by Christian thinkers. If many of the readings are concerned with themes and issues that preoccupy the mind of the whole church in every place, this is not at all surprising. It is due to the global nature of the issues that affect people living in the Third World, and partly also to the impact of the Asian church on the ecumenical movement, as well as to the positive influence of that movement in the Asian church. For a number of years now, the ecumenical movement has been stressing the point that the kind of unity we are seeking is a unity in diversity and not a bland uniformity, each member body through its distinctive heritage contributing to the wholeness of the *oikoumenē*. If Christian theology is to become truly ecumenical, it must express the mind of the whole church in every place. The best Asian theologians see it in this way, not that they are working out "a theology for Asian Christians only"—as necessarily opposed to a European theology, for example—but that they are making possible an Asian development of ecumenical theology—a property of no particular nation or continent or hemisphere, but the heritage of the whole church.

It is equally important that Asian perspectives in Christian theology appear not as a mere appendage to Western theology, still less as a mere adaptation of Western theology to Asian contexts. Rather, it is to be seen as an integral part of the theology of the church ecumenical. Western Christian thought is now only one contribution to the whole, alongside Asian, African, and Latin American contributions. Philip Potter, when asked to describe his vision of the ecumenical church, made this striking reply: "We need to learn together how to celebrate life in all its dimensions—to bring together the contribution of Asian piety, the African sense of community, and the Latin American preoccupation with liberating people from clinging systems of thought and life, and to blend these with the more well-known traditions of Europe and North America."[34] Third World insights into the meaning of the Christian faith are indispensable, and we are already feeling their impact.

It will be evident that a number of the writers in this volume deal with ecumenical themes from uniquely Asian perspectives. These must be judged "in the light of the mission of the church in Asia," says M. M. Thomas, "and need not be brought to any other bar of judgment."[35] Nor must the new theology in Asia necessarily take the form of "systematic" theology if by this is meant the construction of comprehensive, logical systems whose parts stand or fall together. Even if this were the appropriate model, it may not be the proper time. The church fathers came *after* the Apologists! Oral theology, which arises as tools for confessing the faith in specific situations, is often fragmentary and partial in character. It is the raw material for systematic theology. In any case, adds Thomas, taking a lesson from Western thought beginning with Søren Kierkegaard, "we have realized the deadening effect of total systems of thought on human creativity in any field of life, and we are justly suspicious of premature systematization and synthesis."[36] What is "living theology," after all? he asks, echoing the historic 1965 Consultation of the EACC in Kandy, Sri Lanka. It is "the manner in which a church confesses its faith and establishes its historical existence in dialogue with its own environment."[37] Dr. Thomas sees the task of Christian theology in Asia as response to the challenge of resurgent religions and secular faiths and to the new climate of thought and feeling which are part of the Asian social revolution as a whole.

RECENT ASIAN THEOLOGICAL CONSULTATIONS

If theological colloquia are signs of vitality, then the past three years have yielded new growth. In addition to a number of significant seminars and conferences at the national or ethnic level—such as the Roman

Catholic Seminar on "Theologizing in India Today," held in Pune, October 1978,[38] and the Chinese Theologians' Colloquium in Hong Kong, February 1979[39]—at least four important international consultations have been organized in Asia between the years 1977 and 1979.[40] In March 1977, Manila hosted an international Consultation on Theological Education for Ministry in Asia, which had the widest sponsorship of any Protestant/Anglican conference of its kind yet held in Asia. It was jointly sponsored by three regional theological associations—the Association of Theological Schools in Southeast Asia, the Northeast Asia Association of Theological Schools, and the India-Sri Lanka Board of Theological Education—together with the Christian Conference of Asia and the Theological Education Fund. One hundred and ten theological teachers, administrators, and students attended, representing fourteen Asian countries, including Australia and New Zealand. Although this was a Protestant/Anglican conference, Roman Catholics and Independent Catholics (Philippines) were among the speakers, consultants, and worship leaders. The stated purpose of the consultation was to seek answers to three major questions: (1) whether or not there is emerging in the Asian scene some consensus on the nature and agenda of the theological task in Asia; (2) what forms of Christian ministry must be developed to carry out this task; and (3) what kind of theological formation is needed to do it. The central focus was on what it means to be authentically human, and three workshops were organized around Asian man's sense of the sacred, his experience of nature, and his responsibility for society and history. Others have talked in the recent past about the "humanity" of God. Here the focus was upon the "holiness" of the human. Included in this volume is the Workshop Report on "Man and Nature" (No. 9). The full report of the Consultation is published under the title *The Human and the Holy: Asian Perspectives in Christian Theology* (edited by E. P. Nacpil and D. J. Elwood; Orbis Books, 1980). As an extension of the Manila Consultation a series of smaller colloquia on Asian Perspectives in Christian Thought are projected by the Association of Theological Schools in Southeast Asia with the cooperation of the Commission for Theological Concerns of the Christian Conference of Asia. The first of these was held in Bangkok, March 31 to April 6, 1980, under the theme "Methodology and Context in Doing Theology in Asia."

The Asia Theological Association, based in Taipei and related to the World Evangelical Fellowship, held its fifth consultation in Singapore, November 1978. The meeting was held in conjunction with a Pan-Asian Christian Education Seminar under the same sponsorship. Ninety theologians and one hundred Christian educators were present, representing sixteen Asian countries, including Australia and New Zealand. The theme was "The Gospel and Culture," echoing the larger consultation at Willowbank, Bermuda, held in January of the same year and sponsored by the Theology and Education Group of the Lausanne Committee for World Evangelization. Papers were presented on such topics as Contextualization and Syncretism, the Gospel and Islam, the Gospel and Buddhism, the Gospel and Hinduism, the Gospel and Communism, and the Gospel and Secularism. The official report will be published in book form in 1980.

A Roman Catholic International Colloquium on Contextual Theology was held in Manila, June 1978. It was organized by the Association of Catholic Universities of the Philippines in cooperation with the Missionswissenschaftliches Institut, Aachen, West Germany. Limited to East Asia and the Pacific regions, it brought together thirty-five theologians representing Japan, Korea, Taiwan, Indonesia, and Melanesia, as well as the Philippines. Two Protestant theologians were invited to participate. The central question before the Colloquium was, "How can Christianity become part of Asia?" This was the first time theologians from Roman Catholic theological institutions in Asia had come together. Follow-up colloquia are anticipated. The official report of this Colloquium is published in a special issue of *Philippiniana Sacra,* XIV, 40 (1979).

The Asian Conference of Third World Theologians, meeting in Wennappuwa, near Colombo, Sri Lanka, in January 1979, received the most publicity outside of Asia because, although it was organized in Asia by Asians, it was sponsored by the Ecumenical Association of Third World Theologians. The Christian Conference of Asia's Commission on Theological Concerns (Protestant/Anglican) and the Office of Human Development of the Federation of Asian Bishops' Conferences (Roman Catholic) were the Asian cosponsors. The Conference theme was "Asia's Struggle for Full Humanity: The Search for a Relevant Theology." Although the first of its kind in Asia, this is the third such conference of a five-year program, following Dar es Salaam, Tanzania, in 1976, and Accra, Ghana, in 1977. A fourth conference was held in Sao Paulo, Brazil, in February 1980, and finally an intercontinental Third World conference is scheduled for 1981. At the 1979 Asian Conference seventy-three participants represented eleven Asian countries and included theologians, church leaders, and people from grass-roots organizations. The Conference was unique in beginning with a three-day "live-in" experience in villages, slums, and plantations to sharpen the delegates' awareness of the Asian realities and to provide the starting point of the discussions. The delegates agreed to organize an Ecumenical Fellowship of Asia. Although this Conference was "ecumenical" in spirit, only twenty-nine of the seventy-three delegates were Protestant and only one was Orthodox. The Final Statement of the Asian Conference is included in this volume (No. 8). The full report is published by Orbis Books (1980), with the Conference theme as the title: *Asia's Struggle for Full Humanity: The Search for a Relevant Theology.*

RANGE AND SCOPE OF THIS COLLECTION

All the contributions to this volume are written by living Asian theologians. This at once eliminates, unfortunately, some important writings such as those of the late Paul Devanandan, D. T. Niles, and others. Also, most of the essays were written during the last ten years. These are necessary delimitations so as to reduce the collection to the scope of a single volume. This method has enabled us to select from among the best material now available in English and written by living theologians, and to bring together essays and statements from widely scattered sources not ordinarily to be found in any one library. The readings here included are chosen from among hundreds, as the bibliographies indicate. Considerations of geographical representation and thematic distribution also loomed large in the selecting process. Some good articles had to be omitted because they were either too general or too highly specialized for our target audience; others because there were more than enough essays on some themes and too few in other subject areas.

A glance at the Contents will show that the readings are wide-ranging, from discussions of contextual theology in Asia to the classical Christian themes of God, man, and Christ, and to contemporary theological issues including theology of mission, religious pluralism, development, and liberation. Some of the themes, like contextual theology and theology of religious pluralism, though quite new to most Western theologians, have been central concerns for many years to a small number of Asian theologians. It should be understood that neither the inclusion nor the exclusion of any essay in this collection means that the editor, the sponsoring association, or the publisher necessarily agrees, or disagrees, with its point of view. The aim has been to make the collection as widely representative as possible of Christian theological pluralism in Asia today. A few of our authors are not at the moment living in Asia, which may raise the question as to what is an "Asian" theologian. The answer arising from this study is that he or she is not necessarily a theologian now living in Asia. Some of the best contextual Asian theology is being done by Asians who grew up in Asia but are now living outside of Asia proper, such for example as J. Y. Lee, C. S. Song, and Kosuke Koyama. The important point is that the essays selected are written out of an Asian consciousness and are relevant to the Asian scene today.

While there is obvious value in a comprehensive approach to the study of Asian theology, in keeping with the growing sense of Asian solidarity, this should not take the place of a country-by-country approach. Notable examples of the latter include the study of Indian theology by Robin Boyd, and of Japanese theology by Charles Germany.[41] Three comprehensive collections of Asian theological writings have appeared, one in 1968, edited by Georg F. Vicedom, *Beiträge zur systematischen Theologie,* which is Volume III of an anthology of Third World theologians from Africa, Latin America, and Asia including both systematic and biblical essays.[42] This third volume was published in English translation in 1972 under the title *Christ and the Younger Churches.*[43] Four Asian contributions are included, from Kosuke Koyama, Kazoh Kitamori, C. S. Song, and M. S. Rao. More recently published is Gerald Anderson's *Asian Voices in Christian Theology,* a collection of nine essays by as many Asian theologians, all Protestant.[44] Following a historical method, the essays attempt to survey theological developments and trends in each country represented. A third collection was published in Manila under the title *What Asian Christians Are Thinking* (New Day Publishers, 1976), of which the present volume is an updated edition.

In addition, two special collections are worthy of mention. Horst Burkle and Wolfgang Roth coedited, in 1966, a selection of essays on Indian Christian theology under the title *Indische Beiträge zur Theologie der Gegenwart.*[45] Among the authors are four Indian theologians: Surjit Singh, Herbert Jai Singh, Russell Chandran, and John Arapura. An English translation appeared in 1972 under the title *Indian Voices in Today's Theological Debate.*[46] More recently Japanese theologian Seiichi Yagi and Ulrich Luz of Germany collaborated in editing a dialogue volume under the title *Gott in Japan: Anstösse zum Gespräch mit japanischen Philosophen, Theologen, Schriftstellern.*[47]

The present volume is an ecumenical collection of Asian theological writings on a comprehensive scale, representing Roman Catholic, Anglican, and Protestant conservative and mainline communions. It is thematically structured and designed to be used alongside any "standard" textbook in systematic theology, as an introductory textbook for a course offering in Asian theology, or a source book on Third World theologies. It is a collection of twenty-nine readings by twenty Asian theologians representing eight Asian countries with an almost equal number of readings from each major geographical region—South, Southeast, and Northeast Asia. Nine of the readings are theological statements from four Asian ecumenical conferences, from national churches and other Christian groups. All the readings are united by the organizing principle of contextuality and by the fact that all are written by Asians.[48]

This collection, however, does not attempt to document all the forms of theological expression in Asia today; for example, important discussions on indigenous liturgy and Asian expressions of Christian spirituality are not represented. In some parts of the Asian church today theological expression is taking unconventional forms, including declarations of conscience and liturgical protests in situations of conflict.[49] This volume includes five of the most recent statements of national churches and other Christian groups from three Asian countries now under martial law. Christian novelists in Japan are protesting the "Western dress" of Japanese Christianity (Shusaku Endo) and exposing the problems of life in a highly industrialized society (Shiina Rinzo). Both are popular writers of contemporary Japan. The poems and plays of Kim Chi Ha, the Korean Christian political prisoner who was sentenced to death under the Park Chung Hee regime, are a striking example of another mode of theological expression which reflects the Asian reality today.[50] Kim, South Korea's leading literary figure, was nominated in 1975 for the Nobel Prize in both Peace and Literature and has been "adopted" as a Prisoner of Conscience by Amnesty International. Some of the most exciting theology is coming out of the Christian study centers for dialogue with people of other Asian faiths, as well as centers for the study of religion and society.

ACKNOWLEDGMENTS

I wish to acknowledge, first of all, my students and colleagues in the four Asian seminaries in the Philippines and Taiwan where I have been privileged to teach, who have inspired me to inquire further into the thinking of Asian Christians. I wish to acknowledge further the several publishers and authors who have granted permission to reprint these essays and documents, full data on which are given on the first page of each contribution. Finally, I am particularly indebted to the editors of The Westminster Press for their interest in publishing an American edition of a collection of essays which first appeared in Asia.

In such a wide-ranging collection of essays one would expect to find a variety of styles. While each writer has been allowed to retain his own style, an attempt has been made toward uniformity by standardizing the spelling, punctuation, and capitalization according to the policy of The Westminster Press.

In no sense can a source book like this be considered final, for Christian theology in Asia is just coming into its own and new books and articles by Asian theologians are forthcoming. It is hoped that this edition of the collection will help to make seminaries and universities outside of Asia more aware of the contribution Asian theology can make to the thinking of the church ecumenical.

NOTES

1. See Hans-Ruedi Weber, *Asia and the Ecumenical Movement, 1895-1961* (London: SCM Press, 1966). See also WCC (World Council of Churches) and CCA (Christian Conference of Asia) documents and reports over the past ten years, as well as the findings of the ATSSEA (Association of Theological Schools of Southeast Asia), NEAATS (Northeast Asia Association of Theological Schools), and their journals.

2. Barbara and Leon Howell, *Southeast Asians Speak Out* (Friendship Press, 1975); Asia Theological Association, *Voice of the Church in Asia* (Taipei: ATA, 1975); Gerald H. Anderson (ed.), *Asian Voices in Christian Theology* (Orbis Books, 1976).

3. Charles W. Forman (ed.), *Christianity in the Non-Western World* (Prentice-Hall, 1967), pp. 140f.

4. One earlier piece is included because of its continuing interest, namely, that of K. H. Ting on "Christian Theism: A Theology of Society" (1957).

5. M. M. Thomas, *The Christian Response to the Asian Revolution* (London: SCM Press, 1966), Preface. Cf. J. Russell Chandran, "Confessing the Faith in Asia Today," *Southeast Asia Journal of Theology,* XVIII, 1 & 2 (1966), pp. 91–94. See also J. A. Veitch on the distinction between "Asian Theology" and "Theology in Asia," in his article "Is an Asian Theology Possible?" *Scottish Journal of Theology,* XXVIII, 1 (1975), p. 27.

6. Compare the Bangkok Assembly of the EACC (East Asia Christian Conference), in 1950, with the EACC Consultation held in Kandy, Sri Lanka, in 1965.

7. G. V. Job, writing in *Rethinking Christianity in India,* by P. Chenchiah and others (Madras: Christian Literature Society, 1938), p. 15. Cf. V. E. Devadutt, "What Is an Indigenous Theology?" *Ecumenical Review,* Autumn 1949.

8. Walter M. Horton, *Christian Theology: An Ecumenical Approach* (Harper & Brothers, 1955), p. 8.

9. Winburn T. Thomas, "Teaching Theology in Asia," *Theology Today,* XIII, 2 (July 1956), p. 201.

10. See Hans-Ruedi Weber, "Beyond Western Parochialism," in his *Asia and the Ecumenical Movement,* pp. 235–239.

11. Robin H. S. Boyd, *An Introduction to Indian Christian Theology* (Madras: Christian Literature Society, 1969), p. 255.

12. Charles Germany, *Protestant Theologies in Modern Japan* (Tokyo: HSR, 1965), p. 213.

13. S. Paul Schilling, "Living Theology in Southeast Asia," *Religion in Life,* XXXIX, 3 (1970), p. 345.

14. Lynn de Silva, in *The Christian News Bulletin,* Study Centre for Religion and Society, Colombo, Sri Lanka (Sept. 1968). Here is the full quotation: "We have, over the years, come to feel strongly that Christianity in the West is desperately in need of help, and it is the Third World that may provide this help. We have still not lost the sense of the numinous, and quietness and meditation are still part of our life. Our contribution to the total Christian community in the world may well be that of restoring a balance between activism and escapism in religion. Come to think of it, it may be good if more of us Asian Christians sat at the feet of a Buddhist monk and learnt the techniques of meditation. 'In quietness and confidence shall be our strength.' "

15. Paul Verghese (now Bishop Paulos Gregorios), *Freedom and Authority* (Madras: CLS, 1974; an enlarged and revised edition of *The Freedom of Man,* published in 1972 by The Westminster Press, Philadelphia), especially Chapters III and V. The so-called "Death of God" theology, says Bishop Gregorios in another place, "marks the final spasm of the Western intellect trying to deliver itself from the paralyzing grip of its basically corrupt Augustinian tradition of theology"—*Indian Journal of Theology,* XVII, 4 (1968), p. 151.

16. World Council of Churches, *Breaking Barriers* (Nairobi, 1975), p. 66. On this aspect of contextualization see especially Robin Boyd, *India and the Latin Captivity of the Church: The Cultural Context of the Gospel* (Cambridge University Press, 1974).

17. See *Rethinking Christianity in India,* referred to in Note 7, above.

18. Quoted by Seiichi Yagi; tr. and cited by Joseph Spae, *Christianity Encounters Japan* (Tokyo: Oriens Institute, 1968), p. 201.

19. See Shusaku Endo's novels, *The Golden Country; Silence; White Man, Yellow Man; A Life of Jesus;* and *By the Dead Sea.* In *Silence,* for instance, the two foreign apostates are symbols of a Christianity which has failed in Japan because it is so stubbornly Western!

20. Alan Geyer, "Toward a Convivial Theology," *The Christian Century,* April 23, 1969, p. 542.

21. East Asia Christian Conference, *Confessional Families and the Churches in Asia* (Report of the EACC Consultation held at Kandy, Sri Lanka, in December 1965). This part of the report was also printed in *International Review of Mission,* LV, 218 (April 1966), pp. 199–204.

22. Theological Education Fund, *Ministry in Context: The Third Mandate Programme of the TEF, 1970–77* (London: TEF, 1972), p. 19.

23. Ibid.

24. D. T. Niles, as quoted in Chandra Devanesen, *The Cross Is Lifted* (Friendship Press, 1954), p. 11.

25. Kosuke Koyama, *Theology in Contact* (Madras: Christian Literature Society, 1975), pp. 67f.

26. Paul Devanandan, as quoted in Eddy Asirvathan, *Christianity in the Indian Crucible* (Calcutta: YMCA, 1957), pp. 95f.

27. Theological Education Fund, op. cit.

28. W. A. Visser 't Hooft, "Accommodation—True and False," *Southeast Asia Journal of Theology,* XVIII, 3 (1967), pp. 5–18.

29. M. M. Thomas, Foreword to Robin Boyd, *Introduction to Indian Christian Theology* (Madras: Christian Literature Society, 1969).

30. "Confessing Christ Today" (A Plenary Document), in *Breaking Barriers: Nairobi 1975* (Geneva: World Council of Churches, 1976), p. 46.

31. Shoki Coe, "In Search of Renewal in Theological Education," *Theological Education* (Summer 1973), pp. 233–243.

32. A. Lambino, "Theology, Social Change and Christian Conscience," *Impact* (Philippines), XI, 11 (Nov. 1976), p. 375.

33. Theological Education Fund, op. cit. (Note 22, above).

34. Philip Potter, as quoted by David Frost, "Interview with Potter," *Frontier,* XVII, 2 (Summer 1974), p. 95.

35. Thomas, op. cit.

36. Ibid.

37. Ibid.

38. For a brief report see S. Arulsamy, "Theologizing in India Today," *Indian Theological Studies,* XV, 4 (Dec. 1978), pp. 370–382. This seminar was sponsored by the CBCI Commission for Seminaries, and was held at Divine Word Seminary in Pune, October 26–30, 1978. Ninety participants from all over India included teachers, students, sisters, and "free-lance theologians."

39. For a brief report see Peter K. H. Lee, "Chinese Theologians' Colloquium," *Ching Feng,* XXI, 4 (1978), pp. 163–167. This colloquium was sponsored by Tao Fong Shan and the Holy Spirit Seminary, Aberdeen, Hong Kong, where the theologians met, February 2–10, 1979. There were forty-five participants, Protestant and Catholic, from Taiwan, Hong Kong, Southeast Asia, Europe, and North America, ten of them non-Chinese specialists in Chinese Christianity.

40. 1977–1979 are the intervening years between the publication of the Asian edition and the American edition of this collection of Asian theological readings. The Asian edition is titled *What Asian Christians Are Thinking* (Manila: New Day Publishers, 1976).

41. See Notes 11 and 12, above.

42. Hans-Werner Genischen, Gerhard Rosenkranz, and Georg F. Vicedom (eds.), *Theologische Stimmen aus Asien, Afrika und Lateinamerika.* 3 vols. (Munich: Chr. Kaiser Verlag, 1965–1968).

43. Georg F. Vicedom (ed.), *Christ and the Younger Churches* (London: SPCK, 1972).

44. Gerald Anderson (ed.), *Asian Voices in Christian Theology* (Orbis Books, 1976). Includes an extensive bibliography and an appendix on "Creeds, Confessions, and Theological Statements of Asian Churches."

45. Horst Burkle and Wolfgang Roth (eds.), *Indische Beiträge zur Theologie der Gegenwart* (Stuttgart: Evang. Verlagswerk, 1966).

46. Horst Burkle and Wolfgang Roth (eds.), *Indian Voices in Today's Theological Debate* (Lucknow: Lucknow Publishing House, 1972).

47. Seiichi Yagi and Ulrich Luz (eds.), *Gott in Japan: Anstösse zum Gespräch mit japanischen Philosophen, Theologen, Schriftstellern* (Munich: Chr. Kaiser Verlag, 1973). Luz was prompted to publish this symposium during his stay as a lecturer in theology in Japan when he discovered that the European way of "doing theology" was being adopted almost uncritically by most Japanese theologians. Contextual in its purpose, the symposium is intended to show what questions the Christian faith raises in Japan, and how far these questions and answers correspond to the existential questions Japanese are asking today. The volume includes, therefore, contributions from six Christians and four Buddhists. Professor Yagi's essay attempts to relate Christian and Buddhist thinking by means of the key concept of "integration." On the basis of an existential interpretation of New Testament texts, he pictures Christ as "the one who integrates."

48. Obviously there are still untapped resources in the vernacular. Some effort was made to learn of these materials, especially in Korean, Indonesian, and Burmese, and to arrange for translations of some of them for this collection. Unfortunately, some of the translations promised have not yet reached me. This accounts for the fact that a few Asian countries are represented inadequately or not at all. It is hoped that in the future the outstanding essays in the vernacular will be translated for English theological journals in the region.

49. Some of these unconventional expressions of theological reflection are found in T. K. Thomas (ed.), *Testimony Amid Asian Suffering* (Singapore: Christian Conference of Asia, 1977); Marianne Katoppo, *Compassionate and Free: An Asian Woman's Theology* (Geneva: World Council of Churches, 1979); Jae Shik Oh (ed.), *Towards a Theology of People* (Singapore: Christian Conference of Asia, 1977); Charles R. Avila (ed.), *Peasant Theology: Reflections by the Filipino Peasants on Their Process of Social Revolution* (WSCF, Asia, 1976); and others.

50. See Kim Chi Ha, *Gold-crowned Jesus and Other Writings,* ed. by Chong Sun Kim and Shelly Killen (Orbis Books, 1978).

PART ONE
Rethinking Christian Theology in Asia

One

The Confessing Church in Asia and Its Theological Task

Christian Conference of Asia

[This statement grew out of the historic Consultation at Kandy, Sri Lanka, convened in 1965 by the East Asia Christian Conference (since 1973 the Christian Conference of Asia). Concerned with the responsibility to confess their own living faith, these Asian Christian leaders boldly declared that "Christ has more of his truth to reveal to us, as we seek to understand his work among men in their several Asian cultures, their different religions and their involvement in the contemporary Asian revolution."—Ed.]

THE COMING OF THE GOSPEL TO ASIA AND THE ASIAN CHURCHES

The gospel, first proclaimed in Jerusalem and Antioch, has come to us in Asia at different periods and in a great variety of ways. It came in "earthen vessels" formed and shaped elsewhere—from the Middle East, establishing the St. Thomas Christians and the Nestorians; from Portugal, Spain, France and elsewhere, establishing the Roman Catholic churches of Asia; from Europe of the Reformation, through individuals and voluntary societies by the Holy Spirit when their churches were not yet awakened to the demands of the missions, and from the denominational churches of the West.

Missionary enterprises began often in close association with Western colonial expansion. Now, however, when Asian nations have emerged from the colonial period, the gospel must be proclaimed to the peoples of Asia by churches that are part of their own nations, speaking from within their life.

The ways in which the gospel came to Asia inevitably brought to the

Extracted from "Statements Issued by a Consultation on Confessional Families and the Churches in Asia." (Convened by the East Asia Christian Conference, December 1965, at Kandy, Sri Lanka.) *International Review of Mission,* LV, 218 (April 1966), pp. 199–204. Reprinted by permission of the World Council of Churches.

Asian churches a heritage of strength and weakness:

Strength—in the gospel message itself; in the witness of lives devoted to God's mission, in evidence of the Spirit's power, in the Scriptures translated into the languages of Asia, and in the growth of communities of believers, knowing themselves as God's people in the world, met by his grace and salvation in Jesus Christ and committed to making his way known among men;

Weakness—in many cases by reason of a long period of missionary tutelage, a too-great dependence on missionary society leadership and finance, a limited understanding of the gospel in pietistic and individualistic terms, and a view of the church distorted by the divided nature of Western Protestantism.

We express our gratitude to God for the fact and the power of the gospel; for its creation among us by the Holy Spirit of churches confessing the Lordship of Jesus Christ; and for our calling to be his people.

We believe that we can best show our gratitude for the heritage into which God has called us in Jesus Christ, by together seeking to be the one church where we have been set in the world, for the sake of the world; confessing in worship, life, and thought the Lordship of Christ over our lives, our churches, and our world.

CONFESSING CHRIST IN THE ASIAN CONTEMPORARY SITUATION

The faith which the Asian churches have to confess in the midst of their nations is that which the church has always held and which is found in the Scriptures of the Old and New Testaments. This faith, continuously confirmed in the spiritual experience of the church of Christ, is witnessed to and safeguarded by the creeds of the early church.

For Asian churches to be confessing churches in the contemporary world of Asia means that they must extend their worship of God from the sanctuary to the secular world; their creeds and confessions from the liturgy to the life of the whole people of God; and their theology from the study or the seminary to the world of Asian thought, philosophy, and religion—the world of the Asian renaissance and revolution.

Such confession by the churches is part of their essential obedience to God in Christ, so that the effort to relate the gospel to Asian culture generally should not be thought of merely as a technique of evangelism and witness. It is the way to discover yet fuller riches in Christ, to appropriate "those things to come" for which Jesus promised the Spirit of truth "to guide into all truth." This enrichment happens as Christians share in what it means for a Buddhist, a Hindu, a Muslim, to know Christ; or when a convert from another religion brings to Christ the depth of his devotion; or when as Christians we reinterpret, to express our own obedience to Christ, the Asian concern for asceticism and renunciation, its wrestling with the meaning of suffering, and its deep mystical experience.

We have inherited the "great tradition" of the gospel from those who brought the gospel to Asia, but we believe that Christ has more of his truth to reveal to us as we seek to understand his work among men in their several Asian cultures, their different Asian religions, and their involvement in the contemporary Asian revolution. In the past we have been too inhibited by our fear of syncretism and too tied to inherited traditional and conceptual forms of confession to make such ventures. Such formulations have been signposts and pointers to the truth, but we have often interpreted them, or had them interpreted to us, as the final word of truth so that we have encamped around them, forgetting that even as people of other times and cultures made their own confession, we too must do the same in our time and culture. When we make absolute the written confessions of the churches of another culture or age, we become incapable of discovering the new depths of truth God can reveal to us in Christ amidst Asian life.

THE TASK OF THEOLOGY IN THE ASIAN CHURCHES

It is out of this contemporary necessity to confess the faith that there arises the task of theology for the churches in Asia. Theology is a living thing, having to do with our very existence as Christians and as churches. We cannot conceive of it in static or neatly defined final terms. A living theology must speak to the actual questions men in Asia are asking in the midst of their dilemmas; their hopes, aspirations, and achievements; their doubts, despair, and suffering. It must also speak in relation to the answers that are being given by Asian religions and philosophies, both in their classical forms and in new forms created by the impact on them of Western thought, secularism, and science. Christian theology will fulfill its task in Asia only as the Asian churches, as servants of God's word and revelation in Jesus Christ, speak to the Asian situation and from involvement in it. Dogmatic theological statements from a church that stands on the sidelines as spectator or even interpreter of what God is doing in Asia can carry no conviction.

A living theology is born out of the meeting of a living church and its world. We discern a special task of theology in relation to the Asian renaissance and revolution, because we believe God is working out his purposes in these movements of the secular world. The Asian churches so far, and in large measure, have not taken their theological task seriously enough, for they have been largely content to accept the ready-made answers of Western theology or confessions. We believe, however, that today we can look for the development of authentic living theology in Asia in the following directions, though only if certain conditions are fulfilled.

In worship and preaching. The churches' renewal will come from a fresh understanding of Christian worship in its full biblical sense, and from their submission to the word of God. In too many churches in Asia, worship is a dull impoverished thing, and preaching is anemic. Living theology must be grounded in a richer and fuller worship life in congregation. Asian churches and theological seminaries must therefore give immediate and urgent attention to better training and retraining of ministers and lay leaders toward this end.

In various institutions for the study of religion and society. These need to be closely related to the life of a confessing church and its problems, and not abstracted in academic retreat.

In certain committed Christian communities. It is important that their discoveries of the Spirit and obedience be made available to the church generally.

In experiments that are geared to the training of Christian laity for witness in their particular world, especially where such training is done across denominational frontiers. It is at this point that the findings of the ecumenical study on the structure of a missionary congregation will have to be applied.

In seminaries. These must radically recast their traditional or their denominationally oriented curricula, to relate the basic theological disciplines to the Asian scene.

THE CONTRIBUTION OF WORLD CONFESSIONAL ORGANIZATIONS

A *confessing* theology, i.e., a theology which is the result of the wrestling of an Asian church with its Asian environment, will naturally not be specifically confessional even though it may be indebted to many confessional traditions. A *confessional* type of theology, inherited by an Asian church as part of its tradition, is usually a source of division; while a confessing theology will undergird the movement toward unity and union in the churches of Asia.

This raises the question of how world confessional organizations can assist the Asian churches in their theological task and in their responsibility to be "confessing" churches.

We note among ourselves, as Asian churches, a regrettable tendency to look elsewhere for financial security. This needs to be watched by

Asian churches in relation to "the scandal of dependency" and by supporting churches and organizations as a possible threat to a church's responsible selfhood. We urge the churches of Asia to give priority to full participation in local, national, and regional ecumenical organizations, though they may be members of world confessional bodies. While membership in a confessional family of churches can assist an Asian church to a sense of belonging to a worldwide family in Christ, and so assist in overcoming a possible isolation, we believe that world confessional organizations should accept as a basic principle that "membership in confessional families, with financial or other benefits, should not weaken or hinder Asian churches from belonging together in their locality or nation."

In particular, we would offer a strong plea to world confessional organizations:

(a) not to strengthen denominational or confessional theological schools in Asia at the expense of creating or participating in union institutions, with whatever special arrangements, such as the "hall system," as may be thought necessary;

(b) to assist in providing the means and facilities for fuller research into Asian cultures in relation to theological education in Asia;

(c) to encourage Asian churches in the confessional family to join with other Asian churches in the nation to make their own confession;

(d) to encourage any Asian church in the confessional family that wishes to unite with another church or other churches to do so; and

(e) to encourage member churches of the confessional family to have a Commission for Ecumenical Study and Action.

Two

Contextualization as the Way Toward Reform

Shoki Coe

[Dr. Shoki Coe, a Taiwanese theologian and pioneer in the development of Protestant theological education in East Asia, shares his reflections on the now-famous "Working Policy Statement" for the implementation of the Third Mandate of the Theological Education Fund, which he helped to formulate in 1972. He shows how the emphasis shifted from "indigenization" to "contextualization," the former tending to be "past-oriented" because it stresses the relation of the gospel to traditional cultures. Contextualization, however, is "future-oriented" in that it is concerned also with the gospel in relation to social change and the historical situation. He knows the risks involved but he insists that these are risks that have to be taken. Contextualization invites a variegated theology. "There is no colorless theology," he concludes. "But there is all the joy of the multiple colors mobilized for the beauty of the new heaven and the new earth which God has promised." This selection is part of a longer essay by the same title.—Ed.]

THE AIM AND PURPOSE OF THEOLOGICAL EDUCATION

It will be seen from the foregoing that the Theological Education Fund, in spite of its comparatively short life of fifteen years, has changed its emphasis from "Advance" (in the First Mandate), to "Rethink" (in the Second Mandate) and now to "Reform" (in the Third and current Mandate). In 1966, at the inaugural meeting of the Northeast Asia Association of Theological Schools, I gave my personal view of how ideas were moving in an address entitled "Text and Context in Theological Education."[1] In these years of search for renewal I had become more and more convinced that theological education, for better or for worse, occurs invariably as interaction between text and context, and out of this

Parts II and III of an article in *Theological Education,* Summer 1973, pp. 237–243. Reprinted by permission of The Association of Theological Schools in the United States and Canada.

interaction the form is shaped. This means that we must distinguish between theological education as such, and the forms it takes through this interaction, because the latter is an ongoing process, varying according to times and places. Reform and therefore renewal should be a permanent concern, as much for theological education as for the life and mission of the church between the times.

Ecclesia semper reformanda. This is especially so in times such as ours when, having reached the end of an era, another is upon us. We are faced with a radically new context, in which the text has to be reinterpreted. All interpreted texts, at best and at most, spring from the Text which transcends all, because it is directed to and derived from the transcendent reality of God in Christ. But though interpreted texts are mere earthen vessels, they are formed for service to that transcendent reality, and have to be reformed and reinterpreted. By the contexts I mean the historic realities of each situation, all of which are subject to change. Therefore, if theological education is to move forward in renewal and reform, it must simultaneously be involved in a "double wrestle" (these words, incidentally, were the theme of a Consultation on Theological Education, held in Indonesia a year or two ago). By them I mean wrestling with the Text from which all texts are derived and to which they point, in order to be faithful to it in the context; and wrestling with the context in which the reality of the Text is at work, in order to be relevant to it. This "double wrestle" may involve what I call "textual cum contextual criticism." It is in this critical awareness that we are driven to basic questions about the nature and purpose of theological education in the contemporary, revolutionary world. Here the words of St. Paul have for me great meaning and challenge: "I am again in travail until Christ be formed in you . . ." (Gal. 4:19). Is not the purpose of theological education primarily to serve this formation in a threefold way?

1. *Christian Formation.* Again St. Paul's words are applicable: "I live, yet no longer I, but Christ lives in me" (Gal. 2:20). What does this really mean? The life of Jesus was one for others. Can theological education prepare for such a formation? Only if it does will it be able to become part of the ministry of the One who says, "I am in your midst as the one who serves" *(ho diakonōn).* Theological education, as education, is involved in human formation, but with the conviction that the life of Jesus Christ, who lived and died for others, is the authentic human formation. All human development moves toward a centered self, but in that process it faces the predicament of becoming self-centered. How can theological education, as Christian formation, develop an authentic, human formation which is not self-centered, but which is for others? But existence for others could be too general and abstract. The questions raised by the

Third World today are: Who are the others? Are they not the poor and oppressed?

2. *Theological Formation.* Theological education is not something which just provides the student with knowledge. It should develop minds in men and women so that they may genuinely say, "I think, yet not I, but the mind of Christ thinks through me." Theological formation means having "this mind among yourselves, which you have in Christ Jesus" (Phil. 2:5). This comes as a gift, yet at the same time it imposes a rigorous task, for it is no ordinary mind. Its thinking involves praxis, and the extraordinary praxis, at that, of emptying one's self, taking the form of a servant, humbling one's self, and becoming obedient unto death. This mind will only become ours through constant *metanoia.*

3. *Ministerial Formation.* Whoever acquires this life-style and passes through this process will be enabled to say, "I work, yet not I, but the ministry of Christ works through me." There is but one essential ministry of Jesus Christ, entrusted to the church through a variety of gifts (the *charismata*). Theological education is the actualization of these charismata in service to that one essential ministry of Christ, in and for the world. You will see from this that I have come to understand theological education as not primarily for the few who are going into the ordained ministry, but for the whole people of God, of whom the set-apart ministry is one of the charismata, important though it is. In the future, the training of the set-apart ministry must be related to the total theological education of the whole people of God in this threefold formation. The function of such a set-apart ministry would be then to discern the gifts and enable them to be used in a concerted service to the *Missio Dei,* in its concrete, historical context. Moreover, the set-apart ministry may be called to be a pioneer in a new context.

CONTEXTUALIZATION AS THE WAY TOWARD REFORM IN THEOLOGICAL EDUCATION

If this is the aim and purpose of theological education, the urgent question is how and where this is to happen, so far as it lies with us. It was in struggling with this question during the study period required by the Third Mandate that we came upon the two words *contextuality* and *contextualization* as the way toward reform in theological education. They provide the key to the Working Policy document. Since its adoption at the 1972 annual TEF meeting, this has been widely distributed among the schools with which we are in touch, and among mission boards and theological educators. Most of the reactions have been favorable, though there have been some expressions of concern lest the use of these two words might overemphasize the context at the expense of the text. This would be contrary to the intention. If I have indulged in personal reflections, it is because of this apprehension. Although the two words, contextuality and contextualization, came almost in a flash during our long deliberations, I feel that in a way they were the culmination of a long process of historical development, both in the TEF itself, and, speaking for myself, in the personal pilgrimage as a theological educator from Asia. In the remainder of this article I will try to clarify these two words as I understand them, and in doing so I hope others will be stimulated to join in the discussion, because I am convinced we have come upon something vital for the renewal of theological education.

Indigenization and Contextualization

Throughout the three Mandates there has been a continuing concern for indigenization in theological education—a term and a process which have been debated in mission circles of both older and younger churches for a long time. This is understandable, as indigenization is a missiological necessity when the gospel moves from one cultural soil to another and has to be retranslated, reinterpreted, and expressed afresh in the new cultural soil. Why, then, do we now use a new word, contextualization, in preference to indigenization?

Indigenous, indigeneity, and indigenization all derive from a nature metaphor, that is, of the soil, or taking root in the soil. It is only right that the younger churches, in search of their own identity, should take seriously their own cultural milieu. However, because of the static nature of the metaphor, indigenization tends to be used in the sense of responding to the gospel in terms of traditional culture. Therefore, it is in danger of being past-oriented. Furthermore, the impression has been given that it is only applicable to Asia and Africa, for elsewhere it was felt that the danger lay in overindigenization, an uncritical accommodation such as expressed by the culture faiths, the American Way of Life, etc. But the most important factor, especially since the last war, has been the new phenomenon of radical change. The new context is not that of static culture, but the search for the new, which at the same time has involved the culture itself.

Dr. K. Koyama, a longtime missionary in Thailand, and currently the Director of the Association of Theological Schools in Southeast Asia, has put this situation in a graphic way. He says there are two Thailands today: Thailand One, saturated by its nature, the seasons with which the rural community is tied up, symbolized by the leisurely pace of the water buffaloes, and impregnated religiously and culturally by Hinayana Buddhism; Thailand Two, undergoing rapid social change, urbanization, industrialization, modernization, symbolized by the cars crowding the cities and the jet planes coming in from all over the world. He goes on to say that it is as if the Lord of Hosts is conducting the controversy with Thailand One (the unchanging one) through Thailand Two, which is crying out for change.

So in using the word *contextualization,* we try to convey all that is implied in the familiar term *indigenization,* yet seek to press beyond for a more dynamic concept which is open to change and which is also future-oriented.

Contextuality and Contextualization

We who are in the Third World are faced with a new historical reality, where many contexts, old and new, are converging, sometimes in coexistence, sometimes in radical conflict. Dr. Koyama mentioned two Thailands. There are many places with even more overlapping contexts, sometimes in a bewildering state of coexistence as in Hong Kong, sometimes in a revolutionary ferment, as on the mainland of China seen through its cultural revolution. Either by accident or by providence we have used two words instead of one, *contextuality* and *contextualization.* I believe this to be providential.

To take context seriously does not necessarily mean, it seems to me, taking all contexts equally seriously, because all are not equally strategic for the *Missio Dei* in the working out of his purpose through history. By taking context seriously theological education may have to seek the help of other disciplines, such as sociology, anthropology, etc. But that is not all of the task. Behind it all is the missiological discernment of the signs of the times, required of the people of God.

As Dr. Moltmann warned us at the 1971 TEF meeting (the first under the Third Mandate), there is a danger that academic theology may become so contextualized that it becomes fossilized theology, and all the more dangerous because we are not aware of it. But equally there is a danger of contextual theology becoming chameleon theology, changing color according to the contexts. Contextuality, therefore, I believe, is that critical assessment of what makes the context really significant in the light of the *Missio Dei.* It is the missiological discernment of the signs of the times, seeing where God is at work and calling us to participate in it. Thus, contextuality is more than just taking all contexts seriously but indiscriminately. It is the conscientization of the contexts in the particular, historical moment, assessing the peculiarity of the context in the light of the mission of the church as it is called to participate in the *Missio Dei*. Such conscientization can only come through involvement and participation, out of which critical awareness may arise. But it should also engender that capacity to respond and to contextualize. Authentic contextuality leads to contextualization. The two cannot be separated, though they should be distinct. This dialectic between contextuality and contextualization indicates a new way of theologizing. It involves not only words, but actions. Through this, the inherent danger of a dichotomy between theory and practice, action and reflection, the classroom and the street, should be overcome. Authentic theological reflection can only take place as the *theologia in loco,* discerning the contextuality within the concrete context. But it must also be aware that such authentic theological reflection is at best, but also at most, *theologia viatorum;* and therefore contextuality must be matched by the contextualization which is an ongoing process, fitting for the pilgrim people, moving from place to place and from time to time, in awareness that there is no abiding place which is not subject also to the changes of time.

Thus, the Working Policy statement does not speak about "contextual theology" nor "contextualized theology" but about contextualizing theology.

Incarnation and Contextualization

Contextuality-contextualization are, I believe, a missiological necessity. But are they a theological necessity? Contextualizing theology takes the concrete local context seriously. It is rooted in a concrete, particular situation. Is there, then, a danger of losing the catholicity of the gospel? To this there is a counter question: Is there such a theology which is not *in loco* and thus *in vacuo?*—a *theologia sub specie aeternitatis,* as it were —a utopian theology? But the concern for the catholicity of the gospel is a legitimate one, with which contextualizing theology is deeply concerned. And contextualization, I believe, is the authentic way to that catholicity.

Catholicity is both a gift and a task. As a gift, we must see how it was given. This was in a very concrete way, by the Word which became flesh and dwelt among us at a particular time and place. I believe, in fact, that the incarnation is the divine form of contextualization, and if this is so, the way we receive this gift is also through our following his way. That is what I mean by contextualization. As the catholicity of the gospel is given through the Word becoming flesh, so our task should be through our responsive contextualization, taking our own concrete, local contexts seriously. Furthermore, according to the Philippian passage quoted above, in becoming flesh there was even something more involved, of emptying himself, becoming a servant, obedient unto death. That gospel which proclaimed the God who cared for all had, at the same time, a cutting edge, precisely in being for the poor and for the oppressed, for the prisoners and for the neglected. In that way we see how concrete the incarnation is, and the catholicity which it manifests. The true catholicity is a gift which only becomes ours as we draw our basic power from the gospel of the incarnate Word. True catholicity could not possibly be a colorless uniformity, but must be a rich fullness of truth and grace, which unfolds and manifests itself as we take the diversified contexts in time and space, where we are set, and respond faithfully as the Incarnate Word did on our behalf, once and for all. The true and authentic catholicity will become fully ours as we not only draw basic power from the same gospel, but as we are committed wholly to serve the same *Missio Dei* in the diversified contexts.

Of course contextuality-contextualization, as our human response, are at most and at best a provisional and fragmentary witness of that divine contextualization of the incarnation. Ours can only be in following in his steps as an ongoing process of the pilgrim people. But in doing so we can accept our relativity with hope and even with joy, as we see in our faithful responses the sign of the divine contextualization unfolding its purpose for the liberation and salvation of mankind.

What Erik Nielsen often said concerning indigenization is even more valid for contextualization. "The crux of the matter is the resurrection." Through the incarnation and the cross there awaits the resurrection. So, for us, authentic contextualization must be open constantly to the painful process of de-contextualization, for the sake of re-contextualization. Only through the pain of the cross is there the glory of the resurrection.

In this way we can welcome with joy the emergence of black theology, and for that matter, yellow theology, and the theology of liberation, for the sake of the true catholicity of the gospel. There is no colorless theology. But there is all the joy of the multiple colors mobilized for the beauty of the new heaven and the new earth which God has promised. Or to change the metaphor, all the sounds must be mobilized in the great symphony of the Hallelujah Chorus, to be heard not only in heaven but on earth.

NOTE

1. The address referred to, "Text and Context in Theological Education," appeared in *Theological Education and Ministry: Reports from the N.E. Asia Theological Education Consultation,* Seoul, Korea, Nov. 28 to Dec. 2, 1966. (Published by the Presbyterian Bookroom, Tainan, Taiwan.)

Three

The Critical
Asian Principle
Emerito P. Nacpil

[The "critical Asian principle" grew out of a meeting of the Senate of the Southeast Asia Graduate School of Theology, held in Bangkok, 1972. The same principle was adopted by consensus at a Taiwan meeting of the Association of Theological Schools in Southeast Asia, in 1975, as a guideline for theological education in the region. Dean Nacpil considers the following only a preliminary statement of its content and invites readers' comments and suggestions with a view to producing later an official document. He sees the principle as descriptive of the Asian orientation of theological education and the distinctively Asian expression of theological contextualization. "It is critically significant," he says, "not only for graduate theological education in the region, but also for the task of theology and the mission of the church."—Ed.]

As used in the circles of the Association of Theological Schools in Southeast Asia and in the Southeast Asia Graduate School of Theology, the phrase, "the critical Asian principle," seeks to identify what is distinctively Asian and uses this distinctiveness as a critical principle of judgment on matters dealing with the life and mission of the Christian community, theology, and theological education in Asia.

The geographical territory that is immediately meant by the word "Asian" in the phrase is Southeast Asia, since this is the territory in which the Association of Theological Schools in Southeast Asia and the Southeast Asia Graduate School of Theology operate. Asia of course is much bigger than this territory, and so the phrase, by intention, includes all of what is properly Asia, which excludes the Middle East and the Pacific and Australasia.

What is characteristic of this territory?

Without being exhaustive and detailed, perhaps it is possible to men-

This essay was first published in the Asian edition of this collection and is reprinted by permission of New Day Publishers, Manila, Philippines.

tion at least seven features which are characteristic of the region.

First, plurality and diversity in races, peoples, cultures, social institutions, religions, ideologies, etc., characterize this region.

Second, most of the countries in this region have a colonial experience.

Third, most of the countries in this region are now in the process of nation-building, development, and modernization. They want to modernize through the use of science and technology. They want to develop and achieve economic growth, social justice, and self-reliance.

Fourth, the peoples of this region want to achieve authentic self-identity and cultural integrity in the context of the modern world.

Fifth, Asia is the home of some of the world's living and renascent religions, and these religions have shaped both the culture and consciousness of the vast majority of Asians. They represent alternative ways of life and experiences of reality.

Sixth, Asian peoples are in search of a form of social order beyond the current alternatives. There is an apparent resort to authoritarian forms of government as an emergency measure. There are efforts to revise and reformulate alternative forms of socioeconomic systems and adapt them to the Asian context. All this is an indication that the human issues in Asia today are of such a magnitude that none of the current ideological systems seem adequate for dealing with them. And so, like the rest of the peoples of the world, Asians are looking for a form of social order which would enable them and mankind to live together in dignity in a planetary world.

Seventh, and finally, the Christian community is a minority in the vast Asian complex!

Now, what we want to do both in ATSSEA and in the GST is to take these distinctive characteristics of our situation in Asia and use them as a frame of reference in making critical judgments on matters that have to do with our work and decisions as vocationally engaged in carrying out the tasks of doing theology, of Christian formation for leadership and ministry, and of helping the Christian community in Asia assume its missionary responsibility.

The characteristics of the Asian situation which are enumerated above raise many questions and imply many issues for us in ATSSEA and GST to consider. For example: What does Asian diversity and plurality mean for the life of the Christian community? What does the experience of colonialism mean for the understanding of oppression, injustice, and human indignity, and alternatively for understanding human liberation and development? How does one do theology in the context of modernization, and what can it contribute to the search for a new global social order? How does one interpret and communicate the Christian gospel in relation to alternative patterns of experiencing reality and ways of life? What does the experience of being a minority community mean for the life of the church? These are only a few of the many questions raised by the distinctive features of our situation.

As a frame of reference, we wish to use the critical Asian principle in at least four critical areas:

1. As a *situational* principle, by which we locate where we are and thereby indicate our area of responsibility and concern, namely, the varieties and dynamics of Asian realities;

2. As a *hermeneutical* principle, suggesting that we must understand the gospel and the Christian tradition with these realities. Accordingly, we must approach and interpret the gospel in relation to the needs and issues peculiar to the Asian situation. Alternatively, we must also approach and understand Asian realities not only through the variety of academic disciplines available in study and research, but also in the light of the gospel and its traditions;

3. As a *missiological* principle, which aims at equipping people with a missionary commitment that is informed by a missionary theology capable not only of illuminating Asian realities with the floodlight of the gospel but also of helping to manage and direct the changes now taking place in the region along lines more consonant with the gospel and its vision for human life in God;

4. And, finally, as an *educational* principle which should give shape, content, direction, and criteria to our educational task in our member schools and in the Southeast Asia Graduate School of Theology.

From what has been said above, it can be seen that the critical Asian principle is a way of doing theological contextualization. It is primarily a method, and a method is judged by how well it works. Unless it is put to work to produce results, it cannot be evaluated and improved or discarded. It is hoped that we in ATSSEA and in GST will do our theological task experimentally with this method. The time for evaluation will certainly come.

NOTE

A Historical Note: The phrase "critical Asian principle" has its genesis in the meeting of the Senate of the Southeast Asia Graduate School of Theology in Bangkok, 1972. At this meeting, a report on the feasibility of a theology doctoral program in the region was submitted for consideration and action. The report made six points on why there should be such a program and how it is to be carried out. (See the report attached to the *Minutes of the Senate of SEAGST,* Bangkok, Feb. 1972.) Point 2 of the report says that "the degree should be the Doctor of Theology, a professional degree with *a distinctly Asian orientation.*" (Italics added.) In approving the establishment of a doctoral studies program, the Senate on my suggestion made Point 2 (above) of the report as "the *critical principle for the whole program*" (*Minutes of the Senate of SEAGST,* 1972, GS-7208). Thus, the distinctly Asian orientation is to be the critical principle of the whole doctoral studies program. From this was born the phrase "the critical Asian principle." Subsequent developments showed that the phrase is critically significant not only for graduate theological education in the region but also for the task of theology and the mission of the church.

Four

Inquiry Into Indigenous Cultural Energies

Kiyoko Takeda Cho

[This essay is a contribution to the World Council of Churches-sponsored study on what it means to be authentically human. Dr. Cho is a Japanese lay woman theologian who served as one of the six presidents of the WCC from 1971 to 1975. In this essay she is concerned with the complex relationships between Christianity and Third World cultures. Unfortunately, the "younger" churches have been misled into thinking that Western Christian traditions and theologies were universally normative. Although she acknowledges that there are indeed elements of universal value in Western cultural expressions of Christianity, it can no longer be assumed that what is Western is universal. She points out that Third World Christians need to experiment more creatively, so as to demonstrate that there are other cultural expressions of Christianity which are just as universally valid. In the words of Mrs. Cho, they are called in our time "to make a more serious inquiry into . . . the hidden 'Christ' in the midst of indigenous cultural reality and human life."—Ed.]

The Humanum Studies have been a joint search for new ways of deepening our understanding of the gospel in order to become more truly human. This involves participation and commitment in a responsible human partnership which shares human anguish. This is the anguish of poverty, of lack of freedom of choice, of physical and spiritual suffering such as torture, of political imprisonment, and many other forms of social injustice.

We are seeking to be freed from those old, preestablished "Christian" value concepts, or traditional thought forms and styles of life and behavior which often operated as cultural imperialism. We are seeking to be open toward blessed promises found in various forms of culture and to be received through the authenticity of indigenous cultures.

We are seeking to be freed from our own misunderstanding which has

From *The Humanum Studies,* edited by David Jenkins (Geneva: World Council of Churches, 1975), pp. 97–103. Reprinted by permission of the publisher.

led us to treat Western Christian traditions or Western theologies as universally normative. This has happened partly because of our misunderstanding in receiving Western culture or civilization as inseparable parts of Christianity itself. But it is also because of the lack of authentic Christian traditions in younger churches. Often westernized Christian forms have been accepted as being the Christian form. This is due to the Western imperialistic cultural domination and also to laziness or lack of dignity and effort on the side of receivers in the Third World.

We have to be freed from this misunderstanding. We have to free Christianity, the universal values of Christianity, from Western cultural particularism. At the same time we should not fail to recognize that which is of universal value in Christianity as expressed through Christianity particularized and indigenized in Western cultural soil. We need to restore the genuine Christianity, the true universal message of Christianity. We are called to take the incarnation very seriously and to look for a new approach to meet our Lord, quite often hidden in the midst of indigenous cultural and human reality.

I. INDIGENOUS ENERGY

In our search together about the Humanum, we discovered the idea and term "indigenous energies." This term emerged in the course of the final meeting of the Humanum Consultative Group. It served as a crystallizing focus of our thinking. What do we mean by it?

The first source of indigenous energy is the energy of despair. This is the energy of those who, because of desperate suffering and oppressed situations, struggle in anguish with full energy to break through the walls which shut them up in hopeless despair. It emerges under various kinds of oppression and suffering. It is energy resulting from poverty, hunger, and want: an energy for change toward justice and freedom, resisting various forms of social and political injustice. The energy of despair, of want, of change can be found in the people of the so-called Third World as well as in the minority groups or less privileged people in the affluent societies.

The second source of indigenous energy can be found in indigenous cultures of the vast areas of the non-Western world—the traditional moral or religious ethos or philosophical ideas or value concepts which give the traditional understanding of man and interpretation of the meaning of life. Such ethos can be found not only in the sophisticated religious or philosophical ideas but in folk tales, folk arts, poems, literature, or music which bear the significant characteristics and sentiment of the basic culture.

The third source of indigenous energy is the energy of women—not only the women of the so-called Third World but also those of the developed countries. Women are by all means part of the indigenous energies of the above-mentioned two areas, but at the same time it is important to underline that women of the total human race are one unique and significant group or area with full potentialities of indigenous energy which has not yet been fully developed and recognized and used.

These are glimpses of some areas where we can look for resources of indigenous energy. This indigenous energy is found in extremely diverse thought forms, traditions, cultures, attitudes, life situations, and experiences. In their diversity these are full of conflicts but at the same time full of a promised potentiality of the ecumenical activity of God.

II. UNIVERSALISTIC AND PARTICULARISTIC ELEMENTS IN ASIAN TRADITIONAL CULTURE

In our search for new approaches for becoming more truly human, we are called to explore and to venture upon further inquiry into the depths of these diversified cultural and human resources, to dig out our promised indigenous potentialities.

When we carefully examine the traditional indigenous cultural soil of our country I think we can conclude that we find on the one hand the universalistic elements—some elements in the traditional value concepts which are open to or seeking the universalistic value implied in the Christian message. On the other hand particularistic elements are to be found which make oneself absolute and justified in exclusive self-glorifying. Such particularistic elements are apt to lead to various kinds of idolatry whereby one attributes to one's position, tradition, ideas, or ideologies an absolute value. In other words, there are both the positive elements which make men and women more human and the negative elements which hinder men and women from becoming truly human, and these two elements are deeply interwoven as a traditional culture or indigenous energy.

Let me explain what I mean by universalistic and particularistic elements by taking up some examples from my cultural background of Japan with which I am familiar.

A Buddhist priest, Shinran, a pioneer of the Jodo sect (Pure Land sect) said some rather revolutionary words in relation to the moralistic tradition of the Buddhist thought in Japan, namely: "Even a good man can be saved. Therefore a bad man will be surely saved." What he meant was that even a proud man who regards himself as a good man can be saved. Therefore a humble man of repentance who knows he is a bad man can be saved, by the grace of Buddha.

The Rev. Masahisa Uemura, one of the outstanding Protestant pioneers in Japan, wrote about this type of Buddhist understanding of the sinfulness of man and his salvation as a partial grasp of the Christian concept of man and the blessing of the gospel. Uemura thus quoted the passage in Acts 17:23, a part of St. Paul's address to the Greeks at the Areopagus in Athens: "For as I passed by, and beheld your devotions, I found an altar with this inscription, TO THE UNKNOWN GOD. Whom therefore ye ignorantly worship, him declare I unto you."

Toyohiko Kagawa also spoke of this kind of indigenous religious consciousness as an indigenous wild olive branch to be grafted to the root.

This kind of element which we find in our indigenous culture can be regarded as that which is open to universalistic value. However, such elements are not only found in a great Buddhist priest's thought but also in the genuine and pious worshiping hearts of simple men or women who in humble spirit pray to the transcendent being for salvation, or in the ethos of folk tales or folk arts or literature which seek for the meaning of human life or liberation from the suffering reality.

Here, by all means, we have to admit the ambiguity in selecting any universalistic values out of the traditional cultural soil. In recent years in my country we have had an interesting discussion. One popular Catholic writer raised a question about some Japanese who left the Protestant Church and gave up their faith. He suggested that they abandoned their Christian faith because they could not stand under the stern father image of God which they received from the early Protestants. This stern image arose because the first "Samurai" Christians understood the Christian concept of God in terms of their own warrior tradition and in the light of Confucian rigorism. The Confucian tradition stresses the concept of a father with absolute authority.

Therefore this writer emphasizes the need for the element of the mother image with overtones of love and forgiveness in the Christian understanding of God. This suggestion has brought about an interesting challenge.

In accepting this challenge we face another difficulty. If we put too much emphasis on the absolutely all-embracing love of motherhood in our Shintoistic cultural soil, it will lead to an all-embracing syncretism. There will be no room for confronting the issues of righteousness and judgment. In developing an understanding of the Christian concept of God, we are not completely free from the indigenous cultural soil. We have the effects of the family symbolisms in a religious tradition with their corresponding "father image" and "mother image." A Confucian or a Shintoistic thought pattern helps and at the same time hinders our authentic understanding of Christianity.

In our indigenous culture we find at the same time roots of the mystery of evil and various kinds of old and new idolatry. There is not only the idol of worship of primitive religions but also the Emperor worship. Here we find a unique combination of Shamanism, ancestor worship, and the religious and political concept of the traditional communal life and structure. This functioned as the core of absolutistic nationalism and imperialism until the end of the Second World War. This was typical of the particularistic element in the traditional indigenous culture of our country.

In radical student movements of recent years there was a very interesting element of Shamanism by which certain ideological leaders functioned as a kind of religious charisma (a Shaman) of Shamanism and to whose direction all members emotionally submitted themselves in a kind of religious ecstasy without concern for individual freedom or responsibility but with vital explosion of energy. Prof. Ichiro Hori, a leading scholar of traditional religions of Japan, in his article sharply pointed out a queer similarity between the traditional Shamanism and the mentality and behavior patterns of some of the most radical student movements of recent years in my country. At the same time, in these radical student movements, we should not fail to recognize some important elements which seek for universalistic values in their sharp acknowledgment of dehumanizing elements in the nature of the technological civilization of the so-called affluent society as well as in their vital protest against social and political injustice.

Thus indigenous culture is a mixture or interwoven totality of the hidden blessing, the immanent potentiality toward universalism and unique forms of particularism bearing the roots of the unclean spirit, the root of the mystery of evil, in the depth of its cultural soil. This is the concrete human reality in Asia.

Christianity is trying to take root in this indigenous cultural soil. Just as the West has been a place of mutual confrontation and penetration of the biblical understanding of man and of the Hellenistic or other non-Christian and anti-Christian secular understandings of man, other cultural realities of Asia, Africa, and throughout the world are also areas of mutual confrontation and penetration of the biblical elements and the traditional and human indigenous energies which contain the above-mentioned opposite potentialities.

We all agree that we have to cut down the pretensions of formerly normative theologies. The theologies based or originated in Europe are as indigenous as any others.

However, here I would like to add one comment on Western Christian culture. Western Christian anthropology has produced one type of universalistic value. It is true that this anthropology has been produced through indigenization of Christianity into Western cultural and social soil. But we make a great mistake if we fail to recognize its value. Because of the mistakes the Westerners have made and are still making, particularly in their relationship to the Third World, the Western Christians are called upon by themselves to be humble in repentance. I think this is necessary. But at the same time, as an Asian Christian, I honestly cannot help admitting that the Western theologies, particularly Christian anthropology, have revealed one type of universalistic value for humanity and contributed something basically important to the modern transformation of ethics and social systems toward humanization in Asia.

When Mahatma Gandhi, leader of the Indian independence movement, was speaking to a Swiss audience in Geneva, one person asked him, "Is Tolstoi still a teacher for you?" Gandhi answered, "Yes, he is and will be my teacher always." Gandhi told his people in the midst of an independence movement that "unless we fight against the evil within us such as segregation of the untouchables or religious division and hatred between Hindus and Muslims, how can we fight against the evil of the West?"

I think that only in such a spirit we might be able to seek the potentialities and possibilities of universal values which may emerge out of the promise of our Lord in the depths of the particular cultural soil of Asia or Africa.

We the Christians of the non-Western world are called to go into a deeper inquiry and reexamination of the nature of basic culture and indigenous energy, into clearer discovery and understanding of the particularistic and universalistic elements.

We are called to a further venture, namely, our own experiment and demonstration of other types of universal and normative forms of Christianity, expressing the unique fragrance of indigenous culture and a vitality of indigenous energies which is genuinely Christian. This is what is expected of Christians of the Third World in our common ecumenical task of the Humanum Studies.

The ecumenical human search demands that Christians of each cultural background set out to make a more serious inquiry into the incarnation of Christ, the embodiment of his transcendence, the hidden "Christ" in the midst of indigenous cultural reality and human life.

Thus we will begin to be aware of particular forms of sinfulness and will be ready to repent and at the same time to accept the transcending and unifying power of Jesus Christ who has overcome all particularistic self-justification.

Five

Toward an
Asian Christian Theology

Saphir P. Athyal

[This was one of the papers presented to the inaugural assembly of the Asia Theological Association meeting in Hong Kong, January 1974. From the standpoint of conservative Evangelicals in India, the author exhibits a new openness toward the possibilities of a "contextual theology." He goes so far as to say that "Asians should be in a better position than those in the West to develop . . . an indigenous theology based on the Bible," since the context and background of biblical revelation are very similar to traditional life situations in Asia. In spite of the emphasis on the impersonal Ultimate in much Asian thought, he suggests that the starting point for an Asian Christian theology should be the Christian emphasis on the personal nature of God and on faith as a personal relationship with God.—Ed.]

The two major imports of the very term "theology" are, on the one hand, God's eternal self-revelation connoted by *theos,* and on the other, man's understanding of God in categories of one's *logos* or reason. Men from time to time have stressed either of these imports at the expense of the other, as for example, Karl Barth's revelational or transcendental aspect developing what is often termed a "kerygmatic theology," or Paul Tillich's human dimension of revelation leading to his "apologetic theology." The task of theology of any people is to articulate their understanding of the eternal truth in terms of their given locale and context. In this sense we can speak of a German, a British, or an American theology, or of Reformation, nineteenth-century, or contemporary theology, though the core of thought which all these different systems attempt to embody remains the same.

The basic message is something that is already given to us, and it is

A lecture delivered at the Third Theological Consultation of the Asia Theological Association (formerly Theological Assistance Program—Asia) in Hong Kong, Dec. 27 to Jan. 4, 1974. Published in the volume of proceedings, titled *The Voice of the Church in Asia* (Taipei: ATA, 1975). Reprinted by permission.

the fact of Christ, the salvation event, which already stands and which we have no right to modify. It is "delivered once for all to the saints" and it does not belong to us. The problem therefore is not with the content of the gospel, but with the form or the framework in which it comes to each man. While a distinction between form and content may be made, they cannot be separated, and their relationship is a complex matter. This is because the gospel has already taken a particular form in the Bible. What is the eternal core and what is the dispensable form in the written Word itself? And what are they when we apply them to a given situation today? This inquiry is the guiding question in the continuous hermeneutical task of the church.

It has been argued that there is nothing like the pure gospel, and that for the gospel to be indigenous, both the content and the form will have to go through a transformation, just as both the grain and the husk will have to die for the rice to grow. But the point is that out of the death of the rice grain and its husk, no wheat is grown but only rice, and that too not a different type of rice.

The Christian message is not transformed, but it is understood in the points of view of different times and backgrounds. Truth is seen from within one's given situation and experience, and not as a foreign concept thrust upon one. The gospel is actualized when it is heard and appropriated. It never is an abstract truth, but a message that takes concrete forms and continues to have a "dialogue" with the believers in their daily practical situations. One's openness to one's world with its problems and issues helps one to direct the right type of questions to the "gospel" in this dialogue. If the Christian gospel is the answer, one should know what are the real questions, and this is the task of indigenous theology. This type of theology is a contextual theology, its formulations and categories of thought belonging to a given context and experience. It is a confessing theology because it is always "in dialogue" with the contemporary issues and attempts to answer them.

A. WHAT SHOULD CHARACTERIZE AN ASIAN CHRISTIAN THEOLOGY

Guiding principles for the development of any theology cannot easily be set, because theology is something that happens when men attempt to articulate the Christian message in the context of their experience, and no one can predict what will emerge from such attempts. The following may be pointed out as directions that an Asian Christian theology should take:

1. Biblical Basis and Character

If God is the subject matter of theology, and if we know very little of him or of the Christ through whom we know the Father, except for biblical revelation, the Bible should be the very foundation of any Christian theology. But we might speak of three major reasons for a biblically oriented theology being the only valid Christian theology for Asia.

a. *The Christian faith has a historical basis and character unlike most other religions, and the Bible is the only written witness to this specific history of God's salvation deeds.* It is important to keep in mind that the core of Christian theology is Christ incarnate, and not any abstract universal dogma or principle. The transcendent God has already done a concrete and particular work in a specified time and a specific place. The task of indigenous theology would have been perhaps easier if we were dealing with, for example, Plato's "Idea" rather than with the God-Man. The peoples of different nations, who gathered together at Jerusalem for the feast of Pentecost, hearing the disciples, said, "We hear them speaking in our own tongues the mighty acts of God." It is God's great work of redemption in the context of earthly and human scenes which is central to our message and which we should make heard by peoples in their own "tongues."

The historical character of the Christian faith demands that the Bible, as it is the unique witness to and the record of this history, be the source and provide the content of any Christian theology. Any system of thought that does not take the biblical record seriously tends to reduce the Christian message to certain abstract principles and claims as found in many non-Christian schools of thought.

The fallacy of posing some sort of a contradistinction between Christ, the living word, and the Bible, the written word, and asserting that the former is the revelation and the latter at best a fallible witness to revelation, lies in this historical nature of our faith and in the Bible's being the only authentic source of our knowledge of God's acts of redemption.

b. *The context and backgrounds in which God's word came to man during the biblical times are very similar to the life situations in Asia today.* The social-cultural backgrounds of both the Old Testament and the New Testament in many ways are similar to the contemporary Asian situations. If the study of the historical and cultural context of the biblical passages is basic to one's understanding of the biblical message, then at least theoretically speaking, Asians should be in a better position than those in the West to develop biblical scholarship. It is a paradox if the precept, "Honor thy father and thy mother," should be interpreted to Asian Christians by Western scholars. Because the Asian church relives in our times much of the biblical life situation, it ought to have certain advantages over churches in the West in developing an indigenous theology based on the Bible.

c. *The Bible itself provides us with a pattern for indigenous expression of thought.* Israel belonged to a world culture and its religious heritage. They borrowed heavily from their contemporaries; rather, they shared much of their thought and religious practices with those of other nations around and amidst them. But their confrontations only sharpened the cutting edges of their distinctive beliefs, and their claims for Yahweh. The same was true with the New Testament Christians. They belonged to their times, but their gospel always remained a unique proclamation rather than a compromise with the advanced systems of philosophy and religion of the Roman world. When terms or frames of thought were borrowed, they were given new meanings and content.

Confessions of faith in the Bible are not theoretical statements or speculations, but are based on God's redemptive acts and his message as applied to particular needs. Throughout the Bible, God's word is seen as relevant to the situation and tied to the times to which it was spoken. The Old Testament prophets spoke directly to the needs around them. God's message took concrete shape in the context of the evils of monarchy, social injustice, Baal worship, syncretism, the impending judgment of God, etc. The New Testament writers wrote in a context of Gnosticism, Docetism, and polytheism, and not in abstract terms. This character of God's written word gives us a pattern for indigenization.

To give an example, a predominant note in the Bible is the power of God over "the gods of the peoples" and his control over the evil spirits and demons. Unlike most Western Christians, who seem to find this emphasis quite irrelevant today, the Asian Christians who live in situations similar to the biblical world would recapture this particular aspect of the biblical teaching on God's sovereignty and power, which has taken a concrete expression or mode in the Bible similar to what they would want to say.

In the biblical orientation of which we speak, both the Old Testament and the New Testament in their entirety should be taken into account. Without this, an appreciation of the similarities between the concrete human situations addressed in the Bible and those reflected in one's own religious and cultural heritage will be largely lost. Our theologies should be true to the thrust of the total teaching of the whole Bible. In the history of the church, often there has been the temptation to separate the two Testaments and to attempt to relate the New Testament to the scriptures of other religions according to a pattern in which the latter are the expectation and the former is the fulfillment. But the New Testament message makes no sense unless its own claim of inherent relationship with the Old Testament is taken seriously and understood as such.

2. Systematization Around Contextual Issues in Asia

In distinction from the Western theological systems, the systematization of any Asian Christian theology will build around certain emphases not necessarily felt as relevant issues in the West. Not only the priorities will be different, but new areas of discussion and emphasis not dealt with in Western Christianity will be introduced.

Christian theologies of different times and different places, while covering essentially the same general subject matter one way or another, should let their particular contexts decide what particular area of faith should receive special emphasis and perhaps serve as the point which leads to the exposition of the full scope of the field. For Calvin, this central factor in theology was the sovereignty of God; for Luther, justification by faith; and for Barth, the Word of God and the incarnation. It was the context in which they lived and wrote, and the challenges for their times, which dictated their particular emphasis. Many modern evangelical theologies start with the inspiration and the infallibility of the Word of God, because a majority of scholars of the last century raised serious questions about the trustworthiness of the Bible as never before.

Only the keen sensitiveness of the Asian church to the world around it can give it an awareness as to what area of theology should receive primary treatment and serve as the pathway to the total scope of theology. This would also throw light on the methodology which is to be followed. In the context of the many religious myths and the concept of the world as an illusion, should the particular point of Christian theology in Asia be the redemptive acts of God and God's control and plan in history? Or in the light of the general notion of impersonal gods or the idea of religion without God, should the Christian emphasis be on the personal nature of God and on the gist of Christian faith as a personal relationship with God?

A Western systematization of theology may not fit in the Asian scene. Asian theology should take a systematization which is dictated by the emphasis of the culture and leading thoughts of Asia.

A theology in dialogue with its contemporary world around would in its methodology be open to areas where points of contact can be made, and truth can be explained in intelligible terms. At the same time where there are differences, these will be drawn clearly, and stark distinctions will be made. For example, in Western theologies, the concepts of monotheism, the personal character of God, the reality of sin, understanding of the world as God's sphere of action, etc., need not get any thorough treatment at all, while in Asia these might be some of the most alive issues in theology.

Another question relating to the above is the use of theological terms. The selection of terms and the question of their content often are not problems in Western theology because of their general background of Judeo-Christian culture. The Israelites often used terms which they had in common with the Semitic world. The New Testament writers used Greek terms which already carried with them established connotations and meanings. In Asian countries, the Christians often find themselves reliving the struggles which the biblical writers and the theologians of the early centuries of our era went through in spelling out their thoughts in their respective languages, which belonged primarily to non-Christian cultures. Invention of new terms only further complicates communication, yet any transformation of terms, as for example, that given by the apostle John to *logos,* requires a thorough knowledge of what the terms originally mean and generally connote, and also a very clear picture of the new content that is to be added to them.

3. Orientation to Cultures and Religions of Asia

Regarding the question of the relationship between theology and culture in the context of Asia, there are several areas for our inquiry. How is our doctrine of creation and concept of Christ's work in the world to be understood in terms of our own culture as Asians and the social changes that happen around us? What bearing does this understanding have on one's social involvements? What should be the Christian understanding of the non-Christian religions with their recently renewed dynamic and living values?

Western theological systems have taken shape in the general Judeo-Christian cultural background. Western civilization itself, to a great degree, has been the result of Christianity, and Western Christianity in its life and thought have been substantially influenced by Western civilization. Arend van Leeuwen goes to the extent of seeing the Kingdom of God as begun in Western Christian civilization, and as in the process of being established in the world by the technological developments and the conquest of the "autocratic" oriental societies and their cultures. We might say at least that for the Western theologians, though the problem of the relationship between Christ and culture is at times raised, one does not find any real struggle between the two. Niebuhr's classical work *Christ and Culture* summarizes the discussion in the West on the issue.

While in the history of the West, world history and "redemptive history" appear to be already mutually related, their relationship with respect to the history of Asia becomes a perplexing issue to an Asian theologian. The modern Protestant missionaries to Asia generally have held that the national cultures are corrupt and anti-Christian and therefore to be neglected if not opposed by the Christians. Converts to Christianity were "delivered" from these cultures to live protected in isolated Christian communities. At the same time, Roman Catholic missionaries, by and large, held the classical Roman view of Christ as above the culture. There have been only a very few missionaries or Asian Christians who have taken seriously, in relation to Asia, Calvin's conviction that Christ has power to change and transform cultures and social orders.

The Christian church in Asia has always claimed that Christ is given all authority on earth, in Asia, and that he redeems men and makes a new order. The Asian Christians have ceaselessly prayed, "Let thy kingdom come." Now it is for them to spell out the implication of this in relation to the societies and cultures in which they find themselves. When they talk about Christ's work in the world, his works of compassion, his feeding of the hungry, healing of the sick, and setting of the prisoners free, they are speaking of agencies and bodies which would not only consider it an offense to be spoken of as related to Christ's works, but which also are often aggressively anti-Christian in their ideologies. To say that, like Cyrus or Nebuchadnezzar of old, all these also are servants of Christ, whether they know it or not, is to bypass naively the question of the meaning of Christ's Lordship when it is unacknowledged or consciously rejected.

One cannot hold a faith that God wills the total welfare or *shalom* of all men, and have a theory of God's work of renewal and re-creation, without thinking through the question of Christian social responsibility. If our social actions are limited to only certain philanthropic deeds, no problem is raised. But to seek to integrate our concept of social responsibility with our doctrine of creation and our Christian world view is to raise difficult theological problems. To an Asian theologian the issue is all the more difficult as he tries to develop a theology of Christian social concern in a non-Christian and even anti-Christian social and political order. Can we speak of a society or a culture as characteristically Christian or can we speak of one as characteristically anti-Christian, if by "Christian" we mean any shade of Christlikeness? No culture can receive blanket approval and nonblanket disapproval when it comes to Christ's measuring rods.

In biblical exclusiveness, the lines are drawn not between established

Christianity and those outside, not between Christian culture and pagan cultures, but between light and truth on one side, and darkness and falsehood on the other, between those who are in Christ and those who are not. This biblical dualism ought to be kept in mind in our attitude to non-Christian religions so that the issue becomes not the outward contradistinction between established Christianity and non-Christianity. Both in Christian religions and in non-Christian religions there are salient features and, at the same time, degenerated and corrupt features. In all the pious admonitions we hear today from around us that we as Christians ought to be teachable, humble, genuinely loving, and open to what Christ has to say to us through our fellow believers in other religions, there is a failure to distinguish between the truth as revealed in Christ and institutional Christianity. When it comes to the revealed truth and the gospel of Christ, there is no more searching except for further clarity of what is revealed.

Christians have shown different attitudes to the other faiths. Some have envisaged a synthesis of all religions to form a world religion, some others stand for keeping the status quo of all religions, and most others hope that, at least in very large numbers, non-Christians will accept Christianity. People of the last group have generally had a negative attitude to the religions, which meant that they either neglected them entirely or studied them purely to spy out their weak points. When Barth and Kraemer considered the religions essentially as an opposition to God, they were not so much denying the valuable aspects of religions as they were giving the central and the all-important place in Christian faith to God's self-revelation. Any religious systems including those called Christian should be considered not valid if they attempt to circumvent the revelation-fact.

Interreligious dialogue can be quite valuable in several respects. It creates an openness and friendship between people of different religions in the context of communal wars and hatred which have flourished in many parts of Asia in recent years. It helps each participant to understand the basic essentials of his faith whereby religions may be freed from their superstitions and ills. It brings to the forefront the dissimilarities of religions both at their surfaces (these are often obvious enough), and at their depths, if honesty to oneself is maintained by each party involved in the dialogue. Men of different faiths can pursue together their thoughts on matters such as human dignity, the value of labor, and certain areas of social ethics, etc. But in fundamental aspects of the Christian faith which really matter, no common ground is found with other religions for a fruitful dialogue. For example, Christianity has nothing on the basis of which we Christians can, with teachableness, dialogue with the Hindu concept of the nonpersonal deity, the Buddhist idea of religion without God, or their common belief in the unreality of the world and history. Then, what is the need of the Asian Christian theologian for genuinely understanding the other religions? This has now become a more serious and immediate question as the non-Christian religions experience a vital renewal and resurgence, exercising increasing influence on the people of Asia. One might say that the Christian truth comes to a person primarily as a man and not as a Hindu, a Muslim, or a so-called Christian. Yet truth is not like an abstract dictum nor man a simple, pure entity. Everyone is a product of his world, his culture and thought, and truth comes to him through the avenues of his thought patterns. Theology in Asia generally showed some foreignness because of its Western framework and therefore it never became a very well integrated part of the practical understanding and life of the Christians there nor was it easily communicable to others.

In Asia, cultural and religious aspects of life are very closely linked together, and therefore thought patterns and words already have certain religious overtones. That is why no concept can be communicated without understanding the frame of thought which one uses. In the very use of an Asian vernacular language one cannot but face the problem of the interrelation between that language and the religious culture in which it developed.

Western theologies owe much more than is often recognized to Aristotle and ancient Greek philosophy for their thought patterns and structure. Secular thinkers such as Kant, Hegel, and a host of others have immensely influenced the shaping of theologies of the West. Some parallel development in the articulation of the Christian faith in the influential thought-concepts in vogue should take place in Asia.

4. Directed to Practical Life and Mission

Asian theology cannot afford to be purely academic and philosophical. It is valid only if it is produced not primarily in between piles of books but in the "field" where it is put to the test each day. An Asian Christian is always asked to "give a reason for the hope that is in him," and this is the burden of his theology.

The church in Asia finds itself amidst a hostile majority, and in many places it continually pays a price for what it believes. So any theology it develops cannot be pure theory, but must be conviction that has grown deep and has been clarified in the context of needs and challenges.

Much of Western thought does not speak to the issues in Asia. It deals with the questions that are asked in the West and discussed there. Therefore, to a great extent Western thought has remained a good academic exercise for a few Asian theorists and not a living theology for the church.

Theological dilutions and heresies that the Asian church faces and which gnaw at the life of the church are also, just as in helpful theologies, imported from the West. In any genuine development of creative Christian thought, the appearance of certain heresies may be unavoidable, in Asia as elsewhere. But must Asians fight not only these but imported heresies which apart from their Western credentials would not be live issues in the Asian church at all?

One distinctive characteristic of Asian theology should be its mission orientation. The main thrust of New Testament Christianity is its outreach. The Christian church exists for and by its mission. This mission one should understand as our total mission to the total man. Christians in Asia are constantly under pressure to reassert or to reject the Lordship of Christ. It will be increasingly difficult there for mediocre faith to continue as outward pressure increases, and the only way of survival is aggressive outreach and creative mission. The church cannot afford to be an ingrown institution with walls around, doors firmly shut; rather, it will increasingly be a scattered church, the pieces falling in open fields of burning heat and storm to find new life and new challenges. Speculative theology ceases to have any practical value. The church will have to redefine and painfully relearn its claims, life, and goals as the early Jerusalem church did when it was scattered.

B. Asian Theology: Its Bearing on the Asian Church

We might briefly look at only a few areas as examples of how an indigenous Asian theology should make a difference in the life of the church in Asia.

1. In Its Witness and Mission

The famous Indian evangelist-scholar, Sadhu Sundar Singh, spoke of his desire to be able to give to his fellow countrymen "the water of life in an Indian cup." We earlier noted that because the gospel came to man in an already particularized and concrete form and not as an abstract universal principle, the form and content are not two entities that may be divorced from each other. Therefore one cannot easily speak of "the water of life in an Indian cup," nor of the flower pot brought from the West being broken and the plant taking its roots in Asian soil, as D. T. Niles used to say. Yet the form that the gospel took in the Bible is closer to the Asian context than to the Western forms of theology which the church has inherited from its founders.

At present the whole structure, teaching, and practice of the Christian church is looked upon as belonging to the West and not as Eastern in character. This impression is there not merely because Christianity grew in most parts of Asia under the cover of Western colonialism and political dominance. But it is true also with a few exceptions that the churches in Asia, indeed, are counterparts in faith and practice of their mother bodies in the West. This has been the most serious hindrance to its witness, and increasingly is this true in recent years with the rise of nationalism. Today, when Asian countries are free from Western domination, the Christian missionary movement is viewed as a new form of Western imperialism.

This is not to imply that an indigenous Asian Christianity would make the gospel readily acceptable by the Asians and that Asia will in no time be reconciled to Christ. But the point is that so long as the Asian church remains essentially Western in character, it does not even break the ice with, and get access to, those to whom it tries to witness.

An understanding of the gospel as linked and as related to the Asian context and needs would help the Christians to have a clearer and deeper conviction of what they believe, and thus strengthen their own witness.

Because in Asia the religions do have a strong influence upon the people and play an important role in the shaping of men, an essential part of the church's indigenous witness is its sympathetic understanding of the salient features of these religions. Religions represent the sincere search for God by man who is ignorant of God's search for him. They contain his deep longings for his Creator, his world view, and his understanding of himself as well as his society. One who confronts the Christian gospel does not stand naked and simple as if in a vacuum. Paul in his witness to the Jews and the Gentiles, such as the Athenians, dealt with people where they were and as they were. If we insist that the gospel speaks purely and simply to the universal need of all men regardless of who they are, why should anyone become a Jew to win the Jew, and a Greek to win the Greek, and be all things to all men so that by some means he may win some? Indigenous theology will help Asian Christians to be truly Asians so that they may win Asians.

This might also make considerable differences in our methods of witness. To give an example, while the appeal of the gospel is primarily to the individual, for a non-Christian in Asia to leave his religion and become a Christian means a total break with his own immediate family, friends, and home, a disruption of a magnitude unknown in many Western contexts, where the family is not such a close-knit entity. Therefore, in Asia it is especially important that the whole family be the focus of our gospel witness.

2. In Developing an Asian Confession of Faith

The confession of faith of any church ought to be firmly based on the revelation of Christ and the church's life experience in the light of the Word. Creeds such as the Apostles' Creed and the Nicene Creed, which are used universally by all churches, are the products of their times and the end results of battles that were fought against heresies of their periods. They show serious omissions of important aspects of our faith. For example, no mention is made in them of the validity of the written Word, justification by faith, the meaning of the atoning work of Christ, or the mission of the church. No absolute value can be given to the historical creeds, though they continue to be instructive to the church.

When Christians in Asia begin to understand their faith in terms of their life and needs, and from within, a living confession will develop which will try to relate the biblical historical faith to today's life and challenges. This confession will be alert to heresies, taking a lesson from the history of Christianity in forwardness and starkness of distinction. A church that lives in a hostile majority and makes audacious claims for its Lord cannot afford to be vague in its faith and uncertain in its teachings. The Western Christian creeds which we use have not faced the challenges that the church is confronted with in Asia today.

Another aspect of this problem is the diversity of denominational confessions found in Asia. Asian denominational divisions are largely, though not totally, the perpetuation of imported Western divisions, many of which grew out of relatively parochial or trivial issues in Western church development. Denominationalism in Asia has therefore had the especially unfortunate effect of fragmenting a very small minority force of Christians into a large number of separate camps for historically parochial reasons.

The development of an indigenous theology in Asia will encourage unity and cooperation at the level where the church's confession is at work rather than at the level of denominational confessions as mere theological formulations, and it will view confessional differences as a peripheral question. Members of a household can perhaps afford to be fighting with each other if they are at leisure and shut in to themselves. But if they are fighting an assaulter of the family, or called to action by some urgent need, they work as one body. This is the type of unity we should seek in Asia—a unity that is directed to mission, a unity that is purposive, rather than a unity which is an end in itself.

3. In the Total Life of the Church

Indigenous theology as a theology at work goes beyond a purely conceptual level. It affects all aspects of a church's life, such as its leadership, financial independence, music, church architecture, and witness. Generally Asian churches have been remotely controlled by their mother churches in the West, which provided both the key leadership and financial support. This situation is changing fast now. When the churches become free to develop their own expressions of faith, forms of worship, and methods of witness, inevitably we will find many indigenous developments in all these areas. Not all developments, however, will be in the right direction, which should be expected wherever creativity and freedom are at work.

Endless are the possibilities in the use that the Christian church can make of native music, dance, and drama, for its worship and witness. The present forms of worship, which are largely identical to those in the West, will give place to indigenous and therefore meaningful patterns.

In the total structure of the church, also, unlike in the West, perhaps the spotlight will fall on the *laos,* the grass roots of the church, rather than on its hierarchy. The strength of the church, it is hoped, will not be in its imposing structure, its numerical size, or its status and influence in social and political spheres, but rather in the power and mobility of smaller groups of dynamic Christians. The key to the phenomenal growth of Communism in Asia has been its untiring strength and the reckless outreach of its small cell groups primarily at the grass-roots level. The future of Asian Christianity will lie with the laymen and not with its professional leaders, and the type of church development on which we should concentrate is not so much the forming of a world church from the top as the developing of churches that meet in homes, tentmaking ministries, and small but dynamic and functional groups. Of course, only the "professionals" and their united thought, teachings, and efforts can give the kind of depth that laymen should have, lest they fall into shallowness. But in Asia it will not be those in air-conditioned offices of church headquarters nor those behind the pulpit who will determine the future course of the Christian church, but those in the pews (or the straw mats of the church floor), namely, the ordinary laymen who live their faith in a hostile world.

It seems that the church in Asia in many ways lives a life similar to the church of the early Roman Empire. This is very much true with regard to the types of opposition it faces, the gradual shaping of its structures, its urgent sense of immediate mission, the strain it goes through to articulate its faith in a religiophilosophical world, and its all-round steady growth.

Just as it will find its experience to be very similar to that of the church of the early Christian centuries, it will come to have a closer link with the present church of the rest of the Third World. Many of the general characteristics of Asian Christianity can be said to be applicable also to the church of Africa and Latin America. Christians in these three continents share several experiences and aspirations in common, and it will be increasingly fruitful and rewarding to all if they strengthen their mutual ties and find more opportunities to learn one from another.

The church in Asia, as the church anywhere, has to maintain a healthy tension between belonging to its world and belonging to God— that is to say, between its relevance and its uniqueness, which essentially is the problem of indigenization. But belonging to a foreign structure and foreign theology is to be like a plant in a hothouse, secure and comfortable but not related to the soil. Only a life in the open field, with the cold of the nights, the heat of the days, and the storms, will help the church grow steadily with deeper roots.

Six

The Yin-Yang
Way of Thinking

Jung Young Lee

[The author was born and grew up in North Korea, but received his theological education in the United States. The *yin-yang* way of thinking is inclusive and dialectical, embracing the possibility of "either/or" thinking as well. It can therefore help to clarify many of the unresolved issues that have plagued the history of Western Christian thought, such as the nature of divine transcendence and immanence, the idea of God as personal, Jesus Christ as human and divine, and man as body and spirit. This Asian way of thinking reorients us "from a dualistic to a monistic view of the world." In his book *The I: A Christian Concept of Man* (Philosophical Library, 1971), Dr. Lee applies the yin-yang way of thinking to the Christian understanding of man. In his new book, *The Theology of Change: A Christian Concept of God in an Eastern Perspective* (Orbis Books, 1979), he applies it to the Christian doctrine of God.—Ed.]

THE BASIC ISSUE AND RELATED PROBLEMS

The dominant issue in the history of Christian thought is neither the problem of the divine reality nor that of human belief but the Western way of thinking, that is, thinking in terms of "either/or." This was deeply rooted in the Greco-Roman view of the world, which became the general framework for theological thinking in the West from the beginning of Christianity. Its origins may go back to the Persian religion, Zoroastrianism, whose basic characteristic is the ultimate dichotomy between the opposing forces of Ormazd, the spirit of good, and Ahriman, the spirit of evil. It was also directly enshrined in Aristotelian logic, which became the foundation of the "Western" way of thinking. Some obvious examples in the West are easily noticeable to Easterners. We in the West think that what is not good must be evil, and what is not evil

From *International Review of Mission*, LX, 239 (July 1971), pp. 362–370. Reprinted by permission of the World Council of Churches.

must be good; and what is not wrong must be right, and what is not right must be wrong. But it is also possible that what is wrong may be neither right nor wrong, and what is not right may be both right and wrong at the same time. The Aristotelian conception, however, excludes the validity of the middle. The axiom of the "excluded middle," which is based on dualistic absolutism, is quite alien to what the Christian faith presupposes and has to deal with in our generation.

First of all, the either/or way of theological thinking in the West not only promoted but shaped the absolute dogma of God. The God of dogma is not God at all. The God who is absolutized by human words is less than the God of Christianity. That is why Emil Brunner rightly points out, even though he himself was led into the same mistake, that the formation of the doctrine of the Trinity became the norm to test the validity of the divine nature. Thus the doctrine became the judge of the divine. The Word of God became the servant of human words.[1] The absolutization of human words is very characteristic of the either/or way of thinking, and the Western emphasis on the Absolute Reason, from which even the Divine cannot escape, is primarily derived from it. Thus God has been made an idol of intellectual display. [A few notable exceptions to the dualistic way of thinking in Western Christian thought come to mind, e.g., the Pseudo-Dionysius, Nicholas of Cusa, Meister Eckhart, Paul Tillich.—Ed.]

Secondly, the either/or way of theological thinking is responsible for the predicament of Christianity in the world of today. Christianity seems unable to coexist with the different religions of the world. Its isolation from other religions in Japan, in India, in China, and other countries where major world religions are dominant is chiefly caused by the absolute claim of man-made dogmas, based on the either/or category of thinking. This category does not provide any room for the possibility of reconciliation and compromise with different forms of belief. Accordingly, Christianity has no choice but *either* to accept *or* reject them totally. That is why Christian missions in the past stressed conversion rather than cultivation, and total commitment rather than mutual dialogue. Buddhism, for example, existed very successfully alongside other religions in China, Japan, and Southeast Asia for many centuries, because of its middle-way approach to other religions. Yet Christianity either dominates others or is isolated from them. The exclusive character of either/or thinking made the inclusive exclusive.

Thirdly, the either/or way of thinking has made scientific technology possible. Thus Christianity is allied with technology to reject the nonrational aspects of human life. It suppressed occult phenomena and devalued the emotional aspects of religious life. Mysticism did not thrive in the life of the Western church. The Western church considered the exploration of psychic matters as the works of the devil. Her rejection of them is based on the absolute style of either/or thinking, which allows no room for mysticism. Thus Christianity in the West, and especially Protestantism, failed to meet the needs of the whole man whose nature includes mystic elements, and this failure is responsible for youth turning away from the church and seeking to satisfy its spiritual needs in Eastern mysticism.

Finally, the either/or style of theological thought has contributed toward the pollution of our environment. It created the dichotomy and conflict between man and nature, between body and spirit. Man must *either* conquer nature *or* nature will conquer him. *Either* the spirit overcomes the body *or* the body will overcome the spirit. In this kind of relationship we can expect nothing but conflict and war. Man gradually overcomes nature through the use of scientific technology, but he never conquers it completely. Ultimately neither of them survives. Man's conquest of nature is ultimately the conquest of himself. Thus, by this way of thinking, the opposites never come together into a harmonious and peaceful coexistence.

THE TASK BEFORE US

Our task should not be the total elimination of the either/or way of thinking, but the limitation of its function in theological enterprise. Its total elimination might result in the complete renunciation of our theological work. Thus we can summarize our task as twofold: the limitation of the function of the either/or way of thinking in theology, and the search for the most inclusive category of thinking to complement it.

a. *The limitation of the either/or way of thinking.* The limitation of the either/or way of thinking is essential in theology, because of its tendency to absolutize. The divine nature cannot be absolutized by human thinking. Moreover, the absolute category is no longer compatible with the contemporary understanding of the world. Our way of thinking is relative to our understanding of the world, because we think through the use of world imagery. The way of thinking in New Testament times, for example, was based on the world viewed as a three-storied structure. The traditional Western view of the world, to which we are still accustomed, is the Euclidean notion of the world, in which both time and space are infinitely extended. Even Newtonian physics did not offer any radically new world view. The absolute categories of space and time were still maintained. However, the contemporary world view which Einsteinian physics describes is radically different from the traditional Western world view. According to this contemporary view, everything is relative, including time and space. Since everything is relative, the absolute category of either/or thinking is out of harmony with the contemporary world view. Just as Newtonian physics, which presupposes the absolute categories of both time and space, functions well in ordinary mechanics, so the either/or style of thinking can deal with ordinary human situations, with penultimate matters. But just as Newtonian physics is unable to deal with the wholeness of the universe, theology, which deals with the ultimate concerns of our life, cannot be effectively expressed in either/or categories. Therefore, either/or thinking must be limited to penultimate matters only and is useful for the method of analysis and discrimination.

b. *The search for an inclusive category of thinking.* We have to find the most inclusive category of thinking which can be based on the relative world view. And since this relativistic world view, which contemporary physics attempts to describe, has been known to the Eastern people for a long time, it is reasonable to seek the symbol of relativistic thinking in the East. The world view to which Indian people are accustomed is certainly relativistic and inclusive. However, the concept of *maya* has often been viewed negatively by Christians, since it seems to reject the reality of the world. Thus it may arouse suspicion in some Christians if we take the symbol of thinking from the world view of India. However, the way in which the Chinese people have been thinking for many centuries is not only relativistic but is also compatible with the Christian idea of the world. In other words, the Chinese world view is positive and affirmative, just as the Christian world view is. It is then the Chinese world view which can help us to find the symbol of thinking that is most inclusive.

If Christian theology is to be universal in its orientation, it does not make any difference whether the symbol of thinking is taken from China or from the West as long as it satisfies the frame of reference through which Christian truth is conveyed. Furthermore, the Eastern symbol is much more practical than the Western to establish a point of contact between Christianity and other world religions, which have their origins in the East. Through this point of contact a Christian dialogue with world religions is possible. Thus the use of an Eastern category of thinking can be helpful not only for the development of ecumenical theology but for the mutual coexistence of Christianity with other religions in a creative process of becoming.

c. *The yin-yang symbolism as a possible category of theological thinking.* One of the profound treatments of cosmology is the Book of Change or the *I Ching,* [2] which is one of the oldest books in China. Since this book was accepted by both Taoism and Confucianism and became the focal point of the intellectual movement in Neo-Confucian philosophy in the later years, the cosmic view of this book is normative for the Chinese people. The Book of Change views the world as the flux of change, which was reaffirmed by Confucius. He stood by a river one day and said, "Like this river, everything is flowing on ceaselessly, day and night" (Analects 9:16). The concept of change then becomes the key to the understanding of the universe. Because of change everything is relative. Time and space are not absolute but relative, for everything, including themselves, is changing ceaselessly. Time and space are not *a priori* categories of all other forms of existence. Thus the general theory of relativity, which presupposes change, is in conformity with the Chinese view of the world. Since a relativistic world presupposes change, change can become the symbol for the basic categories of all things in the world.

The category of change, according to the Book of Change, is the interplay of *yin* and *yang,* which are the primary categories of all other categories of existence in the world. The idea of *yin-yang* may have a deeper historical root than any other concept in China. It is almost impossible to trace back the origin of this idea, even though the technical use of these terms may come from sometime during the Han dynasty. The concept of *yin* originally came from the imagery of shadow, while that of *yang* came from brightness. *Yin* then came to signify female, receptive, passive, cold, etc., and *yang* male, creative, active, warm, etc. *Yin* represents everything that is not *yang,* and *yang* what is not *yin.* Thus in an ultimate analysis everything, whether spiritual or material and temporal or spatial, can be categorized by the symbol of *yin* and *yang* interplay. The symbol of *yin* and *yang* is then the primordial category of everything that exists in the world. The characteristic nature of this symbol is not the conflict but the complementarity of opposites. It is the category of becoming rather than of being. It is the transcendental category of expression, because it transcends the logical and analytical categories of our rational thinking. It is therefore possible to express the divine nature which transcends every dichotomy and conflict of opposites. The characteristic of transcendence is expressed in the complementarity of opposites. *Yin* presupposes the necessity of *yang,* and *yang* cannot exist without *yin.* The one requires the other. Thus *yin-yang* thinking is a way of both/and thinking, which includes the possibility of either/or thinking. The latter is effective in dealing with penultimate matters, as the former is with ultimate concerns. Since theology is concerned with the ultimate, theological thinking must be in terms of both/and.

The both/and category of thinking, which is based on the *yin-yang* symbolism, is characteristic not only of the Chinese but also of the Indian way of thinking. As Betty Heimann pointed out, "The West thinks in *aut-aut,* the disjunctive either-or." India, on the other hand, visualizes a continuous stream of interrelated moments of *sive-sive,* the "this as well as that, in an endless series of changes and transformation."³ The relativistic world view of India certainly provides this category of both/and thinking which seems to be the general characteristic of Eastern people, and must be adopted by theology.

Scientifically also, the contemporary world view forces the West to think more and more in complementary terms. For example, scientists today do not believe either the wave theory or the quantum theory of light but accept both of them at the same time. In our living, the stress of contextualism tends to avoid ethical absolutes. Thus the both/and category of thinking seems to have a universal orientation. If Christian theology also has a universal implication, I believe that it is to be expressed in this universal category of both/and thinking.

There is a growing interest among theologians in the possible use of the *yin-yang* category of thinking in theology. For example, Wilfred C. Smith of Harvard University says, "What I myself see in the *yang-yin* symbol with regard to this matter, if I may be allowed this personal note, is not an image that would reduce Christian truth to a part of some larger whole. Rather, I find it a circle for embracing Christian truth itself. . . . In this, the image says to me, as in all ultimate matters, truth lies not in an either/or, but in a both/and."⁴ Nels Ferré not only realizes the advantage of using this complementary category of thinking in theology but suggests that this is the only possible category. He says, "There is here no place for paradox, excluded middle, *totum simul* or *Alles auf einmal.* What we need is a . . . contrapletal logic."⁵ Ferré recognizes that the idea of contrapletal logic was already used by Ramanuja in *Vedarthasangraha,* one of the most profound treatises in Indian literature. He says also: "A prime example has been the Chinese use of *yin* and *yang.* Two realities like day and night or light and darkness are contradictory in one dimension and yet fulfilling of each other within their place in nature and man's experience."⁶ The growing interest in the use of the both/and category of thinking by Western theologians will have a profound implication as an impetus for the creation of universal theology.

THE IMPLICATION OF THE YIN-YANG CATEGORY FOR
THEOLOGICAL THINKING

Since the *yin-yang* way of thinking transcends human reasoning, its application to theology not only clarifies some paradoxical issues but provides fresh interpretations of divine attributes. It can, for example, illuminate such concepts as the nature of divine transcendence and immanence, God as personal, Jesus as the Christ, or the relation of body and spirit.

The West, using either/or categories of thought, finds it difficult to express the divine transcendence and immanence together. For the *yin-yang* way of thinking, it is no trouble at all to think that God is *both* transcendent *and* immanent at the same time. He cannot be *either* transcendent *or* immanent. The God of transcendence is *also* the God of immanence.

Similarly, in the West we ask the question, "Is God personal or impersonal?" But God, who transcends all categories, cannot be a personal God *only.* God who is only personal is a limited God. The God of creation is not only the God of personal beings but of impersonal beings as well. To make God personal is to limit him. Thus the use of the *yin-yang* category provides a new understanding of the divine nature.

Further, Jesus as the Christ, as both God and man, cannot really be understood in terms of either/or. How can man also be God? In the West we have to speak in terms of paradox or mystery in order to justify the reality of Christ. However, in *yin-yang* terms, he can be thought of as both God and man at the same time. In him God is not separated from man nor man from God. They are in complementary relationship. He is God because of man: he is man because of God.

Finally, one of the classical dilemmas in theological thinking is the relationship between the spirit and the body (or matter). According to Judeo-Christian teaching, they are one and inseparable. Our spirit is also our body and our body is also spirit. Nevertheless, because Western thinkers have been preoccupied with making distinctions, they have thought in terms of dualistic entities, of dichotomy between the spirit and the body. The *yin-yang* way of thinking clarifies the theological meaning of man and reorients our thinking from a dualistic to a monistic view of the world. It thus renders a great service to the renewed understanding of Christian theology as well as to a universalistic outlook of the Christian message of the world.

CONCLUSION

The use of this transcendental category of thinking has been shown not only to solve controversial issues in theology but often to bring to light new meaning and fresh understanding of theological issues. The *yin-yang* way of thinking applies to ultimate matters which either/or thinking fails to deal with, just as the latter deals with penultimate matters which the former fails to do. We need both the *yin-yang* and the either/or ways of thinking to carry out successfully the theological task. Christian theology becomes universal only when the either/or category is deabsolutized, and it becomes significant only when the *yin-yang* category allows the creativity of either/or thinking. The effective method of theological thinking is possible when both *yin-yang* and either/or categories complement one another.[7]

NOTES

1. See Emil Brunner, *The Christian Doctrine of God: Dogmatics*, Vol. I (Westminster Press, 1950), p. 226.

2. For full explanation, see my *The Principle of Changes: Understanding the I Ching* (University Books, 1971).

3. Betty Heimann, *Facets of Indian Thought* (London: George Allen & Unwin, 1964), p. 168.

4. Wilfred Cantwell Smith, *The Faith of Other Men* (New American Library, 1963), p. 74.

5. Nels F. S. Ferré, *The Universal Word: A Theology for a Universal Faith* (Westminster Press, 1969), p. 80.

6. Ibid., p. 100.

7. The *yin-yang* way of thought is applied as a theological method in my book *The I: A Christian Concept of Man* (Philosophical Library, 1971).

Seven

Doing Theological Reflection
in a Philippine Context
Carlos H. Abesamis, S.J.

[Fr. Abesamis presented this paper to the Ecumenical Dialogue of Third World Theologians meeting at Dar es Salaam, Tanzania, in 1976. He is concerned with methodology in general, and only the final section of the paper deals specifically with the Philippine context. A fundamental distinction is made between theology as something we do and theology as something we study, between the "theologian" and the "student" of theology. The former is theology proper and involves reflection and interpretation of the life experience of a people in the light of their Christian faith. Although he acknowledges that both study and reflection are needed, the way of reflection is seen to be more in keeping with the original spirit of our Christian religion. The basic tools of theological reflection are experience, analysis, and the Bible. Abesamis insists that the "real theologians" are the people at the grass roots of society, and that those formally trained in theology are only the "technicians" who must stand ready to assist them in their theological reflections. Three major stages of theological development are discerned: the Semitic, the Greek, and now the Third World. What is needed today in the Third World church is "a bracketing-off of the Western Greek tradition" in order to make direct contact with the Semitic stage of theology, although Western insights might later on be grafted into an indigenous theology. He concludes that "the procedure is not taking a Western tree and transplanting it on African or Asian soil. Rather it is planting our own African or Asian tree and grafting on whatever is needed for its life and health."—Ed.]

THE MEANING OF THEOLOGY

I understand "doing theological reflection," quite generally, as the activity of reflecting on the contemporary human life situation in the light of one's faith. Those who do theological reflection make an attempt

From Sergio Torres and Virginia Fabella (eds.), *The Emergent Gospel: Theology from the Underside of History* (Orbis Books, 1978), pp. 112–123. Reprinted by permission of the publisher.

to interpret the life experience of their people or community today in the light of their Christian faith.

I take this way of doing theological reflection to be the most in keeping with the original spirit of our religion. For the main focus of our religion in its beginnings is a focus on life experience and events in which our ancestors-in-religion discerned God's saving activity. We learn from certain of their basic religious statements (e.g., Deut. 6:21–23; 26:5–9; Josh. 24:2–13) that their religion was first and foremost concerned with the great saving deeds of Yahweh in their history as a human community. They proclaimed and confessed Yahweh's call and promise in the time of the Patriarchs, their deliverance from the oppression and slavery in Egypt, Yahweh's act to make them his people in the desert, Yahweh's activity in taking possession of a land broad and beautiful. And insofar as these saving deeds of Yahweh constituted a history of saving deeds, their religion and basic confession centered around the history of Yahweh's redemptive activity in their history as a human community. History—life experience, events, history of events—is basic in the Mosaic religion.

Not only their basic creedal statements but also their theology and theological reflection were quite naturally concerned mainly with events and history. The stuff of which much of their theology was made was the interpreted events and history of their life as a people, that is, God's redemptive activity and history with this people. We might recall as examples the religious production of the Yahwist, the Elohist, the Pentateuch itself, the Deuteronomist historian.

What about our ancestors-in-religion in the early church, i.e., the first and second generations of Christians? Their basic confession also centered around history and events. They saw the works of Jesus in their time as the final and definitive saving deed of Yahweh in the history of Israel and the world. They testified that the last saving deed of Yahweh was to be found in the works of Jesus (healings, exorcisms, forgiving of sins, etc.), in his death and rising, and in his coming in glory in the parousia (cf., e.g., Acts 3:11–26). What about their theological reflections and theology? History—the works, death, resurrection, parousia of the Lord, in which Yahweh was exercising his last and definitive redemptive act—is the focus. This can be said to be the main focus of the writers of the body of religious literature we call the New Testament.

People are born, live, love, interact, struggle, hope, die in a given historical context. And God is involved in this concrete historical context. This is the level of concrete *life.* A reflection is made on this concrete life. This is the level of *theology,* more specifically, the level of "doing theological reflection."

THE CHRISTIAN FAITH
AND THE HISTORY OF REDEMPTION

I described "doing theological reflection" as the activity of interpreting the contemporary human life situation in the light of the Christian faith. I would now like to make this more particular by saying that doing theological reflection is above all else "describing" the present moment in the history of redemption (=deliverance, =coming into possession of salvific blessings, =salvation, which, by the way, is total salvation). Why is this? The answer to this question is first another question. What is the Christian faith about first and foremost? It is about the history of redemption. It is a history of salvific actions, of salvific events, especially of course the salvific ministry, death, resurrection, and second coming of the Lord. The salvific events of the promise of land and children, the exodus, the covenant, the conquest of the land, etc., and the *history* that this chain of events formed constituted the main material of the religious confession of Yahwism and Judaism. This confession of salvific actions/events evolved into a hope for the final salvific action/event. This was the case with some of the prophets, the apocalyptic writers, the synagogue religion. (By the way, this salvific action/event, especially among the apocalyptic writers, was to affect not just the individual's soul in its life of sin and grace to prepare it for life after death; rather it was a question of the total salvation of the person—Semitically understood —of humanity, of all creation, from all evils, for all blessings.)

The early Christians confessed that this final action/event of total salvation had been inaugurated in the works, death, and resurrection of Jesus of Nazareth and would be completed in his parousia. These redemptive acts of Jesus, the Messiah and Lord, constituted for them the last phase of this history of salvation.

The Christian faith then is before all else about the history of redemption. (It is also about law, i.e., ethics, morals, law, but we will talk about this later.)

I suggest then that reflecting on today's human experience "in the light of the Christian faith" should mean first of all, though certainly not exclusively, "in the light of or within the context of the history of redemption." The theologian's primary task is to discover the meaning of the present moment, the 1970's and 1980's, within the context of a history of saving deeds/events, a history which begins in the first salvific deed of creation and will be completed finally in Christ's second coming when all things will be renewed in the new heaven and the new earth where there will be no more mourning nor tears nor suffering nor death nor pain (cf. Rev. 21:1–5).

THE TOOLS FOR "DOING THEOLOGY"

In this way of doing theological reflection, what the theologian needs are experience, analysis, and the Bible.

Experience

How can theologians reflect on and interpret the meaning of a particular human life situation unless they have experienced it? Experience is important for doing theological reflection; and without this credential one like me should hesitate to make theological pronouncements today.

The doer of theological reflection is ideally the person whose daily life situation is in all respects the life situation of the people. For example, a worker, not a university professor, is, from the point of view of the need for experience, ideally the best person to reflect on the life situation of workers. Those who have a vicarious and occasional experience of the life of the worker could also (although as a poor second best) do theological reflection, but they must be acutely aware of their very, very serious limitations and be strictly on guard against them.

We should deal with this point more adequately, at least in parenthesis. It happens often enough today that in a dual society—consisting of those who occupy a social position that controls wealth-power-culture and of those who do not control wealth-power-culture (e.g., the worker)—those who do theological reflection are those who occupy neither position, i.e., they occupy a middle position and have little or no experience of the life of the poor. Can such people do theological reflection? Definitely. Will their theology be the theology of the worker, i.e., can it truly express the concerns, the frustrations, the hopes of the worker? Most likely not; in fact, the typical liberalism of their middle-class position makes them run the risk of betraying the worker's cause, not to speak of their penchant to unconsciously "apply" the Western theology that they know "to the present situation" of the worker. Is the situation of middle-class theologians then hopeless? Not completely. Besides of course being able to produce a theology of the middle class for the delectation of the middle class, they can also produce a theology, which, though not a theology of the worker, carries an implicit message to the worker: "I support you and am in solidarity with you, and I invite others of my kind to be in solidarity with you." Or the worker may in effect say to the middle-class theologians: "You have been somewhat immersed in our life situation and we, the workers, commission you to speak for us and with us, as long as you are aware of your limitations."

I would add here another parenthetical remark in response to an objection that could be raised in this present context: How can an ordinary uneducated worker do theological reflection? Passing over the condescending tone of the question, I would for now merely point to a distinction I would make between a theologian and a technician. A theologian reflects on and discerns the meaning of a contemporary human situation. Doing theological reflection is a creative task. It is an art. The technician is the one who has the skill and professional competence in, say, the Greek and Hebrew languages, or in the historicocritical method of exegesis, or in the social sciences (or, also, professional competence in patristics, dogma, history, canon law, etc.). The technician is at the service of the theologian. The theologian can be the same person as the technician, but this would be extremely rare and well-nigh impossible. The task of doing theological reflection would generally be a collaborative task in which the theologians need the assistance of the technicians. So worker-theologians need not be technicians. Although, again, in an egalitarian society of equal opportunities, what would prevent them from being technicians as well?

In any case, my sincere hope is that in the Third World we middle-class "theologians" will be doing the necessary task of transition and then give way to the real theologians of the people. Our role is to fade away. Thank God, I see glimmers of this already in my country.

Analysis

In order to understand and interpret the total life experience of the contemporary human community, the theologian needs, besides experience, a rigorous analysis of the total human situation of the community or society. This is the analysis not only of the intrapersonal and interpersonal (i.e., the psychological or Freudian) factors, but also, especially today, the historical and social (i.e., the economic, political, cultural, religious) factors. Technicians (in the sense I explained above) would ordinarily help the theologians here. Further, because there is no such thing as an objective, value-free social science, the theologians must know whether the tools of analysis being used are First World or Third World tools. They must make a basic option.

Bible

The theologians need experience and analysis. They also need the Bible. They must be able to situate the present in a history of salvation that has a past (the saving deeds of Yahweh, the final saving deeds of Yahweh through Jesus Christ), a present (including the reality of the risen Lord), and a future (the complete deliverance of people and creation from all bondage and decay). It is the Bible (which should be treated not as a dictionary of timeless truths, but primarily as a record of life experiences with God, interpreted in faith, of a people who lived during the founding years of our religion) that contains the record of this redemptive activity and history, both as regards what has already been accomplished in the past and what is to be hoped for in the future.

Here the theologians need the help of other technicians, i.e., the exegetes and biblical scholars. However, even among biblical scholars there are different ways of treating the Bible. For example, one would see in the Bible an arsenal of incipient dogmatic truths. Another would see biblical study to be a handmaid in the service of systematic, dogmatic theology. Another would indeed reconstruct the meaning of the Bible by interpreting it against the background of the literary and the historical contexts, but without sufficiently seeing the broad scope of the history of redemption to which the individual books of the Bible are merely single testimonies through the course of the biblical centuries. Finally, there are the biblical scholars, who, as they do rigorous exegesis, open each book of the Bible as they would different single doors, and as they do so, open up to themselves and to others a whole panorama in which to contemplate the whole history of salvation with its past and its promise for the future. These last are the technicians the theologians are looking for.

The Historical Stages of Theology

If doing theological reflection in the Judeo-Christian context, in keeping with its bias for history, is a reflection on concrete experience (i.e., the experience here among my people which is different from the experience elsewhere, say, in the Western world), then theology, which is the product of theological reflection, cannot but be indigenous.

I would speak very broadly of three (perhaps there are more) major moments in indigenous theological reflection in the history of our religion, corresponding to three major indigenous situations of our religion: These are the Semitic, the Greek, and now the African and the Asian. The theologies of the Yahwist, the Pentateuch, the Deuteronomist historian,

Isaiah, Synoptics, John, even Paul, belong to the Semitic stage. The Greek and Latin fathers, the Scholastics, the contemporary Western theologians (like Rahner, Schillebeeckx), the theology contained in the great conciliar documents, including Vatican II, belong to the Greek stage. Two remarks may be singled out regarding this stage. First, the theology here was, for a long time and in a significant degree, metaphysical and thus ahistorical, i.e., it was often concerned with circumscribing the metaphysical nature of religious realities, e.g., the nature of God as Trinity, the essence of Christ as God and man in one nature, the divine motherhood of Mary, the nature of the sacraments, etc. Second, insofar as it has ceased to be significantly metaphysical and has become existential, experiential, or even historical, as in the case of contemporary Western theologians and Vatican II, it remains a theological reflection arising out of a Western and First World experience and the theological production remains, trunk and root, First World and Western.

And now we speak, and rightly, of an indigenous African or Asian theology. What does this mean? I hope we are beyond the stage where "indigenizing theology" means translating the Western theological works written in Latin, French, German, or English into our native dialects. "Indigenization of theology" is not a question of translation from language to language. Neither should producing an indigenous theology mean "applying" the theology of Athanasius, Ambrose, Pannenberg, Rahner, or Vatican II "to the local situation." Whether metaphysical or historical, their theological productions are Western and we cannot produce our indigenous theology simply by taking over their reflections on their human situation and "applying" them to ours. How can I "apply" the "Theology of the Death of God" and the "Theology on the Use of Leisure" to the situation of my people for whom God is alive and life is difficult? Even the great theology of the historic Vatican II is a theology of the experiences of the First World church, and when it says, "The joys and the hopes, the griefs and the anxieties of the men of this age, especially those who are poor or in any way afflicted, these too are the joys and hopes, the griefs and anxieties of the followers of Christ" (*The Church in the Modern World,* 1), it is the First World church talking with compassion to or about the Third World. It is not the voice of the Third World telling of its own life experience.

THE SEMITIC AND THE WESTERN STAGES OF THEOLOGY

Implied in what I have said (i.e., that the necessary tools for doing theological reflection are experience, analysis, and the Bible) seems to be a bracketing-off of the Western Greek tradition, i.e., the theological production in Europe and America from the second century to the present. Here, I make the following observations:

1. The Greek stage is one of the three major stages in indigenous theological production and it is a valid stage of indigenous theological production.

2. The authentic developments in this second stage are inspired and guided by the Spirit.

3. It is in a significant degree metaphysical in its concerns. For example, whereas, broadly speaking, in the biblical stage the question revolved around: "What is God *doing?*" the significant (and at the time necessary) question in the Greek stage was: "Who is God? What is his *nature?*" To say that theology becomes metaphysical is not necessarily to talk about a fault; it is to talk about a characteristic and a phase in the development of our Christian theological tradition.

4. During this stage the Holy Spirit helped the church to clarify points of doctrine and dogma. These dogmatic and doctrinal clarifications, insofar as they are proposed by the church as articles of faith, are inspired by the Spirit and should be assented to in faith and love.

5. The theological production of this age remains, as any other theological production, culture-bound. This means that the theological problem (e.g., "How do you explain the real presence of Christ in the Eucharist?") arises out of a concrete life situation or culture, is reflected on in thought patterns and categories that are peculiar to that culture and articulated in a language peculiar to that culture (e.g., "transubstantiation").

6. One should study this stage seriously as part of the history of one's religion and should apply all the tools (e.g., scholastic philosophy, contemporary Western philosophy) necessary to understand it. A study of the development of the faith in the Western Greek tradition is part of any theological education. This study can be done either thematically—Christology, Trinity, Mariology, sacraments, etc. Or it can be studied historically—the history of the development of Christian doctrine or dogma. Or both.

7. I make a distinction between doing theological reflection and studying theology, between a theologian and a student of theology. Students of theology must study exegesis, biblical theology, dogmatic theology (thematically or historically), the history of the church, canon law, etc. Theologians, on the other hand, must do theological reflection, that is, they must reflect on contemporary experience. Insofar as in certain and more common instances the students of theology must do the theological reflection, theological reflection becomes one of the tasks of the students

of theology. In fact, in this instance, it is their most important task. And for this they need an understanding of the present life situation of their people through experience and analysis and an understanding of the history of salvation through a study of the Bible. We must today both study theology and do theological reflection. But the two are not exactly the same.

8. Why is the Western theological production not essential in doing our own indigenous African or Asian theological reflection? An initial and superficial answer is because you cannot produce an Asian or African theology by using or applying Western theological production. But isn't the theological production in the Bible equally culture-bound? Yes, and let's not ever forget this point. Having said this and keeping it in the back of our mind always, we must go on to say that if theological reflection is done "in the light of one's faith," we must find this faith and its message somewhere. And anywhere it might be, it is culture-bound; and so we seem to have run into a dead end. Or better, we are forced to choose one of the culture-bound theological expressions of our faith. I choose the Semitic for the following reasons:

a. The Semitic stage (Abraham, Moses, Jesus, early church) represents the primitive years of the founding of our religion. In God's providence, this world religion first took root in a Semitic life experience and culture, and the original meaning and message of our faith was first expressed in a theological production that was Semitic.

b. In it I find the history of redemption depicted *in its integrity:* in its total breadth, i.e., the saving deeds in the history of a human community, from creation onward to the final saving deed(s) of Christ, finally to the full completion at the parousia. I find it *in its fullness,* i.e., in this stage I see depicted God's concern for total life and total salvation for the total person, humanity, and creation, God's concern for all forms of human ills, and God's concern for both this world and the world to come.

c. It is less interested in metaphysical descriptions of the nature of things and more concerned with history, i.e., with human events and God's involvement and activity in them.

d. It is more akin to our oriental spirit and to our Third World aspirations.

9. It is clear that the bracketing off of the Western tradition pertains to the doing of theological reflection, not to the study of theology. Does this, however, mean that the Western tradition is completely excluded from the activity of doing theological reflection? No. First, it could provide examples and models of theological reflection with which we can compare ours. Second, its theological insights could eventually be grafted into our indigenous theology. For example, the theology that comes out

of the life experience of workers would first come to certain core insights and then in the course of later reflections might ask about the role of the sacramental Christ in their lives. At this stage, the clarifications hammered out in the West regarding the Real Presence might prove useful. But one can see that the grafting on is natural, not violent. The procedure is not taking a Western tree and transplanting it on African or Asian soil. Rather, it is planting our own African or Asian tree and grafting on whatever is needed for its life and health.

THE MEANING OF CHRISTIANITY
IN THE PHILIPPINE CONTEXT

In the light of the main outlines of our discussion, we can say that the theological question in doing theological reflection is this: What is salvation today? This is a briefer way of saying: What is the meaning of the present moment in the ongoing history of redemption?

This question can be taken narrowly as the first or core question. Or it can be taken as the broad umbrella that covers the whole process of theological reflection, including and starting with the first and core question. A hypothetical example will illustrate this. For one or other of the industrialized societies of the West, we might have:

What Is Salvation Today? (Broad Umbrella)

1. What is salvation today? (First and core question)
   (Let us suppose that the hypothetical answer is: Deliverance from materialism and atheism.)
2. Then, what does it mean to be church in this situation of materialism and atheism?
3. What does God mean in such a situation?
4. What does grace mean?
5. What does wealth mean? or progress?
6. And so forth.

In summary, we may speak in terms of "method" and "tools" for theological reflection. The method calls for (1) knowledge of the present historical situation (the tools for this are experience and analysis), (2) knowledge of redemptive history (the tool for this is the religious literature called the Bible), and (3) the activity of interpretation or reflection itself.

In our Philippine human community we may say sketchily this: (1) The theologians would see that the present historical situation can be described as a lack of human life due to a social order in which human equality and justice are still mightily to be striven after, in a Philippine —not European, Latin American, African, Japanese, Vietnamese—context of life and meanings. (2) They would plant this situation in the history of God's redemptive activity for total life and total salvation. (3) They would arrive at an interpretation that salvation today means total human development, i.e., concern both for the life of sin/grace and for human dignity, human rights, human sufferings, human life, concern both for the world to come and for this world and its human concerns; and that this is to be done through the transformation of the social order in a Philippine context of life and meanings.

Then related questions will spontaneously surface. For example: What does it mean to be a Christian community in such a concrete setting? What is the meaning of poverty? Of wealth? How does one love? What is the role of the priest? The layperson? What is the meaning of suffering, of struggle, of self-sacrifice, of sharing, of community? Of Philippine values and spirituality? Of life-style? Liturgy or the Eucharist? Catechetics? Land? Work? Folk religion?

I want to make one last remark which unfortunately must be brief. The Christian faith is first of all a *proclamation* of the history of God's redemptive activity. This is the gospel. Secondly, it is also a *teaching* about a way of life, an ethic—more particularly, the ethic of Jesus, and more concretely, the ethic of love. This is the law. And law follows gospel. A more adequate description of doing theological reflection would then be: reflecting on the contemporary human life situation within the context of salvation history *and* in the light of the ethic of Jesus. Theological reflection is interpreting the meaning of life today in the light of the gospel and the law.

Eight

Asia's Struggle for Full Humanity: Toward a Relevant Theology

Asian Conference of Third World Theologians

[Here is the Final Statement of the Asian Conference of Third World Theologians meeting in Wennappuwa, Sri Lanka, January 1979. The title of the Statement was the theme of the Conference. Like those who had met at Dar es Salaam, Tanzania, in 1976 (cf. No. 7, above), these delegates concluded that theology, to be authentic, must "emerge from the people's struggle for liberation." Furthermore, to be truly Asian it must "be immersed in the Asian historicocultural situation and grow out of it." The Statement recognizes that the present role of religion and theology in Asia, though ambivalent, is "dehumanizing." "A truly liberating theology must ultimately be the work of the Asian poor who are struggling for full humanity," though specialists can still be useful as facilitators and catalysts. But the theological work of specialists becomes authentic only when it is "rooted in the history and struggle of the poor and the oppressed." The first of its kind in Asia, the Conference agreed to form an Ecumenical Theological Fellowship of Asia through which to follow up the tasks they have set for themselves.—Ed.]

I. PREAMBLE

We Christians from Asia, along with fraternal delegates from other continents, gathered in Wennappuwa, Sri Lanka, from 7th to 20th of January, 1979, motivated by our solidarity with our people in the struggle for full humanity and by our common faith in Jesus Christ.

Bringing with us the experience of the struggle in our own countries, we came to share in the life and situations of the masses striving for justice in Sri Lanka, through our four-day "live-ins."

During the days that followed, we became more aware of the commonalities and divergences in our background which sharpened our

From *Voices of the Third World,* I, 2 (June 1979), pp. 8–15. Reprinted by permission of the Ecumenical Association of Third World Theologians.

understanding of both the richness and the anguish of our people in Asia.

As Asians, we recognize the important task before us. Our reflections, already begun in our local realities, helped us to enrich the process of interaction and sharing among us who have committed ourselves to the struggle of the poor in Asia. At the same time, we realize that these reflections are only part of the beginning of a collective and continuous search for a relevant theology in Asia.

II. THE ASIAN CONTEXT

Asia suffers under the heels of a forced poverty. Its life has been truncated by centuries of colonialism and a more recent neocolonialism. Its cultures are marginalized, its social relations distorted. The cities with their miserable slums, swollen with the poor peasants driven off the land, constitute a picture of wanton affluence side by side with abject poverty that is common to the majority of Asia's countries. This extreme disparity is the result of a class contradiction, a continuous domination of Asia by internal and external forces. The consequences of this type of capitalist domination is that all things, time and life itself, have become marketable commodities. A small minority of owners dictates the quality of life for the producers (workers, peasants, and others) in determining the price of their energy, skills, intelligence, as well as the material benefits needed to sustain these. What is produced, how and where it is produced, for whom it is produced, are the decisions of transnational corporations in collusion with the national elites and with the overt or covert support of political and military forces.

The struggle against these forces has been courageously taken up by the advocates of socialism. This sociopolitical order corresponds to the aspirations of the Asian masses in both the rural and urban areas since it promises to them the right to take their life into their own hands, to determine both the social and economic conditions that govern their well-being. A very large part of Asia has succeeded, after long struggles, in establishing this socialist order. However, it must be added that the socialist transformation in these countries is not yet complete and that these countries must continue to liberate themselves from all distortions in an ongoing self-criticism.

Neither will socialist movements in Asia be thorough in their struggle for full humanity without an inner liberation from self-seeking and exploitative instincts. The rich traditions of the major religions of Asia (Hinduism, Buddhism, Islam, and Christianity) offer many inspirations. The richness is not only expressed in philosophical formulations but also in various art forms such as dance and drama, poems and songs, as well as in myths and rites, parables and legends. It is only when we immerse ourselves in the "peoples' cultures" that our struggle acquires an indigenous dimension.

However it is equally true that the social function of religions or cultural systems is ambiguous. In the past, religions and cultural systems have played the role of legitimizing feudal relationships, yet the self-critical principle inherent in them can be a source of liberation today from the domination of capitalist values and ideologies.

Hence we feel that the Asian context which dictates the terms of an Asian theology consists of a struggle for fuller humanity in the socio-political as well as the psychospiritual aspects. The liberation of all human beings is both societal and personal.

III. THE ISSUES

We realize that if large numbers of men and women find themselves socially deprived and progressively thrown further and further away from the center of life and meaning, it is not a mere accident or the effect of a national catastrophe. In fact, from Pakistan to Korea, passing through the subcontinent and Southeast Asia, practically all parliamentary governments, with the exception of Japan, have at some time given way to military governments or authoritarian regimes of one form or the other. In these countries not only are political rights suppressed, but so also are the rights of workers to strike in the cities and the rights of peasants to organize themselves in the countryside. Many leaders and people holding political views contrary to the ruling group are condemned to spend several years in prison, often without due process of trial.

Behind the facade of "law and order" are Asia's cheap and docile labor and laws which leave the country open to unrestricted exploitation by foreign capital, with the profit going to a small elite. A deeper logic is to be found in the dual economies of these countries. The industrial sector, monopolized by the national elite, has developed along the lines of an export economy that does not correspond to the needs of the local population. It also depends heavily on foreign capital and technology. And as a result of unequal trade relations and the weakness of these countries their indebtedness and dependence grew to an extent beyond their control. International banks and transnational corporations have become the new masters of Asia's politics and economics.

At the same time the rural sector in these countries has remained stagnant. The so-called agrarian reforms did not change the unequal social relations of production in the rural areas. The benefit of the

"Green Revolution" went only to the middle and big landowners who could afford its technology. A great number of peasants were driven off the land in the process and ended in the slums of the swollen cities of Asia. On the other hand, the rural surplus thus accumulated is often reinvested in crops for export or channeled into urban industries, preventing the growth of production for food. As a result, Asia, which is potentially rich in agriculture, is importing food from outside and the amount is increasing continually at an alarming rate. Hunger and poverty will be the fate of Asian masses for many years to come.

A hopeful sign is the growing awareness among the oppressed peoples which leads to the growth and increase of peoples' organizations in both the cities and the rural areas. The majority of Asian countries have witnessed peasant uprisings and urban disturbances. Put down by bloody oppression and intimidated by imprisonment and torture, many of these movements have gone underground and turned to a protracted struggle as the only means of changing their societies. While not necessarily condoning the use of violence, which is most often unavoidable, we question and object to the enforcement of "law and order" which consolidates the control of the power elites while thwarting the organized conscientious objections of the deprived majorities. When legalized violence leaves no room for peoples to free themselves from their misery, are we surprised that they are so compelled to resort to violence? Have the Christian churches sufficiently understood the message of revolutionary violence in the Asian struggles for political independence, social emancipation, and liberation from the built-in violence of the present economic and political structures?

The youth in Asia, who form a large segment of the Asian population, are continuously victimized. They constitute the growing number of unemployed and underemployed in the labor force. A lack of proper educational facilities and decreasing employment opportunities in the rural areas where the majority of youth come from, lead to the irreversible process of migration to urban centers; while in the urban areas, the youth are the targets of consumer culture and in turn become vehicles of deculturation. We emphasize also that some students, youth, and workers have been playing the important role of a critical and committed force in the struggle for the basic rights of the oppressed people. At the same time, they are also made pawns in the power politics of politicians and other interest groups, thus losing their genuine relevance, and are even sacrificed in abrupt physical violence.

The educational system, linked to the established centers of power, is geared to perpetuate the domination of youth. It serves as a mere channel for the transfer of technical skills and alienated knowledge without reference to humanistic values. The pyramidal elitist structure of education is used to fabricate losers, who are continuously exploited.

We recognized deeply that women were also victims of the same structures of domination and exploitation. In the context of the Asiatic religions and cultures, the relationship between men and women is still one of domination. This situation is worse in the poorer classes of society. Thus women face an unforgivable double oppression.

At the economic level, a male-dominated society reduces the "price" of woman-labor and limits the scope of women's participation in the process of production at all levels—local, national, regional, and consequently the international level. At the political level, women are aware of the political situation in their countries, but here too their competence and activity are greatly stifled.

Women are sexually and intellectually vulnerable in a society where an interaction of traditional and modern forces (especially tourism) compels them to compromise with consumeristic values of capitalist society. It also compels them to prostitution. Instead of condemning the system which forces women into prostitution, it is the women who are condemned by the men who exploit them.

We recognize the existence of ethnic minorities in every Asian country. They are among the most deprived sector at all levels including the economic, political and cultural. They are struggling for self-determination against heavy odds, yet their authentic struggle is often utilized by the centers of power in playing up racial antagonism to camouflage themselves and disrupt the unity among the marginalized.

Mass media, including the printed word, films, television, etc., are controlled by the ruling elite to propagate their dominant value systems and myths, providing a dehumanizing, individualistic, consumerist culture. Despite this domination, we also witness the emergence of a more creative micromedia that portrays realistically the struggle of the dominated people.

We need to mention also the increasing impact of urbanization and irrational industrialization. Women, children and men together face narrowing opportunities for education, housing, and health services as these social needs are determined by market forces. With the transfer of the platforms of production and mechanization from industrialized countries, environmental pollution surfaces in most of the Asian countries, causing ecological imbalances. Here we join with our fishermen in their struggle against the unscrupulous practices of certain countries like Japan, Taiwan, and South Korea.

We realize also the legitimizing role of religion in the course of history within the Asian context. Religions form an integral part of the total social reality, inseparable from all spheres of action. Much interaction has taken place between religion and politics in Asia down the ages, and today there are significant movements of social renewal inspired by religions outside the traditional institutions. We need to stress the critical and transforming element in religion and culture. A serious sociopolitical analysis of realities and involvement in political and ideological struggles should be seen as vital elements of religion in its role as a critic. Here we realize the creative force of culture in bringing people together and giving them an identity within their struggles. Critical cultural action would destroy old myths and create new symbols in continuity with the cultural treasures of the past.

IV. TOWARD A RELEVANT THEOLOGY

We are conscious of the fact that the vital issues of the realities of Asia indicate the ambivalent role of the major religions in Asia and pose serious questions to us, hence challenging the dehumanizing status quo of theology. To be relevant, theology must undergo a radical transformation.

A. Liberation: Area of Concern

In the context of the poverty of the teeming millions of Asia and their situation of domination and exploitation, our theology must have a very definite liberational thrust.

The first act of theology, its very heart, is commitment. This commitment is a response to the challenge of the poor in their struggle for full humanity. We affirm that the poor and the oppressed of Asia are called by God to be the architects and builders of their own destiny. Thus theology starts with the aspirations of the oppressed toward full humanity and counts on their growing consciousness of, and their ever-expanding efforts to overcome, all obstacles to the truth of their history.

B. Subject of Theology

To be truly liberating, this theology must arise from the Asian poor with a liberated consciousness. It is articulated and expressed by the oppressed community using the technical skills of biblical scholars, social scientists, psychologists, anthropologists, and others. It can be expressed in many ways, in art forms, drama, literature, folk stories, and native wisdom as well as in doctrinal-pastoral statements.

Most participants asserted that every theology is conditioned by the class position and class consciousness of the theologian. Hence a truly liberating theology must ultimately be the work of the Asian poor, who are struggling for full humanity. It is they who must reflect on and say what their faith-life experience in the struggle for liberation is. This does not exclude the so-called specialists in theology. With their knowledge they can complement the theologizing of the grass-roots people. But their theologizing becomes authentic only when rooted in the history and struggle of the poor and the oppressed.

C. Liberation, Culture, and Religion

Theology to be authentically Asian must be immersed in our historicocultural situation and grow out of it. Theology, which should emerge from the people's struggle for liberation, would spontaneously formulate itself in religiocultural idioms of the people.

In many parts of Asia, we must integrate into our theology the insights and values of the major religions, but this integration must take place at the level of action and commitment to the people's struggle and not be merely intellectual or elitist. These traditions of Asia's great religions seem to understand liberation in two senses: liberation from selfishness within each person and in society; these religious traditions also contain a strong motivation for personal conversion of life. These religions, together with our indigenous cultures, can provide the Asian sense in our task of generating the new person and the new community. We view them as a potential source of permanent critique of any established order and a pointer toward the building of a truly human society. We are conscious, however, of the domesticating role religions have often played in the past, so we need to subject both our religion and our culture to sustained self-criticism. In this context, we questioned the academic preoccupation to work toward the so-called "indigenization" or "inculturation" of theology divorced from participation in the liberational struggle in history. In our countries today, there can be no truly indigenized theology which is not liberational. Involvement in the history and struggle of the oppressed is the guarantee that our theology is both liberating and indigenous.

D. Social Analysis

Theology working for the liberation of the poor must approach its task with the tools of social analysis of the realities of Asia. How can it participate in the liberation of the poor if it does not understand the sociopolitical, economic, and cultural structures that enslave the poor? The vision of full humanity and the complexity of the struggle leading to its achievement are continually challenged and distorted by the meshing of mixed motives and interests and by the interweaving of the apparent and the real. This analysis must extend to the whole length and breadth, height and depth of Asian reality, from the family to the village, the city, the nation, the continent, and the globe. Economic and sociopolitical interdependence has shrunk the earth to a global village. The analysis must keep pace with the ongoing historical process to ensure a continuing self-criticism and evaluation of religions, ideologies, institutions, groups, and classes of people that, by their very nature, run the hazard of a dehumanizing bureaucracy.

E. Biblical Perspective

Because theology takes the total human situation seriously, it can be regarded as the articulated reflection, in faith, on the encounter of God by people in their historical situations. For us, Christians, the Bible becomes an important source in the doing of theology. The God encountered in the history of the people is none other than the God who revealed himself in the events of Jesus' life, death, and resurrection. We believe that God and Christ continue to be present in the struggles of the people to achieve full humanity as we look forward in hope to the consummation of all things when God will be all in all.

When theology is liberated from its present race, class, and sex prejudices, it can place itself at the service of the people and become a powerful motivating force for the mobilization of believers in Jesus to participate in Asia's ongoing struggle for self-identity and human dignity. For this, we need to develop whole new areas of theology such as understanding the revolutionary challenge of the life of Jesus, seeing in Mary the truly liberated woman who participated in the struggle of Jesus and her people, bridging the gaps of our denominational separation, and rewriting the history of the Asian churches from the perspective of the Asian poor.

V. SPIRITUALITY AND FORMATION

The formation for Christian living and ministry has to be in and through participation in the struggle of the masses of our people. This requires the development of a corresponding spirituality, of opting out of the exploitative system in some way, of being marginalized in the process, of persevering in our commitment, of risk-bearing, of reaching deeper inner peace in the midst of active involvement with the struggling people (Shanti).

Our fellow Christians who have become regular inmates of the Asian prisons bring us new elements of fidelity to our people inspired by Jesus. To them we too send a message of humble solidarity and prayerful hope. May the suffering of today's prisoners in the Asian jails give birth to a genuine renewal of ourselves and our communities of believers.

VI. FUTURE TASKS

Coming to the end of this Conference, we feel the need to continue the search we have initiated here. To keep alive our efforts toward a theology that speaks to our Asian peoples, we see the following tasks before us.

1. We need to continue deepening our understanding of the Asian reality through *active involvement* in our people's struggle for full humanity. This means struggling side by side with our peasants, fishermen, workers, slum dwellers, marginalized and minority groups, oppressed youth, and women so that together we can discover the Asian face of Christ.

2. Our theology must lead us to transform the society in which we live so that it may increasingly allow the Asian person to experience what it means to be fully alive. This task includes the transformation of our church structures and institutions as well as ourselves.

3. We shall continue to assist in the development of a relevant theology for Asia through constant interaction and mutual respect for the different roles we have in the struggle, as professional theologians, grassroots workers, and church people.

4. We seek to build a strong network of alliance by linking groups who are struggling for full humanity nationally and internationally. The following concrete actions taken in the course of the Conference show the beginnings of this network:

   a. a letter of solidarity with seventy-six boat people in Hong Kong who were arrested on their way to petition for better housing.

   b. a public statement by the Sri Lankan delegation pledging to support the Tamil-speaking people in their struggle for their just rights.

   c. a message to Bishop Tji of Korea, supporting the Korean struggle and regretting the absence of the entire Korean delegation at the Conference.

d. a letter to the Kawasaki Steel Corporation, Japan, protesting the export of pollution to other Asian countries.

e. a telegram to the Latin American Bishops as well as to Pope John Paul II, expressing deep concern for the CELAM conference in Puebla, Mexico.

f. solidarity with the Filipino participants in their protest against the pollution caused by the transfer of high-pollutant industries and the erection of nuclear power plants.

5. We are concerned about formation programs in our training institutions and the life-style of our pastoral leaders. The experiences of the Conference make it clear that there must be new emphases in our theological and pastoral policy. We need to evaluate our parish and diocesan structures to assess where they alienate us from the poor masses of Asia and give us the image of might and power. We urge that necessary adjustments be made so that our religious personnel may be more deeply in touch with the problems of our people.

6. In order to facilitate the implementation of our tasks, we have formed the Ecumenical Theological Fellowship of Asia.

For two weeks eighty of us, participants at this Asian Theological Conference, have tried to grapple with the contemporary call of the Asian poor and oppressed.

The prayerful silence in worship and the unity in faith helped to keep our communion in dialectical and creative tension.

As Christians we see the urgent tasks of renewing ourselves and the churches in order to serve our people.

To this sacred and historic task we humbly commit ourselves and invite all Christians and people of goodwill everywhere to participate in this ongoing search.

PART TWO

Man in Nature
and History

Nine

Man
and Nature
A Workshop Report

[This is one of three workshop reports from the Manila Consultation on Theological Education for Ministry in Asia, in 1977, which brought together more than one hundred theological teachers, students, and administrators from eleven Asian countries. The consultation had the widest sponsorship of any Protestant theological conference thus far held in Asia, including the Association of Theological Schools in Southeast Asia, the Northeast Asia Association of Theological Schools, the India–Sri Lanka Board of Theological Education, the Christian Conference of Asia, and the Theological Education Fund (now the Programme of Theological Education) of the World Council of Churches. The report on "Man and Nature," as adopted in plenary session, seeks a middle way between a traditional view of nature as dominating man by its frightening spell, on the one hand, and a materialistic view which reduces nature to a mere "thing" which man can manipulate and exploit at will. Although traditional man in Asia lives in close kinship with nature, relating to it intuitively and mystically rather than analytically, some of his traditional attitudes have led in the past to fatalism and a static view of life which undercut the urgency for social and political reforms. On the other hand, while science and technology free us from the oppressive aspects of our relation to nature, they endanger our relationship to nature and also our understanding of community life which, in Asia at least, is drawn essentially from nature.—Ed.]

Theological reflection in Asia must be concerned with man in his total context, so that such reflection may provide the resources for life and set forth the responsibilities that attend it. Here we deal, however, with the specific question of Man and Nature in the hope that clarification of this relationship will provide insights for the way in which we understand the total situation.

From the official report of the Manila Consultation on Theological Education for Ministry in Asia, in 1977, published under the title *The Human and the Holy: Asian Perspectives in Christian Theology,* edited by E. P. Nacpil and D. J. Elwood (Manila: New Day Publishers, 1978; Maryknoll, N.Y.: Orbis Books, 1980).

The man-nature relationship in Asia is complex because of its characteristic plurality of religious traditions, cultural emphases, social orders, and political persuasions each of which, and in different combinations, exhibits distinctive understandings of nature and man. The situation is further complicated by the pervasive influence of science and technology. In addition to local ethnic expressions of religious belief, many religions and philosophies such as Taoism, Confucianism, Shintoism, Islam, different forms of Buddhism, schools of Hinduism, Christianity, etc., have influenced the overall view of man in relation to nature. Some social orders, politicoeconomic structures, and religiocultural practices which have arisen out of various understandings of nature, have received self-authenticity and express themselves as independent realities.

In this situation, one cannot speak of an Asian attitude to nature without making very broad generalizations. However, it is possible to identify certain tendencies concerning man-nature relationships which arise out of one Asian tradition or another.

TENDENCIES CONCERNING MAN-NATURE RELATIONSHIPS

Some features of Asian approaches to "man and nature." Generally speaking, in Asian religious traditions there is a deep sense of kinship between man and nature. There is a notable absence of the analytic understanding of nature. Instead man's relation to nature is understood relationally, intuitively, mystically, and esthetically.

Nature is looked upon as self-ordered and self-contained, having its own laws based on an organizing principle *(Tao)*. Primary emphasis is placed on the coherent interdependence of nature within itself and in its relation to man.

A number of Asian religious traditions do not place man above or apart from nature; rather, he is part of it, sustaining it and sustained by it. He is expected to live in a reciprocal relation to nature and to learn from it the principles of life, virtue, and wisdom.

Even in those traditions which make a distinction between nature and Ultimate Reality, or God (e.g., schools of Hinduism), God is not understood as "outside" nature, but as manifested in and through it. Thus nature at the popular level is sometimes the object of reverence and respect. In some traditions (e.g., Shintoism), the religious cult is primarily concerned with evoking the right relation between man and the gods expressed in nature.

Philosophical formulations of some religious traditions see man as an integral part of *all* life (as exemplified by the doctrine of transmigration in Hinduism) or indeed as part of the whole cosmic process (e.g., the doctrine of dependent origination in Buddhism).

Some negative effects. The traditional approaches to nature also manifest some dehumanizing and even demonic aspects, both in the life of individuals and of society. Some of the rigid, oppressive social structures (e.g., the caste system) and political systems (political hierarchy; emperor worship) seem to be derived from particular understandings of nature and of the order of the universe (e.g., Confucianism and Shintoism). These understandings are sustained by evoking certain distorted ideas about harmony and stability which are said to be manifested in nature.

Some views of nature lead to fatalism and a static view of life, thus undercutting the urgent need for social and political change and reform. Among still others, superstitious practices and oppressive religious institutions are fostered by particular attitudes of fear and mistrust of the processes of nature. Therefore this whole area of Asian attitudes toward nature has to be redeemed from the grip of the demonic.

THE EFFECTS OF MODERNIZATION

The effects of science and technology and the drive for modernization in most of the Asian societies, attended by the spread of secularism and materialistic philosophies, add to the complexity of Asian attitudes to nature. On the one hand, people are freed from the oppressive aspects of their relation to nature. On the other, however, there is a breakdown in man's relationship to nature and of the understanding of community life that essentially is drawn from nature.

Furthermore, the ecological crisis has begun to threaten Asia as well. Pollution and the rapid exhaustion of natural resources are not only questioning the doctrine of progress in technological development but also raising the specter of an earth which may not be able to support human and natural life. The problem is aggravated by population explosion and the unjust patterns of distribution of available resources.

A scientific view of nature fractures an essentially relational understanding of man and nature by forcing man to think of nature as a "thing" to be used and manipulated. Thus modernization tends to destroy the wider sense of community which is part of the Asian heritage. Particularly at stake are the positive values in the traditional man-nature understandings.

It is in this complex and dynamic context that Asian Christians must seek to define their theological task. In so doing, they need to deal creatively with their given situation on the basis of their commitment to Jesus Christ and also appropriate from other traditions those insights that enliven the faith by mutual interaction. This is not a new task. In the Christian tradition, indeed within the Bible itself, there is a constant wrestling to relate the faith to the living context, which gives both meaning and authenticity to the Christian witness. The Asian attempts to "do" theology are thus a part of this continuous process.

SOME INSIGHTS FROM THE BIBLICAL TRADITION

In the Bible we see many streams of tradition, and therefore a variety of ways of expressing man's relationship to nature. One or another of the traditions received emphasis at different stages of religious history, depending on the situation of the church and the demands placed upon her. There has been, for example, excessive emphasis on the theme of man's dominion over nature (sometimes misconstrued as supporting uncritical technological progress) which has led to a one-sided interpretation of man and nature. Greater use must be made of those traditions within the Bible (e.g., those streams of thought emanating from the Davidic Covenant theology—Psalms, Wisdom literature, Job, etc.) which will serve as a necessary corrective to the present situation.

One seeks in vain in the Old Testament for a clear-cut distinction between history and nature. Quite often "natural events" (the driving back of the sea of reeds; manna in the wilderness; etc.) and "historical events" (e.g., liberation from Egypt) are equally regarded as signs of God's activity. The same easy transition from "nature" to "history" is observable in the Creation Psalms. This relationship must be given prominence, even though the particular symbols of God's relationship with the people are drawn normally from the sphere of political history. In the Creation Psalms (e.g., Psalm 8) there is the sense of the whole of creation (man and nature) "rejoicing" together before God. Creation itself is seen as the manifestation of the faithfulness of God, and as something entrusted to man for faithful and responsible stewardship. In his teaching ministry Jesus drew freely from nature to illustrate and to edify; so do Paul and other New Testament writers. The New Testament, however, is primarily concerned with the inbreaking of the Kingdom of God. The expectation of the impending *eschaton* leads most of the New Testament writings to deal primarily with the tension between the "old" and the "new" order. But even here God's reconciliation is with the whole of his creation which "awaits with eager longing" for its redemption and transformation.

These traditions within the Bible must be drawn and used in the reconstruction of a theology of nature.

SOME THEOLOGICAL ISSUES

The above discussion raises certain particular issues for the "doing" of theology in Asia. As far as the specific area of "man and nature" is concerned, the Asian orientation must result in the broadening, deepening, and indeed the adding of new dimensions to some of the traditional theological concepts. Here are some examples:

First, we need to ask whether there has been an overemphasis on the transcendence or "otherness" of God over man and nature, and on a qualified transcendence of man over nature. Notwithstanding that there are other factors that have contributed to the theological crisis, we need to attempt to enrich and enlarge the understanding of God and his relation to man and nature which will speak meaningfully to the crisis. The Asian cultural emphases on the immanence of the Holy, the self-sufficiency of nature, and the need to have a reciprocal relation to nature must be taken seriously in the way we understand this relationship.

Second, what is the relationship of man to nature? Does the biblical image of responsible stewardship exhaust all that can be said about it? What light does the relational understanding within Asian faiths say about the way to relate man to nature?

Third, in what ways can we accelerate and participate in those processes that liberate man from the demonic manifestations of "nature relationships"? How can we deal theologically with the dehumanizing and "denaturalizing" effects of technology and modernization?

Fourth, how can we understand and evaluate the process of life in Asia today? There are many attempts to understand it primarily in terms of the categories of history. Is this adequate, and true to the Asian reality? What contribution can the Asian cultures which always hold nature and history in tension make to this search?

Fifth, a purely linear understanding of time which is implied in the biblical tradition tends to absolutize a consecutive understanding of processes or events in history and nature. It also fails to recognize the positive values of seeing time in a seasonal sense which implies hopes of repetitive opportunities. It may be helpful to explore ways in which these two experiences of time can be brought together for mutual correction and enrichment.

Sixth, there is a tendency in Christian theology to consider morality and ethics in terms of given codes of behavior. Many Asian religions with their understandings of nature have developed a corpus of moral teachings. There is a theological need to relate these teachings to the biblical Wisdom traditions, which also speak of nature as a teacher.

Seventh, similarly in popular Christian understanding, man's alienation from God (sin) is seen as a failure to obey. Some Asian traditions see this alienation in terms of man's relation to nature as well. What is the understanding of sin in a nature-oriented culture and what new dimension does it open to the Christian concept of sin?

Eighth, the Asian orientation also raises basic questions about the way we understand salvation. On the one hand, the political realities of the society are pressing us to reformulate the concept of salvation. Equally important are the questions raised by attitudes toward nature. Can the search in some religious traditions for a coherent relationship between God-man-fellowman and nature serve as a corrective to the individualistic/communalistic, legalistic, and future-oriented outlook on salvation.

Ninth, what does the nature-man relation in Asia say about life-styles, concept of work, spirituality, etc.?

How to Deal with These Issues.

First, authentic Asian theology concerning man and nature (or any other aspect) cannot arise without informed understanding and meaningful participation in the context itself. We need to reflect on the nature of the essential dialogue and on the ways of exposing Christians to it.

Second, the nature of the authority of Scripture and of its interpretation is a very vital issue. It may be necessary to develop a new cluster of criteria for "doing" theology.

Third, we need to sharpen further the "Asian critical principle" and the mode of its application in different situations.

Fourth, a more sustained effort must be made to gather data and information that would be made available to those reflecting on man-nature issues (e.g., the ecological crisis, population explosion, fertility cults, etc.).

Implications for Theological Education

Theological reflections on man and nature in Asia can meaningfully take place only in an interdisciplinary way. Attempts must be made wherever possible for theologians to work in cooperation with scholars of other disciplines.

Theological education must be broadly based. Studies of other faiths and cultures must form an integral part of the overall program and not be merely an isolated section of the total program.

Theological students must be exposed directly to ecological issues and to the problems caused by absolutizing modernization and technology.

Greater experimentation must be made in the methods of "doing" theology.

The practice of training students to be ministers only in church-directed situations must give way to broad-based training for a variety of ministries. Included in this multiplicity of ministries is the ministry related to problems of ecology.

In some seminaries there is already an attempt to relate theology to life in nature by the inclusion in the curriculum of agriculture. This is to be encouraged.

Theological education has to be more issue-centered and to take seriously the agenda provided by the world it seeks to serve.

We must encourage and foster those "nerve centers" that are dealing specifically with the theological problems relating to man and nature.

Greater emphasis must be given to continuing education of those already in parish situations. Theological education by extension is also recommended as an invaluable tool for education-in-situations.

We should encourage the formation of a theological community concerned with the issues related to man and nature.

Ten

Three Mile
an Hour God
Kosuke Koyama

[In his creative biblical reflections Dr. Koyama has more than once addressed himself to the issues that arise in communicating the gospel to those who are caught up in the technological culture that is rapidly sweeping across the globe. In this essay he is captured by the biblical image of the "wilderness" in which God slowly educates his people to a life of trust in him, at a pace comparable to the human walk. In contemporary society, by contrast, he sees us moving at tremendous speeds—too fast to learn the lessons God would teach us. Koyama seems to be warning us to slow down to a walk, for only at this pace can we hear the word God is addressing to us. God's speed is the speed of love. It is a different kind of speed from the technological speed to which we are accustomed.—Ed.]

A Canaanite woman . . . came and knelt before Jesus saying, "Lord, help me." And he answered, "It is not fair to take the children's bread and throw it to the dogs." She said, "Yes, Lord, yet even the dogs eat the crumbs that fall from their masters' table." Then Jesus answered her, "O woman, great is your faith! Be it done for you as you desire." And her daughter was healed instantly.

—From Matthew 15:21–28

God humbled you and let you hunger and fed you with manna, which you did not know, nor did your fathers know; that he might make you know that man does not live by bread alone, but that man lives by everything that proceeds out of the mouth of the LORD. Your clothing did not wear out upon you, and your foot did not swell, these forty years. —Deuteronomy 8:1–4

From Kosuke Koyama, *Three Mile an Hour God* (Orbis Books, 1980). Reprinted by permission of the publisher.

God wanted to teach his people that "man does not live by bread alone, but that man lives by everything that proceeds out of the mouth of the Lord." This was an extremely important lesson for his people to know and understand before they went into the Land of Canaan. God decided to spend forty years to teach this one lesson. Mind you, forty years for one lesson! How slow and how patient! No university can run on this basis. If God decided that he would use forty years, the subject of the lesson must be of great importance in his view. In truth we are still finding today how critically important this lesson is. Whether we agree with it or not, it seems to me that the history of mankind more or less endorses such an observation.

This lesson cannot be learned easily in a comfortable classroom. The classroom is not free from a "classroomish" distance from the confusing reality of life. In the classroom, theory rather than story dominates. God's people must learn about bread and the word of God realistically and experientially. He took the people into the wilderness. The wilderness is an open space in all directions. It is a place full of possibilities. The mind can stretch out or plunge into deep meditation in the wilderness. But at the same time this open space is a dangerous, desolate space inhabited by demons and evil spirits. It is space not cultivated—not civilized. The wilderness is thus full of promise and full of danger.

Now the people of God found themselves in the wilderness. They were away from their familiar streets, grocery stores, railway stations, dentists, banks, schools, and hospitals. The familiar system and style of life were left behind. They felt increasingly precarious. The wilderness was no longer a phenomenon outside of them. Both promise and danger had come into their souls. ". . . he humbled you." They walked in the wilderness surrounded by danger of hunger and promise of manna. Here God taught his people that "man does not live by bread alone, but man lives by everything that proceeds out of the mouth of the Lord." The people of Israel had this experience on behalf of all of us.

Wilderness, then, is the place where we are face-to-face with danger and promise. And that is an educational situation for the people of God. When danger and promise come together to us, it is called crisis. The Bible does not simply speak of danger. If it did so, the biblical faith would be reduced to a "protection-from-danger religion." The Bible does not simply speak about promise. If it did so, the biblical faith would be reduced to a "happy-ending religion." The Bible speaks about a crisis situation, coexistence of *danger* and *promise*—wilderness—and there God teaches man. In the wilderness we are called to go beyond "protection-from-danger religion" and "happy-ending religion." There we are called to "trust" in God.

Let us consider for a few minutes the subject of God's lesson: "Man does not live by bread alone, but man lives by everything that proceeds out of the mouth of the Lord." "Bread" stands for the things we need. The Bible does not say, "Man does not live by after-shave lotion alone. . . ." Man can very well live without after-shave lotion. But bread is a different story. Man cannot live without bread. But man must not live even by this essential bread alone. Bread alone, shelter alone, clothing alone, income alone, all these "alones" damage man's quality of life. Strangely, these good values contain danger elements too. Man is supposed to eat bread. But what if bread eats man? People are dying from overeating today in the affluent countries. Man is supposed to live in the house. But what if the house begins to live in man? Isn't it true that we are fast forgetting the spiritual and cultural beauty of simple living? What if fashion begins to dictate to man what to wear? Would not this produce indecency and wastefulness? What if income is using man instead of man using his income? Does not this often lead man to strains and mental exhaustion? Man must not live even by all these essentials alone. Man needs the bread plus the word of God.

What a "religious theory"! What a nervous "religious" way to live. Bread is bread, with or without a word of God! We eat bread without theological comment. We need all kinds of essentials and nonessentials. After-shave lotion does occupy an authentic place in our life! Why do we need the word of God over and beyond all our life's essentials and nonessentials? Perhaps we do not need it. Perhaps all by which we live can be expressed by "bread" and "after-shave lotion." But when something happens to us and we are hit by storm and we are thrown into the precariousness of the wilderness . . . should we still say that man shall live by "bread" and "after-shave lotion" alone? Would we say so in the midst of the storm? Perhaps we would say so. But we would be less inclined to say so. In the wilderness our speed is slowed down until gradually we come to the speed at which we walk—*three miles an hour.*

On one of his preaching tours, Jesus walked into the district of Tyre and Sidon. He was met by a Canaanite woman. What we hear is one of the strangest stories we encounter in the Gospel. We do not know much about this woman. Was she poor? Was she fairly well off? What was the size of her family? What did her husband do? Are they happy with each other? Or did they have a different sense of values in their everyday engagement? Are they communicating with their children well? We don't know. But we do know that this woman was hit by a storm.

She "came out and cried, 'Have mercy on me, O Lord, Son of David; my daughter is severely possessed by a demon.' " It is not that someone next door is possessed by a demon, but my daughter. It is not that my daughter once a year suffers possession by a demon. She is severely possessed by a demon. She is exposed to naked threat and danger. How agonizing! Her whole life is now focused on her daughter who suffers. She comes to Jesus believing that she will hear the word of promise in the midst of the danger that is threatening the destruction of her daughter. Strangely, Jesus "did not answer her a word." Can we imagine this? With this cold silence, was not the Canaanite woman taken even deeper into the wilderness where both danger and promise intensify themselves? Read further: "And his disciples came and begged him, saying, 'Send her away, for she is crying after us.' " She is making a wilderness scene right here on the civilized street. True, this woman is literally sandwiched between danger and promise. She is in the wilderness. And here she is clambering after the word of God. . . .

But let's hear more about this woman. Then Jesus spoke. Certainly it must be the word of comfort and healing? "I was sent only to the lost sheep of the house of Israel." What a word! Incredibly disappointing word for the agonizing mother! In effect Jesus said that he is primarily responsible to the people of Israel and not the Gentile people like this Canaanite woman. Did she not believe that the "Lord, Son of David" was the one who would willingly show his mercy upon her if she cried to him? She did not give up. She did not rebel. "She came and knelt before him, saying, 'Lord, help me.' " What a great commitment to Jesus Christ. Why did not she start looking around to find other possible help? Jesus answered—Yes, he did! "It is not fair to take the children's bread and throw it to the dogs." We all would give up at this point. What a cruel thing to say to a woman who was "hit by a great storm." But hear what this Canaanite woman said: "Yes, Lord, yet even the dogs eat the crumbs that fall from their masters' table."

Jesus was deeply moved. "O woman, great is your faith! Be it done for you as you desire."

But what is the matter with Jesus Christ? Why did he not willingly and quickly grant her desire as he did on other occasions? Could he not see at once the faith she had in him? Perhaps Jesus decided to take her into the depth of wilderness so that she might experience the promise of God more deeply and intensively than others. She came out on the other side of "protection-from-danger religion" and "happy-ending religion." She trusted in Jesus Christ. "O woman, great is your faith!" The ending of this story is not a "happy end." It is a "trust end." There is a vast difference between "happy-end religion" and "trust-end faith."

We live today an efficient and speedy life. We are surrounded by electric switches, some of which cost us 10 dollars and others may even cost 2,000 dollars. We want more switches. Who among us dislikes efficiency and a smooth-going, comfortable life? University students use the Xerox machine in their studies. Housewives use "instant pizza" for supper. Men's legs are fast deteriorating from the lack of the most basic human exercise, walking. Automobiles speeding at fifty miles an hour have replaced their legs. We believe in efficiency. Let's not just look at this negatively. There is a great value in efficiency and speed.

But let me make one observation. I find that God goes "slowly" in his educational process of man. "Forty years in the wilderness" points to his basic educational philosophy. Forty years of national migration through the wilderness, three generations of the united monarchy (Saul, David, Solomon), nineteen kings of Israel (up to 722 B.C.), and twenty kings of Judah (up to 587 B.C.), the hosts of the prophets and priests, the experience of exile and restoration—isn't this rather a slow and costly way for God to let his people know the covenant relationship between God and man?

Jesus Christ came. He walked toward the "full stop." He lost his mobility. He was nailed down! He is not even at three miles an hour as we walk. He is not moving. "Full stop"! What can be slower than "full stop"—"nailed down"? At this point of "full stop," the apostolic church proclaims that the love of God to man is ultimately and fully revealed. God walks "slowly" because he is love. If he were not love, he would go much faster. Love has its speed. It is an inner speed. It is a spiritual speed. It is a different kind of speed from the technological speed to which we are accustomed. It is "slow," yet it is lord over all other speeds since it is the speed of love. It goes on in the depth of our life, whether we notice or not, whether we are currently hit by storm or not, at three miles an hour. It is the speed we walk and therefore it is the speed the love of God walks.

The people of God were taught the truth of bread and the word of God in the wilderness as they walked three miles an hour by the three mile an hour God. The Canaanite woman believed in Jesus Christ against all her own speeds by trusting the speed of the promise of God.

Eleven

Indian Christian Theology and the Problem of History

Samuel Rayan, S.J.

[Samuel Rayan, an Indian Jesuit theologian who is one of the Roman Catholic members of the Faith and Order Commission of the World Council of Churches, here challenges our hitherto unquestioned assumption that Indian traditions are lacking in a sense of history, and that therefore "salvation is . . . from history and not of, in and through history" (p. 171 of the volume referred to below). "On the contrary," says Rayan after examining the evidence in the Hindu scriptures, "the religious culture we meet with is open and sensitive to the historical" (p. 179). In any case, even today among European theologians—especially Bultmann, Pannenberg, and Balthasar—the question whether history is linear or cyclic remains unsettled, or rather it begins to appear that "neither model is adequate to describe . . . the complex reality which we call history" (p. 185). The conclusion is that salvation history "lies beyond linear and cyclic thought-patterns and must be described in nongeometrical, positively personal terms" (p. 187). It is at this point that the following selection begins.—Ed.]

For a living and relevant Indian theology it is necessary to go beyond conceptual distinctions (which have their limited importance) and conventional clichés about linear and cyclic historical patterns in an attempt to determine the shape of time and history that is essential and interior to Christian theology. The key to the theological understanding of time and history seems to lie in the fact that the end of history is already present within it. If the Eschaton, the Complete Reality of the End, is present within the tissues of history, and is active in it from start to finish, then history has depths and involutions, and its movement is best described as inward rather than forward. It is best described in personal terms of interiority and relationship rather than in geometrical terms of lines and circles.

1. The risen Jesus is the eschatological reality; God's act of raising

From his essay in *Society and Religion,* edited by Richard W. Taylor (Madras: Christian Literature Society, 1976), pp. 187–193. Reprinted by permission of the publisher.

Jesus is the climaxing activity by which the last enemy, death, is over-come, and God's creative future is grasped as present.[1] But the resurrec-tion is also Christ's way of becoming our contemporary; not only ours but of every man whom he loves and who needs him. It is not a with-drawal from history but a fuller, deeper involvement in it in order to involve it in his own destiny which is not fully achieved without us, which therefore is still in process in history. The resurrection is not only the culmination of the incarnation but the beginning of a more radical one. It means that Jesus Christ is still within space and time, not this or that time and space, but within the totality of space-time, and in the heart of every man as the basis and content of faith and hope. It is thus that the resurrection is a historical event, *the* historical event, the one mean-ingful and meaning-giving center of historical existence. Its historicity is lived and revealed in the faith of the church, in the attraction or repulsion men feel in his regard, in the responsibility of ignoring him or the values which he embodies, and in the Eucharist which reveals him as always coming to birth from the womb of matter. The risen Lord is the depth of history, he has always been that. He who fills the world as the Word fills it as the Word-made-flesh as well, the Flesh become the Word of saving love through the cross. It is the risen Lord that frames and founds human history; and that makes it possible to hold that "creation is an interpretation of the world looked at from its 'neogenesis' in the resurrec-tion of Jesus. The Eschaton, then, is the inner dynamic of the world in process, and of human history moving toward its completion in Christ."[2] It is in some such perspective that all Hindu ideas of religious time and space will have to be understood and evaluated.

2. The Eschaton is God who originated time, holds it in his hands, and dwells in its depths to lead it to himself as its final goal. God is thus continually transforming uniform mechanical Chronos into Kairos or personal, relational time, unique moments of encounter, full of promise and of risks. God is not a "given" which is there, which we could discover and explore at will as an object. He exists not as "datum" but as "donum." We could not have him nor know him as existing unless he gave himself and made himself known. With his self-giving coincides the gift of time and the transformation of time into salvation history. This history is the relationship God establishes with mankind in sum-moning it to the sharing of existence with himself at all levels. The history with which theology, like the Bible, is concerned is human exis-tence addressed by God and enabled to open up to his Word. For theology, therefore, the future of history is a pilgrimage to its Lord who dwells in its depths; it is a matter of chosen relationship, and not of chronological advance. Wherever man existentially responds to God in

faith, time matures and comes to ripeness, and history reaches its end. The fullness of time is had at that Human Point at which there is God's fullest self-utterance and man's completest response, that is, in Jesus Christ.

3. Since God is love, love is the eschatological reality. It is the greatest and the last, it has primacy, and by it is history finally evaluated. Because of man's rootedness in God, "all his responsible decisions are born of love," which consists in "unreservedly being for one's neighbor."[3] Wherever people love truly, they are conveyed to the Eschaton, to the Ending Time and the completion of history. Love binds men together, humanizes them, and conveys them to one another in glad self-giving, and to God in the other, and to their future beyond loss and decay. For love is the power of the future, and is its mother. Self-giving love at any time mediates "the dynamism of the New Humanity" in Christ.[4]

4. It follows that man, the human person, is the eschaton on our earth. God's love makes him a center and an end in himself, a reality to be loved, honored, and served, and never a means to be used for some other end. Time is for man; he or she is its meaning. It keeps flowing toward him and matures in and through his maturation. It becomes itself in his decisions and action, and in his experience of being loved as an end worth loving. He is also *the* sacrament on earth in which God is to be met and served by all. Bound by space and time, man is a particular historical reality, but through thought and faith and love he is universal and fills the whole of history. Man becomes the Eschaton of time as he changes time into history and lends to history its meaning by mastering nature, hominizing the earth, transforming himself from a selfish into a loving person, by weaving relationships and building a community that is truly human.

History has been defined as man creating himself by creating his world. Involvement in history has been described as a movement of human liberation related to human creativity which consists chiefly in the historicization of subhuman nature through technology.[5] But in many parts of the world today man has mastered the earth but has not quite humanized it; he has rather succeeded in polluting it, in rendering it less habitable for man, a real threat to life in all its forms. Much less has man succeeded in humanizing himself. He has often used his technological skill to break up, degrade, and fetter the human in others and in himself; and to build a civilization in which great killers are the ones acknowledged as great, and of which a high achievement is the capacity to commit global genocide. The question of history is a question about the human. History is to be described in terms of the value we put on man and on the human community, and not in terms of mere technology.

There are more ways than the technical of mastering nature, and there are areas to be mastered where technology is of little or no use. Each human group can have its own way of making itself, at its own pace and rhythm, and one may choose to run a mile or swim across the channel while another may prefer to do it on a bicycle or a motorboat. While one concentrates on mastering the subhuman outside us, another may center its concern on the subhuman within, in the conviction that without self-mastery the control of nature could constitute a new force of enslavement and dehumanization. Without suggesting that these alternatives are exclusive we may ask which of these is the authentically history-making choice, the one by which humanity is truly making itself.

The truly historical are the choices and actions by which man becomes increasingly human. The way to the human is not the way of domination, conquest or violence, of enslavement, exploitation or brute strength. Whatever has disturbed the rhythm of human growth, blocked the development of a fraternal society, and humiliated peoples—colonial and neocolonial oppression, slave trade and child labor, sea piracy and war, skill in quietly killing off people with shellfish toxin and various venoms—these things have blocked and destroyed history; the ground from which they sprang lacked historical perspective and all genuine sense of history. If history means free decisions and if free, responsible decisions are born of love, then the taking away of the freedom of peoples, and the plunder of their lands, must be seen as a violent wrenching of history away from its line of growth, and as a brutal destruction of history's possibilities. As Urs von Balthasar explains, time is not neutral; time is either real time which through openness and faith becomes grace, or it is futile time which through unfaith turns into sin. Every decision and movement detrimental to man and creative of unfreedom, suffering, and misery renders time futile, empties it of historical content, and turns its course backward in the direction of initial Chaos. The ruthless greed which marked the colonial adventure and the race to accumulate industrial capital was the great exhibition of Western idolatry in African and Asian lands, and idolatry, like all sins, stultifies history. M. M. Thomas quotes Toynbee's remark that Indian religions, though less heroic, have also been less atrocious than religions of Semitic origin which (like Judaism, Christianity, and Islam) have fostered fanaticism. And fanaticism betrays its defective sense of history in its intolerance of difference and variety, its disrespect for the achievements of others, its insensitivity to other peoples' experience of events, the memory of their past, and their expectations in regard to their future.[6] The foundations of fanaticism and militancy in the West, namely, the claim to possess the monopoly of truth, can be laid only in lands lacking historical configurations and a sense of time and space.

Karl Marx defines every age in which all men are not free, in which not all men are decision makers and shapers of their own destiny, in which some are masters and others slaves, in which a few are affluent and the rest are wretched, in which antagonisms and contradictions exist within productive relationships—he defines every such age as prehistory, for in such a situation men are not yet human, no one is properly man. As long as a single man is in chains, mankind is not free, and those who shut up others in prisons are prisoners themselves. Human history proper will begin only when mankind's brokenness is healed and a society without classes and contradictions has been achieved. The community outlined in Acts 2 and 4, in II Corinthians 8 and 9, in I Corinthians 13, in the commandment to love, in the Bread-breaking ritual, and in the belief in God as Trinity, that community marks the beginnings of true human history. Every effort and movement in that direction has historical significance; what moves away from this ideal of the human is historically negative and preventive of our evolution into the historical age.

What we need now for the making of history is not mere technology and the control of nature, but a new humanity with foundations laid deep in new hearts and new structures. It is our agelong universal experience that nearly all our endeavors tend, as we ourselves do, to decay and death, to futility and impasse. Something is deficient at the heart of our strivings. It is here men have felt the need of a healing which cannot come from man himself. We need God to work with us, take us into partnership with him in redeeming time and rendering it human. History is therefore God's gift and our human task. Our partnership with him is an affair of our hearts and hands, of love and of social action. What we plan and do, the movements we initiate and the structures we create, have their new quality from the quality of the heart addressed by God and made open to him and to his world. The theological problem of history is, therefore, the problem of the inward history of each man, of his heart's experiences, struggles, and decisions, of the captivities and exoduses which occur within his spirit, and of such interior conflicts as are described in Romans 7, in the book of Revelation, and in the opening chapter of the Gita. It is also a problem of the hand and of action to change the old world and build a new one. But it is a partial view of history to describe it exclusively in terms of external action and neglect the crucial role played in it by the heart and by nature. The fact that history is also salvation history and that God is active in the events of our life and struggle is revealed in the first place in the depths of the heart. It is there that history begins. Thence it is communicated socially to become the shared heritage of a group or a race. The resurrection which gives entirely new dimensions to time and history is not a purely external observable fact but a reality of faith. The heart therefore must be taken into account more seriously than till now in all conceptions of history. It is the *Dharma-kshetra* where crucial battles are fought and won or lost.

A historical religion cannot be itself without historical praxis. For Christianity as for Marxism, "truth is known in and through the practice of history and the meaning of this practice is the redemption and fulfilment of man."[7] That reminds us of St. Paul's word about speaking (doing) the truth in love. As Urs von Balthasar insists, time "fulfils itself with eternity only by fulfilling eternity's mission in present time."[8] The implication is that theology will have to spring from the theologian's involvement in actual life, his participation in his group's concerns, dreams, and strivings. His theological vision must become present and active on the political scene where life's decisive battles are fought. The involvement has to be in the concrete history of one's own nation or group, so that a theology may come to birth with the stamp of life's actual experience, with local cultural sensitivity and the capacity to respond to actual needs and possibilities. Authentic involvement in concrete situations will naturally have a universal human quality which will be shared by the theology born of it. Such culture is the only adequate preparation to relate with openness to other committed political theologies born in other situations.

Praxis means further that theology must make its contribution to remake the world and humanize history, so that God's Rule may come. Hearts and lives and economic arrangements are to be reshaped to enable freedom and creativity to grow, to enable man to discover and make himself. As education is the praxis of freedom, as Freire says, so theology is the praxis of salvation, of human wholeness and of ultimate meaning. The praxis, for instance, of the doctrine of the Trinity will go far beyond speculation and press for a socialist society in which all are equal, every man is important, nobody is subordinated or marginated, wealth is held in common, and sacrificial love constitutes the principle of life. If the eucharistic faith is practiced and its power is not prevented from fecundating history, the ritual sharing will become the starting point of an ever-widening activity of sharing bread and wealth in all areas of life, making for a fraternal, eucharistic, socialist community of peoples. Many other aspects of our faith, like the doctrine of Creation, the Incarnation, or the Atoning Death, can through praxis become dynamics of social change and of the evolution and rebuilding of history. And real theology shapes only where history is the practice of liberation. There is thus a dialectical relationship between the praxis of history and the praxis of the faith.

It will not do merely to assert that the consciousness of world history, and the forces that "have transformed all previous history into world history" stem from the Christian faith and have roots in the historicness and universality of the Christian idea of God.[9] Is the universality of the Christian idea of God so clear and beyond question in the context of traditional Christian praxis of both theology and politics? In the biblical view, where injustice is practiced and human relationships are broken or vitiated, God refuses to exist.[10] It is not easy for Asia and Africa and for the wretched of the earth anywhere to associate "historicness and universality" with the God-idea which can coexist with a practice of history in terms of colonial mastery, white overlordship, military-capitalist oligarchies, and racism and apartheid and in terms of used and neglected hungry human masses. Christian faith is more than gnosis and verbalism. There is no faith, no universal and historic idea of God, and no God except in the praxis of all this. Faith lives by building history.

In Christ, God has acted in world history. God has a world history because he makes it in measureless, forgiving, ingathering love, and dwells in it to heal and grace it and give it human wholeness. But for us universal history, and for that matter, all history is a task to fulfill and a mission to accomplish. It is made in the measure in which we love and build up one another to shape fellowship of friends and brothers in which all human diversity and the wealth of human variety are respectfully integrated for the enrichment of all, and the relationship is embodied and expressed in the sharing of all bread and all earth and all power. An ontological understanding of the structure of being may remain unrelated to the problems of life. But so may also theological assertions of historical and social dimensions. What is needed to make both history and theology both possible and authentic is praxis.

NOTES

1. M. M. Thomas, *Man and the Universe of Faiths,* p. 132.
2. Ibid.
3. Rudolf Bultmann, *History and Eschatology* (1957), p. 152.
4. M. M. Thomas, *Man and the Universe of Faiths,* p. 140.
5. Ibid., p. 26.
6. Ibid., p. 43; Arnold Toynbee, *Christianity Among the Religions of the World,* pp. 17, 81–82, 109.
7. Charles C. West, *The Power to Be Human* (Macmillan Co., 1971), p. 126;

M. M. Thomas, *Man and the Universe of Faiths,* p. 128.

8. Hans Urs von Balthasar, *Man in History: A Theological Study* (Sheed & Ward, 1968), pp. 334–335.

9. Wolfhart Pannenberg, *Basic Questions in Theology,* Vol. I (Fortress Press, 1970), p. 69, note 136, with reference to Heimpel, Wiltram, and Gogarten.

10. Micah 3:1–7; Matt. 5:23.

PART THREE

Christ and
the Christian Life

Twelve

On the Meaning of Transcendence
Hideo Ohki

[Professor of Christian ethics at Tokyo Union Theological Seminary, the author is concerned to reinterpret the meaning of transcendence in human experience today. Combining insights from Emil Brunner and Max Weber with those of the Japanese Christian philosopher Seiichi Hatano, he concludes that transcendence must be understood not as "God's being far away from man" but as "God's coming from afar to man." The Japanese concept *shorai* (future), he believes, opens up a new possibility for understanding God's transcendence in terms of time rather than space. To express man's experience of transcendence, Professor Ohki finds "love" to be a more adequate category than "hope." This enables him to see how "God is ultimately transcendent in the cross."—Ed.]

> When Israel sought for rest,
> the LORD appeared to him from afar.
> —Jeremiah 31:3

> Grace and truth came by Jesus Christ.
> —John 1:17

I. A REVERSAL

What is the transcendence of God? By this concept is it generally meant that God is far removed from the human world and maintains an absolute, infinite distance which disallows any approximation from the side of man? My attempt here is to reverse this general conception.

There is a moment for human beings in which the infinite distance between God and man appears to be self-evident and this is said to give

This was originally a lecture delivered at the Lexington Theological Seminary, Lexington, Ky., on Jan. 5, 1973. *Northeast Asia Journal of Theology*, No. 14 (March 1975), pp. 10–19. Reprinted by permission.

rise to the atheistic situation articulated in such expressions as "God's silence,"[1] "the eclipse of God,"[2] or "God is dead."[3] Some believe this to be a basic characteristic of the modern age. Indeed, the modern age has not yet got over the stage of philosophical premonition in relation to a truly atheistic situation, if what we mean by a really atheistic situation is the kind of unendurable condition ancient Israel suffered in Egypt or that the modern Jews suffered in Auschwitz. In such situations there comes a time when the atheistic character of the situation in which man exists becomes unbearably apparent. And at such a time, truly at such a moment, God comes to man transcending that infinite gap between God in his otherness and man in his present reality. If and when this happens, how exciting the experience is! What does the existence of Christians mean in this atheistic, or preatheistic, modern age? It is nothing else than the empirical manifestation of the reality of God's coming into the midst of the modern world.

Abraham Joshua Heschel, a famous contemporary Jewish philosopher, has spoken of revelation as "a moment in which God succeeded in reaching man."[4] It is this act of God "reaching" to us that we call God's transcendence. Revelation is the reality of the act of God's transendence. Transcendence means, thus, not to be far away from one, but to come near to one from afar. This reversal of the more usual interpretation may sound strange to the ears of modern men, since they are more accustomed to interpret the word "transcendence" with such connotations as "distance" and "distinction."

Barth's *Romans,* published in 1922, deeply impressed men of the early twentieth century with such an interpretation of God's transcendence. The overwhelming power this book exerted can be attributed in large measure to the discharge from the bow of his stern logic of the notion of "the infinite qualitative distinction between time and eternity" and the recurrent theme that "God is in heaven, and thou, man, art on earth."[5] We have been habituated to this idea now for over fifty years. Even more than that, Barth advocated the logic of the infinite qualitative distinction on the precedent not only of Kierkegaard, but also of Kant and Plato. Certainly it goes back at last to Plato, and from Plato it has come to us down the centuries, forming a long custom of thought which has dominated the Western mind. It is never easy to challenge such a long-dominant habit of Western theological thinking. But is this habit of thinking truly suitable to the biblical God, to such a concept of God, for example, as that stated by Heschel above? Or, rather, hasn't the traditional notion of transcendence created a centuries-old misunderstanding of the biblical God?

We hear many voices deploring the loss of the dimension of the supernatural.[6] But do we really need to restore the Platonic theory of two worlds again in the midst of the modern age? Rather, must we not develop a new, or must we not return to an old, biblical understanding of God's transcendence, which reaches back beyond the traditional misconception of Western theological thinking? The God to whom the Bible witnesses is one who crosses the infinite distance between God and man, and immerses himself in man's atheistic situation. This is precisely the true reality of the infinite qualitative distinction between God and man. And when the atheistic situation is experienced with sufferings, when aspiration after salvation becomes man's sole and his greatest concern, this transcendence of God's coming will be experienced as nothing but the reality of salvation. God's transcendence is a soteriological reality.

Only when God is understood as the one who comes all the way to man, only then does it become apparent to the eyes of man, with awe and gratitude, how tremendous is the abyss between God and man.

II. "God from Afar"

There are several influences that have led me to this reversal of the more common understanding of transcendence. The greatest of them was my teacher Dr. Emil Brunner's later thought. When he published the second edition of his celebrated book *Truth as Encounter,* in 1963, he emphasized his discovery of the "coming-character," as he called it, of biblical truth, quoting the Johannine passage "Grace and truth came by Jesus Christ." He wrote:

> The transcendent ground of truth moves from a hidden transcendence into history. . . . That the Ground of all being should come to man, and not be found by him, this is what the Gospel tells us, and in so doing, it expresses the difference between the Biblical understanding of truth and all others.[7]

All that I have tried to do here is to draw the implications of the "moving" and "coming" that Brunner stated here for the concept of God's act of transcendence. This was my starting point.

But I have also learned something important from a Japanese Christian philosopher, Seiichi Hatano. Especially his unique understanding of time in terms of *shorai* (future), which was developed in his last work *Time and Eternity,* [8] helped me in conceptualizing God's transcendence.

Here, however, I want to mention another figure who was no less helpful to me, that is, Max Weber. Above all, I have found useful his unique sociological conception of the biblical God as it is found in his book *Ancient Judaism,* namely, the notion of God as a "god from afar." His sociological interpretation of Yahweh-God helped me in theologically clarifying the meaning of God's transcendence.

It is in a section of his book devoted to the discussion of the important subject, "The Uniqueness of the Relation of Israel to Its God," that this interesting concept of a "god from afar" appears. He writes:

> But Yahweh was a god in a quite special sense. He was—and that remained a conception fraught with consequences—a "god from afar," holding sway from his remote mountain seat near heaven and on occasion personally intervening in the course of events. . . . It was no local or tribal deity familiar of old, but the sworn Israelite confederacy.[9]

This sociological concept is pregnant with meanings which illumine the problems of the origin and also the character of Israelite religion. The significance of this concept will become immediately clear when compared with Japanese mythology. Gods of Japanese mythology cannot be thought of as gods from afar. The Japanese nation is regarded in these myths as a descendant of the gods as the gods themselves, in turn, were born from gods. Between gods and men there is a native, or natural, continuity. But to say that Yahweh is a god from afar means that there is no such native, natural bond, nor, to speak in a more sophisticated manner, any ontological relationship, nor even *analogia entis* between him and the world. Yahweh is, as Weber said, "no local or tribal deity." Israel was not born from Yahweh. His relationship to Israel is, so to speak, a relationship of "adoption." Originally there was no "blood" and "land" tie between them. If both parties do not have any natural tie and yet will to establish a relationship, that relationship must be a covenant which can only be entered into by voluntary personal engagement. Here is the explanation why the idea of "covenant" occupies such an important place in Israelite religion.

Though we have only referred to a few implications of the idea of "a god from afar," this is certainly, as Weber says, "a conception fraught with consequences." We cannot, however, dwell on this discussion. Let us simply indicate a bit further how this idea illumines our understanding of God's transcendence.

That God is a god from afar implies that the religious bond between God and man is only effected by God's coming all the way into creaturely existence—that is, in himself crossing the great gap between God and man. God is for Israel a "foreign" one, to use a New Testament image —foreign like a "good Samaritan," but this means one who approaches and becomes "intimate." This metaphor is very powerful when it is interpreted in such a Far Eastern country as Japan. God comes as far as Japan and does the work of salvation there. We have seen it with our eyes, we have looked upon it, we have touched it with our hands. In

Japan, Christianity is generally regarded as a "foreign" religion. This is true, but not in the sense that is generally assumed. We must ponder this fact: Hasn't faith in this God been a "foreign" religion not only to Japanese, but even also to the Israelites from the beginning? God came to Egypt from afar and rescued Israel by his mighty acts, and thus entered into a covenantal relationship. This original Israelite experience is reflected in our own experience. Our Japanese experience of salvation is thus better clarified by applying Weber's idea of a "god from afar." Based on this experience, we interpret God's transcendence not as God's being far away from man, but as God's coming from afar to man. In these terms God's transcendence is nothing but the enactment of his grace, the reality of his salvation.

III. God's Transcendence and Man's Transcendence

We began our discussion of the meaning of transcendence immediately with a discussion of God's transcendence. The stated reversal in the customary meaning of God's transcendence will come as a stumbling block to any attempts which begin by discussing man's capacity for self-transcendence. But we deliberately did so, for the reason that we have to deal with transcendence where it is presented in a concretely authentic manner and not rendered ambiguous and merely hypothetical. This means that the actual fact, though it is often hidden, is that we cannot reach God via man's transcendence but rather that man's transcendence as such must be conceived as grounded in God's transcendence. This may need some further explanation.

Among Western theologians it is often presupposed that man's capacity for self-transcendence and freedom is a universal fact of human nature. They are inclined to build a logical structure on this basis ascending toward God in a manner typically stated in the words of Augustine's *Confessions:* "Our hearts are restless till they find their rest in thee." But if we take a wider, transcultural perspective, we can easily find that the various concepts of man's self-transcendence and freedom do not always converge. For example, Max Weber compared conceptions of salvation in Judaism and Hinduism at the beginning of his *Ancient Judaism.* There we can learn what a fundamental difference lies between them. In Hinduism, and also generally in Oriental civilization, man's aspiration after salvation does not take the form of "emancipation" as it does in Judaism. But rather, salvation is conceived more in terms of a state of "resignation." If we hold this difference in view, we must consequently recognize this fact, that the notion of man as a free being, and the content of this freedom as "emancipation," is not a universal but rather a specifically

Jewish-Christian heritage. If it is not exclusively a Jewish-Christian possession, certainly it is a basic element in Jewish-Christian belief. If God
is not the one whose freedom in coming to his people gives them the
freedom to leave Egypt, isn't it a wiser policy to rebel against Moses'
leadership in the wilderness and to return to Egypt and be obedient to
Pharaoh and be content with the "flesh pots" which comfort the fatigued
bodies of slave labor? Or might it not be interesting to speculate according to Hindu philosophy that they who arrogantly exploit us will be
reborn slaves in the world to come, and we who now obediently suffer
will be reborn masters? No one can escape the *Karma,* and the *Karma*
is a revenger. When we view from another cultural perspective Western
thinkers' presupposition of man's freedom and his capacity for self-
transcendence, these ideas will be immediately revealed as historically
circumscribed. Such notions are not universal at all, nor do they have
universal validity by themselves. They are, in fact, merely the historical
product of a particular religiocultural tradition, even though through the
expansion of Western civilization they are now widely spread over the
world today.

It is quite natural that a concept of transcendence based upon this
historical development is restricted in scope by the historically structured context in which it has emerged. Therefore it is no wonder that the
concept of man's transcendence takes a direction and a character which
are covertly determined by this historical derivation. So, attempts of this
sort to frame a universal notion of human self-transcendence on the basis
of immediate self-understanding commit in fact, if not in logic, the
mistake of a *petitio principii.*

We may note in this connection Gordon D. Kaufman's *God the
Problem* (1972), as an important recent addition to the discussion of the
meaning of transcendence. Professor Kaufman distinguishes two models
of transcendence. One he calls the "teleological" model, and the other,
an "interpersonal" model. The attempt to develop a concept of transcendence on the basis of man's capacity for self-transcendence may be
classified as representative of the "teleological" model. Kaufman's contribution is aimed more in the direction of a clarification of the "interpersonal" model. He bases this model on the "experience-of-inaccessibility-
except-in-moments-of-revelation"[10] as these occur in the process of
interpersonal knowledge. We admit with appreciation that this interpersonal model of transcendence is effective in many respects in explaining
the biblical conception of God. At the same time, however, we also notice
that an ingredient in this model is, in hidden outline, the Western historical bias which construes the experience of Western man as typical of all
human experience. Thus it is simply a matter of course that this model

suits such experience properly, for this model originally comes from it. Kaufman's discussion remains exclusively on the level of "model" analysis and does not probe to the level of the "ground" for the construction of all theological models. The recurrent motif in Kaufman's discussion seems to be an attempt to provide a nonmythological idea of transcendence through analysis of the process of interpersonal knowledge. But if we go deeper, namely, to the very ground of the idea of personal being, that with which the biblical witness is concerned, we have to question seriously whether this understanding of man as "person" can possibly be spoken of without basing it upon (albeit mythological) statements concerning God's self-revelation.

Professor Kaufman's discussion seems to resemble Emil Brunner despite the fact that he does not mention Brunner in this book. Because of this similarity, we are all the more interested in an important difference between them. Brunner peered deeper into the fundamental problem of the ground of personal existence in his discussion of the personalistic philosophy of the I-Thou relationship. For a personalistic understanding of man must needs go, if deeply pursued theologically and historically, finally to the question of the ground of personal existence in order to conceive what it means for man to be "person." Brunner says:

> "The First Person," as we say in grammar, is the I that alone can truly say, "I," because he alone is independent, self-sufficient, without other foundation, and self-positing. This I discloses itself as an I by addressing us as Thou. And we, "the Second Person" through the word "Thou" of his address spoken to us, become true selves dependent on the Self.[11]

Here we notice a deepening of the discussion, a pressing beyond an epistemological level of interpersonal knowledge to an ontological search for the ground of personality. If, then, in a biblical perspective we must conceive this ground as nothing less than God's self-revelation, we naturally come to see that this ground is nothing other than that mysterious divine act of "coming," that graceful divine act of "transcendence," which establishes man as "person," as partner of God's covenant.

Is this, then, still a third model of transcendence? No, this is really the *basis* of the two models we have considered.

IV. "Shorai" (Future) and "Agape" (Love) as the Most Adequate Categories of God's Transcendence

God comes from afar. And his coming is consummated in Jesus Christ. Psychologist Erich Fromm interpreted the revelation of God's name "I am what I am" (or "I will be what I will be") to show his "anonymity," rather than his "name."[12] This is meaningful for theology, too. Anonymity is symbolic to Israelite experience of the God who comes from afar. It negates a feeling of natural intimacy. But this anonymous God becomes known to us as he names himself in Jesus Christ. In Jesus Christ, God has made concrete what it means to be God.

God's transcendence is suggested in that anonymous self-introduction, "I will be what I will be." God is essentially self-transcending. When his self-transcending is set before us in the concrete form of Jesus Christ, this reveals to us at one and the same time what a tremendous gap does exist between God and man and what God has done and does to reach man. It is an absolute abyss, to use the Barthian expression, "the infinite qualitative distinction," which only God can and which he does cross. In this act of transcendence, God is the absolutely other *(das Ganz-Andere)* who is beyond the world and man, and in relation to whom there is no *analogia entis* between himself and man. And yet also in this act of transcendence and as its primary character, God the absolutely other is "full of grace and truth." It is true that grace reveals sin. The event of God's transcendence reveals the infinite qualitative distinction between God and man.

We try to conceptualize God's transcendence formally by the concept of *shorai* (future) and materially by the concept of *agapē* (love). We employ these two concepts as the most appropriate categories for God's transcendence.

1. *Shorai* is a Japanese word which describes a unique dimension of the future. There are two Japanese expressions which describe the dimension of the future: *shorai* and *mirai*. *Mirai* means literally the future "not yet come." *Shorai* is something "about to come." The English word "future" approximates the meaning of *mirai*, but there is no English equivalent for *shorai*. The German language uses two words for future, *Futur* and *Zukunft*. The latter, *Zukunft*, may be a closer approximation to *shorai*. But *shorai* has a unique nuance which even *Zukunft* cannot convey. For it implies a posture of forward-bending, rather than merely a "coming-to," that is, *Zukunft*.

The Japanese Christian philosopher Seiichi Hatano has made it clear that there are opposite directions in time-vectors between *shorai* and *mirai*. *Mirai* suggests a time-ray which started from the past but which does "not yet come" to the future. The time-vector here takes a direction from the past to the future. But *shorai* signifies a direction from ahead, that is, from the future to the present. In *shorai* the ordinary direction of the time-vector is reversed. *Shorai* is a time which is about to come, that even now is facing us.

Now, let us apply the category of *shorai* to God's transcendence. It will open up a new possibility for conceiving God's transcendence *temporally* as over against a *spatial* conception such as, for example, in the Platonic two-world theory. God (the "I will be what I will be") cannot be grasped as something static in spatial terms. He is essentially the dynamic one who is about to come—*shorai*. The event of Jesus Christ is the presence of the *shorai* of God.

We agree with Moltmann in designating *Zukunft* as the "new paradigm of transcendence."[13] The only difference between Moltmann and us lies in the content of the notion of God's transcendence which is to be conceived in terms of *shorai* or *Zukunft*. Moltmann interprets it by the concept of "hope." But we envisage "love" as a more adequate descriptive category.

2. The *shorai* of God (the "I will be what I will be") cannot be rightly interpreted anthropomorphically, for example, in terms of God's walking in the garden of Eden. God's *shorai* is nothing but God's self-dedication. Brunner once said, "true self-communication would be self-dedication." Let us thus boldly say, "God's transcendence is God's becoming love through dedicating himself out-and-out to man." Needless to say, this love is named by the New Testament *agapē*, which cannot be interpreted simply by analogy to the human love experience. "God is *agapē*" (I John 4:8). God's transcendence is this movement from the "I will be what I will be" to the "God is *agapē*." In Jesus Christ, Yahweh-God has become *agapē*. The presence of God's *shorai* is his *agapē*.

Why cannot man express *agapē*? Because man cannot transcend himself in the same way in which God does. In *agapē* God's self-transcendence is consummated as he decisively comes to save man. God's transcendence is nothing less than his forgiveness and love to sinners, in which he infinitely surpasses the limits of human being. The ultimate manifestation of the transcendence of God took place in the cross of Jesus Christ, for there God decisively reached man by coming all the way over the infinite qualitative distinction between God and man. We have to return to a *theologia crucis* as a corrective to the recent excessively emphasized theology of resurrection, for God is ultimately transcendent in the cross rather than in his work of resurrecting Jesus from the dead. He who is so powerful to suffer the cross is able to do the work of resurrection. Thus, in the suffering of the cross, God revealed his true transcendence, for this act of self-giving love was solely a possibility for God.

Twentieth-century history of theology seems to have followed a dialectical course from an emphasis on faith by neo-orthodox theology to the counter emphasis on hope by the younger generation of the 1960's, but this dialectical development must be fulfilled now in the recovery of the "greatest of these," that is, the reality of the love of God.[14] This is not a return to the nineteenth-century liberal ethic of love. The recovery of this truth must be conducted by experiencing deeply the presence of God's *shorai,* that is, the reality of God's transcendence in *agapē.* "God is love, and he who abides in love abides in God, and God abides in him" (I John 4:16). We must grasp this presence—not a future but this presence-in-*agapē*—as the act in which God arrives from afar. The presence of God's *shorai* in *agapē*—the reality of God's transcendence—is the "step" by which we alone will be able to transcend the bondage of the "Slough of Despond" (Bunyan) which surrounds us everywhere today in these closing years of the twentieth century.

NOTES

1. Cf. Shusaku Endo, *Silence* (Charles E. Tuttle Co., 1969). Endo is a Japanese Catholic writer.

2. Martin Buber, *Gottesfinsternis: Betrachtungen zur Beziehungen zwischen Religion und Philosophie* (1953).

3. Cf. the writings of Friedrich Nietzsche.

4. Abraham J. Heschel, *God in Search of Man* (Farrar, Straus & Cudahy, 1956), p. 199.

5. Karl Barth, *Der Römerbrief* (1919); 2d ed., 1922 (E.T., *The Epistle to the Romans,* London: Oxford University Press, 1933). Quoted from Preface to the Second Edition.

6. Cf. a very interesting book by the American sociologist Peter L. Berger, *A Rumor of Angels: Modern Society and the Rediscovery of the Supernatural* (Doubleday & Co., 1969).

7. Emil Brunner, *Wahrheit als Begegnung* (1963); E.T., *Truth as Encounter* (Westminster Press, 1964), p. 4.

8. Seiichi Hatano, *Time and Eternity* (Japan Publications, 1963).

9. Max Weber, *Ancient Judaism* (Free Press, 1952), Ch. V, p. 124.

10. Gordon D. Kaufman, *God the Problem* (Harvard University Press, 1972).

11. Brunner, *Truth as Encounter,* p. 23.

12. Cf. Erich Fromm, *You Shall Be as Gods* (Holt, Rinehart & Winston, 1966), Ch. II.

13. Jürgen Moltmann, *Religion, Revolution and the Future* (Charles Scribner's Sons, 1969).

14. [Cf. Gustaf Aulén, "The Sovereignty of Love," pp. 121–130 in his *The Faith of the Christian Church,* 2d English edition (Fortress Press, 1960).—Ed.]

Thirteen

The Unbound Christ:
Toward a Christology in India Today

S. J. Samartha

[This important essay, like the book from which it comes, is significant for three main reasons: (1) "The primacy of Jesus Christ to Christian faith and practice," which assumes special importance "at a time when the traditional religions are being pushed back to examine ... the basic beliefs at the very center of their life"; (2) "the amazingly persistent response of Hindus to Jesus Christ in spite of the avowed self-sufficiency of modern Hinduism"; (3) the "need for systematic formulations of Christian theology in India, taking into account the living categories of Indian life and thought." The insights of the Christian faith in Jesus Christ as Lord and Savior can help Hindu spirituality to recover a sense of the personal, the historical, and the social. On the other hand, the Hindu insight into "the larger unity of all life" can help Christianity to overcome "a narrow view of revelation as confined to the historical, thus isolating it from nature and from human consciousness." "The affirmation of the Lordship of the crucified and risen Christ over all life," concludes Dr. Samartha, "does not involve any exclusiveness. On the contrary, it is the declaration of the universality of the unbound Christ."—Ed.]

Christology is the task of the church. Its central effort should be to acknowledge the mystery and explain the meaning of the person and work of Jesus Christ. Its starting point is the total commitment to Christ as the crucified and risen Lord. Its context is one of sharing and involvement. It is only as we share in the struggles and conflicts and tragedies of our national life and, in that context, seek to answer what it means to affirm that Christ, crucified and risen, is the Lord of all life that we can hope to make the gospel trustingly relevant to human need in contemporary India. It is my conviction that unless Indian Christian theo-

Extracted from the author's book *The Hindu Response to the Unbound Christ,* Inter-Religious Dialogue Series, No. 6 (Bangalore: Christian Institute for the Study of Religion and Society, 1974), pp. v, 1–2, 7–8, 184–200. German edition, *Hindus vor dem universalen Christus: Beiträge zu einer Christologie in Indien* (Stuttgart: Evang. Verlagswerk, 1970), pp. 181–197. Reprinted by permission.

logical thinking takes *advaita*[1] seriously in both its classical and modern forms, it is not likely to make any effective contribution to the quest for resources to undergird our national life.

It is the further conviction of this writer that Christ has already made, and continues to make, an impact on the heart and mind of India and that the church should take into serious account this prepared ground and fertilized soil to understand the nature of its mission and to fulfill it. This means that Christianity need not be in *competition* with the whole range of Hinduism for the allegiance of the hearts and minds, but that in certain areas *cooperation* with it should be possible in the common quest for fullness of life. It also means that Hinduism need not necessarily continue on its lonely pilgrimage in suspicious mistrust of Christianity and proud of its own self-sufficiency, but that in partnership with Christianity it can seek the meaning of the material, the personal, and the historical within the structure of its own spirituality. Whether it is in the attempts to redefine the goals of life or in the effort to meet human needs in the dust and heat of the plains, wherever two or three Hindus and Christians are gathered together in his name, there one need not doubt the presence of the living Christ in the midst of them. In this cooperative quest it is obviously necessary to take into account the particular historical context in which India finds itself today, struggling to reach its national goals for the renewal of man and the remaking of society.

Once the centrality of Jesus Christ is acknowledged, the particular expressions of Christology might vary depending upon particular situations and in relation to particular cultural positions. The fact that the sympathetic Hindu response to Christ is already there should be helpful to the church in this task. . . . Without theological backbone we are in danger of becoming spiritual jellyfish. But it should not be assumed that the theological enterprise is the work of a few individuals who, with some knowledge of Western theology and Indian philosophy, can juggle terms from both, and talk in terms of a precarious synthesis. Theology cannot be produced to order. It is the function of the church and, therefore, must grow out of the mature soil of the church's spiritual and intellectual life. If Christology is concerned with the question, What does it mean today in India to affirm that Jesus Christ is Lord and Savior? then any significant answer to that question can come only insofar as the church shares in the struggle of the people desperately demanding freedom from all manner of bondage, seeking personal fulfillment, social reconstruction, and national renewal. One can wholeheartedly agree with M. M. Thomas when he makes the following observation: "True theology is not a means of enhancing self-righteousness and political messianism but a spiritual source of constructive and discriminating participation."[2]

THE NATURE OF JESUS CHRIST

The connection of Jesus Christ with God on the one hand and with man on the other raises the question of his nature. The older discussions of this question usually deal with the two-nature theory, struggling to answer the impossible question how the same person can, at the same time, be both God and man. A purely academic discussion on what the concepts of divinity and humanity mean and how they can be brought together will not be particularly helpful in this connection. Neither will it be specially illuminating to discuss whether the divinity of Jesus Christ is to be seen *in* his humanity or *through* it. It is more important to ask what is the Reality that one encounters in Jesus of Nazareth as the living and the risen Lord, in the totality of his life, death, and resurrection, and how, through him, a renewal of human life is possible. The "new creation" in Christ has first to be understood in his own life and work, and then accepted and appropriated in faith and through grace in personal and social life. Therefore the question is about Christ and the being of God on the one hand and Christ and human existence on the other. From the New Testament it is quite clear that his "humanness" was as real and natural as his conscious acceptance of, and therefore identity with, the will and purpose of God. While acknowledging that the consciousness of another person always remains a mystery to others in spite of its occasional, revealed meaning, one must accept that the New Testament portrait of Christ gives no hint of any conflict in his consciousness; on the contrary, the unity of his personality and the unambiguous centrality of his purpose as being one with that of God are clearly indicated. Further, the expression of God's will and purpose, his love and compassion, are manifest in Jesus Christ not just through his consciousness but through his decisions and acts, through obedience even unto death, through acts of mercy and healing bringing wholeness not to humanity in the abstract but to men and women in their concrete personal existence, anxious, guilty and mortal, living, struggling and dying, seeking, doubting, and finding, hoping for the Kingdom to come but not yet knowing that in Jesus Christ it has already come.

The later attempts by the church to safeguard the humanity and divinity of Christ's nature in one person must be considered in the proper historical perspective. The Chalcedonian statement (A.D. 451) was an attempt to guard this unity. One is familiar with the declaration:

> We all with one accord teach men to acknowledge one and the same Son, our Lord Jesus Christ . . . of one substance with the Father . . . , of one substance

with us . . . ; recognized in two natures, without confusion, without change, without division, without separation . . . ; not as parted or separated into two persons, but one and the same Son and Only-begotten God the Word, Lord Jesus Christ.[3]

This statement has been severely criticized in recent years. William Temple said that the Chalcedonian definition of the nature of Christ "represents the bankruptcy of patristic theology."[4] G. L. Prestige is even more critical when he remarks that in the Chalcedonian formula the living figure of the Redeemer is obscured by formalism and "Jesus Christ disappears in the smoke-screen of two-nature philosophy."[5] Bishop Robinson compares the two-nature theory to an unstable mixture of oil and water, and goes on to say that a doctrine of incarnation, based on the two-nature theory, "conjures up the idea of divine substance being plunged in flesh and coated with it like chocolate or silver plating."[6]

These criticisms are valid but perhaps are not sensitive enough either to the historical situation of the time, when the substance theory of reality was accepted, or to the purpose of the Council in making the particular formulation, which was mainly to guard against any heresy endangering the humanity and the divinity of Jesus Christ. In India today this type of formulation which one encounters even now in Christian preaching and in the answers of theological students in examinations is both meaningless and irrelevant. For one thing, the metaphysical doctrine of substance on which the two-nature theory is based is different from the understanding of reality in Hindu thought. For another, in the context of an *avatara* doctrine where the immanence of God is taken for granted, the two-nature theory can be dangerously misleading. To these must be added another important reason. Today the whole conception of the human self, of the ego and personality, is changing. The Hindu understanding of the *atman* as the essence that remains when everything else is stripped away is also changing in the modern *neo-advaitic* pattern of thought. It is true that the interiority of the self as an autonomous, undefinable, thinking subject is there, but stripping away all that adheres to it in experience and beholding it in its uncontaminated purity and splendid isolation is in itself no virtue. The shift of emphasis from the self to personality as the more significant category in history should also help one to understand the *relational* aspect of the self rather than to think of it in terms of localized interiority.

> The self is not an experience within the experiences, nor can it be equivalent to the whole experiential flux, but is "something else," a plus—which connects, leads, and gives sense to it. . . . The self is not changeless but is

permanent. It is always present and what it experiences both modifies and gives stability to it.[7]

It is important to note this permanent, autonomous character of the self. One must avoid the rather loose thinking that characterizes some of the discussion on this subject where terms like the self, the ego, individuality, personality, etc., are being used without precise definition, and often with different connotations—but at the present juncture, where the understanding of these terms is in a state of flux and where there are controversial opinions, it is perhaps better not to insist on precise definitions.

This discussion is in connection with the nature of Jesus Christ, his relation to God and to man understood historically. Both the existential understanding of the self as "a Being-next-to-God," as Heidegger remarks,[8] and the mystical description of the *atman* as being identical with *Brahman* himself do not seem to give sufficient importance to man as a historical personality, where his ego is a permanent center of responsible freedom and where personality should be considered as the product of the moral ego, exercising its freedom in relation to concrete historical situations and therefore moving in a state of continuous relationships. The whole question of the nature of Jesus Christ may therefore be understood in this sense. To describe him as an *advaitin,* one who had realized his identity with the *Brahman,* would limit one's understanding of him to the interiority of his consciousness without giving sufficient weight to the social, historical dimension of his life and work. It is true that the consciousness of Christ, as far as one can infer from the New Testament, exhibits "a unique interiority" and there is no reason to deny it. But it is also clear that it was not just a state of being-in-God but one of personal relationship where actualization of decisions takes place historically both in his own life and in his relation to others. Overholser is therefore right in his observation on this point when he writes:

> In the historical rather than the speculative sense; in the mood of open affirmation, and not strict definition; in the involvement of personal awareness, as against the fiction of impersonal detachment; in faith, but not without reason; in the sphere of the coincidence of knowledge and worship—the Christ of the New Covenant is to be equated with the God of creation and providence.[9]

There is, however, a further question which has been hovering over this discussion and which cannot and should not be avoided. This is the question of the divinity of Christ himself. For even if one is constrained to revise the God-man formula devised by Western theology or to reject the *advaita* category of the realization of immanent divinity as unsuitable for the purpose of Christology in India, the question of the status of Jesus Christ still remains. For one thing, it must be said that even though it is recognized that the distinctive feature of the New Testament estimate of Christ is historical, it must also be noted that one is driven beyond the historical categories in looking at the fullness of Christ. Being grasped by Christ through faith, experiencing God's grace in him, and having the very center of one's life transformed—all this is not the result of just responding to a historical teacher in the past. It is much more than that. To be in Christ is to be grasped by God who is larger and deeper, who, while being active in history, is beyond the categories conditioned by time, in his fullness and mystery. For another, while it would be unwise to formulate the question in such bald terms as "Is Jesus of Nazareth God?" one cannot ignore the fact that in the New Testament divinity is attributed to Christ. Ultimately one's answers to this question will depend on one's conception of God, but in the context of Christology, where both the meaning and mystery of God must be acknowledged, the understanding of God will be conditioned by what is revealed in Jesus Christ. It will be too much to expect a full-length treatment of this theme in this section. What can be done is just to indicate the lines of approach to this question under the guidance of New Testament scholarship.

In the New Testament it is not difficult to find considerable evidence to support what is usually described as "a subordinationist Christology." It may be recalled that Ram Mohan Roy in his time, and many others today, whether they are articulate or not, maintain this position. Quite a few verses in the Gospels as well as in the epistles may be put forward to support this view. In many places Paul speaks of God as the Father of the Lord, thus lending himself to this view (Gal. 1:1; Phil. 2:11; Rom. 1:7; etc.). But it would be a mistake to forget that Paul is not subordinationist, for in many other passages the terms God and Lord are used synonymously; at least there is obviously a *functional* similarity (II Cor. 8:9; I Thess. 2:19; Rom. 1:5; etc.). Two points in Paul's thought have to be specially noted in this connection. First, even though to Paul the divine disclosure in Jesus Christ is undoubtedly decisive, he is also aware of the fact that the divine reality that has been revealed in Jesus Christ is *not exclusively* present in this one event (Rom. 1:19–20; 3:21; I Cor. 10:4; etc.). Secondly, Paul looks forward to a time when the Christian dispensation must come to an end and God alone will be all in all. "When all things are subjected to him, then the Son himself will also be subjected to him who put all things under him, that God may be everything to every one" (I Cor. 15:28). Still, as Ogden points out, to Paul the reality signified by "God our Father" is the same reality designated by "our

Lord Jesus Christ." "What it means to have God as Father is existentially the same as having Jesus Christ as our Lord."[10] Too often expositions based on inadequate exegesis, sermons which lack theological precision, and pronouncements about Christ noted more for their zeal than for their humility create confusion and misunderstanding in the minds of the hearers.

Oscar Cullmann, after a careful examination of the designation of Jesus as God, makes the following observations:

> The fundamental answer to the question whether the New Testament teaches Christ's "deity" is therefore "Yes." But to this "yes" we must further add: "on condition that we do not connect the concept with later Greek speculations about substance and natures, but understand it strictly from the standpoint of *Heilsgeschichte.* "[11]

Cullmann argues that "salvation history" is definitive for Christology, and that without it, it would not make sense to speak of Jesus' deity. He also points out that it determines the specific subordination, in the New Testament, of Christ to God—"not in the sense of later so-called 'subordinationism,' but in the sense that Jesus Christ is God only in his revelation of himself . . . but it does not exhaust the nature of God the Father."[12] Without necessarily subscribing to the "salvation-history" scheme one must recognize Cullmann's point that the divinity of Jesus Christ must be understood only in his revelation of himself, and also that there is no need to maintain that the nature of God is completely exhausted in the life and work of Jesus of Nazareth. It is important to emphasize this point in the context of *advaita.*[13] Too often the way in which statements about Christ's divinity are formulated or the manner in which God's revelation in Jesus Christ is described lends itself to serious misunderstanding. The easy equation of Jesus of Nazareth with God Almighty is also misleading. Without minimizing the importance of the divinity of Christ, it is necessary to state it in such a way as not to give the impression that Christians know everything there is to know about the inexhaustible depth of God. The Bible, with so much of emphasis on the revelation of his love and purpose, still speaks of the "hiddenness" of God. "Thy footprints were unseen" (Ps. 77:19). "Truly, thou art a God who hidest thyself, O God of Israel, the Savior" (Isa. 45:15). "No man has ever seen or can see" the Sovereign, the King of Kings and Lord of Lords, "who alone has immortality and dwells in unapproachable light" (I Tim. 6:16). St. Augustine points out that that which one can comprehend is not God if, by comprehension, one means complete and adequate grasp of the totality of God in his infinity. This is not to say that the "hiddenness" of God should be overemphasized against his revelation in Jesus Christ, but to indicate that even while accepting the revelation of God's truth and love in Jesus Christ, the sense of the mystery and depth in God should not be eliminated through any cheap formulations of Christology in India.

THE CROSS AND THE RESURRECTION

The necessity and the meaning of Christ's work of salvation, particularly the significance of the twin themes of the cross and the resurrection, must now be considered in the context of *advaita.* Anyone who has some understanding of its structure as a system of philosophy, an attitude toward life, and a means of realization can immediately raise the question of the need for and the credibility of a savior in this pattern. If some of the Hindu thinkers have spoken of Christ in this connection, it is not as one who *brings* salvation but as one who has realized the potentialities already within man and so *became* his own savior. Nevertheless, it would be helpful to bring out the insights of Christ's work in such a situation also.

It has already been pointed out that the *advaita* emphasizes the unity of all life and thinks of nature, man, and God within the everlasting process that has its beginning, sustenance, and end in the *Brahman.* It is a neat and clearly worked out scheme where the individual, the historical, and the cosmic closely fit into a harmonious process. It begins with God, marches through the gradations of existence, through matter, life, mind, and spirit, till finally man returns to the starting point of the whole journey. The "push of process" rather than the "pull of purpose" is the determinative factor here. Fulfillment therefore is a return to the original perfection. Ignorance of man's true nature rather than sin and guilt is the state of bondage from which man has to be liberated. And this liberation, which confers true freedom on man, is to be achieved through the acquisition of the knowledge of the *Brahman.* It is only he who knows the *Brahman* that can *become* the *Brahman.* The crucial law that inexorably operates in this process, governing not only the life of man but also that of the whole cosmos, is the law of *karma-samsara,* the law that lays down that "according as a man acts, according as a man conducts himself, so does he become. The doer of good becomes good; the doer of evil becomes evil. One becomes virtuous by virtuous action and sinful by sinful action."[14] It further connects the fruits of one's actions with the chain of births and rebirths so that not only human life, and therefore history, but also nonhuman existence, and therefore nature and the whole cosmos, come within the scope of its operation.

And as a caterpillar, having come to the end of the blade of grass and having made an approach to another, draws itself together toward it, even so does this Self: having thrown off this body and dispelled all ignorance, and having made another approach toward another, (it) draws itself together toward it.

And as a goldsmith, taking a piece of gold, turns it to another shape—a newer and more beautiful one—even so does this Self: having thrown off this body and dispelled all ignorance, (it) makes for itself another shape, a newer and more beautiful one. . . .[15]

It is not necessary to repeat that some of the fundamental categories of this structure are being reinterpreted today. It is necessary, however, to point out that in this scheme, as it is and as it influences the life and thought of many people, the following categories do not receive sufficient attention: the freedom and responsibility of the individual personality; the social and historical dimensions of human life; the possibilities for the emergence of the new both in nature and in history; the fact of tragedy and evil within human spirituality sometimes masquerading as goodness; the persistence of sin, guilt, and death in human existence, particularly at a time when with new weapons of total destruction at the disposal of man, which may be willfully used or accidentally released, there is the possibility of human existence coming to an abrupt *finis* without ever having an opportunity of reaching its *telos.* It is in this context that one ventures to suggest that the cross and the resurrection of Christ manifest the power to overcome evil and tragedy in human life and the hope of reaching a consummation which is not a return to the old but a bringing in of the new. But, at the same time, one must hasten to add that a narrow interpretation of the saving work of Christ as a kind of "emergency measure" or "a rescue operation" decided on at a policy committee meeting in the high heavens after "the Fall" of man must be corrected by the larger view of the unity of all life coming under the all-embracing love of God. The scope of the saving work of Christ is larger than the redemption of individuals. As the Agent of creation and as the Savior of mankind, his work is continuing until all things are summed up in him. Here therefore the *advaita* emphasis on the unity of all life, where history and nature are seen together in the totality of the life of God, is not irrelevant.

There is no doubt that both in the New Testament and in subsequent Christian history all the lines of personal and social transformation converge on and diverge from the crucifixion and the resurrection of Jesus Christ. The influence of the saving power of the cross on the lives of many Hindu thinkers has already been noted. In the New Testament it is clear that it was after the resurrection of Jesus Christ that the disciples began proclaiming the good news "with power." It was the consciousness of the abiding presence of the living Christ and a recognition of the continuity between the crucified Savior and the risen Lord that endowed them with power, granted them peace, and gave them a purpose that transformed their lives. Too often, Christian attempts to *explain* the mystery of the cross and the resurrection have led to unnecessary misunderstandings. While it should not be forgotten that in the very character of the crucifixion-resurrection event there is a quality which questions man's sense of pride, it should not be so stated as to obscure its own power to make it luminous. Paul's words still remain true, not only in the context of *advaita* but in every human situation, that the word of the cross can be a stumbling block and foolishness to people. But the "offense" of the cross need not be stated in an offensive way. The following points should be particularly avoided: the tendency to describe the resurrection as a kind of happy ending to an otherwise tragic story; theories of atonement based on outmoded ideas of sacrifice which make little sense today; the tendency to remain weeping at the foot of the cross for a longer time than seems necessary, enjoying the emotional *catharsis* but refusing to move out into the light of the resurrection; an overemphasis on "original sin," stated in a crude manner, which deprives man of his spiritual dignity and which compels sensitive Hindu friends to cry out, "It is a sin to call man *sinner*"; the stress on feelings of sin and guilt as prerequisites before the saving power of the cross can become operative in the life of men; the obsession with symptoms of sin rather than with the root of sin in what is described in Sanskrit as *ahamkara* ("I"ness or pride); and the tendency to defend and *explain* the meaning of the crucifixion and the resurrection rather than to allow Christ to unveil his own mystery.

There is a further point which should be stressed in discussing the meaning of the crucifixion and the resurrection in this context. This is the matter of the persistence of tragedy in human existence, the presence of evil in history, and sorrow in personal life. No talk about the larger perspective and the cosmic context can minimize the intensity with which an individual person suffers, sometimes through his own fault, sometimes through the vindictiveness of others, and sometimes simply because he is helplessly caught up in the clash of social and economic forces which, as an individual, he is unable to control. The question of the source of such suffering and the way out of it therefore becomes important. The doctrine of *karma-samsara* is one way of neatly solving it, by fixing the responsibility on actions done in a previous birth and by holding forth the hope that the possibility of overcoming suffering and going beyond tragedy lies within the power of man himself. In such a context a savior is not necessary, for, if one person should suffer for the sake of others, it would upset the principle of justice that each man should reap the fruit of his actions and that the innocent should not suffer for the sins of the guilty. It is also possible to deny the very reality of suffering by denying that it exists and by pointing out that it is only due to one's *avidya,* ignorance, that one merely *thinks* that one suffers. The solution is to destroy this ignorance through correct knowledge that the soul itself does not suffer. But this is obviously small comfort to those to whom suffering is very real and intense. The interdependence of all life in its personal and social aspects, the possibility of the self transcending its particular situation, the fact that certain people voluntarily suffer and die so that others may live to enjoy the values of life—these are not matters that can be dismissed as insignificant in human life. When Gandhiji was assassinated there were certain hints here and there which unobtrusively raised the question of the meaning of *karma* as a law of justice, not in the abstract but in relation to his one, concrete human life. It was recognized that, surely, Gandhiji's cruel and untimely death could not have been the result of any bad actions of his in *this* life. The possibility of pushing back the reason to a *previous* life was doubtful because, obviously, it would involve the question of memory which should connect action with its results through a principle of justice. There is little doubt therefore that in the minds of thoughtful people it raised a number of questions about oversimplifying the possible answers to the tragic element in human life. Mere suffering for the sake of emphasizing a spirit of renunciation is no virtue in itself. Tagore brings out this point clearly when he says:

> However unpleasant it may be, we must admit that neither the capacity nor the effort to bear the sorrows of others, intrinsic in the love of God, is widely evident in our country. . . . We have sought the delights of divine love to the exclusion of its pain. . . . There is no spirituality in the cultivation of suffering for some ultimate gain; true spirituality lies in suffering for the sake of love.[16]

Tagore goes on to say that "the spiritual seed from the tree of Christ's life" is "the ability to find strength through suffering." This is a matter not of ignoring suffering or transcending it, but accepting it and using it to fulfill the purpose of love. It is well known that in the Gospels a proportionately large place is given to narratives of the sufferings and death of Christ as well as his resurrection. There is affirmation of facts as well as theological reflection on the part of the disciples on the total life of Jesus Christ culminating in the cross and the resurrection. In the New Testament one can discern a threefold emphasis on this theme. Christ's suffering and death was *voluntary.* He willingly accepted suffering and death even though it would have been possible for him to postpone it or to escape it. He "set his face toward Jerusalem" when he could have gone elsewhere. "For this reason the Father loves me, because I lay down my life, that I may take it again. No one takes it from me, but I lay it down of my own accord. I have power to lay it down, and I have power to take it again; this charge I have received from my Father" (John 10:17–18). Secondly, it was *vicarious* in the sense that there is a deliberate recognition that it was for the sake of others. The theological interpretation of this and the later theories of atonement are not particularly important. What is significant is the fact that through an act of historical decision Jesus Christ took upon himself the sins of others and suffered and died for their sake. "For the Son of man also came not to be served but to serve, and to give his life as a ransom for many" (Mark 10:45). In India, during the monsoon season, heavy rains swell the rivers, which gather mud and dirt and carry them to the sea. Standing on the shore, one can make out that the waters of the sea are muddy for several miles. But it is always possible to look beyond and see the line of blue which never gets blurred, whatever be the volume of muddy waters the rivers might carry to it. The cross brings out the depth of human evil which, however, does not succeed in overcoming God's love in Christ. Thirdly, it is also pointed out that without the light of the resurrection the shadow of the cross would remain unillumined and would be taken as a failure. Therefore, the cross cannot be understood apart from the resurrection. It was only because of the resurrection that the death on the cross could justifiably be described as a *victorious* death; otherwise death in itself is the doom of all beings, the final separation, the ultimate in loneliness. "Why do you seek the living among the dead?" (Luke 24:5). "But thanks be to God, who gives us the victory through our Lord Jesus Christ" (I Cor. 15:57). It is in acknowledging the crucified and risen Lord and in obedience to him, participating in his suffering struggle to transform evil, that the church is called upon once again, if necessary, to die, in order that it may also share in the power of his resurrection. It is significant that Hindu friends in the context of present-day national reconstruction, which involves the removal of human suffering, challenge the church to a life of crucifixion-resurrection. Ashok Mehta, formerly Minister for Planning in the Union Cabinet of the Government of India, speaking to a group of Christians, made the following statement:

> We must reclaim 900 million people of the world who are today in a state of abject depression. This human reclamation requires a peculiar type of social engineering. This is, to my mind, the big challenge that all people, all men of religion, all men of God have to face. And if it is the proud claim of

the Christian churches that they have the spiritual understanding, the spiritual agony, and that their spiritual outflow is going to be greater than of other men of God, well, it has got to be proved in the crucible of life itself. If it is the claim of the Christians that even to this day they feel the agony of Christ on the Cross whenever humanity suffers, as it were, it has to be proved in action, not by any statement.[17]

The cross and the resurrection of Christ, taken together, far from being irrelevant to human need, today provide the inspiration and power to a life of worship and service, of suffering and victory. Without this anchorage in the crucifixion and without the hope of the resurrection, one is liable to be overcome by the very human suffering which one may try to remove. Therefore Paul is quite right in his statement of priorities when he says that his sole desire is "that I may know him and the power of his resurrection, and may share his sufferings, becoming like him in his death, that if possible I may attain the resurrection from the dead" (Phil. 3:10–11). To accept the Lordship of Jesus Christ means that one must be prepared to obey God's demand in Christ to crucify the self in its desire for isolation and in its feeling of self-sufficiency, in order that the promise of renewal in the resurrection might become operative in human life. Wherever the Christ event is recognized, and wherever people are prepared consciously to die with him and to be raised again with him, there God's work of reconciliation takes place.

Further, the New Testament also teaches that God's work of reconciliation and renewal extends beyond history to the cosmos itself. He who is the crucified and risen Lord is also the agent in creation, and so there is a wider range to the scope of the saving work of Christ. The recent emphasis on the "Cosmic Christ," in both Catholic and Protestant theology, is an indication of the fact that the narrow view of salvation as being limited to saving man is being supplemented by a recognition of the work of the "larger Christ." The consummation of all life, the disclosure of the ultimate meaning of creation, and the final destiny of nature and history must lie in the womb of the future, but he who is now acknowledged and accepted as the Lord is also the one in whom the divine activity is so focused as to provide a clue to the future consummation. "Beloved, we are God's children now; it does not yet appear what we shall be, but we know that when he appears we shall be like him, for we shall see him as he is" (I John 3:2).

In modern Hindu thought there is a good deal of discussion on the goal to which men are looking forward in hope and toward which humanity is moving—the ideal which would ensure personal, social, and cosmic fulfillment, going beyond the conflicts and tragedies of existence. Gandhiji spoke of *Ramarajya,* the kingdom of Rama, where truth and righteousness would be established forever and where life would proceed in harmony and love. To Gandhiji the way of nonviolence and the pursuit of truth were the means of attaining it. Radhakrishnan elaborates the idea of the *Brahma loka,* the world of the *Brahman,* to which the whole cosmic process after its long pilgrimage would return at the end. History, included in the cosmic process, would reach its fulfillment as part of the total process initiated by God, sustained by him, and being received by him again at the end. Aurobindo, making use of the well-known concept of *loka sangraha* (the gathering up of the world), enriched its content by pointing out that nothing in existence would be discarded, but everything would be transformed and gathered up in the final consummation toward which not only humanity but the whole cosmos is moving. In this context, God's activity in Christ, expressing itself in the continuing act of creation and redemption and moving toward fulfillment, has a significant role. Ultimately, it is God who brings about the consummation of all creation. "The mystery of his will" and the purpose he has set forth in Christ as "a plan for the fulness of time" is "to unite all things in him, things in heaven and things on earth" (Eph. 1:10). But this consummation should not be regarded as a return to the beginning, but as an enrichment and a fulfillment, moving through struggles and conflicts, overcoming evil in love, gathering up values, reaching out, and finding final fulfillment in the fullness of God himself.

This affirmation of the Lordship of the crucified and risen Christ over all life does not involve any exclusiveness. On the contrary, it is the declaration of the universality of the unbound Christ. There is no need to enter into any controversy on this question. One can wholeheartedly agree with Devanandan when he makes the following observation on this point:

> Christians believe that with the coming of Christ, God Almighty identified Himself for a while with man in all man's struggles for perfection and the realization of his true nature. Such identification initiates a new era in creation. It marked the beginning of a redemptive movement, which takes humanity in its entirety, that is the whole community of mankind inclusive of all peoples, whatever their beliefs, language or race. So that, far from shutting others out from participation (which would be being exclusive), the Christian wants the world of men to share his faith in this all-inclusive cosmic process of a new creation.[18]

This emphasis on the universality of God's love in Christ is necessary to point out that Christ transcends all cultures. For the question may rightly be raised: Having acknowledged the Hindu response to Christ, and after having stressed that it is the unbound Christ who has elicited that response, does it mean that he is now tied down to another world view like that of the *advaita?* Is Christ to be unbound only to be bound again by other cultural ropes and so become provincial? Far from it. In all human efforts there is the persistent temptation to succumb later to the very slavery from which man tries to free himself. This is true of all major experiences of history, whether it is in the attempts to meet modern man satisfied with his post-Christian, secular ideology or the self-sufficient Christian who, living in a world that has supposedly come of age, has accepted the demise of the Almighty, or the Indian Christian who, torn between his identification with the culture of his own country and his participation in the heritage of the world church, is struggling to bring out the distinctive meaning of Christ in the Hindu context. Not to succumb to this temptation needs that kind of Christian liberty which Martin Luther was talking about in his exegesis of Galatians, a liberty that has to do with the freedom of the son rather than the obedience of the slave. Christ is always involved in human situations wherever the struggle for justice, freedom, and truth is going on and demands from his followers participation in his crucifixion and resurrection, with the assured hope of renewal, partially perhaps in history, but certainly, fully, beyond history. But at the same time, Christ in his unbound freedom can never be identified with any particular system of thought, for Christ "is our hope, not our possession." Therefore all Christological efforts should be humble enough to recognize that they constantly stand under the judgment of God and that they need the continuing grace of God to be instruments of renewal and advance.

NOTES

1. [Nonduality; Shankara's system of Vedanta, which draws together God, world, and man in a single conception of unity.—Ed.]

2. M. M. Thomas, *The Christian Response to the Asian Revolution* (London: SCM Press, 1966), p. 22.

3. Henry Bettenson, *Documents of the Christian Church* (London: Oxford University Press, 1944), p. 73.

4. See the essay by William Temple in *Foundations,* ed. by B. H. Streeter (London: Macmillan & Co., 1913), p. 230.

5. G. L. Prestige, *Fathers and Heretics* (repr. London: S.P.C.K., 1948), p. 146.

6. J. A. T. Robinson, *Honest to God* (London: SCM Press, 1962; Philadelphia: Westminster Press, 1963), pp. 66–67.

7. "The Self as Structural Function Within the World," by Risieri Frondizi,

in the *Proceedings of the Tenth International Congress of Philosophy,* Vol. I, Fasc. 1, p. 368.

8. See Martin Heidegger, *Being and Time* (London: SCM Press, 1962); see also Karl Jaspers, *Philosophical Faith and Revelation* (Harper & Row, Publishers, 1967); and Rudolf Bultmann, *The Presence of Eternity* (Harper & Brothers, 1957), *The Theology of the New Testament,* Vols. I and II (Charles Scribner's Sons, 1951 and 1955), and *This World and the Beyond* (Charles Scribner's Sons, 1960).

9. James A. Overholser, *A Contemporary Christian Philosophy of Religion* (Henry Regnery Co., 1965), p. 119.

10. Schubert Ogden, *The Reality of God* (London: SCM Press, 1967), p. 201.

11. Oscar Cullmann, *The Christology of the New Testament* (Westminster Press, 1959), p. 306.

12. Ibid.

13. [Nonduality, non-otherness, or at-one-ness. Refers to Shankara's philosophy (9th century A.D.), which draws together God, the world, and man in a single conception of unbroken unity.—Ed.]

14. *Brihad,* IV.iii.33.

15. *Brihad,* IV.iii.30–31.

16. Rabindranath Tagore, *Towards Universal Man* (New Delhi: Asia Publishing House, 1961), p. 167.

17. Reported in *The Guardian,* Madras, June 22, 1967, p. 197.

18. Paul D. Devanandan, *Preparation for Dialogue* (Bangalore: Christian Institute for the Study of Religion and Society, 1964), pp. 137–138.

Fourteen

Christian Art in Asia: Signs of a Renewal

Masao Takenaka

[The medium of visual art is an exciting and significant way of interpreting the Christian message in Asia today. This selection is excerpted from a longer essay introducing his book *Christian Art in Asia* (1975). A project of the Christian Conference of Asia, with Dr. Takenaka as General Editor, this book represents the first time the works of Asian artists on Christian themes have been compiled and published. The collection includes 120 works of 107 artists from eighteen countries. They speak vividly of what the biblical revelation means to them in the Asian context. "I became convinced that artists are pioneers of the renewal of the church in Asia," says Takenaka, "since they exhibit in a concrete way a visible sign of the Christian presence in Asia today" (p. 9). He develops here a typology of Asian Christian art, classifying the works as "Passing Forms" and "Coming Forms." Under the former we have "syncretistic," "superficial," and "separation" types; under the latter we have "controversial," "contextual," or "confessional" types. "Authentic Christian art contains a confession of Christian faith as the personal response of the artist in a particular situation."—Ed.]

I. BACKGROUND

Throughout the history of Christianity, as God's people encounter the power of the gospel in each cultural and social context, we see new visions and hear new songs. One sees an exciting correlation between Christianity and culture, and particularly between faith and art. The power of Christ is an illuminating power, stimulating the vision of those who have artistic gifts in every generation. Whenever the inner life of people is inspired we see the vigorous development of religious art in various forms.

In Asia, one acknowledges the existence of rich traditional art. These

Excerpts from the Introduction to his book, *Christian Art in Asia* (Singapore: Christian Conference of Asia; Tokyo: Kyo Bun Kwan, 1975). Reprinted by permission of the Christian Conference of Asia.

art forms are often connected with a religious background. Increasing numbers of people from around the world are making pilgrimages to the Ajanta Cave in India, Borobudur Temple in Indonesia, or Nara Dai Butsu in Japan.

One naturally asks about the contributions of Asian Christians in this realm of art. What kind of artistic formulation is made when Asian people from such an artistic tradition are confronted with the gospel? How are the struggles and joys of being a Christian in Asia expressed through art forms? What are the unique gifts Asian artists are contributing to the whole *oikoumenē?*

Quite often when the gospel dwells among the people, it stirs up the minds of the people to bring forth their own expression of new being in Christ, both in music and in the visual arts. There is an irrepressible creative urge among people. People are not like stones or machines. Stones may be arranged to tell a message; but the stone itself does not initiate creative formulation. Machines may be used to produce goods; but the machine itself does not create the original idea. It is people who speak through stones and people who use machines. People have intuitive initiative and freedom of creativity. But if people lose this gift of human creativity, "the stones will cry out" (Luke 19:40). And if people lose their courage, "Leviathan will rise up" (Job 3:8). Yet people are people. Even if they are silent, they are struggling and yearning. Even if they are suppressed, they never cease to see visions.

During the long period of feudalism and colonialism most Asian people have never been silent. They have continuously engaged in the creative process in the area of culture. But often these energies of people are utilized for the ruling class, either for feudal lords or for foreign bosses. The history of Asian art is not simply the history of the search for beauty, but is a part of a complex history bound up with the economic and political forces of the period.

II. Signs of a Renewal

Among the various elements in the immense change that has taken place in Asia since World War II, it is important to discern the correlationship between national independence and cultural renaissance. The attainment of national liberation has brought an appreciation of the people's selfhood that has helped release the energy and creativity which had long been suppressed. To be sure, the directions and patterns are different in each country, yet there is a common trend of cultural renaissance in Asia.

Certainly Asian nationalism includes a desire to develop economic and political power. Also there is taking place in Asia today the painful struggle against suppressive elements of traditional customs and values. Yet it is a very superficial observation to equate nationalism with antitraditionalism. The basic concern of nationalism is the selfhood of people. It is not just a matter of technological efficiency. It concerns the whole outlook of a people to see themselves not as the objects of others but as a community of selves responsibly participating in the course of their own history. It is a somewhat liberating experience, and one which is shared by those who have been suppressed under feudalism and colonialism.

To illustrate this, let us look at one concrete example. On April 27, 1521, Ferdinand Magellan was killed by Lapu Lapu on the shores of Cebu, Philippines. On the site where Magellan was killed there are now two monuments. One was erected by the Spanish government in 1886 under the reign of Isabella II. The other was put up by the Philippine Historical Society in 1951. The former monument sees history from the point of view of the Spanish Empire, and thus glorifies Magellan as the great leader of the Spanish expansion. The latter, which interprets the same event from the perspective of the Philippine people, commemorates Lapu Lapu as the hero who said no to Western aggression. The color of the Magellan Monument is white and its form is typical of Spanish architectural style. On the Philippine Historical Society monument are painted the faces of Lapu Lapu and his people, as they fought against the invaders. This does not mean necessarily that the Lapu Lapu memorial is artistically superior to the Spanish-style Magellan memorial. But it does point out that the national liberation attained in the postwar period provides the Philippine people with a different perspective from which to see the event.

A similar insight can be drawn from the magnificent painting by Vincente Manansala on the "Planting of the First Cross in the Philippines" (No. 97). The artist reveals sharply the direct relationship between the missionary movement and imperialism by painting the priest blessing a huge cross which has just been planted on the Philippine shore by native workers, while the Spanish soldiers direct them with spears and an armed black boat awaits just offshore. It is a powerful picture, in terms of not only its technique but also its sensitivity. It echoes the voices of the Philippine people as they critically reflect on past history. Great art quite often emerges out of struggle and conflict with what has preceded it. This has been true with many of the Christian artists in Asia.

In 1922, during the time of Dutch colonialism in Indonesia, a nongovernmental school was founded in Jogjakarta by a prominent educator named Ki Hadjar. It was called *Taman Siswa,* meaning "Pupils' Garden." It emphasized education in the context of the people's lives, and helped "to foster in the children a free, humane, creative, and at the same time, nationally conscious attitude. While initiative and self-reliance were encouraged, the pupils were also led to take pride in their Indonesian cultural identity."[1]

It is not mere coincidence that a number of Indonesia's contemporary painters, such as Sudjojono, Basuki Resobowo, Rusli, and Alibasjah, at one time or another were students, teachers, or both at Taman Siswa School. With regard to the tendency toward beautiful, romantic painting, Sudjojono, who initiated new movements among Indonesian artists and took an active part in the independence struggle, has expressed his deep concern as follows: "A new generation is coming up, a generation which carries the living seeds of a people who will live and who, together with other peoples, will soon arise, a generation with new and fresh ideas."[2]

This is the new generation of people who have regained selfhood and who are no longer satisfied at being treated as objects of others but who dare to say, "This is how we are," meaning, "This is the condition of our life and our joy and our struggle, and our reality and our aspiration." When he was twenty-four, Sudjojono and the painter Agus Djajasuminta organized a group called *Persagi* (an abbreviation of *Persatuan Ahli Gambar Indonesia,* "Union of Indonesian Painters"), which had twenty members. Soon thereafter they opened an exhibition at Kolff, one of the bookstores in Djakarta, to open a new road for Indonesian painters. It was not a simple road toward a single goal, but a complex road with a lot of tortuous twists and turns. Yet the central concern was clear, namely, to encourage Indonesian artists to depict reality in their works and to express their Indonesian identity.

III. ARTISTS AND CHURCHES IN ASIA

In the climate of the cultural renaissance today, the churches in Asia are increasingly recognizing the creative gifts of artists and appreciating their contributions in the life and mission of the churches.

One of the earlier attempts by the Asian churches in this realm of art was the collection and publication of Christian music in Asia. The *EACC Hymnal,* published by the East Asia Christian Conference in 1962, was the first regional attempt of the churches in Asia to come to a common expression of their praise to the Lord. It has manifested the growing expression of indigenous music and Christian poetry written by Asians. D. T. Niles, then general secretary of the EACC, acted as chief editor. Based on his conviction concerning the selfhood of the church,[3] he made a continuous effort to stimulate and encourage indigenous expression of the Christian faith in Asia. This was made concretely in the Consultation on "Confessing the Faith in Asia Today" held in Hong Kong, October 26 to November 3, 1966. This was a most significant regional attempt on this theme, and one which still holds a continuing influence in the ecumenical movement.

The basic thrust of that consultation was stated in the following:

> The Christian community finds itself set within a particular cultural flux, shaped by and shaping the life of the larger community with all its particular historical and social complexities. The gospel enables the Christian to live joyfully, though not uncritically, in that culture into which he is born, and which itself is a part of God's creative gift to man. The churches in Asia cannot truly be confessing churches as long as they remain societies apart from the mainstream and common life of Asian nations. Jesus Christ is the Lord of the Church, as well as the world. Both the churches and their settings of culture are under His lordship.[4]

That statement was based on a Christological conviction which places the realm of culture under the Lordship of Christ. Whereas man is often tempted to place culture at the center of his activity and values, here it is acknowledged as a gift of God and a means to his glory. Therefore the use of indigenous forms of painting and sculpture which carry and express the Christian message naturally are encouraged. These cultural expressions by Asian artists help to communicate the message to contemporary Asian people.

Especially in this technological age, an increasing significance is recognized in human communication through image, as in Marshall McLuhan's statement, "The medium is the message."[5] The image cuts across linguistic and cultural differences and goes beyond the sphere of the printed word. Hans-Ruedi Weber, through his experience in Luwul-Banggai, Indonesia, has hinted at the importance of communicating the gospel among illiterates through the use of pictures.[6] In this sense, Christian art which was formulated in the Asian context with Asian sensitivity contains a significant possibility for the communication of the gospel in today's context, not only in Asia but also elsewhere.

Furthermore, concern for indigenous culture should not be considered only for the sake of communication of the gospel. It has much deeper implications. The EACC statement on "Confessing the Faith in Asia Today" makes this important point: "The responsibility of interpretation goes further, in discovering the thought-forms in our cultural heritage and investing them with new meaning and new depth in the light of the gospel as the Christian community confesses its faith in its setting."[7] The one decisive event happened in Jesus Christ, which was proclaimed by the Scriptures. The power of the gospel contains the illuminating power to invite manifold responses and interpretations. Accepting the rich traditions of various images in the history of Christianity, Asian Christians are beginning to interpret the gospel in Asia today—an Asian response to Jesus Christ as they meet with him in an Asian context. This is increasingly recognized in the fields of theology and church structure, which arise out of the experience of the Christian community in a particular place, at a particular time. The Bangkok Assembly, organized by the Commission on World Mission and Evangelism of the World Council of Churches in January 1973, stated this issue as follows:

> The problem of personal identity is closely related to the problem of cultural identity. "Culture shapes the human voice that answers the voice of Christ." Many Christians who have received the gospel through Western agents ask the question: "Is it really I who answer Christ? Is it not another person instead of me?" How can we ourselves be fully responsible when receiving salvation from Christ? How can we responsibly answer the voice of Christ instead of copying foreign models?[8]

At the Bangkok Assembly, special workshops were held on such subjects as "Salvation and Art," "Salvation in Visual Art," and "Songs of Salvation," in order to grasp the meaning of salvation today.

Churches in Asia also responded to the theme by giving the delegates copies of *New Songs of Asian Cities,* which had just been published by the East Asia Christian Conference. This was a collection including forty-nine new songs from an Asian city context, together with artistic illustrations.[9]

In recent years, although patterns are different, we see a variety of developments of Christian art in Asia. In Korea there is the Association of Korean Christian Artists, which was organized in 1963. This group, which has an annual exhibition in Seoul, has been a major source of stimulation to the public on Christian art and also a means of mutual encouragement among the artists. Outstanding Christian periodicals such as *Kidokkyo Sasang* ("Christian Thought") have been printing the works of Christian artists on their covers.

In Thailand, the Student Christian Center in Bangkok has been playing a remarkable role in stimulating Christian art in that country. On August 15, 1974, the Center celebrated the fifteenth anniversary of its annual exhibition of students' works by displaying the outstanding art works of the previous exhibitions. From these exhibitions have come some of the outstanding contemporary Thai artists such as Tawan Duchanee and Praphan Srisouta. The wall of the dining hall of the Center is decorated by a large-scale mural on creation done by Tawan Duchanee (No. 1).

Since 1966 there has been an annual exhibition of Christian art in Japan, sponsored by the Waseda University Student Center with the help of the Audio-Visual Aid Commission of Japan. A group of prominent artists representing both Catholic and Protestant churches has been actively participating every year. The publication of *Seisho no Kotoba, Creation and Redemption Through Japanese Art* by the present author in 1966 has introduced many Christian artists to the public. Christian periodicals like *Fukuin to Sekai* ("Gospel and the World") and *Shinto no Tomo* ("Friend of the Laity") have been utilizing the works of Christian artists in color on their covers.

In the Philippines there is no special Christian artists' association as such, but many of the prominent artists share a Christian perspective. A careful look at a book on contemporary Philippine art reveals the impact of Christian faith on practically every page.[10]

Types of Relationships

If Christian art in Asia is beginning to show signs of renewal and to exhibit a variety of expressions today, one naturally asks how the artists' works dealing with Christian themes can be classified in terms of the relationship between artistic quality and Christian faith. H. Richard Niebuhr made a typological analysis between Christ and culture, in which he described five types of relationships.[11] In his stimulating analysis of Christian form and modern art, Paul Tillich discerned four types of relationships between Christian faith and culture.

Typology is a working hypothesis; it is not the definitive way to draw a demarcation line. Yet it suggests the basic characteristics out of the variety of expressions. In this sense the following six types are suggested. We may subdivide them into two categories, those belonging to "Passing Forms" and those belonging to "Coming Forms." The former represent trends from the past; the latter indicate constructive forms seriously to be considered in the future.

Passing Forms

1. *Syncretistic.* This is a rather artificial combination of Christian faith and Asian culture. It lacks spontaneous vitality. Here Christ is covered by an Asian gown—which is as unnatural as would be Confucius put in Western dress. There are two elements in syncretism: the element

of mixed artificiality and the element of relative mediocrity. Both lack natural and authentic expression. It is unfortunate that, so many times in the past, Christian art in Asia has been represented by this type of art. But it would appear that, as seen in this book, the mainstream of contemporary Christian art in Asia goes beyond this type.

2. *Superficial.* This type indicates an inadequate representation in terms of the quality of art work. Christian art should be art before it is called Christian. Not everything which deals with a Christian theme should be called Christian art. Unfortunately much "Christian art" in the past is of this category. Paul Tillich called this kind of art a combination of religious content and nonreligious style.[12] As an illustration of this type, Tillich refers to a portrait of Jesus painted by Hofmann, who gives a soft and tender touch to the figure of Christ. At least in its style it does not exhibit the real depth of the person of Jesus Christ. Religious vitality should be matched by artistic quality.

3. *Separation.* This does not mean the artist lives geographically out of his home country. To look outside of one's country does not make one less Asian. It has been said, "You can take a Filipino out of the country, but not the country out of a Filipino."[13] "Separation" means here that, regardless of the artist's physical location, his basic concern is outside of the national and local context. He is no longer Asian in his thinking. Some of the early Christian artists in Asia fell into this category by primarily imitating Western models. This happened not only in the realm of art, but also in the field of theology.

The above three types are fortunately becoming less important in the Christian art of Asia. The following three types seem to contain creative value and positive challenge for the growth of Christian art in Asia for tomorrow.

Coming Forms

1. *Controversial.* Some people insist that unless the artist is Christian his work should not be called Christian art. They make a very clear distinction. But it is perplexing to see a naive mediocre painting of Christ which might even be classified as anti-Christian art. Although it is painted by a baptized Christian and its theme is explicitly Christian, its form and style do not reflect the power of Christ.

On the other hand, there are many creative works of Christian art done by non-Christian artists. Many of them have read the Bible thoroughly and have come to admire Christ personally. Richard W. Taylor, who has done the pioneering research on these painters who have been expressing what they know and feel about Christ, writes that "many of the most intellectually lively and artistically exciting of these painters are not Christians."[14]

K. C. S. Paniker, one of the most outstanding contemporary Indian painters, is an example. Paniker's artistic contribution to modern Indian painting is well known. After working first in the Indian Telegraph Department and then in an insurance office, he decided to devote himself solely to art by entering Madras Art School at the age of twenty-six. He has won prizes and medals in many exhibitions both in India and abroad. In 1954 he was nominated by the government of India as one of nine Eminent Artist-Members of the Lalit Kala Akademi. Later he became the principal of Madras Art School, succeeding Devi Prosad Roy Choudhury, the renowned sculptor under whom Paniker studied. Paniker is regarded as one who carries on the spirit of India in a modern form. Ludwig Godscheider, a noted art critic, described Paniker as follows: "Your paintings are not translations from the French: neither are they enlarged Indian miniatures, or reduced Indian rock-paintings. They are as competent as anything done by the younger European painters, and at the same time, they are very Indian."[15]

In 1964, after his retirement as the principal of Madras Art School, Paniker started a commune of young artists at Cholamondal, outside of Madras. Paniker himself is a liberal Hindu but has a deep admiration for the life of Christ. He encountered Christianity while studying at Madras Christian College. He was attracted by the living person of Christ who manifested in a natural way love and justice. Paniker produced several paintings and sculptures on Christian themes, such as "Blessed Are the Peace-Makers," "Woman Taken in Adultery," "Healing of the Leper," "Christ," and "Sorrow of Christ" (No. 74). The present author visited Paniker's studio at Cholamondal outside of Madras, where he has been building a commune with a group of progressive painters. ("Children of Light," No. 93, was a product of S. J. Ravivarma, who is one of these painters.) Upon being asked why he had painted so many pictures of Christ, he replied, "I have been attracted by the agony of Christ. We talk about love and peace. We are meditating, fasting with austerity. But we are not involved in physical agony. Yet in Christ I meet the man who manifested love by shedding his own blood."[16]

Paniker has not only technical competence but also the genuine spirit of the artist, who is not content to stay in the same place, but always strives to move forward into the frontier. It is especially significant to recognize the challenge of non-Christian artists like Paniker in the midst of the cultural renaissance in India. In a similar way, competent non-Christian artists like Krishna Hebbar and Shiavax Chavda became interested in painting Christ. What M. M. Thomas wrote in *The Acknowl-*

edged Christ of the Indian Renaissance has an implication here, namely, within the total renaissance in India, Christ is being acknowledged and responded to by the heart and mind of Indians.[17]

2. *Contextual.* It is recognized that technology is universal but culture is local. Christian art in Asia becomes very vital when it is formulated out of the local context utilizing the local texture. Here the rich traditional art becomes the means to express the Christian message.

Bagong Kussudiardja is an artist who combines the gifts of traditional Indonesian art, namely, batik painting and Indonesian dancing. In 1958 he founded PLT, the Dance Training Center, in Jogjakarta, the cultural center of Indonesia. National guests come to Jogjakarta to admire his dance performance and batik work. Expressing his personal vocation and religious conviction with regard to art, he says: "It is really God's mercy that has given me skill in dancing and the art of painting. I feel there is a strong vocation in me that, every time I produce works of art, I should offer them for the advance of my fellow men and above all to the greatest and most beloved God."[18]

He has produced batik works on Christian themes such as the Nativity (No. 25) and Crucifixion (No. 67). Christ's crucifixion is expressed through the figure of a traditional puppet, which intensifies the feeling of tragedy. Yet the mysterious use of color, Christ's head covered by green light against the background of darkness, gives the contrasting effect. Christ is expressed here not through the symbols of foreign art, but through Indonesian art in an Indonesian context.

In this category should be mentioned the use of flower arrangement by Gako Ota (No. 89), the paper stencil by Sadao Watanabe (No. 16), woodcarving by Paul Navaratra (Nos. 21 and 111), and the traditional Bali painting technique by Ketut Lasia (No. 44). In his or her own way, each expresses the Christian faith, utilizing the texture of the local culture. In this universal technological era, such local cultural expressions of the Christian message have increasing significance.

3. *Confessional.* Authentic Christian art contains a confession of Christian faith as the personal response of the artist in a particular situation. It is part of a living witness to the power of Jesus Christ. It derives from the existential experience of the artist who encounters Jesus Christ and expresses in a very personal and unique way the meaning of his experience.

There is a parallel here with theological formulation. In expressing the theological concern of Asian churches, the East Asia Christian Conference used the phrase "living theology in Asia." Participating in the emerging theological discussion of churches in Asia, M. M. Thomas has summarized the thrust of "living theology in Asia" in the following way:

1. A living theology is always "situational" or contextual.

2. The content of a living theology is the discernment of what God-in-Christ is doing in the situation and the interpretation of the truth and meaning of Jesus Christ in terms of the situation and self-understanding.

3. The stuff of living theology is the life and witness of the laity in the lay world and the fellowship of the churches' congregations responding to Christ to save the secular neighborhood.

4. There is the need of a new understanding of the meaning of orthodoxy and heresy with respect to Christian theology.[19]

The direction of living theology has developed further at the above-mentioned EACC Consultation on "Confessing the Faith in Asia Today" in 1966. In the field of urban industrial mission in Asia, a similar emphasis was made at the Workshop on "Theology in Action" held in Manila, September 1972. In the report of that workshop the following was stated: "We see that God-understanding is based on God-practice. That is to say, theology lives, grows and becomes powerful as it is engaged in by involved Christians. Theology begins with the experience of the actual struggle, suffering and joys of particular communities."[20]

Quite often, Christian artists in Asia also formulate their artworks out of their own concrete experience of encounter with the gospel in their daily life. They reflect a sort of "confessing the faith" through art in Asia today. They may be said to be living Christian art in Asia.

Tadao Tanaka was born in 1903 in Sapporo, Japan, the son of a minister of a church in that city. He was brought up in the Christian community, and in his younger days he wanted to be an artist to design stained-glass windows for the churches. Yet, it took some years before he devoted himself entirely to Christian themes. During World War II, artists were not given the opportunity to paint freely since they were mobilized in the national interest. Shortly after the war, while passing through the streets of Tachikawa City, a military base of the occupation forces, he saw a number of prostitutes. They reminded him of the gospel story of Jesus meeting with the prostitutes of that time. More than ever before, Jesus became near to him in the dark and somewhat confusing situation of the period immediately after the war. After that he decided to devote himself to painting explicitly Christian themes. He is one of the founders of Kodo Art Association. Widely respected by his colleagues, he has served as president of the All-Japan Artists' Association.

Junkichi Mukai, a well-known contemporary Japanese artist, writes: "Through his family background and education, Tadao Tanaka has a deep devotion to and insight in religious art. Avoiding the traditional formalism, he brings the story of the Bible anew into the contemporary Japanese situation. Combining the bright color and strong tone, with a fresh understanding he recaptures the biblical figures in the midst of today's confusing and struggling society."[21]

These three elements, namely, artistic competence, genuine Christian commitment, and critical social sensitivity, are necessary but uncommon requisites for good Christian art. Usually artists are quite lonely and struggle for their daily living. Therefore to foster Christian artists, the network of mutual encouragement and pastoral care among them needs to be strengthened. Tanaka as an elder Christian artist in Japan has been playing such a role.

Hope for the Future

In the period of social change, everyone is looking for something new to transform the old, and for something reliable in the midst of uncertainty. No one is sure what the shape and pattern of the coming civilization will be. But for Christians, one thing is sure, that Christians always open themselves toward the future with hope. A true Christian constantly places himself under the disposal of grace in the process of transformation. Christians in Asia have been learning the meaning of the firstfruits, a Christian presence in a minority situation. The firstfruits are a small bundle. They are a small minority in number, yet they are a pledge of the Holy Spirit that a great harvest is to come. This combination of the two elements, Christian hope and artistic creativity, orients people into the future. It is a blessing and a promise to the community of firstfruits, to whom St. Paul wrote, "If any one is in Christ, he is a new creation; the old has passed away, behold, the new has come" (II Cor. 5:17).

NOTES

1. Claire Holt, *Art in Indonesia: Continuities and Change* (Cornell University Press, 1967), p. 195.

2. Ibid., p. 196.

3. D. T. Niles, *Upon the Earth* (McGraw-Hill Book Co., 1962), pp. 139ff.

4. *Confessing the Faith in Asia Today* (Redfern, Australia: Epworth Press, 1966), p. 51.

5. See Marshall McLuhan, *Understanding Media* (McGraw-Hill Book Co., 1964); also Marshall McLuhan and Quentin Fiore, *The Medium Is the Massage* (Harmondsworth, England: Penguin Books, 1967).

6. Hans-Ruedi Weber, *The Communication of the Gospel to Illiterates* (Lon-
1: SCM Press, 1957).

7. *Confessing the Faith in Asia Today,* p. 53.

8. *Bangkok Assembly 1973,* Minutes and Report of the Assembly of the Commission on World Mission and Evangelism of the World Council of Churches, Dec. 31, 1972, and Jan. 9–12, 1973, p. 73.

9. I-to Loh (ed.), *New Songs of Asian Cities* (Tainan: East Asia Christian Conference, Urban Industrial Mission Committee, 1972).

10. Manuel D. Duldulao, *Contemporary Philippine Art* (Quezon City: Vera Reyes, 1972).

11. H. Richard Niebuhr, *Christ and Culture* (Harper & Brothers, 1951).

12. Paul Tillich, "Existential Aspects in Modern Art," in Carl Michalson (ed.), *Christianity and the Existentialists* (Charles Scribner's Sons, 1956).

13. Duldulao, *Contemporary Philippine Art,* p. 56.

14. Richard W. Taylor, "Some Interpretations of Jesus in Indian Painting," *Religion and Society,* Vol. 17, No. 3 (1970), p. 1.

15. Quoted in *Paniker,* Contemporary Indian Art Series, No. 4 (New Delhi: Lalit Kala Akademi, 1961), p. iv.

16. Interview with K. C. S. Paniker, July 25, 1974.

17. M. M. Thomas, *The Acknowledged Christ of the Indian Renaissance* (London: SCM Press, 1969).

18. *Bulletin* of Bagong Kussudiardja, The Dance Training Center, Jogjakarta.

19. Thomas, *The Acknowledged Christ of the Indian Renaissance,* pp. 306–312.

20. Oh Jae Shik and John England (eds.), *Theology in Action* (Tokyo: East Asia Christian Conference, Committees on Urban Industrial Mission and Christian Education and Lay Training, 1972), p. 25.

21. From the catalog of a one-man show by Tadao Tanaka at Aoyama University, Tokyo, 1970.

PART FOUR

Theology
of Christian Mission

Fifteen

The Divine Mission of Creation

Choan-seng Song

[In this essay Dr. Song lays the foundation for a radical reconstruction of Christian missiology, from the standpoint of the biblical doctrine of Creation. If we can relate redemption in Christ to the whole process of God's creation, it will liberate us from the "religious isolationism" and "spiritual provincialism" that have called the Christian mission into question, especially in religiously pluralistic Asia. "The biblical faith is, in the last analysis, the faith which transcends the boundaries of race, nationality, culture, and even religion." Therefore, "God is not to be identified *simply* and *solely* with a particular form of his manifestation and with a particular expression of man's response." Song discusses three areas in which the reconstruction of mission theology may take place—namely: culture, history, and politics. What he calls "mission-compound Christianity" is here challenged by a cosmic view of mission.—Ed.]

> The heavens tell out the glory of God,
>   the vault of heaven reveals his handiwork.
> One day speaks to another,
>   night with night shares its knowledge,
> And this without speech or language
>   or sound of any voice.
> Their music goes out through all the earth,
>   their words reach to the end of the world.
>   —Psalm 19:1–4, NEB

I. Creation and Christian Mission

What I propose to do in this chapter is to discuss the meaning of the story of creation in the first chapter of Genesis in the Old Testament for the Christian mission in the post-Western missionary era. I am conscious

---

Chapter 2 of the author's *Christian Mission in Reconstruction: An Asian Attempt* (Madras: Christian Literature Society, 1975). Reprinted by permission of the publisher.

of the fact that this may immediately provoke some questions: What, one may ask, has the story of creation to do with Christian mission? Isn't the main burden of Christian mission related to redemption and not to creation? Is it not true to say that in the Bible, accounts are chiefly given to those men and women who have come to experience the wonderful love of God in many different ways? In other words, does the Bible not deal with God's salvation and that alone?

It goes without saying that our answer to these questions is yes. From beginning to end, one basic theme which runs through the Bible is the theme of God's personal dealings with man and the world *redemptively.* God, as the Bible tells us over and over again, does not deal with man without specific aim and purpose. He does not relate himself to man and his world in a general sort of way. Whenever he acts, he acts personally, directly, and concretely. He does not act in a vacuum. He addresses himself to man with particular concern, needs, or interests. At every turn the Bible tries to communicate this, and it is really remarkable that it succeeds in doing so. Just read a few psalms in the Old Testament, and you will be so impressed with the personal and intimate tone in which psalmists pour out their hearts to God and the way in which God listens to them and participates in the agonies of their hearts. To give just one example:

> Hear my cry, O God, listen to my prayer.
> From the end of the earth I call to thee with fainting heart;
>   lift me up and set me upon a rock.
> For thou hast been my shelter,
>   a tower for refuge from the enemy.
>
> (Ps. 61:1–3)

The Bible thus gives us insight into the divine-human drama unfolding itself before our eyes around the theme of redemption.

Furthermore, God's dealing with man is radical in the sense that he goes to the root of man's need, namely, the need of being right with God and with his fellow creatures. Thus, God's timely act of redemption brings about new relationships in the ordering of the whole of creation. As a result, a new creation comes into being. In this way, the experience of redemption is an experience ultimately related to the experience of creation. Can we not, therefore, relate the story of creation in the book of Genesis to the experience of God's saving acts in behalf of the Jewish people in exile? As we shall see presently, for them to be able to relate redemption to the entire process of God's creation serves to liberate them from their religious isolationism and spiritual provincialism. They find themselves staring at the unfathomable depth of God's mystery in creation and redemption. They are led to the beginning of all things, which is their present suffering and liberation. They realize that the darkness had to be there, that chaos seemed to be gaining the upper hand, that the order of the cosmos and the being of man were threatened. Can we not, therefore, conclude that the story of creation in Genesis 1 does not have much to do with the primeval history of the universe? Rather, it seeks to express the joy of redemption from the tyranny of chaos. It tries to convey the exuberance of being which is set free from the sinister power of destruction. In Karl Barth's words:

> But what makes non-being a menace, an enemy which is superior to created being, a threatened destroyer, is obviously not its mere character as non-being, but the fact that it is not elected and willed by God the Creator but rather rejected and excluded. It is that to which God said No when He said Yes to the creature. And that is chaos according to the biblical term and concept.[1]

In short, in the first creation story in Gen. 1:1 to 2:4a, redemption is seen in the perspective of creation.

We may reinforce what we have just said by referring to the circumstances in which the first story of creation gets to be written. As we all know, the creation story is the production of the religiously creative mind of the Jewish people taken captive to Babylonia by King Nebuchadnezzar in 587 B.C. The Babylonian captivity seems first to put an end to Israel as a political and religious entity distinct from other nations. It is reasonable to assume that her spiritual force must have eroded from its very foundation. But through this traumatic experience of national disaster, she learns to perceive another dimension to the faith she has inherited from the past. As John Bright observes:

> When one considers the magnitude of the calamity that overtook her, one marvels that Israel was not sucked down into the vortex of history along with the other little nations of western Asia to lose forever her identity as a people. And if one asks why she was not, the answer surely lies in her faith. . . . Yet this answer is not to be given glibly, for the exile tested Israel's faith to the utmost. That it won through was not something that transpired automatically, but only with much heart-searching and after profound readjustment.[2]

Perhaps one of the most profound readjustments they have had to make is related to their understanding of Yahweh, their God. An infinitely rich dimension of God's relation with the world has been revealed to them in the totally new situation. They have begun to take a fresh look at the saving acts of God in the context of the whole of creation. A new understanding of the place and mission of Israel among the nations thus becomes possible.

To be sure, there are those among the exiled in Babylonia who find it difficult to sing "the Lord's song in a foreign land" (Psalm 137). Nationalism is not discarded as an old garment. The nostalgia for the land of promise is not buried out of sight. There is still strong inclination to interpret the nature and acts of God exclusively in favor of Israel as a privileged nation. But the deepened perception of the redemptive works of God under the form of creation affected their spirituality in such a way that fundamental change cannot but take place in their orientation toward the purpose of God for the nations. The culmination of this spiritual reorientation is to be seen in the great missionary called the Suffering Servant in the Second Isaiah. He is not chosen only for Israel in exile. He is to live and die even for those beyond the boundary of his own race and nation. This is why he, in accepting the divine call, proclaims:

> Listen to me, you coasts and islands,
>   Pay heed, you peoples far away:
> From birth the Lord called me,
>   He named me from my mother's womb.
>   —Isa. 49:1

The election of the Servant is thus an "ecumenical" event, which must be acknowledged and celebrated by all nations. No one can afford to be indifferent to it, for the mission of the Servant is of ecumenical significance. There is already a distant echo of this in the call of Abraham. It is through Abraham and his house that "all the families of the earth shall bless themselves" (Gen. 12:3, RSV). In the person and work of the Suffering Servant, this distant echo becomes a clear and loud proclamation; it has become a reality which will have a profound impact on the spirituality of mankind.

The biblical faith is, in the last analysis, the faith which transcends the boundaries of race, nationality, culture, and even religion. The Creator-Redeemer God is not to be captured by and crystallized into one particular racial and cultural texture. On account of this, we can only speak of a national or state church with great caution. A state church tends to become so closely related to the political and cultural interests of the nation that she begins to identify the cause of her nation as the cause of God. The faith in the Creator-Redeemer God permits no such nationalization of God. A nationalized God ceases to be relevant for other nations and peoples. It is therefore understandable that the people of the Third World[3] have become extremely restless with what they call the "white" God who comes with everything which the white West stands for. They have begun an earnest search for "black" God or "yellow" God. Is God colored? Yes and no. Yes, because God seems to make himself known in different ways to different peoples in different places. Consequently, responses to this God must take different forms and expressions. But at the same time we must say no, because God is not to be identified *simply* and *solely* with a particular form of his manifestation and with a particular expression of man's response. God has the whole of creation to deal with. He cannot be bound by any nation or any culture. God is the God of freedom. Much of the agitation against "white" Christianity in the Third World springs from the perception that the white West has imprisoned God and thus deprived God of his freedom. That is why God is preached and presented everywhere as the "white" God.

After a century of expansion from its Western base, Christianity is said to have failed in no small degree in crossing the self-imposed boundaries of Western culture. To be sure, Western missionaries have had to cross the geographical boundaries. Beyerhaus, professor of missiology at the University of Tübingen, pointedly says:

> It must in fact be questioned how many missionaries today really do cross any decisive frontier. For it is a dreadful possibility that they have traversed continents and oceans and still never left their home, because in their mission stations in Bangkok or Botswana they busily reconstruct their little Bielefeld, Birmingham or Boras. In this way they prevent themselves from achieving that which is the real mark of having crossed the frontier: the missionary identification.[4]

This is a severe criticism with much justification, particularly when directed to the life-style of missionaries. The question of the missionary identification is the question of life-style. But if we press the question further, we will realize that there is something much deeper and much more fundamental than just a matter of life-style. It is the question of whether most missionaries ever think deeply about the meaning of God and what he does in a different cultural context, whether they have seen the necessity of correcting and even discarding some basic elements in their faith in the light of their new experience.[5] In short, it is the question of whether their faith is shaken to its foundation. Only after this shaking of the foundation can a reconstruction of Christian faith begin. And the reconstruction may take place at least in the three areas of culture, history, and politics corresponding to the aspects related to God's creation.[6] In the following discussion we will endeavor to see what implications the consideration of these areas of creation may have for the reconstruction of the Christian faith in the non-Western lands.

II. Cultural Dynamic of Creation

The concept of culture is not easy to define. What you mean by culture depends very much on the world view in which you believe. If you are a staunch materialist, you may look upon culture as visible and tangible forms through which man's endless pursuit for a reconstruction of the physical world is given expression. On the other hand, if you happen to be a consistent idealist, you may regard culture as a bundle of ideas projected in terms of the spaciotemporal framework. Or you may try to understand culture from the point of view of psychology, anthropology, or sociology. In the contemporary world, which is fashioned very much by the progress in science and technology, culture tends to be interpreted in relation to the process of modernization. It is clear that no matter what definition you may give to the concept of culture you have to realize that no definition can exhaust the meaning of the concept, that each definition will have both merits and demerits. Fortunately, for our purpose here we are not required to side with one particular definition of culture to the exclusion of all other definitions. Nor is it necessary for us to come up with a supposedly new definition in order to proceed with our discussion. All we have to do here is to look upon culture as comprehensive expressions of the creative dynamic released from its origin. In the human realm, the release of creative dynamic takes forms in painting, sculpture, music, architecture, technology, and so on. This power to create becomes imprisoned, so to speak, in the multidimensional structure which serves as media for man's self-expression. Thus, tension develops between man's creative dynamic and the structure through which his dynamic has to be expressed. The tension testifies both to the greatness of man and to his finiteness.

The above consideration leads us to speak of the cultural dynamic of God's creation from which man's creative power is derived. Culture as a whole is none other than the manifestation of God's creative power translated into actual forms and events. Thus, creation may be regarded as God's culture in its totality. The writers of the first creation story present us with a superb picture of God's power of creation becoming cultural dynamic, giving forms, order, and above all, life to that which is formless, chaotic, and without life. That is why each creational act of God is punctuated with the exclamation that God saw the work of his hand as good. This is the unqualified affirmation of what God has done. The "good" here does not imply moral judgment passed on God's work. Good in this particular context should not be contrasted with bad or evil. Even a genuine work of art fashioned out of man's mind and hand may transcend the boundary of good and evil. Is it not true then to say that evil loses its power over the creative dynamic of the truly artistic mind? If this is the case with man's work of art and culture, how much more so with God's creation! Creation may become corrupted and may decay, but it never comes under the dominion of evil. It remains God's creation no matter what. Bonhoeffer is therefore right when he says:

> That God's work is good in no way means that the world is the best of all conceivable worlds. It means that the world lives completely in the presence of God, that it begins and ends in him, and that he is its Lord. Here is meant the goodness which is undifferentiated from evil, whose goodness consists in its being under the dominion of God.[7]

This is an insight which very often got lost in the course of the development of Christian thought in the West. And a reintroduction of this insight into Christian theology by theologians such as Bonhoeffer becomes a starting point for many new movements in contemporary Western theology laying emphases on secularization, the immanence of God, Christian responsibility for the world, and so on.[8]

This affirmation of creation being under God's dominion is very important for our understanding and appreciation of culture, especially when we find ourselves confronted with cultural expressions and activities different from those to which we are accustomed. This provides the basis on which we may enter into meaningful, intercultural experiences. Let us face the fact that each and every one of us is tainted with cultural provincialism. Can we call this cultural chauvinism? A story is told of a man who had grown up and lived in a country whose traffic law required its citizens to keep to the right and who happened to be in another country, for the first time, where different traffic regulations were practiced. As soon as he saw people driving on the left side of the road, he exclaimed: "They are driving on the *wrong* side of the road!" Needless to say, this was a judgment passed on a different set of traffic regulations on the basis of his own. This kind of cultural confrontation will never pass into fruitful experience of intercultural exchange. Basically, this is the hopeless and at the same time harmful "my country, right or wrong" attitude.

The more intense a form the cultural dynamic of man's spiritual activities takes, the more dangerous and futile cultural confrontation becomes. Here we are especially referring to religion. We can agree that in religion we have the intense concentration of man's cultural dynamic and creative energy. Religion is in a true sense a synthesis of culture. In religion the communion between the divine and the human gets expressed in visible and audible forms in an extremely heightened degree.

Can we therefore not say that it is man's religious genius that gives birth to culture? In other words, is the source and origin of man's cultural dynamic not to be found in man's communion with the cultural dynamic of God become embodied in his creation? Gerardus van der Leeuw, great phenomenologist of religion, puts it beautifully when he speaks of Bach's *Mass in B Minor* in the following words:

> In Bach's *Mass in B Minor,* the Credo is a glorious piece of music, an expression of beauty and an expression of holiness. All the voices speak, one after another: "Credo . . ." It is as though all the stops of human piety and human sense of beauty were released. We fear a letdown immediately. Then the violins begin, high and radiant, the old intonation of the liturgy. Now it is as though the mystery were revealed; here God speaks.[9]

That is why Van der Leeuw finds it possible to speak of the holy in art. In the holy, God's speech and man's response are joined together for the communion of spirit. With uncontestable eloquence, Van der Leeuw muses:

> The dance reflects the movement of God, which also moves us upon the earth. The drama presupposes the holy play between God and man. Verbal art is the hymn of praise in which the eternal and his works are represented. Architecture reveals to us the lines of the well-built city of God's creation. Music is the echo of the eternal *Gloria.* [10]

What seems to happen in culture is that the divine Spirit of creation makes impact on the spirit of man to translate the heavenly into the earthly.

This last statement, it seems to us, has universal validity, for if Christian expressions of cultural dynamic are the end results of spiritual interaction between heaven and earth, how can one deny such spiritual quality to expressions of cultural dynamic working in other contexts, Buddhist for example? It is said that "the minds of the medieval Japanese artists have always been trained in the nature-mysticism of Buddhism."[11] Without this basic perception, it will be difficult for anyone, especially those from different cultural backgrounds, to appreciate the beauty and genius of culture brought into being in predominantly Buddhist Asian countries. But once one is able to identify and appreciate this spiritual quality deep-rooted in the being of the Asian, one begins to understand the hopes and meanings in which the spiritual quality concerned comes to expression. Japanese architecture, for instance,

> is utterly unlike the Gothic. Its chief beauty consists in the long, curving, horizontal lines of the eaves, and in the gentle slope of the roofs. Such forms harmonize well with the hills and trees, and such buildings become a part of

the landscape instead of appearing like gigantic and laborious constructions built in defiance of nature.[12]

To a considerable degree this is true of most of the expressions of Asian cultural dynamic. The unfortunate thing is that Western missionaries generally have never truly grasped this basic quality of the Asian mind. They have endeavored to establish Gothic theology, that is, Gothic understanding and interpretation of Christian faith, in lands where the shape of spirituality is not only foreign to it but entirely incompatible with it.

Thus, we must speak of the cultural task of Christian mission. It consists in an effort to search for and appreciate different shapes which the cultural dynamic of God's creation takes in different cultural and historical contexts. Christian mission goes about this cultural task with the basic assumption that diversity in shapes of culture is not witness against the unity and sovereignty of God's creation. Rather, it is an affirmation of the richness of God's nature and his relation to the world he has brought into existence. It follows that there is no justification whatsoever for Christian mission to work and operate with the dichotomy of Christian and non-Christian cultures. The message of the Bible, particularly that of God's overarching relationship to every aspect of his creation and his dominion over it, tends to be distorted on account of such a dichotomy. It simply will not do for Christian mission to pose itself as the guardian of the so-called Christian culture against what is often carelessly labeled as non-Christian culture.

Christian mission must, therefore, be first of all a critique of cultures. If the word "critique" sounds a little too judgmental in connotation, we may call it "theology of cultures." It is a theological perception and interpretation of the spirituality of a particular culture in the light of the biblical faith in God as the creator. This ought to be a theological task vigorously pursued by those engaged in Christian mission. It is a task that requires an open mind and cheerful willingness to let new light shine into the citadel of the Christian faith. At the same time, through such an effort the Christian and the people of other faiths are ultimately drawn into the question of truth. And insofar as it is the question of truth, it has to be stressed that no one possesses the final answer. Those who are primarily concerned with Christian mission must be humble enough to acknowledge this. They have to present their case for Christian faith with conviction and assurance, but they must do this without claiming to have sole access to the whole truth of God. Such an attitude is required of them by the very nature of the truth they seek to serve and witness. The truth of God does not permit man's total penetration. The attempt to defy this basic human limitation and trespass this boundary of man's knowledge causes man to fall from the truth.

It follows that we must be content with speaking of "degrees of truth." At most, all we can say is that in and through Jesus Christ we believe we are given access to considerable degrees of God's truth, particularly when it is made known to us in the form of God's love for the world in creation and in redemption. A perception such as this will not lead us into the temptation of putting Christian religion on top of all other religions, and it will keep us from confusing the Christian way of life as the embodiment of the whole truth of God.

Christian mission as a theological task related to the search for truth in cultures is thus entrusted with a twofold responsibility. On one hand there is the negative responsibility of bringing into light how the love of God for man and the world is misapprehended, distorted, and even corrupted in cultures. But to stop at this negative aspect is to make caricature of God's Lordship over his creation. This would tacitly mean that at last evil is a viable form of being, posing as a threat to God's being. If we believe in the "goodness" of God's creation, we cannot regard this as the final word. There should be at the same time a positive responsibility on the part of Christian mission to fathom how this same love of God is reflected in the life and work of those who live in different contexts of culture and ethos. To use the analogy of architecture again, Christian mission in the non-Western lands, especially in Asia, should not emulate the defiant spirit of Gothic architecture with emphasis on contradiction and incompatibility. Christian mission should be more like Asian architecture which seeks to express the spiritual yearning for harmony in the midst of agony and pain. For centuries Asian peoples have continued to live and experience great turbulence of history. Their lot has not been an easy one. Disorder in society, disruption of family life, dislocation of people, caused by war and natural disaster, have been and still are the order of the day rather than the exception. In the midst of all this, the Asian cultural and religious genius has never ceased to search for inner tranquillity and harmony of nature. It is to this kind of situation that Christian mission has to address itself. Thus, only in developing empathy for different cultural dynamic manifested in non-Christian contexts, are Christians enabled to come to grips with the mystery of the divine cultural dynamic at work in creation. This, I believe, is the prerequisite of Christian mission. Is this not basically the reason why the Bible begins with the story of creation and ends with a vision of a new creation? Let us remember: new creation is not to be the total destruction of the old creation, but fulfillment or completion of it. This is the divine mission of creation and redemption; Christians are called to take part in this divine mission. And this essentially is Christian mission.

III. HISTORIES AS CONTINUATION OF CREATION

Increasingly, Christian mission finds itself faced with impacts of historical pluralism and is forced to take them seriously. This is significant when we consider that in this day and age there seems to be emerging a world culture built on science and technology. The language of science and technology is cut and dry. It permits little equivocation. Consequently, its symbolic character is reduced to a minimum. Particularly in contrast to poetic language, the language of science and technology is factual and not emotive language. Thus, the probability of misunderstanding is greatly reduced. At last in this language modern man seems to have achieved what those unfortunate builders of the tower of Babel failed to achieve, namely, one world with one language, one history, and one culture.

But the fact remains that this is a short-lived dream of modern man. After all, we in this age of science and technology do not seem to fare any better than the builders of the tower of Babel. The fact that the use of electricity, for example, is now almost universally a routine matter for most of the inhabitants of the earth does not automatically mean that they can communicate with one another without difficulty. Nor does the shortening of geographical distance by modern means of transportation and communication at once result in the coming into being of a world community with some historical uniformity. The truth of the matter seems just the opposite. Nationalism is certainly not a by-product of science and technology, but without the challenges posed by scientifically and technologically advanced nations, nationalism would not have been stimulated into assuming a prominent role in Third World politics. And as people find themselves more and more in international contexts, the problem of their historical identity becomes very much sharpened. Especially when issues of justice and human rights increasingly become the focus of men and women striving for their own destiny, the question of historical identity inevitably comes more and more to the fore. Therefore, it is extremely doubtful whether a concept such as one world culture has any substantial meaning. In fact, we live in a world of pluralism. It is this reality of historical pluralism that needs to be taken into consideration when we face the world of our present day.

The church in the West has, through her theology and practice of Christian mission during the past century, failed to do justice to the reality of historical pluralism. Her aim consists in "Christianizing" the non-Western lands with the hope of creating one historical entity which can be identified as Christian. Simply put, the planting of the Kingdom of God in other parts of the world is understood as an extension of Western Christendom. What constitutes the theological basis of such Western Christian mission is the highly monolithic interpretation of the relation between revelation and history. Most Western theologians will, with a few exceptions, find themselves in full agreement with Christopher Dawson when he says:

> It is very difficult, perhaps even impossible, to explain the Christian view of history to a non-Christian, since it is necessary to accept the Christian faith in order to understand the Christian view of history, and those who reject the idea of a divine revelation are necessarily obliged to reject the Christian view of history as well.[13]

In accordance with this statement, revelation, faith, and history are set in a well-defined logical order. A certain way of responding to revelation, which is Christian faith in this case, is made a *sine qua non* for the understanding of the meaning of history.

To press such a theological assumption to its logical conclusion, we shall be driven to assert that from the Christian point of view, communication on the meaning of history between the Christian and the people of other faiths has to be suspended. All discussions on the important subject among the Christian thinkers become intramural conversation. This has largely been the case in the past; and it is likely to continue, if the apprehension of the meaning of history is conditional upon the embracing of the Christian faith. This is to limit the faith in Christ as the bearer of God's love to the narrow confines of the religious phenomenon called Christianity and the institutionalized religion called the Christian church. Against such a view, I would like to argue that faith in Christ does not serve as the point of departure in interreligious encounter but as the focal point through which the meaning of history is understood and interpreted in the contexts of historical pluralism. It is, therefore, more correct perhaps to say *meanings* of history instead of meaning of history. There is no reason why Christ should provide only one way of looking at the unfolding of the mystery of God's dealings with man in different spaciotemporal contexts.

The truth of the matter seems to be that the presence of Christ opens up the real possibility of men and women responding to God in different historical contexts. Far from suppressing these responses as having little to do with God whom he represents, Jesus Christ commends them. He, for example, is astonished at the faith exhibited by the Roman centurion by saying that he did not find it even in Israel (Matt. 8:5–10). This is the faith that cannot be explained by the norms of religion accepted by Israel. It has its origin outside the confines of the Jewish religion. Throughout his ministry, Christ more than once uncovers this latent faith which comes to sudden manifestation in his presence. Does this not indicate that there is apprehension of the meaning of history outside the realm of Christianity not unrelated to the work of God in Jesus Christ? It is true that the name of Jesus Christ is unidentified, but the reality of his presence in and through the Spirit cannot be denied.

By a stroke of religious genius, John, the author of the Fourth Gospel, gives us insight into the mystery of the relation between creation and incarnation. This is an eloquent testimony of how the interpretation of the meaning of history gets broken away from a narrow religious background and set in the wider context of creation. According to the prologue in John's Gospel, the Word of God becoming flesh is not an isolated moment in the history of the interactions between God and man. This event of the incarnation reaches far back to the very beginning of time. Not only this, the Word that became flesh was neither something that resulted from the divine act of creation nor a silent and passive spectator of the creation. As John's testimony has it, the Word was actively involved in the process through which the creation came into being. It is this Word, it is this Christ who at the appropriate moment in the history of the world "became flesh, . . . came to dwell among us" (John 1:14). If we acknowledge as we must do the profound meaning of such a statement, we can no longer say, as Christopher Dawson did, that it is not possible to explain the Christian view of history to the people of other faiths. It becomes impossible to do so when the incarnation is seen in separation from creation, and history is viewed as essentially unrelated to God's act of creation in the beginning of time. When the event of Christ is divorced from the total process of creation, Christianity becomes armed with historical particularism bent on claiming universal validity for its particular view on history. In this way the church fails to realize that different particulars in different historical contexts may have inherent meaning derived from the common denominator which is the whole complex reality of creation-incarnation. Historical particularism advocated by the expanding Christian church thus easily takes on a militant attitude toward other historical entities.

We must stress that the intrinsic meaning of each historical entity has its origin in God the Creator. Insofar as this is true, evaluation and judgment of that historical entity has to be based on this dimension of the divine creation as well as on the particular view of history formulated within the tradition of Christianity. Take for instance the traditional Chinese concept of the imperial ruler as the son of Heaven. The emperor is called son of Heaven because his sovereign power is granted him by virtue of the decree of Heaven. He sums up in himself all people and all things in his domain and even beyond. China is thus regarded as the Middle Kingdom occupying the place of centrality and eminence in terms not only of geography but also of culture and religion. The well-being of all nations depends largely on the degree in which they come into beneficial relation with China. This is a magnificent picture of heaven and earth converging on the person of the son of Heaven. He is chosen and elevated to this awesome height of power and sovereignty to execute the will of Heaven. He is thus expected to go about his duty in fear and trepidation. He is to rule and govern with human-heartedness, justice, and wisdom lest he should forfeit the decree of Heaven. When he misuses his power and departs from the royal virtues such as human-heartedness and justice, Heaven discloses its displeasure by inflicting natural disasters and social unrest within his domain. Then the people under some other charismatic leader rise to overthrow him. This is the revolution which signals the transfer of the decree of Heaven from one ruler to another. Revolution is therefore a religious as well as a political event. Through it, the decree of Heaven continues to be administered without interruption. This ancient Chinese ideal of a ruler as the son of Heaven reflects to some degree the biblical picture of man as one who is given the responsibility of carrying out the will of the Creator.

The will of the Creator for the human creature is given in unambiguous terms in the creation story. Man is to be the maker of civilizations and histories in accordance with the purpose of God's creation. As Ethelbert Stauffer puts it:

> God's will is carried out in and through the will of the creature. The creative act of God was continued in a history for which man's will was responsible agent. It was man's duty to fill the earth and give names to the animals; he had to subject land and sea to himself as farmer and worker and king. . . . This makes very clear what the divine conditioning of history originally was. History is the continuation of the work of the creation put into the hands of man who is possessed of a will.[14]

This is a very important statement, particularly the last sentence regarding the nature of history. On account of overemphasis on Jesus Christ as a particular historical event in the history of the Jewish nation, history both personal and of the world as a whole tends to be thought of as having its point of departure in that calendar year marking the end of B.C. and the beginning of A.D. The massive concentration of Western theologians on the history of Israel and the history of the Christian church in their interpretation of the acts of God in the world has thus made it difficult for them to allot a positive place to the histories of nations in their theological systems. Western Christian mission during the last hundred years or so is this highly segmented theology of history in action. This is by no means to say that Jesus Christ should be given a more qualified place in the Christian understanding of history or in the carrying out of the mission of the church. On the contrary, Jesus Christ should be released from the captivity of the so-called *Heilsgeschichte*[15] and set in the process of history as the continuation of the work of the creation.

It is, therefore, urgent that this dimension of creation be restored to the mission of the Christian church. Through the theological movement toward secularization in the contemporary theological scene, creation, the incarnation, and history at least get related again in a very vital way. This theological movement which claims its origin in Bonhoeffer's concept of "religionless Christianity" and is given tremendous impetus by Harvey Cox's *The Secular City*[16] will continue to mold and remold Christian understanding of the creation and history. It goes without saying that the missions of the church cannot remain unaffected by the current opening up of new theological frontiers. It is not simply the geographical frontiers that we are dealing with here. It is the frontiers of meanings with regard to the histories as the continuation of the creation that should occupy the theologians in the non-Western nations. The task of the mission of the church, among other things, is thus to extend continually the frontiers of meanings in the histories of nations as witnesses to the acts of God in creation and redemption. When these two foci, creation and redemption, are brought to bear at the same time on the histories of the nations, the artificial distinction and the arbitrary separation of the Christian and the non-Christian, the sacred and the profane, the Jew and the Gentile, will lose its meaning and validity. We may call this the secularization of the Christian mission.

IV. POLITICAL IMPLICATIONS OF GOD'S CREATION

As early as in the beginning of the 1950's, Canon Max Warren, then General Secretary of the Church Missionary Society, hit the nail on the head when he pointed out the basic weakness of the missionary Christianity to be its schizophrenic tendency to shy away from the political implications of the nature and task of the church. To illustrate his point, he referred to a young Muganda woman studying at an English university who on some occasion said to her English audience:

Many Africans are seeking answers to their questions but the Church is not playing its full part in helping young people to face the problems of society.

To them God is the God of the Church; he is not the God of politics and social life. They need help to see him as one God: to see that the church is concerned with the whole of life.

Commenting on the above highly poignant remark, Canon Warren goes on to say: "The God of the church: he is not the God of politics—so, apparently they have learned Christ, these Africans, and discovered in him not integration but divorce, not atonement but separation. A great gulf is fixed between the scripture lesson and education for career, between what happens in the church and 'the high tumultuous lists of life.' "[17]

The issue brought up here by Canon Warren is the issue which still causes the Christian community everywhere to be divided into two camps under the grossly misleading labels of "liberal" and "conservative." Although there is much shadowboxing in this polarized state of the Christian community, the issue is serious enough to have created a great gulf among the delegates to the Uppsala Assembly, in 1968, in the section on Renewal in Mission. Lesslie Newbigin, sensing a great detriment here to the cause of Christian mission, issues a warning and a plea:

> To establish communication across this gulf is surely one of the most urgent tasks of the ecumenical movement. So long as it remains unbridged, the call to mission will be heard—on both sides—as a call not to unity but to separation.[18]

It is lamentable that polarization does exist here at the heart of Christian mission. It has divided the Western Christian mission into camps which vie for dominance in the non-Western lands. This is a divided mind of the church in the West coming to visible expression. It has vitiated much of the good cause of the gospel in the eyes of "pagans" whom Western missionaries want to reach. By becoming in this way a call to division and separation instead of a call to unity and solidarity, the Western Christian mission has betrayed its cause. It has preached a lie in place of truth. Bitter bickerings among Christians of different persuasions have made the love of God appear to be diminutive and hollow. To make the matter worse, converts in Asia and elsewhere are all too quickly processed into one camp or the other, thus perpetuating the practice of making the salvation of God a caricature.

We would like to assert that the choice between the God of politics and the God of the church is a false one. The fact is that the God of politics is the God of the church, that the God of the church is the God of politics. This implies that the church is a political existence. The church is part and parcel of this total political world. Political impacts between the church and the world are mutual. Neither the church nor the world can escape this mutuality in political involvement. The Bible itself is a perennial witness to this. The history of Israel was motivated politically as much as religiously. The Old Testament prophets constantly made trips between the Temple and the palace. The mission of the prophets was thus in a true sense a political mission. It had to do not only with the order and worship within the religious community but also with love and justice in the social order. The famous exchange between Jesus and the Pharisees on the question of paying taxes to Caesar is a very telling example of the tension that exists with regard to the church and politics (Mark 12:15–17; Matt. 22:15–22; Luke 20:20–26). The answer of Jesus is often regarded as a clever way out of a difficult dilemma. In that case the answer can only be regarded as a prevarication. Then one would be prompted to press the question and ask what should be the practical standard to make a distinction between the things that belong to Caesar and the things that are God's. It is precisely so difficult to make such a distinction that from the biblical and therefore theological point of view, it is wrong to try to keep politics out of the church. The answer of Jesus to the questioning of the Pharisees is no equivocation of the issue. Rather, it is more correct to say that Jesus by answering as he did threw the question back at the questioners, challenging them to make a decision in their own political-ecclesiastical contexts. It was a matter of decision of faith on a particular political issue. It follows, therefore, that any decision to which one may come would be a political as well as a religious decision. This only goes to underline the obvious fact that the church is in the world and that the world is in the church. Any theological position which does not do justice to this plain reality cannot be a guide to the church in her efforts to serve God and man.

We can go back, I believe, to the very root of our faith in God's creation to substantiate what has been said above. The act of creation, we may say, is a political act. Here we are using the word "political" in a broad sense having to do with power. Politics cannot be divorced from power. It is a manifestation, organization, and mobilization of power for a certain definite purpose in the ordering of human society. Obviously, this is a platitude. But we need to be reminded of this again and again lest we forget it or take it for granted. When asked why he wanted to run for the presidency of the United States, John F. Kennedy was reported to have said that the White House was the place where the power was. And he was right. Just think of the power released from that massive citadel of power, both to construct the bridge of peace in the world and to shatter it with demonic force! This in essence is the demonic nature of power in the hands of man. Each and every government has, with differing degrees, power to build and to destroy. You simply cannot govern without power. A government without power is a chimera. This is equally true for individual persons. Each and every person has some power according to his status, wealth, and occupation. The relation between the ruler and the ruled, the dominator and the dominated, the superior and the inferior, is determined on the basis of power. We may thus go so far as to say that the phenomenon of politics, whether of international, national, or social nature, is the phenomenon of power. Can we not say then that in a very true sense politics is the phenomenology of power?

In this analogy we would like to stress that creation as the political act of God is the manifestation of the divine power. The creation stories in the first and the second chapters of Genesis are no other than phenomenologies of the power of God. The creating power of God, taking the form of Word and Spirit, brings into existence the whole creation. And it is this same divine power which continues to become concretized into the ordering of the cosmos with all things and all beings in it. What a tremendous exhibition of the divine power this is! In traditional theology the word "omnipotence" is used to describe the Creator-God. To coin a term, what we have here is a cosmic politics. This is the politics which affects the whole of the cosmos. Paul is very much aware of the cosmic dimension of God's creational activity. That is why for him salvation involves no less than the whole universe. In writing to the Christians in Rome, Paul could not refrain from saying that "the whole created universe groans in all its parts as if in the pangs of child-birth," and that "the universe itself is to be freed from the shackles of mortality and enter upon the liberty and splendor of the children of God" (Rom. 8:20–22). In the same spirit, John, the elder of the earliest Christian communities, exiled to the island called Patmos, envisions the restoration of the creation in terms of a new heaven and a new earth taking the place of the first heaven and the first earth (Rev. 21:1). This grandiose picture of God's dealing with his creation is a powerful affirmation of God's politics of power in the universe.

To interpret the creation of God in terms of power is very timely and important especially for the churches in the Third World. Too long the stories of the creation have been understood by the Asians, for example, either literally as eyewitness accounts of how the universe came into being, or simply as myth or legend. Seen as a literal record of the origin of the universe, they only serve as a defense mechanism for the self-styled defenders of the faith against the "impious" scientists. Treated as legend or myth, they are regarded as not more than a literary and religious device which has no substantial role to play in the unfolding of the history of Israel and the nations. But the truth of the matter is that creation as the manifestation of God's power plays a crucial role at each moment in history. History can be said to consist of events as witnesses either for or against God's power of creation. To put it differently, it is when the church is confronted with happenings in the world that she begins to know what it means to speak of God's revelation and acts in the world.

This leads us to examine further the concept of omnipotence mentioned earlier. According to John Macquarrie, God's omnipotence means

> that he, himself, not any factual situation, is the source and also the horizon of all possibilities and only those are excluded that are inconsistent with the structure and the dynamics of God himself.[19]

I think here is a clue to understanding the mission of the church having to do with the politics of God and the politics of man.

First of all, there are possibilities in the course of history which can only be regarded as ambiguous. Any historical possibility is ambiguous because it turns into an actuality as the result of man acting on the power released by God. Once released, God's power comes, in a very real sense, to be disposed of by man. That is why man is supposed to have dominion over the earth and its creatures. To be sure, the power man has is a delegated power, and the authority he possesses is a delegated authority. He can only have limited use of that power and authority. Nevertheless, it is real power and real authority. For this reason ambiguity sets in and takes hold of the structures of power which man builds around himself. It is always an open question as to whether a particular structure of power is, to use Macquarrie's expression, consistent with the structure and dynamics of God.

To ask this question, to probe into the nature of the structures of power exhibited in different situations, is precisely the mission of the church. Perhaps we can call this the political mission, not because she lets herself become part of the struggle for political power, but because she is expected to direct critical questions to the use and forms of power in given human situations in the light of the structure and dynamics of God. This is the function performed by the prophets in the Old Testament with regard to their own nation and also other nations. And at critical turns in history, some astonishing judgments are made by the prophets. The Persian Cyrus, who made his entry into Babylon in 539 B.C. and put an end to the Neo-Babylonian empire by expelling its last king, Nabonidus, is hailed as an instrument of God for the future destiny of Israel. Second Isaiah actually regards him as God's shepherd who will fulfill all God's purpose (Isa. 44:28). In this particular instance, the political power exercised by Cyrus is an extension of the politics of God.

The political mission of the church to discern and interpret the will of God in and through political structures of powers that be is faced with great difficulty when confronted with the powers that seem to pose themselves against God. Since all power comes from God and belongs to God, it follows that all political power, including that which is against God, ultimately has its source and origin in God. Jesus makes this clear when he is confronted with the political power and authority represented by Pilate. As a ruler over the defenseless, colonized Jews, Pilate is very much conscious of the power he has in determining the fate of his subjects. He therefore reminds Jesus somewhat sadistically that he has authority to release or crucify Jesus. But Jesus gives a startling answer. "You would have no authority at all over me," he said, "if it had not been granted you from above" (John 19:11). In the book of Revelation, the author seems to go so far as to suggest that the beast with its destructive power derives its authority from God himself (Rev. 13:1–8).

It is Paul who has drawn a logical conclusion with regard to a Christian attitude toward political authorities in the famous thirteenth chapter of his letter to the Christians in Rome. His advice to them carries the air of conclusiveness. Every person, he exhorts,

> must submit to the supreme authorities. There is no authority but by act of God, and the existing authorities are instituted by him; consequently, anyone who rebels against authority is resisting a divine institution, and those who so resist have themselves to thank for the punishment they will receive. (Rom. 13:1–25; cf. I Peter 2:14)

Is Paul advocating unconditional civil obedience? Is he ruling out the possibility of rebellion against any political authorities? Is he denying Christians the right and responsibility to dissent under any circumstances? Unfortunately, it has sometimes been interpreted this way. This explains why some Christians, and especially these Christians in Asia constituting the minority of the population, tend to adopt a passive attitude toward state authorities. This is unfortunate because if we read Paul's letter a little further we realize that Paul bases his argument on the assumption that the cause of right is the key to the whole question of state authorities and civil obedience. If you do right and good, so he seems to be arguing, state authority as a divine institution would not wield its sword to intimidate and terrify you.

Paul does not go on to state the case on the reverse side. That is, supposing you do right and good, and state authorities wield their power and sword to crush and destroy you. Would Paul still exhort you to do nothing but obey? Probably not. When the powers that be come to stand for injustice, it is apparent that the power that comes from God is abused and thus becomes corrupted. Paul would be the last one to argue that Christians owe obedience and respect to the abuse and corruption of power.

The implication here for the mission of the church is this. On one hand, it is the joyous task of the church to make explicit the will and purpose of God in the powers of this world when they reflect the structure and dynamics of God—that is to say, when they reflect the love and justice of God. On the other hand, it is the responsibility of the church not to keep quiet when the powers of this world have fallen short of the structure and dynamics of God. Thus, the church lives in tension. She cannot be a partisan to any political power. She maintains creative tension with it in order that her prophetic vision is sharpened as events unfold themselves before her eyes to shape the destiny of men and women.

It has to be pointed out that there has been a tendency to identify democracy with divine sanction of power and to regard Communism as total aberration of the divine power. That is why powerful nations can wage war against Communist countries in the name of democracy and by invoking the name of God. It becomes a religious war. Western Christian mission in Asia has, in the last two or three decades, echoed and given spiritual support to this Western political ideology. It has, therefore, failed in its prophetic task. The church in Asia has to be set free from the contamination of this pseudo interpretation of political power systems and political history which have shaped and continue to shape the structures of politics in various countries in Asia. It should be stressed that we can no longer think of and practice the Christian mission in separation from this political mission of the church. In other words, we have learned in Asia through painful experience that Christian mission understood and practiced in the narrow sense of converting pagans to Christianity has isolated the Christians from the political life of the nation of which they are supposed to be responsible citizens. To use a very graphic expression of an Asian churchman addressing a group of his prominent American counterparts, Asian Christians in the midst of political uncertainty and economic depravity after World War II were given sleeping pills by the churches in the West to have a false sense of security and to get much-needed sleep at night. By sleeping pills, he meant the aids from the Western churches. But now, he said, we no longer want these sleeping pills. We need to wake up from our sleep to become actively involved in the formation of the political destiny of our country.

He was so utterly right. Christian mission does not consist in counting the sleeping heads of converts in the security of mission compounds. This kind of what I would call mission-compound Christianity will do more harm than good to the cause of Christian faith. Within its boundaries one can hardly perceive the creative dynamics of God at work. One also does not find the confrontation there with the power of this world that comes ultimately from the Creator-God.

But things are beginning to change. An increasing number of Christians in Asia are finding themselves thrust more and more into the vortex of actions in which the power of the Creator-God and the powers that be intersect and interact. Out of this involvement the church will learn to redefine her mission and reshape her style of life. This will call forth a new chapter in the history of the Christian church in Asia and in other parts of the non-Western world.

NOTES

1. Karl Barth, *Church Dogmatics* III.3 (Edinburgh: T. & T. Clark, 1961), p. 76.

2. John Bright, *A History of Israel* (Westminster Press, 1959), p. 328.

3. The term "Third World" is not used only in a geographical sense. Nor is it used only of the underdeveloped nations from the economic standpoint. It also refers to the men and women, whether in the West or in the East, who are deprived of human rights and social justice.

4. "The Ministry of Crossing Frontiers," in *The Church Crossing the Frontiers,* Essays on the Nature of Mission, in honor of Bengt Sundkler (Uppsala, 1969), pp. 44f.

5. [Three notable exceptions come to mind: Yves Raguin, Karl L. Reichelt, and Joseph J. Spae.—Ed.]

6. [In his book Dr. Song discusses also a fourth area under the heading "The Impact of Social Change," omitted here.—Ed.]

7. Dietrich Bonhoeffer, *Creation and Fall: A Theological Interpretation of Genesis 1–3,* tr. of *Schöpfung und Fall,* 1937 (London: SCM Press, 1959), p. 22.

8. In summarizing Bonhoeffer's contribution to the radical understanding of the Christian faith, John D. Godsey accurately predicted: "In the final period of his theology Bonhoeffer was breaking fresh ground in his concept of 'worldly' Christianity, and it is here that he is helping the church to a new understanding of the relation between God and the world. In the long run this will undoubtedly be Bonhoeffer's greatest contribution, and it is possible that his thought will lead to a significant revolution of the understanding of the Christian faith" (*The Theology of Dietrich Bonhoeffer,* Westminster Press, 1960, pp. 280–281).

9. Gerardus van der Leeuw, *Sacred and Profane Beauty: The Holy in Art,* tr. by David E. Green (Abingdon Press, 1963), pp. xii–xiii.

10. Ibid., p. 265.

11. Masaharu Anesaki, *Art, Life, and Nature in Japan* (Marshall Jones Co., 1933), p. 22.

12. Ibid., p. 18.

13. Christopher Dawson, *The Dynamics of World History* (Sheed & Ward, 1957), p. 235.

14. Ethelbert Stauffer, *New Testament Theology,* tr. by John Marsh (Macmillan Co., 1955), p. 62.

15. The term *Heilsgeschichte,* in spite of its wide use, is not without some opponents, H. Richard R. Niebuhr among them. As Isaac Rottenberg points out, Richard Niebuhr attacks the concept of *Heilsgeschichte* "because in his judgment it completely severs the ties between 'regular history'—the history of 'objective occurrences'—and 'sacred history.' " (Isaac Rottenberg, *Redemption and Historical Reality,* Westminster Press, 1964, p. 49.)

16. Harvey Cox, *The Secular City* (Macmillan Co., 1965).

17. Max Warren, *The Christian Mission* (London: SCM Press, 1951), p. 9. Quoted by Paul Lehmann in *Ethics in a Christian Context* (Harper & Row, 1963), p. 81.

18. Lesslie Newbigin, "Call to Mission . . . A Call to Unity?" in *The Church Crossing the Frontiers,* p. 257.

19. John Macquarrie, *Principles of Christian Theology* (Charles Scribner's Sons, 1966), p. 189.

Sixteen

Evangelism Today: The Sinners and the Sinned-Against

Raymond Fung

["In our evangelistic messages we deal with man *the sinner,*" observes Raymond Fung, "but not man *the sinned-against.*" Too often the church has been content to understand the poor only as sinners. We are here challenged to see them also as victims of the sins of others. The message which deals only with man as sinner conveys too much "condescension" to be credible to those who suffer indignity and injustice. The missing ingredient is "compassion," which is the key element in the way Jesus communicated the good news. Compassion is possible only when we perceive people as "the sinned-against." An evangelist who is not aware of the "sinned-againstness" of man cannot communicate good news to those who have been sinned against. This paper was presented at the Workshop on Evangelism sponsored by the WCC Commission on World Mission and Evangelism, at Bossey, Switzerland, in June 1979.—Ed.]

When Christians talk about evangelism, we think of a person as a sinner rebelling against God, needing repentance, and, in response, receiving forgiveness. This is as it should be. But I want to stress that a person is not only a sinner, he is also the sinned against. I would like to stress that for the purpose of evangelism, the fundamental reality of a person is that he or she sins and is sinned against. If evangelism seeks to speak to the very depth of a person through the proclamation of the gospel, evangelism must recognize and deal with the fact that a person is an object of sin as well as a subject of sin.

When I refer to "the sinned-against," I would leave open the specificity of the question of "by whom." Suffice it to say that it has to do with the principalities and powers of the world, demonic forces which cast a bondage over human lives and human institutions, infiltrating their very textures. I am using this rather broad understanding because I do not wish to exclude in our consideration of evangelism the reality that the

From *A Monthly Letter About Evangelism* (Geneva: World Council of Churches), No. 7/8 (July-August 1979), pp. 2–9. Reprinted by permission of the World Council of Churches.

poor are sinned against by economic and political systems; neither do I wish to exclude the reality that the affluent are sinned against by the same or less identifiable forces. My emphasis at this point is that people are not only willful violators of God's will, they are also the violated. This realization must have a bearing on our evangelism. To the sinner in the person, the gospel says: "Know your sinfulness. Bow in humility before God, and receive forgiveness." To the sinned-against in the same person, the gospel says: "Know that you have value. Stand in defiance against the forces which deprive you of it, and receive strength."

I do not think I need to argue that man is sinned against. The Scriptures are full of references to this effect. And daily experience confirms it. But somehow we have missed taking this fundamental human condition seriously, if at all, into our evangelistic consideration. In our evangelistic messages, we deal with man the sinner but not man the sinned-against. We talk about the bondage of sin, but we only pay lip service to it, believing that individual piety can set our lives and institutions free from the principalities of this world.

This very shallow understanding of sin, in my opinion, is damaging to evangelism. Let me make a few observations out of my experience in Hong Kong in particular, and Asia in general.

1. *A gospel which does not address man as the sinned-against poses no problem for those who do not feel that they are the sinned-against—*mainly people in the upper brackets of society, people who benefit from the social, economic, and political system. Sinned-againstness is not part of their experience. And so, looking at themselves, they can honestly say, "We have become Christians because of hearing the gospel, and the same has made us prosper. What can be wrong with it?" They do not acknowledge that they are the sinned-against, or for that matter, that anyone else is the sinned against.

2. *A gospel which does not address man as the sinned-against poses a lot of problems for those who are the sinned-against—*mainly the poor. There are often two kinds of responses from the poor to the gospel— outright rejection of the gospel, or, accepting this gospel, accepting also the sinned-against fate as something outside of the bearing of the gospel. In the first case, no evangelism takes place. In the second, religion serves as an opiate.

Let me illustrate with an experience. As a result of helping out in a labor dispute, I came to know a textile worker in his early forties. He would occasionally come to my office for a chat when he worked night shift and could afford the time. At one point, we touched on the subject of Christianity, and he tried to provoke me, in a friendly way, by dismissing it as a foreign religion. I asked him if he had ever read the Bible. He admitted that he had not. So I told him to shut up, also in a friendly way, and that until he did, he had no right to criticize my faith. He said: "Okay, I don't want to read the Bible because I don't read books anyway. But I will come to your church for once." I was caught and couldn't say no. He did, the coming Sunday, at the cost of a day's wages. After the service, he took me to lunch and he said, "Well, the sermon hit me." It had been about sin. "You know, what the preacher said is true of me— laziness, a violent temper, and addiction to cheap entertainment. I guess he was talking about me all right." I held my breath, trying to keep down my excitement. He continued, "But there is nothing there about my boss —employing child labor, not giving us legally required holidays, putting on false labels, and forcing us to do overtime." My heart sank. Not simply because this friend of mine is most unlikely to go to church again, but more because there are quite a number of factory owners in the congregation who should benefit from the textile worker's observation.

An evangelistic message which does not speak to the sinned-against-ness of man does not speak to those who have been sinned against. Furthermore, my friend the textile worker might agree with the diagnosis of the church, "You are a sinner," but he rejects the church which provides the diagnosis.

Given the middle-class character of most churches, at least the middle-class character of those who control the articulation of the evangelistic message, the gospel which ignores man the sinned-against may work among the middle class (this is happening in some parts of Asia, especially among the ethnic Chinese in urban centers, but not quite—witness the dropout rate of those who fail to go into universities, the professions, or executive-level jobs). But it cannot possibly work among the overwhelming majority in Asia—peasants and workers who are the poor. The evangelistic message which deals with man as the sinner but not the sinned-against, coming from a middle-class institution whose members benefit from the status quo, simply conveys too much superiority, condescension, yes, even pity, to make sense, let alone to become credible to those who suffer indignity and injustice every day. The one element necessary in the message and its transmission is absent, namely, *compassion*.

When I look at the Scriptures, I find that compassion is the key element in the good news of Jesus Christ, and in the way he communicated the good news. I discover that every time the gospel talks about Jesus having compassion on the people, he had compassion on the people primarily because they were the sinned-against.

Matthew talks about Jesus going ashore and seeing a great throng, "and he had compassion on them, and healed their sick" (Matt. 14:14).

And Jesus told his disciples to feed the people: "I have compassion on the crowd, because they have been with me now three days, and have nothing to eat; and I am unwilling to send them away hungry, lest they faint on the way" (Matt. 15:32). Luke paints a similar picture. When the Lord saw a woman whose son had just died, "he had compassion on her and said to her, 'Do not weep' " (Luke 7:13). And when the Samaritan saw the man beaten and wounded by robbers, "he had compassion, and went to him and bound up his wounds" (Luke 10:33). The parable of the prodigal son makes the same direct connection between compassion and man as the sinned-against. Luke reports: "But while (the son) was yet at a distance, his father saw him and had compassion, and ran and embraced him and kissed him" (Luke 15:20). And when Matthew summed up the work of Jesus in the first stage of his ministry in Matt. 9:36, he put it this way: "When (Jesus) saw the crowds, he had compassion for them, because they were harassed and helpless, like sheep without a shepherd." In short, Jesus had compassion on people because they were the sinned-against. And yet, even more significantly, immediately after this summary, Matthew recorded Jesus' appeal to his disciples for evangelism: "The harvest is plentiful, but the laborers are few; pray therefore the Lord of the harvest to send out laborers into his harvest" (Matt. 10:37–38). It is clear that the call to evangelism is a response to the call to having compassion on the sinned-against. Mark, in his corresponding passage in Mark 6:34, omitted the "harassed and helpless" reference, but he made the necessity for compassion in evangelism even more clear. Mark reported, "(Jesus) saw a great throng, and he had compassion on them, because they were like sheep without a shepherd; and he began to teach them many things."

I think I am prepared to make a bold suggestion: that compassion for people is possible only when we perceive people as the sinned-against. If we look at people as sinners (as distinct from the sinned-against), we may have concern for them, affection or pity, but no compassion, i.e., "suffering together with another; fellow-feeling, sympathy" (Oxford English Dictionary). Many evangelists of today have little perception of people as the sinned-against. Most evangelistic activities are devoid of compassion. We must recover compassion in our evangelism. To do that, I think, we need to sharpen our understanding of people as the sinned-against, not in a behavioristic sense, but in a theological sense, in terms of sin, the domination of sin, and of our "struggle against sin . . . to the point of shedding (our) blood" (Heb. 12:4).

How do we come to understand people as the sinned-against? Again, let us look to Jesus. If we go back to the passages I just quoted, we will find that every single reference to compassion informs us that Jesus saw the people. Jesus saw the people, Jesus saw a great throng. The Lord saw the woman whose only son was about to be buried. Jesus saw the crowd. The good Samaritan saw the half-dead man. The father saw the wayward son and had compassion.

So we must see the people at close range. We must be near them so that we can feel their pulse and read their sighs. So near that the people become "you" and not "they"; they are those right in front of us, whose eyes we must look into, whose voice we cannot but hear, and whose very presence lays claim to our friendship. In short, we must be involved. I would submit that this is the way we can come to understand people as the sinned-against, and the way we can begin to be compassionate.

I cannot overemphasize the importance of compassion in our faith and in the communication of our faith. Compassion, not the popular, unexamined notion of being sentimental and soft, but—in the proper sense—suffering together with, fellow feeling, sympathy. Compassion is important because it is the way to live out the Christian life, and because it works for evangelism.

Compassion is important to the Christian life because there is the element of suffering in it, and suffering is what makes the church authentic. If the church is to be the church, it must have the marks of Jesus Christ upon it—the marks of the beatings, the nails, and the crown of thorns—the signs of the cross. With this, the church is authentic, not only to God but also to those who suffer, people who are sinned against.

Compassion is important to Christian life and evangelism because there is the element of involvement in it, and the compassion born out of involvement bestows authority on our word and our deeds. When John the Baptist sent his disciples to check on Jesus' messiahship, Jesus answered them, "Go back and tell John what you hear and see; the blind see again, the lame walk, . . . and the Good News is proclaimed to the poor" (Matt. 11:5, JB). So Jesus based his authority on his involvement with the poor. He who gave up equality with God and entered into human suffering has a special right to be heard. And Jesus was heard. He spoke as no scribes spoke. It seems all too clear then that if an evangelistic message is to have authority, it must be based on experience of involvement. It must come from persons who know what they are talking about when they speak words of comfort and of judgment.

Thirdly, compassion is important to evangelism for a strategic reason. Since compassion presupposes fellowship with the sinned-against, the sinned-against, even before they decide to be Christians, are already inside some kind of a Christian community. So, the communication of the gospel takes place in a context of trust and solidarity. The nonbeliever can judge Christianity at work from the inside, and not from outside looking in. Compassion on the part of the Christian enables the non-believer to examine Christianity from within rather than from without. It invites people to look at Jesus as "you" rather than "him." This is how faith in Jesus Christ becomes possible.

Two experiences are illustrative of the above. I was present when an evangelist, having been invited by his factory-manager friend, preached to shop-floor workers on the theme: "Man does not live by bread alone," over a loudspeaker system. It was plain that, without really listening to him, the workers thought he was talking nonsense. Next day, the loud-speaker wire was found cut. Yet, the same Scripture, given by an industrial missioner, found positive acceptance. "Right, poor as we are, money is not everything."

On a separate occasion, I was invited to a luncheon meeting of a group of prosperous managers. They had some interest in evangelizing their workers. I told them that Jesus had to humble himself and become a human being before he could reach men and women with the gospel. What made them think they can do the same to workers from their managers' glassed-in offices? (I also told them that their job is to evangelize their fellow managers, and learn how to be a Christian in a manager's role.) This is an extreme case, but I hope it illustrates why compassion for the sinned-against is so important to biblical and effective evangelism.

I am aware that without actually announcing it, I have been focusing more and more on the poor, whose sinned-againstness is obvious. That is because I happen to know something about the poor in Asia. I'd like to think too that the theological understanding of men and women as the sinned-against, the attitude of compassion, and the method of involvement, are also applicable in the evangelization of the affluent. Sinned-againstness is part of their reality, too, maybe less obvious to others or to themselves. But it is there. Evangelism must therefore deal with this aspect of their life if the gospel is to be fully meaningful, if the affluent converts are to see that they share the common destiny of the sinned-against with the world's poor, and if they are to understand that while they are the sinned-against, they are at the same time sinning against the poor. So I would like to suggest that the concept of the sinned-against is applicable in the evangelization of both the poor and the affluent. After all, the evangelistic message to the poor and to the affluent is basically the same message. The call of the Lord that those of low degree be exalted is the same call that the proud be scattered and the mighty put down from their thrones. The promise to the hungry that they will be filled with good things is the same promise to the rich that they will be sent empty away (Luke 1:46–55). The Lord's command to the paralyzed man, "Rise, take up your bed and go home," is at the same time a reminder to the scribes of the evil in their hearts (Matt. 9:1–8). The parable which tells the unemployed that the master of the vineyard cares for them is also the parable which shows those who have already made it their own selfishness. So the evangelistic message, in compassion, says words of comfort to the sinned-against, and the same becomes words of judgment, also said in compassion, to the sinning. Conversion depends, and begins, on their separate response. In this way, the evangelistic message coincides with the prophetic message. They are indeed one and the same message. The evangelist and the prophet are the same person.

What about the "sinner" or the "sinning" aspect of the poor, the sinned-against? Shouldn't evangelism deal with that, too? Yes, of course, the poor are certainly sinners. Evangelism must help a person come to a knowledge of his own sinfulness, and of the fact that he must have a personal relationship to the Lord and Savior Jesus Christ. I have not talked about this at length up to now because the concept of the sinner in evangelism is fairly well accepted. I have, however, described the abuse of it in practice as I observe it in Asia. But the question remains: in the case of the poor, what is the connection between his realization of his sinned-againstness and of his own sinfulness? In my experience of ten years working among industrial workers, sharing their struggles and asking them to share my Christian faith, I believe strongly that there is a relationship, and a direct one. When the gospel addresses itself to the sinned-againstness of a person, that person will also allow the gospel to deal with his own sinfulness. Or, from the perspective of that person, awareness of his sinned-againstness comes first, followed by awareness of his sinfulness. I am not saying that the process will complete itself every time. Much depends on the gospel's human agent and the person's response. But there is enough evidence in the urban-rural mission experience in Asia to support the validity of this evangelistic process. Let me illustrate by reading a worker's testimony. This is one out of many.

> I've been a worker for over ten years. I am writing this testimony with joy and thanksgiving.
>
> Born in a very poor family, I began at Primary 5, helping my father in the factory where he worked as a cook. I worked half-time and went to class half-time, until I finished Primary 6. My father told me he could not afford to send me to secondary school. I was thirteen years old. So I became assistant to my father at the factory kitchen.
>
> In the next year, I witnessed a labour dispute. A worker at the plant inadvertently broke a trolley. He was asked to pay a hefty sum for damage. Most other workers downed their tools in sympathy. Everybody was sacked. I was young, but I could feel an injustice had been done. The worker did not break the trolley deliberately. Furthermore, the thing hadn't been installed

properly. I don't think I can ever forget the scene: the exploitation, the solidarity, the high cost of standing up.

Soon my sister was born. There was no room in our cubicle, so I began sleeping in the factory and picked up bad habits. Then I left the kitchen and went on the shop floor. Another dispute took place. A new law was passed, providing for four rest days a month. But the boss allowed us only two. So we demanded the legal provision. The boss refused.

Over lunch, we decided on strike action the next day. It was to be my first participation in industrial action. The next day, we struck. But quite a number of those who had agreed to strike turned tail. I felt betrayed. Eventually the dispute was settled. Later on, the strike leaders were dismissed. I somehow stayed on. There would be other disputes to follow, in some cases with the boss calling in the police, and with the boss pitting workers against workers.

Then my father, together with a number of workers, was told not to report to work again. There was no formal notice of dismissal, and no advance notice. My father was simply informed on payday that the company kitchen was to be abolished. After ten years working for the boss, my father was discarded, with only two months of wages. It was so sudden and unfair.

I got the dismissed workers together; I had known about industrial mission, so I suggested that we seek help. But they were hesitant. "We are no Jesus-believers. They won't help us." I decided to try it anyway. So I took my father to the industrial mission office. The staff there explained the law to us and taught us the procedures and other things. My father won his case. I was angry that so many workers dared not raise their voices. I felt deeply the oppression between man and man.

My father became unemployed. An industrial mission staff asked if he would cook several meals at a workers' Gospel camp. He went and I went along to help out. There, for the first time, I came to hear about Christianity. My father couldn't go to the third Gospel camp, so I took his place. There I got to know other workers. I was invited to take part in the evening group discussions. We were invited to reflect on our own lives. One told us he had no home of his own, and that he was bullied by his boss and also his relatives. I felt deeply moved. After the Gospel camp, those interested could come for a regular Thursday evening Bible study; I began to go regularly. Strangely, the Bible studies there seemed to have a lot to do with workers.

Later on, my next-door neighbor moved out and he left some books behind, one of which was a Bible. I took it home and read it, especially the passages I had studied with the Thursday group. Several texts talked about the cost of following Jesus. This reminded me of my first dispute and how the workers had to pay a price.

Then there were texts on sin. I didn't quite understand it, but when I read about Jesus being crucified, I began to understand. At once across my mind flowed pictures of my own cowardice, how I kept my mouth shut, afraid to pay the price, bitter at others not caring for me, but never thinking of caring for others.

From that time on, Christianity stuck in my head. It was always there, but I couldn't make up my mind. This went on for a whole month. One evening, having nothing to do, I went up to the industrial mission office. There was no course on, no Bible study, and no one to make jokes with. So I just sat and began to think about Jesus. I felt a sense of urgency and I remembered something about prayer. So I prayed and decided to follow Jesus. Later, I told two mission staff about it. They laughed and we embraced. The following Easter, I was baptized.

Let us compare this testimony with the story of the textile worker who went to church with me. The textile worker was informed of his sinfulness: He agreed, and he responded in effect with a "So what?" The other realized his sinfulness in the midst of his sinned-againstness. In such situation, he cannot say "So what?" He has to take his own sinfulness seriously and deal with it. This man testified: "I didn't quite understand (sin), but when I read about Jesus being crucified, I began to understand. At once across my mind flowed pictures of my own cowardice, how I kept my mouth shut, afraid to pay the price, bitter at others not caring for me, but never thinking of caring for others. I began to think about Jesus. I felt a sense of urgency and I remembered something about prayer. So I prayed and decided to follow Jesus."

I am ready to suggest that in evangelism, especially of the poor, we focus primarily on man as the sinned-against. This is not to take lightly the fact of sin; this is to take sin seriously, in all of its deadly forms. This is not to absolve a person from personal responsibilities, but on the contrary, this is to make him see how he can be personally responsible.

Finally, what does the good news do to man the sinned-against? The gospel does not do away with the powers which sin against man. It does not provide ready answers for their destruction. What the gospel does is to demythologize these powers so that man the sinned-against can be clear about them, get hold of them, see himself in relation to them, and see his own sinfulness in the very midst of these powers. In short, evangelism to man the sinned-against frees man to deal with the powers which sin against man, and it also frees man to deal with his own sinfulness. In practice, the evangelistic focusing on man the sinned-against means a community which identifies with and accepts nonbelievers on the basis of sinned-againstness, and, in the common struggle against the forces which sin against man, confronts all those involved in the struggle of their personal sinfulness, and experiences God's forgiveness and Christian oneness.

To conclude, I would like to see churches make a clear and unambiguous, systematic and long-term commitment for the evangelization of the poor. This is no more and no less than how Jesus described his ministry.

Our evangelism has to become a lot more biblical and effective, and the best way this process can begin, I believe, is to focus on the poor. Evangelism of the poor will demonstrate clearly the false dichotomy between doing evangelism and doing justice. In fact, it demonstrates the necessity of both in calling men and women to God. And, if I may speak only of Asia and in terms of the church's self-interest, a middle-class church in a sea of peasants and factory workers makes no sense at all.

I further hope that the World Council of Churches might be an instrument in facilitating the global evangelization of the poor. I am aware that the WCC may not be the best-known body for evangelism. I am aware there are more famous ones whose reputation rests on their plans and strategies for world evangelism. But, as far as my knowledge goes, the ecumenical tradition, imperfect though it is, remains that which possesses a record of understanding of people as the sinned-against, a record, again imperfect, of commitment to the poor and their causes, and a willingness to risk the displeasure of the powerful for what it believes to be the just and the humane. Hence this hope. For evangelism is costly (and I do not mean money). This ministry which deals directly with sin demands compassionate involvement with the sinned-against, and that means it also demands compassionate denouncement of the forces which sin against man. Evangelism is costly. An evangelism which does not cost the church something is cheap evangelism.

PART FIVE

Theology of
Religious Pluralism

Seventeen

Christian Encounter
with People of Other Beliefs
Christian Conference of Asia

[This statement was prepared by a Commission of the Third Assembly of the East Asia Christian Conference, held in Bangkok in 1964. Our common humanity is the meeting point for the presentation of the gospel to others instead of the points of similarity between religious traditions. It follows that the concern of the Christian should be "to confront men with the event and person of Christ," and not merely to confront them with Christianity. Because Jesus Christ is Man among men and also the Savior of men, he makes possible "an unveiled and honest openness between men."—Ed.]

The Christian encounter is, by its nature, a meeting of men with men. Christian men meet with and are met by their fellowmen in the normal converse of life. The increase of life in the cities makes this meeting inevitable and even irritating. Life in the village, too, is no longer the life of a harmonious community; it involves a great deal of mutual questioning. It is from within this life together that Christians seek to transmit, interpret, and give evidence of the good news of God's purpose for all men and for all the world as it has been made manifest in Jesus Christ.

That this witness of the Christian community to the gospel becomes at all possible or meaningful is due to the fact that God himself in Christ encounters men and that this encounter is constantly renewed in the living traffic of prayer. In the encounter of the Christian with men of other beliefs, God, who sent his Son for all men, continues this mission by the power of the Spirit. It is to this primary reality of God's action that the Christian encounter points. Indeed, it is this which makes the use of the term "Christian encounter" both permissible and necessary.

The Christian Community Within the Human Community. Statements from the Bangkok Assembly of the E. A. C. C., 1964, pp. 9–16. Reprinted by permission of the Christian Conference of Asia.

THE AMBIGUITY OF RELIGION

Inasmuch as God has made man in his own image, he is constantly at work seeking to win men's allegiance to himself as their Creator and Lord. Since God takes the initiative, men must respond; but as they are already in a state of estrangement from God, even their response to him is shot through with disobedience. There is always in a man's faith in God that element of sin by which he seeks to deny his creatureliness. Men attempt to transcend their position as creatures before their Creator, either through attempts to make God serve their own purpose, or by claiming that they have found God as the result of their own search, or by seeking some kind of equality with God whereby either God's graciousness toward them is earned by a life of good works or God himself as "other" to men is denied. Man in his deepest nature contradicts himself.

Here lies the importance of recognizing that "religion" is not necessarily the point of meeting between those who would present the gospel and those to whom it is to be presented. Indeed, there is enough evidence to show that there are communities which are farthest from God specifically at the point of their religious life. Religion is not necessarily a good thing. The conversation about the Christian faith is often most meaningfully conducted in the simple perspective of men in their secular lives. In the last analysis, the Christian encounter is an encounter with men as men both in their religious life and in their nonreligious life, both in their belief and in their unbelief, both in what they hold to be sacred and in what they hold to be secular.

This means that to present the gospel of God in Jesus Christ to men is to challenge them with God's searching judgment of all religions, including Christianity, which is implicit in the gospel. Without this, the new life offered to men in Jesus Christ must remain incomprehensible. Indeed, no conversation concerning the gospel can have true seriousness unless those who take part in it, Christian or not, religious or not, recognize that the gospel is addressed to them precisely as they are, to each in his condition of alienation from God, and that it comes to them with the invitation that they live by God's forgiving mercy as it is offered to them through Jesus Christ, the risen Lord who died for them. It is Jesus whom men must encounter. The concern of the Christian is to confront men not with Christianity but with the event and person of Christ.

THE ADDRESS OF THE GOSPEL

The conception of man as man, however, on the basis of which the Christian encounter must take place, includes not only a judgment of men in their religiousness and in their sin, standing within the saving action of God. All men are created by God through Jesus Christ. When they are illumined, it is he who illumines them. In his light they must walk, by it they are exposed. The life he lives is the light of men. When men hear the news of God's love for them in Jesus Christ, the Holy Spirit seeks to bring them to obedience to this love, and summons them to participation with Jesus Christ in his continuing life and mission in the world.

Jesus Christ has died for all men; so that men, though they are in a state of rebellion against God, are nonetheless also within the working of the reconciling ministry of Christ. The proclamation which the church makes of forgiveness and renewal of life in Jesus Christ is part of this reconciling ministry. Through it are offered to men the gifts of repentance and of faith whereby they are incorporated in him.

All men live by the providence of God. He provides for all. "He makes his sun rise on good and bad alike, and sends the rain on the honest and the dishonest." His love broods over all and is present in the life of each person, both in judgment and in mercy. In spite of men's rebellion against God, all history is held within the Lordship of Christ. He is the destination toward whom all history and histories are set. By him all men will be judged at the last and through him all things will be brought to their consummation. The Christian encounter takes place within this universality of meaning.

THE NATURE OF THE CONVERSATION

There is not only a Christian understanding of man; there is also an understanding of man peculiar to each religion and each ideology. True conversation cannot take place unless each party to it can speak in terms of his own total system of thought and experience. The question which is posed for Christians is how they reconcile their own position as witnesses to the truth in Jesus Christ with the necessity of subjecting themselves to that process of mutual correction and learning which belongs to a conversation when it is truly open. There has been given to them a certainty concerning the Lordship of Jesus Christ, but this confers on them no superiority over those to whom they go. On the contrary, the Scriptures teach that God may use these others to correct them.

And yet, there is a truth in which to abide, a faith in which to stand firm. The very concern of Christians to enter into a true conversation with men of other beliefs, whether religious or irreligious, is rooted in a commitment which must withstand all temptation to compromise. Christians must recognize, however, that the very nature of conversation demands that they be ready to bring both Christian truth and themselves out from under the protecting wall of their own dogmatically congenial thinking. The Christian must learn to speak to others out of his own experience in the language of everyday life.

Whereas many Christians, when they think of an encounter with men of other beliefs, tend to conceive of that encounter largely in terms of such doctrines as those concerning sin, atonement, and so on, much in the hold of other faiths on their adherents lies outside the intellectual encounter. It lies at the point where the mystery and burden and responsibility of human existence are felt. This is equally true of men who deny that they hold to any faith. This is why, while men are conditioned by their systems of belief and practice, no man can be estimated simply by the faith which he professes or denies. Men cannot be merely intellectually encountered or rationally confronted. Should one seek to do this, one not only would not carry conviction; he would not even minister.

There is a further difficulty in presenting Jesus and his gospel to men of other beliefs. There is a real distinction between Jesus Christ as the church proclaims him and Jesus Christ as men of other beliefs think of him. To them he is the founder of a specific religion, the person whom a certain group of men and women claim to be God, and, therefore, one whom they insist on interpreting in terms of the life and practices of the Christian community, down the centuries and today. The result is that a constant ambiguity arises whenever Christians speak with men of other beliefs concerning Jesus Christ.

All this but underlines, in the first place, the absolute necessity of studying and understanding the beliefs and practices of devotion of those with whom Christians would converse; not simply the classical formulations of their beliefs but the actual ways in which men hold their convictions and live their lives. In some parts of Asia the issues which divide men are primarily religious, in others primarily cultural: Christians must learn to bear witness to the gospel in both circumstances. There is the added complication that everywhere in Asia there are cultures that are passing away as well as cultures being born. The Christian responsibility is in terms of these emerging cultures.

In the second place, there is common ground in the questions to which men are seeking answers, just as much as there is wide divergence in the answers themselves. Besides, there is the disturbing fact that when Christ is met, he raises new questions in addition to demanding that old questions be answered at deeper and deeper levels.

In the third place, there is the necessity that Christians so share with others a common secular life that there is established with them a relation of friendship and mutuality. In particular, there are many services to the community as a whole in which men of all beliefs can act together in fruitful cooperation. There are also the many problems posed by a rapidly changing world and its technological developments which ought to be studied and solved together by men of all persuasions.

Knowledge of one another's beliefs and convictions and a life shared together will then enable each party to the conversation to enter into the feel of the other, so that prejudices can be allayed, historic misunderstandings can be avoided, and all postures of superiority can be eschewed. That this whole attitude and approach involves risk is true, but it is the kind of risk without which theology becomes disloyal to the adventure of the incarnation and the exposure of the cross.

THE NEW CREATION IN CHRIST

Indeed, it is in the fact of the incarnation, and the power of the cross, that there lie the resources for that openness which the Christian encounter with men of other beliefs demands. Inasmuch as Jesus Christ is Man among men—the Son of man, and is also the Savior of men—the Son of God, he makes possible an unveiled and honest openness between men when they seek to converse concerning him or concerning the world within which he has wrought the new creation. He is open to men and to the world: and in him is the only true way for the Christian to be open to secular and religious men in truly Christian encounter.

When Christians are aware of the wonder of the treasure which they have in Christ they will be able, not with fear, but with joy and expectation, to enter into the lives of those of other beliefs so as to discern in them their treasures. This is not to say that one would naturally turn first to a study of religions and to fellowship with religious men to discern what God is doing in his world, for religion can also be the sphere of the demonic. The point is that Christians must learn to discern the working of God wherever it may be, whether through the religious or the secular life. Asian churches are gravely weakened in their witness by their lack of knowledge of and even interest in the cultures of their people. The discernment of God's working and the responsibility which it involves is part of the calling of those who in Christ are the firstfruits of the new creation, the trustees, on behalf of all men, of all that is from God and belongs to God.

In thus resting the promise of mutuality that belongs to honest open-ness in love on the fact of the new creation, acknowledgment is made of the work of the Holy Spirit. In his work lies the relation between the light of Christ, of which no man is left without evidence, and witness to that light by the church's proclamation of the Word. In his work lies also that obedience of faith by which men serve Christ through their service "to the least of his brethren."

The new creation is his creation, and those who are in him must seek from him the eyes to see the signs of his creating activity wherever and in whomsoever they may be.

God's new creation brings into being a new community and, there-fore, the encounter of which we speak is not simply one between in-dividuals but is the encounter of this new community with other com-munities. That is why, where it takes place, the demand and the promise are made: "Believe and be baptized, and you will receive the Holy Spirit." It was their experience of the power and presence of the Holy Spirit, in mission on which Jesus Christ had launched them, which established the people of the early church in their conviction that Jesus is Lord. Because of this conviction the church became not communal but missionary. Through the Holy Spirit, they were enabled to proclaim Christ's Lordship and have it accepted. By the working of the Holy Spirit they were able to manifest the powers of the New Age. The Holy Spirit led men into their involvement in the continuing mission of Christ in the world and distinguished them by their participation in the fellowship of his sufferings and the power of his resurrection.

The continual renewal of this common life of worship, faith, and witness in the power of the Holy Spirit is integral to the Christian proclamation. Only so will men recognize the Christ of whom we speak. Since the worshipability of God, as he is and as he is known in Jesus Christ, is what makes the Christian a witness, the encounter with men of other beliefs cannot be a pure question of verbal conversation. The disposition of God toward men in Jesus Christ cannot, in the last analy-sis, be communicated apart from a life which makes it credible. It must be demonstrated by those who bear his name.

This demonstration must go hand in hand with the work of interpreta-tion. With what boldness did men like John and Paul press into the service of the gospel the terminology of Greek philosophy, the symbols of the mystery religions, and the structures of thought of the Gnostics. The Christians of Asia must live more actually within the cultures of their own peoples. This may involve the abandoning of much that is familiar—a kind of self-emptying which will be both painful and danger-ous. But it is only so that the Spirit will show how the faith may be restated in the idiom of the indigenous cultures, in forms of community life where the faith becomes luminous, and in actions relevant to the needs of contemporary society.

CONCLUSION

Scripture affirms that the mission of the church is an expression and consequence of the Lordship of Christ. "All authority has been given to me—go ye therefore." It is by this authority that all men are claimed for Jesus and asked to become his disciples. It is by this authority that the Christian community seeks to bring all forms of human community to an acceptance of Christ's Lordship. It is by this authority that the love of God in Jesus Christ, both in its wrath and mercy, is set forth as the final answer to the hopes and fears of human existence. It is by this authority that the totality of human history is declared as held within his rule and set toward the manifestation of his glory.

The dialogical situation within which the Christian encounter takes place is characterized, therefore, by the universality of the gospel as it encompasses all men, the mutuality that is promised when the dialogue takes place in honest and loving openness, and the finality of Christ himself who alone is Lord.

Eighteen

Emergent Theology in the Context of Buddhism
Lynn de Silva

[This comprehensive essay is in some ways the culmination of a lifetime of theological reflection on Christian themes in the context of Buddhist thought. Dr. De Silva attempts here to restate in summary fashion the fundamentals of Christian faith in relation to the Theravada tradition. His purpose is not only to communicate the Christian faith more effectively to Buddhists but also to draw from Buddhist philosophy spiritual resources that enrich contemporary Christian theology. "There are deep insights in Buddhism that can enrich Christian thinking," he declares, "but Christians have been afraid of having anything to do with Buddhism." Beginning with an analysis of our human predicament —a meeting place for Christians and Buddhists—De Silva moves on to a discussion of the doctrines of creation and redemption, sanctification and eternal life, spirituality and the Christian ethic. He advocates a "common spirituality linking inwardness with action, solitary contemplation with mutuality, and transcendence with social involvement."—Ed.]

INTRODUCTION

Theology is a living thing and has to do with our very existence as human beings in a particular situation and therefore must be related to the traditional beliefs, classical expressions of faith, and cultural forms. Theology is not an intellectual activity that takes place in the seclusion of a classroom, but a human activity that takes place in a culture; it is not a theoretical science with a fixed structure of thought applicable to all times and all places, but one that is dynamic and mobile and adaptable to changing circumstances. No doubt there are elements of constancy and continuity and an unchanging content in any theology, but the form or the modus undergoes changes in relation to the context. Although no

Emergent Theology in the Context of Buddhism (pamphlet) (Colombo, Sri Lanka: Ecumenical Institute for Study and Dialogue, 1979). Reprinted by permission of the publisher.

theology is derived from the culture alone, it does take form and is shaped in the particular situation or context. Authentic, living theology arises from an interplay between the *"logos"* and the culture in which it seeks to express itself. The theologian, being part of the culture himself, cannot but speak from its context and in its terms.

The need for restating Christian theology in relation to the faiths in Asia has been stressed over and over again. We have an imported theology that does not make much sense in the context in which we are living in Sri Lanka. There are deep insights in Buddhism that can enrich Christian thinking, but Christians have been afraid of having anything to do with Buddhism. In contrast we see how Buddhism, wherever it spread, adapted itself to the different cultures. The Buddha himself boldly took over and adopted terms, concepts, beliefs, and practices from the religious milieu at that time. Numerous examples can be given: the most obvious is the term *karma* and its corollary rebirth to which the Buddha gave a new interpretation. Similarly, he took over the term *nirvana* and gave it a new meaning. The *pañcasīla* has roots in Jainism, and the four *Brahma Viharas* were practiced long before Buddhism arose. Such adaptation has not taken place in Christianity. But today, Christian theologians, appreciating the values in other religions and cultures, have begun to rethink Christian theology in relation to the different contexts. In this paper an attempt is made to restate briefly the fundamentals of Christian theology in relation to Theravada Buddhist thought, speaking from its context and its terms, with the practical aim of harnessing spiritual resources for the well-being of humankind.

TILAKKHANA AND THE HUMAN PREDICAMENT

Buddhism begins with an analysis of the human condition. This is the right starting point for theology, for a living theology must begin with living existential realities and not with metaphysical speculations. The Buddha in his diagnosis of the human predicament discovered three marks *(Tilakkhana)* or characteristics of all existence. They are *anicca, dukkha,* and *anattā.* These three terms indicate the fundamental "marks" or "characteristics" of all existence in the space-time order of reality. They are the hallmarks of existence which point to the fact that all existence in its absolute entirety is but a flux-in-process *(anicca),* having nothing permanent or enduring in the process of change *(anattā),* and hence inherently incapable of producing any lasting satisfaction *(dukkha).* *Anicca* means impermanence, *anattā* means soul-lessness or self-lessness, and *dukkha* means all aspects of suffering. *Dukkha* is a word that has varied shades of meaning and defies precise definition.

Perhaps "existential anxiety" covers much of what *dukkha* means (see Note 5).

In my opinion in the *Tilakkhana* analytic we have a comprehensive analysis of the human predicament, in which the anthropological, empirical, and experiential problems converge embracing the whole breadth of human existence, which can provide a basis for an indigenous Christian theology.

It is important to note that the understanding of the human predicament in terms of the *Tilakkhana* arose, not from a theoretical interest but from an existential concern. This concern is reflected in Prince Siddhartha's experience of seeing the three sights—an old man, a sick man, and a corpse—signifying the fact of negativity, nihility, or mortality, inherent in all existence. The three sights correspond to the three signs mentioned above. When he saw each sight he asked the question "Will this happen to me?" That is the question "Everyone" asks in silence or articulates in different ways. There was also a fourth sight which the Prince saw—that of a serene hermit. This signifies to him that there was a transcendent state beyond conditioned existence. This experience of Prince Siddhartha is a paradigm for understanding the human predicament and finding a solution to it.

There is a striking parallel to this experience in Nietzsche's *Zarathustra* in the chapter "The Preachers of Death," in which he refers to three ways in which the threat of the possibility of nonbeing or of ceasing to be comes to man: "They meet an invalid, or an old man, or a corpse—and immediately they say: 'Life is refuted!' "[1] It is significant that the distinguished theologian Paul Tillich refers to this passage and sees its existential significance.[2] We could relate this to what the father of modern existentialism, Søren Kierkegaard, said. He pointed out that a man who comes to realize that "all men are mortal" knows the universal essence of all existence, but what is needed is that he should apply this truth to himself and come to the conclusion in his own case, "I too must die." It is then that an individual will feel the need to find a purpose, a plan, and a destiny in life. Kierkegaard's aim was to help men to come to that conclusion and thus experience the truth—one might say the truth of *anicca, dukkha,* and *anattā*—in their own individual existence so that they will seek for a rationale for true living. This was exactly the aim of the Buddha too—to help people to understand the real nature of existence and seek for a rationale of authentic living which can bring liberation from conditioned existence.

Modern existentialist writers describe the human predicament in terms of anxiety. Paul Tillich describes the nature of anxiety as follows:

The first assertion about the nature of anxiety is this: anxiety is the state in which a being is aware of its possible nonbeing. The same statement, in a shorter form, would read: anxiety is the existential awareness of nonbeing. "Existential" in this sentence means that it is not the abstract knowledge of nonbeing which produces anxiety but the awareness that nonbeing is part of one's own being. It is not the realization of universal transitoriness, not even the experience of the death of others, but the impression of these events on the always latent awareness of our own having to die that produces anxiety. Anxiety is finitude, experienced as one's own finitude. This is the natural anxiety of man as man, and in some way of all living beings. It is the anxiety of nonbeing, the awareness of one's finitude as finitude.[3]

In the light of this passage we could understand anxiety in terms of *Tilakkhana*. Anxiety is "the state in which a being is aware of its possible nonbeing" (i.e., the possibility of *anicca*). This awareness is due to the fact that "nonbeing is part of one's own being" (i.e., man is *anattā*). It is an "existential awareness" because "Anxiety is finitude, experienced as one's own finitude" (i.e., the state of *dukkha*).

If, as John Macquarrie says, "by 'existentialism' is meant the type of philosophy which concerns itself with human existence and which tries to understand this existence out of the concrete experience which, as existents, we all have," then we could speak of a Buddhist existentialism as some writers have done.[4] An Asian Christian theology should begin where Buddhism begins, by trying "to understand this existence out of the concrete experience which, as existents, we all have."[5]

THE BIBLICAL UNDERSTANDING OF TILAKKHANA

The polarity of conflict between being and the possibility of nonbeing that lies at the core of human existence, the mood of anxiety, the finitude and precariousness of man's life, is a familiar theme that runs through the Bible. There is no systematic exposition of this human condition in the Bible as is found in the Buddhist texts. The biblical writers were concerned only with stating facts of experience and not with systematization. The task of systematization belongs to the theologian. For this task of doing theology in the context of Buddhism the theologian could employ the *Tilakkhana* analysis of existence, as has already been indicated.

There should be no difficulty with regard to *anicca* and *dukkha*. There are a number of passages which speak of the transitoriness and suffering and anxiety of human life (Ps. 144:3–4; Eccl. 2:11; II Cor. 4:18). But, *anattā* may present some difficulties, because the notion of an immortal soul is deeply embedded in Christian thinking. However it is now seen that this notion is an alien infiltration from Greek philosophy, into Christianity. Modern studies in biology, psychology, and physiology are all agreed in rendering incredible the doctrine of the immortality of the soul, and modern biblical theologians are in agreement with this view.[6] For example, Karl Barth says: "We necessarily contradict the abstractly dualistic conception which so far we have summarily called Greek, but which unfortunately must also be described as the traditional Christian view. . . . It was disastrous that this picture of man could assert and maintain itself for so long as the Christian picture. We must earnestly protest that this is not the Christian picture."[7]

There are two important passages in the Bible where the undertones of the terms *anicca, dukkha,* and *anattā* occur together.

The first is Psalm 90: Man is turned back into dust from where he came (v. 3)—Man is *anattā.* His life is like a dream, like the grass that withers (v. 5). He is *anicca.* Even the short span of life is full of toil, trouble, and anxiety (vs. 9–10—the Jerusalem Bible uses the word "anxiety"). Life is *dukkha.*[8]

The other passage is Rom. 8:18–25. In describing the human predicament St. Paul uses three terms in this passage, namely, *mataiotēs, pathēmata,* and *phthora,* which have close approximations to the Pali terms *anicca, dukkha,* and *anattā* respectively. The Buddhist overtones of the Greek words are striking. There are three things that stand out in this passage. *(a)* The whole creation is subject to vanity *(mataiotēs).* This means that all things are subject to corruption and decay; they are perishable since they are impermanent *(anicca). (b)* The whole creation is groaning in travail *(pathēmata).* That is what *dukkha* means. *(c)* The creature is subject to corruption *(phthora).* The Greek word means that the creature is subject to mortality, to decay and death *(jāti, marana).* This means that man is *anattā.*[9]

All in all, the Tilakkhana emphasizes man's nonegoity (*anattā*-ness). This concept is the bedrock of Buddhism. Man must realize his nonegoity and free himself from the false notions of I, Me, and Mine if he is to gain final liberation. Christian mystics also, as we shall see, stress this point. It has had a deep significance in Christian spirituality, which we have lost sight of.

It is in the Buddhist *nāma-rūpa* analysis that the fact of nonegoity is clearly shown. This is an analysis that Christian theology can assimilate.

According to the biblical view, man is a psychophysical unity, of "soul" *(psychē)* and "flesh" *(sarx).* This bears a close resemblance to the Buddhist analysis of man in terms of *nāma* (name) and *rūpa* (form). *Psychē,* like *nāma,* corresponds to the psychical aspect of man, which represents more or less those processes that come within the field of psychology, and *sarx,* like *rūpa,* corresponds to the physical processes with which the biologist is concerned. Both the Buddhist and the biblical views of man agree that there is no distinguishable, immortal soul within this psychophysical *(nama-rūpa)* aggregation which constitutes a person.

The Creature and the Creator

Buddhism and Christianity come to a realization of nonegoity in two different ways. Christianity begins by stressing the greatness and majesty of God the Creator in relation to whom man is insignificant, fragile, and weak, and apart from whom man is nothing. Buddhism begins by looking inward and seeing man's nothingness, and then something beyond is sought for. Perhaps the Buddha declined to say anything about God, because to assume that there is such a reality, which gives a sense of security, could be an obstacle for one [seeking] to realize and understand the fact of nonegoity or self-emptiness. The Christian view however is that man understands his creatureliness—nothingness—in relation to the Creator. Man is nothing-at-all in relation to the Creator, who is all-in-all.

The biblical doctrine of creation is a doctrine concerning the relationship between God the Creator and man the creature. It is not a phenomenological account of how all things were brought into being. Its primary interest is in the Creator-creature relationship and not in an empirical description of the tangible world of sense experience. The interest in the empirical world is that it is the environment in which the creature is placed, and the nature of which the creature shares. It is preeminently a religious affirmation about the sovereignty of God and the absolute dependence of the creature. The intention of the creation story in Genesis 1 is not to analyze man's essence or to define God's nature, but rather to indicate man's task and his relationship as creature to the Creator.

The Creator-creature relationship is best expressed in the doctrine of *creatio ex nihilo.* This doctrine has a twofold significance in the context of Buddhism. It implies the absolute impermanence *(anicca)* of all things apart from the Creator who maintains them in existence by the power of his word. As they were created out of nothing at his word, so they can vanish into nothingness at his word. As all things, including man, have been created out of nothing, so all things including man stand vis-à-vis the threat of nonbeing *(anattā* and *anicca*). On the other hand it implies the absolute Lordship of God over existence. In other words God is the Uncreated, man is the created; God is the *Asamkhata* (Unconditioned), man is the *saṃkhata* (conditioned).

It is significant to note that the first meditation in the *Introduction to the Devout Life*, by Francis de Sales, is on creation, in which man's "nothingness" before the Creator is stressed.[10] Thus we see the existential and spiritual significance of the doctrine of creation.

MAN'S NEED OF GOD

I believe that the biblical understanding of the Three Signata, especially *anattā*, can enable us to understand what the term "God" means. It is my contention that, if *anattā* is real, God is necessary; it is in relation to the Reality of God that the reality of *anattā* can be meaningful. Because man is *anattā*, God is indispensable; because man is absolutely *anattā*, God is absolutely necessary. The conditioned *(saṃkhata)* man has nothing to hope for unless there is an Unconditioned Reality *(asaṃkhata)*. It is in relation to the Unconditioned (God) that the full depth and significance of *anattā* can be understood.

To assert that man has within himself the intrinsic self-derived power to transcend conditioned existence is to deny the full import of *anattā*. If man can save himself, *anattā* is not real. Christianity takes the meaning of *anattā* in all its seriousness and denies any form of intrinsic power in man—be it karmic force or the power of mind, *viññāna*—by which he can save himself. For Christianity *anattā* means *anattā* in its fullest sense. As Karl Barth puts it, "Man without God is not; he has neither being nor existence."[11] I AM is the name of God (Ex. 3:14). It is he alone who can say "I AM." Therefore all that man can say is, "I am not."

To explain what this means we could employ the famous Udāna passage in the Pataligama Vagga of the *Khuddaka Nikāya:*

> Monks, there is *(atthi)* a not-born *(ajātam)*, a not-become *(abhūtam)*, a not-made *(akatam)*, a not-compounded *(asaṃkhatam)*. If that unborn, not-become, not-made, not-compounded were not, there would be apparent no escape from this here that is born, become, made, compounded. But since, monks, there is an unborn, unbecome, unmade, uncompounded, therefore is apparent the escape from this here that is born, become, made, compounded.

This is a passage that has deep implications for Christian theology. Firstly, this passage makes a distinction between the Transcendent (the not-born, the not-become, the not-made, the not-compounded), by whatever name it is called—Nirvana or God—and the transient (the born, the become, the made, the compounded), the existential components of which are *anicca, dukkha,* and *anattā*.

Secondly, the dimension of the Transcendent cannot be found in the transient, the finite, the linear, the purely human. It is something to which man can aspire to; not something that arises from the human condition.

Thirdly, the transient being has no hope apart from the Transcendent. This is strongly implied in the passage. It implies that the Unconditioned Reality *(Asaṃkhata)* is indispensable if man is to find freedom from conditioned existence; apart from the Unconditioned there is no escape for the conditioned. To put it in another way: if man is truly *anattā,* the hypothesis of the Unconditioned or some such hypothesis becomes absolutely necessary if the error of nihilism *(ucched adiṭṭhi)* is to be avoided. Apart from the Unconditioned Reality, there can be no emancipation for that which is conditioned; all that can be expected is total annihilation.

Finally, in spite of man's transience he can affirm that there is *(atthi)* a Transcendent Reality which stands beyond the flux of things. This affirmation cannot be self-derived; there must first be a Transcendent in order to affirm it. The Transcendent is prior to our affirmation of it. Man can affirm the Transcendent because man exists in relationship with the Transcendent. This is what enables me, against the threat of emptiness, meaninglessness, nothingness, and death, to affirm my identity, and the significance and value of my existence which drives me to find fullness of being. My awareness of my finitude drives me to search for plenitude. For the Buddhist the term Nirvana, and for the Christian the term God, signify that plentiude, although the two terms are not identical. The Christian finds this plenitude in a relationship with God.

MAN'S RELATIONSHIP TO GOD

Though man is *anattā,* he is able to ask the question about his destiny, analyze his nature as nonbeing, and evaluate the flux in which he is involved, and thereby transcend himself. He has a sense of the Transcendent. If man is aware of his nothingness *(anattā),* he must be something more than nothing. Man transcends his *anattā*-hood by questioning his very nature of finitude. In other words, there is a transcendental quality in man which enables him to rise above his finite existence and affirm the Transcendent. But this transcendental quality is not a natural property of the human structure as such. It cannot be identified with any natural self-derived power in man. If there is some such power, it would nullify and contradict our insistence on the truth of *anattā.* If *anattā* is understood in its final depth, this transcendental quality cannot be found as a natural quality in man himself or derived from existence itself. This sense of transcendence is derived from the Transcendent. If there is no

Transcendent Reality, there can be no awareness of it. The Transcendent is prior to our awareness of it.

This transcendental quality is to be found in man's relationship to God. This is what is meant when we say that man is created in the image of God. "Image" does not mean physical likeness. It means that man has a relationship to God. To signify this relationship the distinctive word *pneuma* (spirit) is used in the New Testament (the parallel Hebrew word in the Old Testament is *ruach*). This word is used in different senses. When used with the article *pneuma* denotes the Spirit of God; without the article it denotes the dimension *created* in man which enables him to have communion with God. The human spirit is never used in the sense of a divine spark within man. As an ordinary element in man, which has no divinity in itself, *pneuma* in man has nothing common with the Divine Spirit, except that it can be energized by the Divine Spirit. The spirit in man is not a thing or some kind of substance; it is not a soul entity. It is a dimension in man which makes him more than a mere psychophysical organism, differentiates him from animals, plants, sticks, and stones, and makes it possible for him to enter into a relationship with God. We could thus say that spirit is the principle of man's relation to God in which alone he can find authentic being.

This principle has two aspects: mutuality and transcendence. It is in mutuality that a person as a person emerges in community. The self-integration of a person as a person happens in the encounter of person with person and in no other way. Personal life cannot be actualized apart from community. In this personal-communal relationship, a person reaches beyond himself to the other with whom he is related. In this reaching out he transcends himself. But this is the work of the Divine Spirit who grasps him and lifts him to a transcendent state. It is only through the Divine Spirit that the self can go beyond the self as self. The Divine Spirit is the Unconditional in the conditioned, driving the conditioned beyond itself; it is the Uncreated in the created, grasping and drawing the creature out of itself into a relationship with God and man.

Anattā and *pneuma* are interrelated. The more one realizes one's self-emptiness (*anattā*-ness), the more one realizes one's spiritfulness (*pneuma*-ness). Taken together, *anattā-pneuma* helps us to understand the true nature of the self or personhood. There are three aspects in which we could see the mutual relation of *anattā* and *pneuma,* each enriching, deepening, and filling up the gaps in the other.

There is firstly the psychophysical or *nāma-rūpa* aspect. Here *anattā* means rejection of *atta* or an eternal self or soul. Buddhism is unique in its rejection of any permanent entity within man. This is a corrective to the wrong notion that has invaded popular Christian thinking. Christian theology can be greatly enriched by the absorption of the *anattā* doctrine into its system of thought. However, the *pañcakkandha* analysis seems to reduce man to a psychosomatic organism. But *pneuma* points to a dimension of reality which cannot be exhausted by a scientific or psychological analysis of finite life; it signifies that extra dimension of finite life which is constitutive of authentic being which makes a person more than a bundle of aggregates or merely a psychophysical organism or an unusually complex animal. *Pneuma* is not some kind of "thing" or a substance parallel to the substance of physical entities; it is a dynamic quality of being which lifts man above finite existence through his relationship with the Divine Spirit.

There is secondly the ethicosocial aspect. Ethically *anattā* means nonattachment, particularly to the false notion of the self or soul, which is the root cause of all evil. Relinquishing self, abolishing self, is therefore the primary concern in Buddhism. It is the concern of every religion. But Buddhism stands unique in its ethical discipline designed to root out everything that inflames the self. But, overstressing nonattachment from a purely individualistic point of view can lead to isolation and a socially irrelevant ethic. *Pneuma* affirms this social dimension. It signifies the fact that to be is to be related: "all existence is coexistence." Man is therefore a socially responsible being. Authentic being is not what one attains for oneself, but something that is shared; something that brings persons into relationships with one another. Love is the basis of this shared life. It is love alone that is capable of uniting persons in such a way as to negate exclusive individuality and to complete and fulfill personality. But if one is not disciplined in nonattachment and forgets the ideal of self-obliteration, one will turn love, and interpersonal relationship into a selfish game. Therefore *anattā,* with its stress on nonattachment, will always be a safeguard against such a danger, and *pneuma* with its stress on mutual relations is a safeguard against individualism.

There is thirdly the transcendental aspect. *Anattā* implies the realization of emptiness; the fully realized man is totally emptied of self. That realization is *Nirvana.* It is an experience in which self has been completely transcended; an experience of supreme bliss when nothing of self remains. Buddhism stresses that this does not mean annihilation. How can we understand this paradox? The *pneuma* concept provides one way of understanding it. *Pneuma* signifies that capacity for transcending oneself, of going out of oneself and beyond oneself, of losing oneself in communion with Reality. The more a person goes beyond himself, the more is the spiritual dimension of his life deepened, the more he becomes a true person. In transcending oneself one ceases to be a self-contained entity; but selfhood is always being fulfilled by being transcended.

Pneuma signifies communion, not union or absorption. The underlying principle is that communion differentiates by negating exclusive individuality and by perfecting personality. Personal identity will be retained in a complete harmony without that identity being expressed in the exclusiveness of self-contained individuality.

Anattā serves to stress the nonegocentric or selfless aspect and *pneuma* the relational and transcendental aspects of personhood. Thus, the *anattā-pneuma* formula captures in a nutshell, as it were, the essence of the nature of man. It points to three dimensions in man: selflessness, mutuality, and transcendence—the inward, the horizontal, and the vertical—which are essential in man's quest of a full humanity.

Meaning of the Term "Christ"

For the Christian the eternally existent unborn, unbecome, not-made, and Unconditioned—the Logos, the Word, the Dharma—was fully manifest in Jesus Christ. He is preexistent and eternally present reality— "Before Abraham was I am." In him, in his incarnation, there was a unique relation between the conditioned and the Unconditioned. This truth can be best understood in the light of the well-known passage, Phil. 2:7-11, in which St. Paul speaks of the *kenōsis* of our Lord. The deep significance of kenotic Christology can be understood in terms of the *Tilakkhana* when it is seen not as the emptying of the divinity of our Lord, but as the negation of the self in which the divinity of love is disclosed. In this self-emptying there is nothing of self to be seen—no notion of I, Me, Mine—but only the Ultimate, Unconditional love of God.

The essential principle of the divine *kenōsis,* based on the conception of self-emptying, is that Christ negated himself without losing himself. By his identity with conditioned existence he negated himself; but because of his identity with the Unconditioned (God), he did not lose himself. This identity was a relationship between the conditioned and the Unconditioned. But it was unique in that it was a relationship concerning the unconditioned identity of the conditioned and the Unconditioned. This is the principle of *kenōsis,* which has affinities with the Buddhist doctrine of *Sunyatā* (the doctrine of the void).

The kenotic principle must be understood in the light of the death and resurrection of Jesus Christ. In Christian piety this has meant that one must die to self in order to rise to new life. The ethical aspect of this truth is well expressed in the words of Jesus: "If any man would come after me, let him deny himself, and take up his cross and follow me. For whoever would save his life will lose it, and whoever loses his life for my sake will find it" (Matt. 16:24–25; Luke 9:23–24). William Barclay commenting on this verse says:

> To deny ourselves is to say, "I do not know myself." It is to ignore the very existence of oneself. It is to treat the self as if it did not exist. Usually we treat ourselves as if our self was far and away the most important thing in the world. If we are to follow Jesus we must obliterate self and forget that self exists.[12]

In the words of Jesus there is implied the principle of negation ("he that loseth himself") and elevation ("shall find himself"). This is the universal principle in all religions—negation-elevation or death-resurrection—which is particularized in different ways. Authentic life consists in the activation of this principle in theory and practice. Self-negating (or self-effacing) and self-elevating love is the moving pattern of the spiritual life. Negation-elevation is not an experience exclusive to Christians. It is a universal experience. But for the Christian it is an experience grounded on the fact of the death and resurrection of Jesus the Christ, which for him is ultimately archetypal.

To be in Christ, to lose oneself "for my sake," means to experience negation *(sunyatā)* and elevation *(puññatā)*. It is the experience of emptiness and fullness *(sunyatā-puññatā)*. It is when we are empty of self-fulness that we can be filled with truth-fulness. Although we can experience negation and elevation in varying degrees in everyday life, it is through progressive sanctification that perfection can be reached.

PROGRESSIVE SANCTIFICATION

Modern theologians have found the notions that at death a person passes into either everlasting happiness in heaven or everlasting damnation in hell as literalistic distortions of biblical symbols. Today theologians speak of progressive sanctification which begins here and now and continues after death.

Heaven is a symbol for the fruition of life toward which a person advances till he reaches the goal which is identified with the "beatific vision"—that direct and indubitable awareness of God. Man advances toward this goal by overcoming self-centeredness—the egocentric notion of I, Me, Mine. He must realize that he is *anattā*. In the words of Romano Guardini, "death upon death has to be endured so that new life may arise."[13] It is by transcending the self that one grows into the likeness of Christ and so becomes "perfect as (our) heavenly Father is perfect."

Rightly interpreted, then, heaven is neither mythological nor egocentric but the progressive fruition of life, the upper limit of which is fullness of being or perfect communion with God.

Some, mainly Protestants, prefer to call "progressive sanctification after death" the "intermediate state," and some, mainly Roman Catholics, "purgatory." In spite of the aversion Protestants have to the idea of purgatory, mistakenly thought of as a state of mere suffering, it is being increasingly recognized that this notion, when rightly understood, is entirely appropriate, for it points to the process by which one is purged of all egocentric elements, purified, and fitted for one's ultimate destiny. Hell, heaven, and purgatory are not sharply separated states, but form a kind of continuum through which one passes from even the "utter state" of near-annihilation which is called hell, to the closest union with God. Thus hell is also a phenomenon within this continuum and can be experienced here and now, and even after death, in varying degrees.

Progressive sanctification is the Christian alternative to the theory of rebirth. If *anattā* is real, there cannot be natural survival. From the Christian point of view, to affirm the continuity of one's own karmic force or memory contradicts the truth of *anattā*. If *anicca* and *anattā* are real, there can be nothing in man that can survive death. In the Christian view, it is only by an act of re-creation that continuity beyond the grave is possible. This is what resurrection means. Resurrection is most meaningful in the context of *Tilakkhana.*

RESURRECTION

The doctrine of resurrection contradicts the notion of the immortal soul within man which survives death. It emphasizes the fact of man's mortality, that man comes to a total end at death. Therefore he has to be recalled to life by a new act of creation. As Oscar Cullmann puts it: "Resurrection is a positive assertion; the whole man who has really died is recalled to life by a new act of creation by God. Something has happened—a miracle of creation! For something has also happened previously, something fearful: life formed by God has been destroyed."[14]

There are two well-known and significant Scripture passages which have a particular relevance in this connection. They are I Cor. 15:35–58 and II Cor. 5:1–5. The fact of *anicca* is stressed in these passages. Man by nature is perishable and "mortal" (I Cor. 15:53, 54). He is like a *tent,* fragile and temporary, which will be destroyed at death (II Cor. 5:1). And in this tent man experiences the fact of *dukkha,* for "here indeed we groan" and "sigh with anxiety" (II Cor. 5:2,4). There is no suggestion or hint in these passages that man has an immortal soul. We, like Adam, are of "dust," and "flesh and blood cannot inherit the kingdom of God," neither does "the perishable inherit the imperishable" (I Cor. 15:47, 48, 50). Thus man is *anattā*. These verses also stress that there is no natural survival. Man never rises from the dead; he is raised (I Cor. 15:42–44). And when he is raised God gives "a body as he has chosen" (I Cor. 15:38) and not one that develops naturally from the previous one. When this earthly tent is destroyed "we have a building from God, a house not made with hands" (II Cor. 5:1). It is all God's doing.

The analogy of the seed (I Cor. 15:36–37) may give the impression that the dead body has the power of germination in it like the seed. Strictly speaking, the seed does not die in the way that a man dies, and there is nothing that sprouts up from the dead body as a shoot sprouts up from a seed. We must not press this analogy too far and read something into it which Paul did not have in mind. All that Paul wants to say is that there is an analogy in nature to show that death is not the end. He did not believe that there was a power of germination embedded in the dead body from which would sprout up or grow another kind of body by a natural process of development. He stresses that it is by a miraculous act of creation that a person is raised from the dead, and not by any inherent power which he possesses as a natural right.

This does not mean that this earthly body is unimportant. The spiritual body, though it is not the natural outcome of the physical body, is related to it, for God gives a body as he has chosen, "to each kind of seed its own body" (I Cor. 15:38). What we do in our body is important, "For we must all appear before the judgment seat of Christ, so that each one may receive good or evil according to what he has done in the body" (II Cor. 5:10; see also Rom. 2:6–7; Gal. 6:7–8; Col. 3:24–25; I Peter 3:17; Rev. 2:23).

The word "immortality" occurs twice in I Cor. 15:53, 54. It occurs only once more in the New Testament, and that is in I Tim. 6:16, where it refers only to God. For Paul it is clear that immortality does not belong to man by nature; it is "put on" when man is raised from the dead. The notion of an immortal soul finds no place in these two passages. In Paul's thought, resurrection is not the result of immortality; immortality is what is *given* in the resurrection.

Thus we see that the Christian hope of survival rests solely on the doctrine of God and not on any theory of man's intrinsic capacity to survive death. There is nothing in man, however noble, which does not bear the marks of *anicca, dukkha,* and *anattā* in the strictest sense of the words. Thus the doctrine of resurrection is wholly in keeping with the doctrine of *anattā*.

ETERNAL LIFE

The Bible teaches that man was created for communion with God but he has fallen short of the ideal. The goal of life is to enter into perfect communion with God. This can be done through progressive sanctification in which the egocentric life of craving and self-interest come to an end with the realization that separate individuality bound up with the notion of I, Me, and Mine is a false notion. This realization in one sense could be called *nirvana*. Therefore progressive sanctification is a process of "nirvanizing" oneself: continually realizing one's nonegoity, and the consequent sense of bliss.

In the Christian tradition there is something strikingly analogous to the Buddhist view of the need to strip oneself of the notion of I, Me, and Mine. Summarizing this central feature of Christian mysticism, Evelyn Underhill says:

> All mystics agree that the stripping off of personal initiative, the I, the Me, the Mine, utter renouncement, or self-naughting—self-abandonment to the direction of a larger Will—is an imperative condition of the attainment of the unitive life. The temporary denudation of the mind, whereby the contemplative made space for the vision of God, must now be applied to the whole life. Here, they say, there is final swallowing up of the wilful I-hood which we ordinarily recognize as ourselves. It goes for ever, and something new is established in its room. The self is made part of the mystical Body of God; and, humbly, taking its place in the corporate life of Reality, would "fain be to the Eternal Goodness what his own hand is to a man."[15]

The "unitive life" in which I-hood is swallowed up does not mean absorption but communion or participation. Communion is not absorption into distinctionless union, but is participation in which the person retains his differentiation as a person without the mark of exclusive individuality being expressed in it. The person loses his exclusiveness completely through participation but discovers his authentic selfhood through communion. The I-Thou relationship in which alone a person exists on earth will be perfected and fulfilled in the end when the I and the Thou meet inherently in union and distinction. In communion, individual identity is preserved within a harmony without the implications of exclusiveness that the notion of I, Me, and Mine entails. In the end we shall be fully persons and cease completely to be individuals in the exclusive sense. We shall retain identity within a complete harmony. The relationship in which we live on earth will be progressively sanctified until we reach perfect communion with God. This relationship is like the relationship of the center to the circle within which it is. The center is identifiable only within the circle. There is no question of dualism here. The I and the Thou meet inherently in union and distinction.

A Socially Relevant Ethic

What bearing has the theology we have outlined for a socially relevant ethic and for practical, meaningful living? What is human nature? From our earlier discussion three points emerge—three aspects or dimensions of human nature. Christianity emphasizes *mutuality*, the I-Thou relationship; Buddhism emphasizes *selflessness* (non-egoity or *anattā*-ness), and both emphasize *transcendence*, an ultimate reality toward which man inclines. They are, as already indicated, the horizontal, the inward, and the vertical dimensions.

By mutuality we mean right-relatedness. That means to be rightly related to one another, overcoming alienation of man from man. It means to be other-oriented. Secular ideologies have stressed this aspect of man's mutuality. Karl Marx said: "The human essence is no abstraction inherent in each single individual. In reality it is the ensemble of social relations."[16] Marx's social philosophy was based on an anthropology according to which man is a species being. Marx, being a Jew, owed much to the biblical view of man. Martin Buber refers to his view of man, as a species being existing in relationships, as a Copernican revolution of modern thought. The man who is rightly related is one who has a deep concern for social justice and the removal of those things that create divisiveness between man and man. Thus, we could say that the concern of a Marxist for the abolition of class distinctions is a spiritual concern. Anything that is done compassionately to remove alienation of man from man, whether by the so-called religious men or by the so-called secular men, is spiritual.

This understanding enables us to see morality in its right perspective, not as the observance of rigid absolute laws but as responsible living for the good of one another. Morality is not the adherence to inflexible absolute laws. Moral principles are situationally adaptable for responsible living for the common good of man. This is what it means to be a socialist man. In Christian terms this is what "love thy neighbor" means. In the parable of the good Samaritan the "neighbor" was a *victim*. Today we should specially think of our neighbors as *victims* of oppression and exploitation. To love one's neighbor therefore means to have empathy with these victims and uphold their cause in word and deed.

By selflessness or nonegoity we mean the realization that one is nothing in himself. It means that man is *anattā*. It means overcoming the notion of I, Me, and Mine that stands in the way of right relationships.

To be rightly related to others one must be rightly related within, because the causes that separate man from man are within man himself. "What causes wars, and what causes fightings among you?" asks St. James; "Is it not your passions that are at war in your members? You desire and do not have; so you kill. And you covet and cannot obtain; so you fight and wage war" (James 4:1–2). In one word it is selfishness or *tanhā* and everything that promotes selfishness that must be removed.

Right-relatedness means a fundamental change in attitude, a basic change in mind, a prerequisite for change in society. Revolutionaries and peacemakers have recognized this principle. The well-known Cuban revolutionary, Ché Guevara, recognized this truth. It is said that his whole outlook was governed by one fundamental principle, "that no matter how much you change society, no matter how much you restructure it, unless you create a new man, unless you change his attitudes, it all ends up in greed, lust and ambition."[17] There can be no new society without a new man. A statement of the purpose of UNESCO reads, "Since wars begin in the minds of man, it is in the minds of man that the defence of peace must be constructed."

To this end it is necessary that the egocentric life of craving and self-interest be conquered by the deliberate denying of the self. Arnold Toynbee sees the overcoming of self-centeredness as the key to peace. He says:

> For a true and lasting peace, a religious revolution is, I am sure, a *sine qua non*. By religion I mean the overcoming of self-centredness, in both individuals and communities, by getting into communion with the spiritual presence behind the universe and by bringing our wills into harmony with it. I think it is the only key to peace, but we are very far from picking up this key and using it, and until we do, the survival of the human race will continue to be in doubt.[18]

As seen in the above passage, overcoming self-centeredness also implies transcendence. This is the third dimension—transcendence. It is in the very nature of man to transcend himself, to incline toward an ultimate reality—Nibbana, God. Carl Jung pointed out that inborn in man is a psychic aptitude for the beyond, the transcendent. The love shining from the eyes of a bride; a scientist's devotion to his research; a mother's concern for her son; the haunting sweetness of music; the sense of wonder at the radiance of the sunset; the sense of immensity at the sight of the starry skies; the compulsion to reason, to question; the never-ceasing creative urge in man to create something new and higher and not remain satisfied with what is; the experience of nullity or "*anattā*-ness" which makes him realize that there is something beyond the born, the made, the created; and the quest for meaning—these are all experiences that bring us to the threshold of something more. Even in atheism there is a dimension of transcendence, for atheism is a protest in the name of hope for the not yet comprehended. Man inclines toward this something-more, "the spiritual presence behind the universe" in veneration, aspiration, hope, and worship. In Marxism and other social ideologies, transcendence finds expression in faith-decisions made in hope oriented toward a glorious future; it creates a sense of glory. In religions this hope is oriented to a glorious future even beyond the grave. This also creates a sense of glory which finds expression in worship. In theistic religions transcendence is based on a personal God. Transcendence is a summons from the Beyond that enables man to go beyond himself, by which alone he can discover authentic selfhood.

The quality of transcendence is in every man, whether he be a materialist, a Marxist, a Hindu, a Buddhist, a Muslim, or a Christian. There is a beyond in science: the wonder and mystery of the immense range of depths in physical matter. There is a beyond in reason: an ever-receding something beyond the grasp of the mind—the inexplicable—what Buddhists have called *avyakata*. These point to an ultimate Beyond which gives meaning to the proximate beyonds—the experience of transcendence in everyday life. Even after a hearty meal in a classless society there will still be a hunger for something MORE—for the BEYOND.

Religions have generally tended to emphasize inwardness (a characteristic particularly of renascent religions) to the neglect of social action, and social ideologies have tended to emphasize social action to the neglect of inwardness. The understanding of human nature consisting of the three dimensions of mutuality, selflessness, and transcendence will perhaps lead us to participation in a common spirituality linking inwardness with action, solitary contemplation with mutuality, and transcendence with social involvement. A living theology should help to link these two aspects, which are essential for the realization of full humanity.

NOTES

1. Friedrich Nietzsche, *Thus Spoke Zarathustra,* Pt. I, Ch. 9.
2. Paul Tillich, *The Courage to Be* (Yale University Press, 1952), p. 27.
3. Ibid., pp. 35–36.
4. John Macquarrie, *Studies in Christian Existentialism,* pp. 115–116.
5. Edward Conze describes *dukkha* as existential anxiety, accepting that "the existentialist diagnosis of the plight of human existence agrees with that of

the Buddhists." See his *Thirty Years of Buddhist Studies,* p. 210. A. D. P. Kanansuriya draws parallels between Buddhist existentialism and modern existentialism. See *Buddhist Annual* (Colombo: M. D. Gunasena & Co., 1967), pp. 75, 77.

6. See Lynn de Silva, *The Problem of the Self in Buddhism and Christianity,* Ch. 8.

7. Karl Barth, *Church Dogmatics* (Edinburgh: T. & T. Clark, 1960), III, 2, pp. 380, 382.

8. For a detailed exposition, see Samuel Amirtham (ed.), *A Vision for Man,* pp. 89–90.

9. See the exposition of this passage in *Asian Voices in Christian Theology,* p. 44.

10. St. Francis de Sales, *Introduction to the Devout Life,* p. 48. There is a meditation on death too, p. 55.

11. Barth, *Church Dogmatics,* III, 2, p. 345.

12. William Barclay, Daily Study Bible, *The Gospel of Luke* (Westminster Press, 1956), p. 122.

13. Romano Guardini, *The Last Things,* p. 46.

14. Oscar Cullmann, *Immortality of the Soul or Resurrection of the Dead?* (Macmillan Co., 1958), p. 27.

15. Evelyn Underhill, *Mysticism,* pp. 497–498.

16. Karl Marx, *Selections in Feuerbach,* p. 244.

17. *Venceremos! The Speeches and Writings of Che Guevara,* ed. by John Gerassi (Simon & Schuster, 1969), p. 48.

18. A. J. Toynbee, *Surviving the Future,* pp. 44–45.

Nineteen

Toward an Asian Theology of Liberation: Some Religiocultural Guidelines

Aloysius Pieris, S.J.

[Fr. Pieris' paper has been called "the richest single dish" on the menu at the Asian Conference of Third World Theologians, and yet also one of the most controversial because it does not rest content merely to apply Latin American liberation theology uncritically to the Asian scene, as other delegates seemed so ready to do. Any theology that is contextually Asian, says Pieris, must grapple with two interpenetrating realities: Asia's poverty, which identifies her with the Third World, and her religiosity, which defines her specific character as Asian. It is the latter pole, however, that offers the greatest potentiality, in his view, for creating an Asian theology that will radically differ from both Latin American and African theologies. This selection includes Parts I and III of a longer paper, Part II focusing naturally on Buddhism as a paradigm of Asian religiosity. He points out that "a 'liberation theopraxis' in Asia which uses only the Marxist tools of social analysis will remain un-Asian and ineffective till it integrates the psychological tools of introspection which our sages have discovered" (p. 43). This leads to a discussion in Part III of the Asian style of doing theological reflection which, he concludes, "is itself Asian theology." In Asian terms, "theopraxis is already the formulation of theology."—Ed.]

TOWARD A DEFINITION
OF THE RELIGIOCULTURAL DIMENSION

This being a *Third World* theologians' *Asian* consultation, I presume that the theological axis of our deliberations should have, as its two poles, the *"Third World-ness"* of our continent and its peculiarly *Asian* character: two points of reference we must never lose sight of. Spelt out in more realistic terms, the common denominator between Asia and the rest of the Third World is its overwhelming *Poverty;* the specific character which defines Asia within the other poor countries is its multifaceted

Parts I and III of an article in *Dialogue* (Colombo), VI, 1 & 2 (Jan.–Aug. 1979), pp. 29–52. Reprinted by permission of the Ecumenical Institute for Study and Dialogue.

Religiosity. These are two inseparable realities which in their interpenetration constitute what might be designated as the *Asian Context* and
which is the matrix of any theology that is truly Asian.

We must immediately warn ourselves that Asian poverty cannot be
reduced to purely "economic" categories—as much as Asian religiosity
cannot be defined merely in "cultural" terms. They are both interwoven
culturally and economically to constitute the vast sociopolitical reality
that Asia is. Hence an Asian theologian can hardly ignore Roy Preiswerk's appeal[1] that the "dependency theories" of the Latin Americans
(Cardos, Frank, Furtado, etc.), which offer valid explanations of and
useful strategies against the increasing poverty in the Third World, ought
to be complemented (and, I would add, even corrected) by the "cultural
approach" of social scientists.

This is nowhere more applicable than in Asia, for there is in our
cultural ethos "a yet-undiscovered point" at which *Poverty* and *Religiosity* seem to coalesce in order to procreate the Asian character of this
continent. In fact, history attests, as we shall indicate later, that the
theological attempts to encounter Asian religions with no radical concern for Asia's poor and the *ideological* programs that eradicate Asia's
poverty with naive disregard for its religiosity have both proved to be a
misdirected zeal. Hence the theologies now prevalent in the Asian
church and the secular ideologies presently operating in this continent
have all to be judged in the light of this axiom, as will be done in the
course of our discussion.

Without, therefore, diluting or deemphasizing the economic features
that define the "Third World-ness" of Asia, I am compelled here, by the
organizers, to concentrate on the "religiocultural" dimension of the
Asian context. As it might be objected that such a dimension exists also
in all other poor countries, let me straightaway name three distinctive
features which clearly demarcate the religiocultural boundaries of Asia
within the Third World. They are: *(a)* linguistic heterogeneity; *(b)* the
integration of the cosmic and the metacosmic elements in Asian religions; and *(c)* the overwhelming presence of non-Christian soteriologies.

Linguistic Heterogeneity

Asia is diversified into at least seven major linguistic zones, the highest
that any continent can boast of. There is, first of all, the *Semitic* zone,
concentrated in the Western margin of Asia. The *Ural-Altaic* group is
spread all over Asiatic Russia and Northwest Asia. The *Indo-Iranian*
stock alongside the *Dravidian* races have their cultural habitat in Southern Asia. The *Sino-Tibetan* region, by far the largest, extends from

Central Asia to the Far East. The *Malayo-Polynesian* wing opens out to the Southeast. Last but not least is the uncatalogable *Japanese,* forming a self-contained linguistic unit in the Northeastern tip of Asia.

The first theological implication of this linguistic heterogeneity derives from the very understanding of "language." According to a nominalist view, a truth is apprehended intuitively and is *then* expressed outwardly through a language. If this were true, communal disturbances between linguistic groups—such as those in Sri Lanka or Cambodia or Burma—would have to be explained purely in terms of political and economic factors, which is not the case.

The fact, however, is that each language is a *distinctly new way* of "experiencing" the truth, implying that linguistic pluralism is an index of religious, cultural, and sociopolitical diversity. Zaehner seems to be implying this when he, too easily perhaps, typifies the whole Western religiosity as "Semitic" and the Eastern religiosity as "Indian."[2] I think it is only partially true to say that religion is an "experience" of Reality and language is its "expression"; the converse is closer to the Truth: *language is the "experience" of Reality and religion is its "expression."* Religion begins with language. Would it be wrong to say that language is a *theologia inchoativa*—an incipient theology?

And what is the fundamental Reality that a particular culture grasps through its own language and symbol? Read what the Asian proletariat has produced over the centuries, and not merely the sophisticated writings such as the Vedas and Upanishads, the Tripitaka, the Torah, or the Tao Te Ching. Learn, first, the folk language. Assist at their rites and rituals; hear their songs; vibrate with their rhythms; keep step with their dance; taste their poems; grasp their myths; reach them through their legends. You will find that the language they speak puts them in touch with the basic Truths that every religion grapples with, but *each in a new way:* the meaning and destiny of human existence; Man's crippling limitations and his infinite capacity to break through them; liberation both human and cosmic; in short, *the struggle for a full humanity.*

Every Asian culture, therefore, has grown round a soteriological nucleus which has not yet been assimilated into the Christian conscience. The Asian theology of liberation lies hidden there, waiting to be discovered by whoever is ready to "sell all things." For a recovery of an ancient revelation is indeed a new creation.

This means that the task of the Asian theologian is more complex than that of his colleagues in the North Atlantic region and the Southern Hemisphere. After all, do not the European theologians communicate in the same Indo-Germanic languages? Even liberation theologians think, act, and speak in a common Latin idiom. They are all within reach of one another by means of a European medium of communication. Such is not the case here.

It is therefore regrettable that Asians (like the Africans at the Conference in Ghana) are not able to consult each other's hidden theologies except in a non-Asian idiom, thus neutralizing the most promising feature in our methodology. We Asians professionally theologize in English, the language in which most of us think, read, and pray. The theological Language in a "continent of languages" has been grossly underestimated, and our stubborn refusal to consult each other's treasures directly in each other's linguistic idioms, or even to be familiar with *one's own cultural heritage,* will remain one major obstacle to the discovery of a truly Asian theology. This is not an appeal for chauvinism but a plea for authenticity imposed on us by what we have defined as the Asian Context. The foundation for a genuinely *Asian* consultation must be laid here at this Conference.

Integration of the Cosmic and the Metacosmic in Asian Religiosity

The institutional framework within which Asian religiosity operates is composed of two complementary elements: a *Cosmic Religion* functioning as the foundation, and a *Metacosmic Soteriology* constituting the main edifice.

By the term "cosmic religion" I wish to designate that species of religion which is found in Africa and Oceania and has been *pejoratively* referred to as "animism" by certain Western authors. Actually it represents the basic pyschological posture that the *homo religiosus* (residing in each one of us) adopts subconsciously toward the mysteries of life; a sane attitude which an unwise use of technology can disturb. They relate to the cosmic forces—heat, fire, winds and cyclones, earth and its quakes, oceans, rains and floods—which we need and yet fear. They serve as ambivalent symbols of our own subconscious powers, symbols freely employed in ordinary speech and in sacred rites, as expressive of our deepest yearnings. Even in the West where these natural elements serve man through technology, can the Christian celebrate the Paschal mystery without using fire and water? After all, if the theory of evolution is really true, we were all once a mountain, the crust of the earth, the water and the fire, and all that we now carry with us as our material substratum, by which we become sacramentally present to others and to ourselves. We cannot be fully human without them.

In our cultures these natural elements and forces merge into the mysterious world of invisible powers which maintain the cosmic balance.

They may appear in various guises in various regions: *devas* in the Indianized cultures of Southeast Asia; *Nats* in Burma; *Phis* in Thailand, Laos, and Cambodia; *Bons* in Tibet; *kamis* in Japan; and, of course, in the Confucianist world view, the departed *ancestors* belong to this invisible sphere. Rites, rituals, and a class of mediators form the constitutive elements of this religiosity.

The characteristic feature of Asian religiosity is that, unlike in Africa or in Oceania, this cosmic religion does not appear in its pure and primordial form except in certain isolated pockets which anthropologists frequent. It has practically been domesticated and integrated into one or the other of the three *metacosmic soteriologies,* namely, *Hinduism, Buddhism,* and to some extent *Taoism.* The summum bonum they present is a "Transphenomenal Beyond" which is to be realized here and now through *gnōsis.* This justifies the existence of a certain spiritual elite, the wise men, who become the personal embodiments of the *mysticomonastic* idealism held out as the climax of human perfection. They serve as models and the symbols of "liberated persons."

Hence it is also true that the metacosmic soteriologies mentioned above are never found in abstract "textual" form but always "contextualized" within the world view of the "cosmic religion" of a given culture, creating a twofold level of religious experience well integrated into each other. Here the Asian Context differs from the African, because, owing to this superimposition, cosmic religions, unlike in Africa, are *not regarded as salvific.* This is of great consequence for Asian theology. Let me mention in passing that it is invariably at the cosmic level that both technological and sociopolitical activity affect the major religions: a fact which we shall discuss later.

(One might say, parenthetically, that the establishment of biblical religions, such as Islam in Indonesia and Catholicism in the Philippines, was easier partly because "cosmic religions" were found there in almost pure forms at that time; whereas in Sri Lanka, India, Burma, and other countries, neither Islam nor Christianity could sweep over these cultures because the aforesaid gnostic soteriologies had already domesticated cosmic religions into a well integrated cultural system.)

These facts have hardly engaged the attentions of Asian theologians but have been a major preoccupation of anthropologists doing fieldwork in Asia.[3] The terms "cosmic" and "metacosmic" used here, however, have not been borrowed directly from anthropologists but derived from a Buddhist self-understanding of the two levels: *Lokiya* (Sinh. *Laukika*) and *Lok'uttara* (Sinh. *Lokottara*). Buddhists recognize the two dimensions and explain their own religious experience in terms of this distinction.

My reference to Buddhism here is not accidental. To sharpen our focus on Asian religiosity, it is only reasonable that I should concentrate on one of the major religions. If my choice falls on Buddhism, it is not only because I would be traversing familiar grounds, but even more because it is the one religion which is *pan-Asian* in cultural integration, numerical strength, geographical extension, and political maturity. Though an integral part of the Indian heritage, now preserved in its Indian form only here in Sri Lanka, it had penetrated practically every linguistic zone—even the Semitic, for a brief period.[4] In other words, Buddhism is not limited to one language or national group—as in the case of Hinduism and Taoism. By allowing itself to be shaped by the various "cosmic religions" of Asia, it has in turn molded several Asian cultures. Thus today there is an Asian Buddhist for every Roman Catholic in the world. There are at least twenty political territories in Asia where Buddhism is either the official religion or a culturally influential factor. It is the one religion that can boast of an Asia-wide ecumenical organization such as the World Fellowship of Buddhists (WFB), or the World Buddhist Sangha Council (WBSC), or the World Buddhist Social Service (WBSS), all of which look to Sri Lanka for leadership. It is also politically the most resilient of Asian religions with a major role to play in the development and liberation of Asia—for it has a rich experience of Western colonialism as well as of Marxism. Hence no Asian theology of liberation can be construed without consulting Asian Buddhism.

While Buddhism, we grant, does not exhaust the whole phenomenon of Asian religiosity, it will nevertheless serve us as a mere paradigm to demonstrate how the interplay of the cosmic and the metacosmic levels of religious experience gives a new point of departure for politicosocial change and technocratic advancement in the very process of Asia's liberation; something that neither Western technocracy nor scientific socialism has sufficiently appreciated and which Asian theologians cannot underestimate.

The Overwhelming Presence
of Non-Christian Soteriologies

Asia is the cradle of all the scriptural religions of the world, including Christianity which, however, left Asia very early and forced its way back several centuries later as a stranger and an "intruder" whom Asia consistently refused to entertain. Thus with four centuries of missionary presence the Christians are numerically and qualitatively an insignificant minority: a sheer 2 percent of the Asian masses. A good half of this Christian population is in the Philippines, which, in the process of becoming Christian, was forced to cut off its Asian roots. The Philippine church is only a magnified version of most Christian communities scattered in the Asian Diaspora. Can a Christianity that has lost its "Asian Sense" presume to create an Asian theology? Even the churches of the Oriental Rites have frozen their early enthusiasm for the Asian Reality.

However, this limitation is also the greatest potentiality the Asian church possesses of creating a Third World theology that will radically differ from the South American and the African theologies. The liberation theologians of Latin America can speak of Christ and his liberation as a national and continental concern because of their traditional Christian heritage. This is why they are able to offer us a relevant Christian theology in place of the classical one of the European churches. So can the Africans become soon, numerically and qualitatively, a powerful Christian voice within the Third World. But Asia, as circumstances clearly indicate, will remain always a non-Christian continent.

This situation is ambivalent. It creates enormous opportunities for more creative modes of Christian presence in Asia by humble participation in the non-Christian experience of liberation; or it can repeat past mistakes in radically new ways.

THE ASIAN SENSE IN THEOLOGY

To predispose ourselves to receive the *Asian Sense* into our Christian consciousness, certain inhibitions inherited from the local churches of the West need first to be eliminated. Consistent with the methodology so far pursued in our investigation, this review of our theological past must also be made *(a)* from the *Third World point of view* in general and *(b)* from the *Asian point of view* in particular. The content of an Asian theology, however, does not concern us here. All we hope to achieve by this critique is to discover the *Asian Style of doing theology.*

A Third World Critique of Our Theological Past

In the course of our discussion we met two "secular" movements engaged in liberating us from our "poverty"; both have originated in the West; the first is *Marxist socialism;* and the other is the *development ideology* associated with capitalist technocracy. The West is also "spiritually" present through the church which, for the most part, is an extension of Western Christianity. Thus the church too reflects, in her own *theological* self-understanding, the *ideological* conflicts of the West.

The Asian church, for the moment, has no theology of her own, though the cultures that host her teem with them. She is today caught between two "theologies" which are as "Western" as the secular ideologies just mentioned. The first is the *classical European theology,* which, in its various brands, is officially taught in all major institutions of the Asian church. The second is the *Latin American theology,* which is also making itself felt in certain theological circles. These theologies, of course, are diametrically opposed to each other, as are also the secular ideologies mentioned above.

Classical theology in the West, which went through the mill of renewal since the nineteenth century, is said to have made a major "breakthrough" in the middle of this century, climaxing in modern theology with its openness to the "world." The chief centers of this renewal were the French and Geman linguistic zones, according to Mark Schoof, because, to quote his own words, it was there that "the theologians seem to have the necessary scientific tradition and sufficient creative energy at their disposal."[5] One major source of inspiration for Catholic renewal of European theology is traced back to Protestant Germany, according to the same author.[6]

This close-range view of European theology justifies Schoof's title of his thesis: *Breakthrough.* But an Asian looking from a critical distance sees quite another picture. The real breakthrough in Western theology came with the Latin American critique of that same "scientific tradition" which Schoof proudly alludes to. The openness to the world which European theologians achieved up to the 1960's by dialoguing with contemporary *philosophies*[7] is only a mild reform compared to what the Latin Americans achieved from the 1960's onward. The latter effected a complete reversal of method. They seem to have done to European theology what Feuerbach did to Hegelian dialectics. They put theology back on its feet. They grounded it on theopraxis. What was formerly revolving round a Kantian orbit was made to rotate round a Marxian axis.[8]

For us Asians then, liberation theology is thoroughly Western, and yet so radically renewed by the challenges of the Third World that it has a relevance for Asia which the classical theology does not have. The Ecumenical Association of Third World Theologians (EATWOT), which is now holding its Asian Consultation here, is perhaps its first tangible fruit in Asia. In the churches of the East this *new method* has already begun to compete with the traditional theology. What the Latin Americans claim, and what we Asians must readily grant, is that it is not perhaps a new theology, but a theological *method,* indeed the *correct method* of doing theology.

The features of this methodology peculiarly relevant for us in Asia can be selected from Sobrino's presentation.[9] The first feature is that the

Kantian attempt to "liberate reason from authority" paved the way to a theological preoccupation with harmonizing "faith with reason," while the Marxian attempt to "free reality from oppression" did not receive theological attention in Europe until the South Americans made an issue of it.[10] Thus the use of "philosophy" to explain away "suffering" rationally, or to define God and his nature in such a way as to justify the existence of oppression and injustice, was understandable in a European sociopolitical context, while substitution of philosophical speculation with "sociological" analysis to *change* rather than explain the world of injustice has become the immediate concern of liberation theology. Such a concern cannot come within the "scientific" purview of European theology, whether Protestant[11] or Catholic.[12]

The second feature, quite important for Asians, is the primacy of praxis over theory. Spirituality, for instance, is not the practical conclusion of theology but the radical involvement with the poor and the oppressed, and is what creates theology. We know Jesus the *Truth* by following Jesus the *Way*.

Thirdly, this Way is the Way of the Cross, the basis of all knowledge. Thus, the growth of the world into God's Kingdom is *not* a "progressive development" but a process punctuated by radical contradictions, violent transformations, and death-resurrection experiences—what Sobrino calls the "ruptura epistemologica"—scripturally founded in the "Transcendence of the Crucified God."[13]

Fourthly, we see that it is not a "development theology" such as would justify and perpetuate the values of an "acquisitive" culture, but a "liberation theology" demanding an asceticism of renunciation and a voluntary *poverty* that sneers at acquisitiveness. This resultant "spirituality" is not self-enclosed, motivated as it is by the desire to bring about the Kingdom of God here on earth. What it inculcates is not merely a *passive solidarity* with the poor in their poverty and oppression but also a *dynamic participation* in their struggle for full humanity. Indeed, a dynamic following of Christ![14]

Finally, the encounter of God and man, i.e., the interplay of Grace and Liberty, is seen as man's obligation to use all his *human potentialities* to anticipate the Kingdom which, nevertheless, remains *God's gratuitous gift.* This explains the liberation theologian's political option for socialism, i.e., for a definite social order in which oppressive structures are changed radically, even violently, in order to allow every person to be fully human, the assumption being that no one is liberated unless everyone is.

This theology, and also its European predecessor, receive their contextual significance in Asia precisely in relationship to the aforesaid

Western ideologies with which they are very closely connected. Our earlier criticism of how these ideologies operate in Asia has clearly situated the two theologies, too, in the context of Eastern religiosity. Hence our task is to complement the Latin American method with an Asian critique of classical theology.

The Asian Style as Asian Theology

Peking's recent prediction about the future of Buddhism runs as follows:

> The Communists hold that, as a *religion* Buddhism will gradually die out, as history moves forward; but as a *philosophy* it merits careful study.[15]

This sort of apocalyptic optimism which turns hopes into predictions is not new in the history of Asian Buddhism. For instance, the Christian missionaries in Sri Lanka used to pronounce such prophecies in the last century,[16] when the whole colonial state machinery was backing their missions against the Buddhists.[17] Buddhism, however, has lived to tell the tale. The analogy with the Chinese situation need not be labored here.

The Marxists seem to grant that it is "religion" that will die and not the "philosophy," which merits study. Here again, I cannot help drawing a parallel with the theologians of the West, who, too, have detached religion from philosophy in their "theology of religions." In fact, the inherent incapacity of both classical Marxism and classical theology to grasp the Asian Sense, as revealed in the multifaceted religiosity of our people, is ultimately rooted in this unhappy dichotomy which both have inherited from a tradition which began perhaps with the early Western encounters with non-Christian cultures.[18]

Let me then put things back in focus. In all the nonbiblical soteriologies of Asia, *religion* and *philosophy* are inseparably interfused. Philosophy is a religious vision; and religion is a philosophy lived. Every metacosmic soteriology is at once a *darśana* and a *pratipadā,* to use Indian terms; i.e., an interpenetration of a "view" of life and a "way" of life. In fact, the oft-repeated question whether Buddhism is a philosophy or a religion was first formulated in the West, before it reached Peking via Marxism. For in the Buddha's formula, the fourfold salvific *truth* incorporates the Path as one of its constituents while the Eightfold *Path* coincides with the realization of the Truth.

Here let me refer to the current trend of *using* "Buddhist techniques" of meditation in "Christian prayer" without any reverence for the soteriological context of such techniques. For, the naive presupposition is that the (Buddhist) *Way* could be had without the (Buddhist) *Truth.* It is time to impress on our theologians that in our culture the *method* cannot be severed from the *goal*. For the word "technique," now misused in task-oriented cultures to mean a mechanical action which, when done according to set rules, produces predictable results, must be traced back to its original Greek sense. *Technē* is not a mechanical action, but a skill, an art. In our traditions, the art of doing a thing is itself the thing done. The *goal* of life, in Buddhism, is the *art* of living it. The Perfection to be achieved is the style of achieving it! The obvious corollary is that the Asian method of doing theology is itself Asian theology. *Theopraxis is already the formulation of theology.*

Thus the mutuality of praxis and theory which defines the Asian Sense in theology is the missing ingredient in the theology of religions which we have uncritically accepted and which hampers our task of acquiring the Asian Style.

This inadequacy seems to have been introduced by the early fathers of the church who, in their dialogue with the nonbiblical systems, restricted their interest to the *philosophical* rather than the *religious* plane.

They further impressed this dichotomy in the Western theological tradition when they took "pagan" philosophy out of its religious context and turned it into an intellectual weapon serving Christian apologetics against those very religions! Thus philosophy became the handmaid of Christian religion, *ancilla theologiae,* as already noticed in the writings of Clement of Alexandria and Peter Damian.[19] It is in this play of circumstances that one can understand the two permanent dents which Western theology of religions has received very early in history.

First, the use of philosophy minus religion imparted a *cerebral thrust* to the theology of religions. This emerged side by side with an abhorrence of "pagan" religious practices: an old Semitic intransigence continuing up to the apostolic era. Nevertheless, in the course of time these religious practices did influence Christian liturgy and ethics—even though theology held fast to her *ancilla!* Thus from the very inception, theology and theopraxis parted ways. The God-talk of theologians and the God-experience of the monks ran parallel. The former was working on "pagan" thought and the latter on "pagan" spirituality! The academicians and the mystics lived in mutual suspicion.

The second dent is even deeper. It is the apologetical technique of using a non-Christian religion against itself. This later became a missiological strategy, still resorted to in our theology of religions. It began with the way a "pagan" philosophy was removed from its original religious context and made to serve Christianity, not merely to enrich Christianity with an intellectual equipment but also to counteract the "pagan" religions. This process of "instrumentalization" is not absent even in De Nobili and Ricci, the missionary innovators of the seventeenth century in Asia. What the early fathers did to nonbiblical philosophy, these men did to Asian *culture*. They truncated it from its religious context and turned it into a means of conversion. It was a step forward, no doubt, but in the same direction! To this category must be relegated also the Christian "guru" who, as we mentioned earlier, plucks Zen and Yoga from the religious stems which give them sap, and adorns Christian spirituality with sapless twigs!

This species of "theological vandalism" has been euphemistically expressed by a new Christian usage of the word "Baptism." One hears of "baptizing" Asian cultures, and now, after Vatican II, "baptizing Asian religiosity." Baptism which, in its scriptural usage, expressed the most self-effacing act of Christ, first in the Jordan where he knelt before his precursor (Mark 1:9–11), and then on the cross (Mark 10:38; Luke 12:50) where, as the Suffering Servant, he ended his earthly mission in apparent failure, has now come to mean Christian triumphalism which turns everything it touches to its own advantage, with no reverence for the wholeness of another's religious experience.

Conclusions

1. Our theology is our way of sensing and doing things as revealed in our people's struggles for *spiritual* and *social* emancipation and expressed in the idioms and languages of the cultures such struggles have created.

2. Theology then is not mere God-talk; for, in our cultures, God-talk *in itself* is sheer "nonsense." As evidenced by the Buddha's refusal to talk of Nirvana, all words have *Silence* as their Source and Destiny! God-talk is made relative to God-experience. The word game about nature and person or the mathematics of one and three have only generated centuries of verbosity. It is word-lessness that gives every word its meaning. This inner *Harmony* between *Word* and *Silence* is the test of Asian authenticity, indeed it is the Spirit, the Eternal Energy which makes every word spring from Silence and lead to Silence, every engagement spring from renunciation, every struggle from a profound restfulness, every freedom from stern discipline, every action from stillness, every "development" from detachment, and every acquisition from nonaddition. Since, however, Silence is the *Word Unspoken* and the Word is *Silence Heard,* their "relationship" is not one of temporal priority but dialectical mutuality. It is the Spirit of Buddhist Wisdom and Christian Love. If there is Harmony between our Speech and our Silence, whether in worship or service or conversation, the Spirit is among us.

3. The same *Harmony* reigns between *God-experience* which is Silence and the *Man-concern* which makes it Heard. One is not temporally prior to the other. It is, rather, the mutuality between Wisdom and Love, Gnosis and Agape, Pleroma and Kenosis, or as the Buddhists would put it, between "Knowledge that directs us to Nirvana and the Compassion that pins us down to the world."[20] For liberation praxis is at once a withdrawal into the metacosmic and an immersion into the cosmic.

4. The most subtle point of this dialectic is between *authority and freedom.* The magisterial role in the Asian church has to be earned by the Master's *competence to mediate liberation.* Authority makes no external claims. Authority is competence to communicate freedom. He who lacks competence uses power. "With whose authority . . . ?" asked the power-thirsty clerics of the Son of Man, who submitted himself to that very power in order to vindicate his authority. His *authority was his freedom,* available to all who touched him. It is a self-authentication derived from a liberation praxis; it is a Man-concern testifying to a God-experience: the two prongs of a liberation struggle.

5. To regain her lost *authority,* therefore, the Asian church must abdicate her alliances with *Power.* She must be humble enough to be baptized in the Jordan of Asian *Religiosity* and bold enough to be baptized on the cross of Asian *Poverty.* Does not the fear of losing her identity make her lean on Mammon? Does not her refusal to die keep her from living? The theology of power-domination and instrumentalization must give way to a theology of humility, immersion, and *participation.*

6. Hence our desperate search for the Asian Face of Christ can find fulfillment only if we participate in Asia's own search for it in the unfathomable abyss where Religion and Poverty seem to have the same Common Source: God, who has declared Mammon his enemy (Matt. 6:24).

7. What then is the locus of this praxis? Certainly not the "Christian life lived within the church in the presence of non-Christians"; rather, it is the "God-experience (which is at once the Man-concern) of God's own people living beyond the church" and among whom the church is called to lose herself in total participation. That is to say, *Theology in Asia is the Christian apocalypse of the non-Christian experiences of liberation.*

NOTES

1. Roy Preiswerk, "La Rupture avec les conceptions actuelles du développement," in *Rélations inter-culturelles et développement* (Geneva, 1975), pp. 71–96.

2. R. C. Zaehner, *Foolishness to the Greeks: An Inaugural Lecture Delivered Before the University of Oxford on 2 November 1953* (Oxford, 1953), p. 17.

3. For the most recent discussion on the matter, cf. H. Bechert (ed.), *Buddhism in Ceylon and Studies on Religious Syncretism in Buddhist Countries* (Göttingen, 1978), specially Part III, pp. 146–339.

4. Rock Edict XIII of Asoka speaks of Buddhist Missions to Syria. A complement to this is the Aramaic Inscription found in eastern Afghanistan in 1969.

5. Mark Schoof, O.P., *Breakthrough: The Beginnings of the New Catholic Theology* (Dublin: Gill & Macmillan, 1970), p. 17.

6. Ibid., pp. 22–30.

7. It is observed (ibid., p. 26) that the new theology began by making the "whole life of the Church" the locus of a theological reflection, specially, "the world in which this community (of the church) lived, specially, *the world of contemporary philosophy*" (emphasis and parenthesis mine). The way *the world in which the church lived* is filtered into "the world of philosophy" would not escape South American criticism.

8. For a lucid exposition of this Latin American breakthrough, cf. Jon Sobrino, "El conocimiento teológico en la teología europea y latino-americana," in *Liberación y cautiverio: Debates en torno al método de la teología en América Latina* (Mexico City, 1975), pp. 177–207. For a neat summary of it, cf. Alfred T. Hennelly, S.J., "Theological Method: The Southern Exposure," *Theological Studies,* XXXVIII, 4 (Dec. 1977), pp. 708–735.

9. Loc. cit., passim.

10. However, a relatively early example of a pioneering, and perhaps premature, but certainly praiseworthy, attempt at a Christian assessment of the Marxist challenge can be found in R. B. Y. Scott and G. Vlastos (eds.), *Towards the Christian Revolution* (London: Victor Gollancz, 1937).

11. According to the thesis put forward by W. Pannenberg (*Theology and the Philosophy of Science;* Westminster Press, 1976), the main task of theology is to establish rationally the truth of theological propositions.

12. For a self-understanding of Catholic theology as a "scientific pursuit," cf. Y. Congar, O.P., *A History of Theology* (Doubleday & Co., 1968), pp. 221ff.

13. Here Sobrino (loc. cit., p. 201) quotes Moltmann. Cf. Hennelly, loc. cit., p. 721.

14. Hennelly, loc. cit., pp. 710–713.

15. *Peking Review,* No. 47 (Nov. 24, 1978), p. 31. The emphasis is mine.

16. Cf. K. Malalgoda, *Buddhism in Sinhalese Society 1750–1900: A Study of*

Religious Revival and Change (University of California Press, 1976), pp. 173–174.

17. Ibid., pp. 191–196.

18. Cf. Aloysius Pieris, S.J., *Western Christianity and Eastern Religions: A Theological Reading of Historical Encounters* (Pro Manuscripto), a paper read out at the German Theology Professors' Seminar, Bossey, Switzerland, Sept. 27–30, 1978.

19. Cf. Pannenberg, *Theology and the Philosophy of Science,* p. 10.

20. *Nibbānābhimukho paññāya, samsārābhimukho karunāya.* For a lengthy excursus on the dialectics between *paññā* and *karunā,* see *Itv A* I 15–16, *Cp A* 289–290, *Pm* 192–193.

PART SIX

Theology of Development
and Liberation

Twenty

Christian Theism:
A Theology of Society

Kuang-hsun Ting

[The author of this remarkable essay is the former President of Nanking Theological College in Nanking, China, and here is one of his earlier addresses to the graduating seminarians. He is currently Vice-President of Nanking University and Director of its newly established Centre for Religious Studies. In a recent interview with Bob Whyte in Toronto it was disclosed that Bishop Ting lectured on Christian Theism as recently as May 1979 to ninety members of Nanking University, mostly staff, indicating his continued interest in the theme. In the essay before us he skillfully answers the charge of the Marxist that "religion is the opiate of the people" by turning the charge back upon the Marxian dogmatist. While belief in God sometimes becomes an opiate, he admits, one must also consider "how often refusal to believe in God becomes an opiate—how many men there have been who drugged themselves by a denial of God's existence."—Ed.]

Our Christian belief in God is in general not the result of reasoning or persuasion, but of spiritual experience. This is not surprising. We know our mother not because we have been persuaded by some argument or demonstration, but because from childhood up we have felt her love. Many carpenters who have never heard that pi equals 3.1416 still know that the circumference of a circle is a little more than three times its diameter, and this is enough for the practical needs of life.

But for a theological student or church worker today, to know only that he believes in God and not to know how to give a reasoned explanation of this belief is not enough. Theological discussion today is too important to be neglected. We know that the various atheistic theories are wrong, but we must also know wherein they are wrong and, still more, what the right view is. We must think deeper and strengthen our

From *Documents of the Three-Self Movement,* edited by F. P. Jones and Wallace Merwin (National Council of Churches, U.S.A., 1963), pp. 156–167. This piece is from *China Bulletin* (Dec. 9 and 23, 1957; Jan. 6, 1958). Reprinted by permission of the National Council of Churches.

faith, so that when we go out to preach the truth of the gospel our works may carry weight because of their reasonableness. In I Peter 3:15 we read, "Be ready always to give an answer to every man that asks you a reason for the hope that is in you, with meekness and fear."

CHRISTIANITY AND THE
IDEALISM-MATERIALISM QUESTION

Is Christianity idealist or materialist? Many people both within and without the church are interested in this question. Some Christians are concerned to deny that Christianity is idealist, because to be idealistic is to be backward; some are trying to prove that Christianity is materialistic, because to be materialistic is to be progressive.

Some people think that materialists are of necessity progressive and idealists backward, or even reactionary. But the situation is not as simple as that. The early Taoists, and Lao-tzu, and Chuang-tzu, did not believe in God or any spirits, but explained everything by the heavenly Tao resident in all nature; they had thus a strong tendency toward atheistic and materialistic thought. But at the same time they had a strong aristocratic spirit, and represented aristocratic interests. Wang Yang-ming's doctrine of an instinctive conscience would seem to be idealistic [and thus defective—Tr.], but it encouraged a spirit of individual initiative, a recognition of right and wrong, and a questioning of tradition, which both in this time and since has had a forward-looking influence too important to be neglected.

It is not according to Christian reasoning to divide all thinking into the two categories of materialist and idealist, with a deep gulf between them. People ask if Christianity is materialist or idealist. I reply that the question itself does not correspond to Christian reality. Other people may ask the question if they like, but we are not obliged to answer it. To accept such an obligation and try to answer that question is unconsciously to step outside the realm of Christian thinking. We Christians do not as Christians ask that question.

There are many ways of dividing mankind. Some are universally recognized, and others may be questioned. No one questions the validity of dividing all mankind into two categories of men and women, or of dividing the present generation into those born in either the nineteenth or the twentieth century, for a twenty-first century birth is still to come, and all those born in the eighteenth century are now dead. (Although Russian newspapers reported recently the death of a man 157 years old!)

But there are other classifications that are more doubtful, to which some people may object, because they do not include all individuals. For example, some Westerners, in order to vilify Communism, would classify all Communists as either Stalinist or anti-Stalinist. But this classification is not an inevitable one, and is in fact only intended to confuse the mind and break up Communist fellowship. Again, the Jews considered circumcision very important, and divided all men into two categories, the circumcised and the uncircumcised. But Paul said, "Neither circumcision avails anything, nor uncircumcision, but a new creature." As a Christian, the question which he raised was whether a person had or had not become a new creature.

We Christians do not think that it is satisfactory classification to call all shades of thought either materialistic or idealistic. It is a hopeless simplification of the facts. Would it not be truer to say that there has never been a hundred-percent materialist or a hundred-percent idealist? Idealism and materialism not only stand opposed, they also interpenetrate each other; they are not only mutually exclusive but mutually influential as well; they have not only points of disagreement but also of agreement. There is some idealism in all materialism, and some materialism in all idealism. Someone has said: "Tao Hsing-chih was once an idealist, and then his name was T'ao Chih-hsing. Afterward he became a materialist, and changed his name to T'ao Hsing-chih." But I cannot think of Mr. Tao as simply as that. Man is the most complex of animals, and his thinking is very complex. In all thinking there is development. A man may change his name, but intellectual development cannot get away from the fact of a certain continuity in the process. The Soviet Philosophical Dictionary describes Pavlov as follows: "Great Russian physiologist and thinker . . . inheritor of nineteenth century Russian materialistic philosophy and the progressive traditions of a naturalistic science. . . . His theories deal a deathblow to idealistic psychology, and laid the foundation for a true materialist psychology." And yet we know that Pavlov was at the same time a devout member of the Orthodox Church. Evidently the coexistence of materialism and idealism is as common as their mutual opposition.

It is still more impossible to classify Christianity as either idealist or materialist because, although it is in form the product of history, it is in essence not an ideology, not a structure built upon an economic base. Its true substance is revelation, the incarnation, and thus it transcends all human lines of division. Some Christians today do not understand this point, and so they try to draw a line between idealism and materialism, and say, "We are not idealist," or even say, "We are materialist." This is all very unnecessary, because we do not need to accept the classification itself.

Christianity in its organization, its thought, its ceremonies, and its formal structure has of course been deeply influenced by human history, but in itself it is not the fruit of history, and the gospel is not an ideology. The gospel comes from the free revelation of God. This gospel is Christ himself, through whom all things were made. A theologian of Western Europe has said, "The greatest danger facing Western theology today is that of reducing Christianity to an ideology and thus of placing it in opposition to another ideology—Communism." This is true. We must ever remember that what we preach is the gospel, is Christ, something in nature entirely different from an ideology, something which moves in a different orbit from any system of thought, and then we will have a clear understanding from which to perceive that all talk of comparison of Christianity with Communism, of likenesses or differences, is beside the point and superfluous.

IS CHRISTIANITY AN OPIATE?

"Religion is the opiate of the people." This sentence of Marx is sufficiently cutting and clear. But regardless of how applicable this saying is to Christianity, let us note first of all that the point of criticism is directed against the religion of certain times or of certain persons, and not against religion itself.

To analyze the effect which religious belief has had upon some individual is one thing. But the question whether God exists or not is an entirely different thing. Let us grant for argument's sake that you have discovered that the religion of certain individuals has had a narcotic effect upon them. But this discovery does not at all prove that the universe is without a Creator. The mental state of some believers may be unstable, so that they seek for an anesthetic, and use religion as an opiate, and some preachers may even present religion in this light, and of course this is not good. But what does this prove regarding the existence of God? The thinking of some religious believers is backward and needs help, but the fact that these backward believers use religion as an opiate has no bearing on the question of the being of God. Similarly, if they were progressive, that would not prove that God exists. The existence of God is a different and independent question.

There are many things in the world which are used as opiates, and not just religion. Literature, art, science, all can become means of intoxication and escape from reality. The other day we had a meeting with some students from the University of Nanking, and some of them were students of astronomy. I said to them: "Let us imagine a man who because of some great grief has become very pessimistic about the world, his country, and his family, and so he seeks for an escape from reality, in order to benumb his mind. Is it not possible that such a man would choose astronomy as his opiate? Day and night he might sit at his telescope, drawing calmness of mind from the great emptiness of space. But the fact that he was using astronomy as an opiate would not mean that the sun, the moon, and the stars which he saw through his telescope did not really exist. On the contrary, it is possible that his observations might make a great contribution to the advance of astronomy. His subjective psychological state is one thing, the objective existence of the universe is quite another thing."

If anyone on discovering that certain religious believers in certain periods of history have used religion as an opiate should draw the conclusion that therefore God does not exist, we should say to them: "Your logic is not good. You have no right to draw that conclusion from that premise."

Certainly it is a painful fact which we cannot and need not deny, that religion has been preached by some preachers and received by some believers as an opiate. "Religion is the opiate of the people." This forceful statement was made some time before Marx by an English clergyman, Charles Kingsley, a man who had great sympathy for the downtrodden working classes. At the time the destructive features of capitalism had begun to appear, the life and security of workers was without protection, and even five- and six-year-old children had to work in the factories under inhuman conditions. In the face of such conditions the church of that day did nothing but urge people to control themselves and accept tyranny, saying that after this life they would enjoy happiness in heaven. That was why Kingsley made this stinging statement. But the use of Christianity as an opiate is an accident, and does not belong to the essence of Christianity. In Matt. 27:34 we read that when our Lord hung upon the cross "a well-meaning individual, wishing to relieve the pains of Christ's death, offered him a cup of some opiate, which when he had tasted he would not drink." Did he not have the right to drink it? Why did he refuse? Our Lord at the end of his human life, at the most important moment when he was bearing the sins of all mankind upon the cross, wanted to keep a clear mind to the very end. He was not willing to use a drugged and benumbed mind to complete the work which his Father had given him to do. See, how without hesitation he refused the opiate. Consider, if he had consented to drink the drug. He might have escaped the pain, but then he would no longer have known what was going on around him, the Seven Great Words from the cross itself would have been left unsaid, and the meaning of the cross itself would have been dark and unclear.

What Christ gives men is forgiveness, consolation, and strength, not a numbed spirit. We pray, "Thy will be done on earth as it is in heaven." Where is there any opiate in that prayer? This is the highest religion, the religion of revelation, that is Christianity. St. Ambrose (340–397) once said: "You rich men, when will your greed end? Will it continue until there is nothing left on earth but yourselves? How do you dare to take all nature as your own? The world was made for all men, how can you claim it as your private property? Nature does not recognize the rich; it produces the common man. The products of nature are for the use of all, and God wants the world and all it contains, to be for the use of all." The saint who said this was not a man who had been benumbed by some opiate. In the museum at Prague there is a statue of John Hus, on which is carved this memorable saying of his: "Woe to me if I keep silent. If I do not speak out against the greatest evils, then I become an accomplice of sin and hell, and it were better had I never been born." Who dares to say that a man who talks like this has been drugged with opiate? People do not take the primitive nature of early Communist society as a reason for distrusting the future of the Communist world; they do not because of the absurdities of alchemy look down upon modern chemistry, nor because of the superstitions of old-time astrology despise modern astronomy. In the same way you cannot take such ideas as opiate to weigh the gospel of Christ.

One should study religion concretely, and not proceed from a priori definitions; otherwise one will fall into the error of dogmatism. Feudalistic barons or bandits said they were acting for heaven, and then proceeded to oppress the people. The Taiping leaders also said they had been appointed by heaven to liberate the people, and they really did liberate them. Both used the word "heaven," but with what a different meaning. In the Middle Ages the contending schools of nominalists and realists were both faithful to Roman theology, but anyone with even a moderate knowledge of philosophy knows that we cannot consider them alike, and without discrimination mark them both unacceptable. The idea of paradox is entirely a theological idea, but it cannot be denied that ever since science was liberated from obscurantism the idea of paradox has had great influence in it. If we say that religion is by its very nature reactionary, so that its progressive manifestations are for that reason more dangerous than its reactionary manifestations, then what shall we say of the Chinese Christian church today, which has shown itself to be patriotic and which upholds socialism?

ENVIRONMENT AND SIN

Modern atheistic thinking has a tendency to attribute all the ills of society to a bad social system, as though there could be no other source for them within man himself. For Christians themselves this tendency is an important and useful corrective. In the past we thought little about the social order. Our bias was simply to attribute all evil to man's sinful nature. We said, the question of sin is the only question; once that question is solved, any social system will be good; and if it is not solved, no social system will be good. Today we must acknowledge our mistake. It is true that the question of sin is fundamental. But we cannot expect everybody to repent at once, and thus solve the problem of sin. It is still necessary for men to live together before they have all repented and been regenerated. What kind of society will be best for our common life? That is an important question which cannot be neglected. The difference between socialism and capitalism is very great. Our studies during the past few years have shown us the superiority of socialism. We certainly cannot think of the two systems as of equal value.

But can we deny the existence of sin? Certainly not. In New China the level of morality has been greatly raised. Does that mean that the question of sin has been solved? Decidedly not. The fact that man must come into a good environment (New China) in order to manifest a better standard of action does not mean that man is now without sin; rather it is a demonstration that man is carrying a heavy load of sin, so that he is not able to overcome his environment. Consider your old grandfather or grandmother, crippled with rheumatism so that they cannot move around at all in the winter. Then spring and summer come, and they become more lively. Does that mean they are now well? No, it only emphasizes the weakness of their bodies.

Not long ago I went to visit some country churches, and on the bus I sat by the driver, watching him as he alertly turned the wheel, now this way and now that. And I wondered, if the road were perfectly straight and perfectly level, would it be possible for the driver to be not alert. Could he after setting the direction take his hands from the wheel and sit there reading a book? I answered my own question, No. Even if the road were as straight as a ruler, and as level as a pane of glass, yet there is bound to be a certain amount of play in the setting of the wheels. And if there is àny play at all, even if it is too small to be measured, yet the results would be that without the steering of the driver the car sooner or later would go into the ditch. As a saying in one of the old classics has it, "A mistake of a thousandth of an inch can put one wrong by a thousand miles." Of course the straighter and smoother the road the better. But the most up-to-date factory cannot produce a car which will obviate this weakness inherent in the nature of the car. Man's life in the world is like this. We must work for an improved social order and environment. But man's sin is not thereby cancelled out; we still need a Lord to come and hold the steering wheel of our life.

In a school where I once studied, we had in the gymnasium a ball about the size of a basketball, but much heavier, and with an off-center weight in it. The result was that no matter how you tried you could not roll it straight. It was very exasperating. Is not man's life like that? In the presence of God, man yesterday, today, and tomorrow still can be described in the words of Isaiah, "All we like sheep have gone astray; we have turned every one to his own way" (Isa. 53:6).

In today's society the level of moral action has been raised, and this is a fact which we Christians should welcome. We should not go around looking for flaws, trying to make someone lose face, as if the only way to satisfy us were to discover that someone else was wrong. We should welcome a social system that shows itself able to raise the level of moral life. But the change of social system can only limit the effectiveness of sin, it cannot solve the problem of sin. Sin can only be healed by forgiveness, salvation, and grace. It is not a matter of social progress. These two matters should not be confused.

Perhaps someone will accuse me of having too pessimistic a view of man. But I ask you, what pessimism is there in this view? It is instead the greatest optimism. When the prodigal son came to understand his own sin, our Lord said of him, "He came to himself" (Luke 15:17). Evidently in his sin he was not himself, but when he repented his true self showed itself. From this we see that the Lord Jesus had a very high view of man, one which cannot be called pessimistic.

THE REASON FOR UNBELIEF

Other people are always analyzing us Christians, to explain why we believe in God, saying that we are looking for an opiate. I have already said what I want to on that subject, but now let us do some analyzing ourselves, and find out why it is that from the beginning of the world there have been people who would not believe in God. There are two reasons: the first a general and universal one, the second one that applies particularly to this century.

1. Moral and spiritual reasons. To believe in God or to believe that there are living beings on Mars may seem both to be acts of believing, but they are vastly different. To believe that there is life on Mars, if you

believe it, you believe it; and if you don't, it makes no difference in your moral or spiritual life. It makes no demands upon you; whether you believe or do not believe, your life, your thinking, your actions will be the same.

Belief in God is a different thing: if you don't believe, that is all there is to it; but if you do believe, the consequences are great. Adam sinned and then when Jehovah drew near, he hid himself in the trees because he did not dare to look upon the face of Jehovah. We can imagine how happy he would have been then, if there had not been within or without the universe any such thing as this Jehovah. And if he had remained hidden for a long time, would not he and his children have come to believe that Jehovah after all did not exist?

Peter knelt at Jesus' feet saying, "Lord, depart from me, for I am a sinful man" (Luke 5:8). Since he knew Jesus to be Lord and himself to be a sinner, should he not instead have repented? Why would he ask Jesus to depart? Yes, we have all had this experience of both wanting the Lord and not wanting him. The Lord is what we want, but yet he demands that we repent. If we are not willing to repent, if we are unwilling to pay the moral and spiritual price, we can only ask this Lord to leave us, and even wish that he did not exist.

Belief in God sometimes becomes an opiate, that is true. But consider how often refusal to believe in God becomes an opiate. How many men have there been since the beginning of history who have drugged themselves by a denial of God's existence, so that they could continue to sin, avoid responsibility, and stifle the reproaches of their conscience? Sometimes we meet people like this within our churches. They are morally reprobate, but refuse to repent, and the result is that having departed from God they gradually come to deny his existence. The only way they can recover their faith is first to repent of their sin.

2. The church's failure to manifest God. Another reason why the world refuses to believe in God is the failure, the darkness, the sin of the churches. The Lord Jesus said, "Let your light so shine before men, that they may see your good works, and glorify your Father which is in heaven." But we do not do this. From the life, the thinking, and the work of Christians, people are not able to see Christ's Father, full of love, justice, and purity. What men can see in the church is instead a God whom their own sense of morality and justice does not allow them to believe in. This is an important reason why people today do not believe in God.

French Catholic writer Jacques Maritain, in his *True Humanism,* says: "What is the source of Communist atheism? It is that the Christian world was not true to its own principles, thus arousing the hostility of

Communists, who then went on from hating the Christian world to hating Christianity itself."

Berdyaev, a Russian theologian who moved to Paris after the October revolution, in his book on *The Rise of the Russian Revolution,* writes as follows: "There are some Christians who condemn the Communists for their atheism and their antichurch activities. But we must not place the main responsibility for this upon the shoulders of the Communists. Christians themselves must bear the larger part of the blame. Christians should be not only condemners and judges, but also penitents. Had Christians in their social life tried hard to put their Christian principles into practice? The sins of Christians and of the historical church have been very great and they have brought a just punishment."

The Armenian Christian Tiran Nersoyan, in his book *A Christian View of Communism,* says: "Atheism was a necessary tool for the Communist to use in order to liberate the proletariat from the reactionary influence of the clergy. . . . Atheism was the most radical way of sweeping away the lack of fellowship between people of various sects."

We need not agree entirely with all the above quotations. But because of the sins of the church and especially because the church in the field of politics was always on the side of the enemies of the people, the church lost its ability to show God forth. This point is one which we in the Chinese church can appreciate. Now the Three-Self Patriotic Movement has called the whole church out of bondage to imperialism, which makes it a movement of great significance.

In their criticism of religion, people have fortunately centered their attention on some of the evil results of religion in personal and social life, such as its inhibiting influence on civilization, its harmful effect on health, its upholding of private property, its perversion by enemies of the people, but have not touched upon the substance of our faith. Some of the things criticized are foreign and now a thing of the past, while others are Chinese in origin, and are still a problem. These should rouse us to greater vigilance and self-examination, amending what is wrong and strengthening what is right.

Twenty-one

Notes for a Theology
of Development

C.G. Arevalo, S.J.

[A continuing interest of Jesuit Fr. Arevalo has been the Christian perspective on development and liberation. Professor of Theology at Loyola School of Theology, in Manila, he first presented reflections on the theme at the Asian Ecumenical Conference on Development held in Tokyo in July 1970. The paper before us was presented to the Philippine AECD Echo Seminar held in Manila three months later. After carefully establishing the Christological basis for a theology of development, Arevalo, following Latin American signals, reviews the three basic kinds of institutionalized violence which today crush the underdeveloped part of mankind. He reflects on the question, "Must Christian churches of Asia align themselves unequivocally with the poor and the victims of social injustice . . . against unjust structures which impede justice and development?" His answer is a qualified "yes," qualified by the consideration that "to stand on the side of the poor is not to take a stance of enmity or hate against those who possess wealth and power . . . but rather to take issue with attitudes of selfishness and the structures which institutionalize egoism. . . ."—Ed.]

I. On the Christological Foundations
of a Theology of Development

A

For the Christian it is fitting that a vision of development should begin with Christ (St. Paul to the Colossians 1:15–20). The perspective of his faith suggests this from the start. "Jesus Christ . . . constitutes, according to the scriptures, the origin and foundation of being, the archetype and prototype, the light and power, the meaning and the value, the support and purpose of creation."[1]

The New Testament texts with this burden are many; we can only touch on a few.

From *Philippine Studies*, XIX, 1 (January 1971), pp. 65–91. Reprinted by permission.

From I Corinthians: "Yet for us there is one God, the Father, from whom are all things and for whom we exist, and one Lord, Jesus Christ, through whom are all things and through whom we exist" (I Cor. 8:6).

"All things are yours, and you are Christ's, and Christ is God's" (I Cor. 3:22–23).

From Hebrews: Jesus Christ is the one "whom (God) appointed the heir of all things, through whom also he created the world. He reflects the glory of God and bears the very stamp of his nature, upholding the universe by his word of power" (Heb. 1:2–3). And it is said of him, "Thou, Lord, didst found the earth in the beginning, and the heavens are the work of thy hands" (Heb. 1:10).

From John: "All things were made through him, and without him was not anything made that was made. In him was life, and the life was the light of men" (John 1:3f.).

Their concern, of course, and that of the sacred writers, is not to speculate on the origins of the universe. Rather, their message is that it is in the light of the redeeming task, it is in the light of man's fulfillment by God *in and through Christ the Savior* that creation is to be seen. In God's design it is in Christ the *Redeemer* that man is to find salvation and fulfillment and that the universe is to find completion, as it is *in Christ* that man and the world were brought into being. Christ the incarnate Son is the reconciler of men, and the key to man's fulfillment and to the completion of the rest of the universe, just as he was with the Father in the creation of all things.

Thus the three "moments" (so to speak) of God's action in man's regard—creation, reconciliation, and the final fulfillment of all things—take place in and through Christ; they take place *for* Christ. "The total action of man's God," someone has written, "is christoform: it starts with Christ, proceeds through Christ, and is completed in Christ.... The whole of the world order in which we exist is christoform: created through, reconciled from its sinfulness by, finally to be fulfilled in Christ." Christ came to save and fulfill what was basically already his.[2]

This is what the great Christological canticles tell us in the majestic texts of Paul to the Ephesians and Colossians, as well as the difficult passage from Romans 8. Nothing of course surpasses the statement on the cosmic place of Christ in the hymn in the first chapter of Colossians, where Christ is spoken of as the image of the invisible God, the firstborn from among the dead.[3]

a. *Image of the invisible God and firstborn of all creation.* For Paul, recalling the texts of Proverbs, Christ "the son of the Father's love" is God's Wisdom, collaborating with the Father in the work of creation. Perfect self-expression of the Father in his whole being, he is *his* fullest revelation. And thus in fashioning the universe and man, it is the Son who serves as the pattern of his work, the model of its shaping, the "showing forth" of his glory. In Christ, through him, and for him the whole world was made; all things have him as their meeting point; all things are joined and hold together in him; all things refer to him as to the one through whom they shall come to fullness. Distinct from things heavenly and earthly, yet he is their *sense,* the intelligibility of each and of the whole. He is present to them all, he gives meaning to the *cosmos,* and it bears his imprint from its first beginnings.

From the first, then, the universe is not devoid of pattern or meaning; finally (contrary to the pessimism of the existentialist), it is not absurd. Finally it has purpose and its thrust is not blind: it is moving toward the term God has set for it, toward Christ as end, as its fulfillment. To seek to know the earth, then, is to seek the Wisdom of God; to listen to the earth is to cup one's ear to his Word; to seek to develop the earth is to bring it to its glory and completion in Christ; to love the earth, truly and rightly to love it, is in the final showing to love the "Son of his love."[4]

And man, in Christ the new man, is a creature larger than any horizons he might set for himself: he is made unto the image of God's own Son, and destined to be, in him, also the son of the Father and sharer in the inner life of God in grace and glory. To seek to affirm man and the true fullness of human life, of human peace and joyousness, then, is to proclaim Christ and to hymn his glory.

b. In the text from Colossians (1:15–20), *Christ is the Savior too, the firstborn from among the dead, the head of the church which is his body.* In the incarnation of the Son, man—in both his wonder and his lowliness —has been assumed by God; in the Christ the new man, the fullness of God's gifts, finds a dwelling place in the midst of men, in the very heart of the world.

And in Christ's work, what sin has sundered, God puts together again: through Christ's blood on the cross he reconciles all who are at enmity, all who are estranged; he directs men to growth and to fullness, to forgiveness and acceptance of each other, to love. God in Christ is reconciling all men to himself and to each other, bringing them into the sweep of convergence in Christ, in whom they—we—become part of each other. Thus all things come together, through man, in the crucified and risen one, in his risen body, in the fulfillment of the creative task that was from the first, as the redeeming work was itself, through Christ and for him and in him. "The mystery (which it was God's purpose to reveal) is Christ among you, your hope of glory. This is the Christ we proclaim, this is the wisdom in which we thoroughly train everyone and instruct everyone to make them all perfect in Christ."

This vision of Christ the principle of creation, of Christ at the heart of things, Christ the center point and norm of history, Christ at work in the healing and shaping of the human community, Christ the pattern of man's growth and progress and peace, must be for the Christian the vision of development. Our involvement in the task of development is a seconding of three "moments" of God's action in man's regard: it is to be our affirmation of Christ in the world of things and the world of man, in the world of power, technology, politics, human relatedness, human oneness in justice and in peace. It is our sharing in God's "opening up of spaces" for human knowledge, freedom, creativeness, community, love, and fullness of life; our call to share in the world's making and in the building up of the city of man.[5]

B

Some Latin American theologians, as we know, prefer not to speak of "development" but of *"liberation."* They feel that the notion of development, as it is accepted in much current talk, has built into it a prejudgment, on the part of much of the developed world of the affluent West —a prejudgment of what it means to be "modern man and modern society come to fulfillment," with its focus on the TV set and the burdened table, the air-conditioned house cum swimming pool, an evening with the beautiful people, a seat on the 747 to Paris. Whereas liberation asks that the Latin American be allowed the freedom to grow toward what he himself would want to become, toward the society expressing the *configuration* of values he himself chooses, toward the good life for man as he sees it, not as he is told to see it by others. For these thinkers are alive to the reality of a cultural imperialism which Harvey Cox has described as using massive means to brainwash Latin Americans on what they must want (multicolored toilet tissue, Barbie dolls in ski togs, Max Factor cosmetics, and all the rest), a cultural imperialism which is, he says, hastening *mis*-development in that continent, which is establishing what he terms "a whole diabolical system of empire."[6] And so liberation means that each people is progressively freed, politically, economically, culturally, so that it can have "the room and space and air" to realize its own vision of a world of human friendship and communion. Liberation, as one writer tells us, means that the Latin American can say, to the economic and cultural imperialist especially: *"Let us be. Let us find our own ways.* Let us shape our own future as we choose to."[7]

The understanding, from the part of a man of the Third World, that *development is liberation,* can be rooted in the Christian understanding of what it means for the church to be truly *catholic,* and what it means for Christ to be at the heart—at the root—of all honest human approaches to truth, all true human values, all true human culture, all genuine human development.

For the church to be truly catholic, as we understand it, means that the community that is God's people on pilgrimage is open to all that is positively human, and therefore that whatever is true and good in man has a place in her existence—for all of man and human life is to be brought to fulfillment in the restoration of all things in Christ. "All things are yours, and you are Christ's, and Christ is God's." The church thus "strives constantly and effectively to gather all humanity and all its riches under Christ its head, in the unity of his Spirit" (*Lumen Gentium,* 13). This is a theme that the documents of the Second Vatican Council take up, but these texts have a solid parentage in Christian tradition.[8]

The people of God, in the Second Vatican Council's decree on the church, is said "to take to its heart (the qualities and values of every people)" and "purifies, strengthens, raises up and consecrates them all. In this, the church is mindful that she must work with and for that king to whom the nations were given for an inheritance, to whose city they bring their presents and gifts" (*Lumen Gentium,* 13). "For thus each nation strives to express Christ's message in its own way. At the same time, a living exchange is fostered between the church and the diverse cultures" (*Gaudium et Spes,* 44).

The catholicity of the church is thus an expression of the transcendence and universality of Christ's double task at work within the world and in all peoples, opening the Christian community to a wonderful universality and pluralism in its life: all human cultures, all human civilizations, modes of thought, feeling, and expression, are seen in Christ, *fons et finis:* he is at their root, he is the term of their completion.

The Christian vision of development can thus be a liberating leaven; it is of its essence "nonimperialist," it can find the space for genuine nationalism and the search for national identity that plays so large a role in the growth of the new nations, the space for the yearning in Asian man and Asian peoples to be free to find their own ways and perfect their own cultures and traditions. There is space in the Christian vision for this, because it believes that Christ is "behind, beneath, and ahead of" all this, penetrating the dynamism of growth, informing the thrust toward freedom and toward the future from within.

The Christian vision of development, of liberation, is thus essentially *optimistic,* hope-filled, and fruitful for joy, because it sees the process bathed in the light of Christ's redeeming victory. It believes that Christ, crucified and risen, has freed the world already from the slavery of sin; that in Christ redeemed man has broken through already to the new life, that this liberation is being brought to completion even now by "Christ in us, the hope of glory."

Hence this vision is one of *joy*, an opening out to what Chesterton called the gigantic secret of the Christian. At a conference two years ago a Christian from Europe spoke of his experience "of Asian Christians who have found in Christ a new life of immense gratitude and joy."[9] He spoke of a transparent, contagious joy that he met among Christians in our own host country, and how this gave him the realization of the "newness" of Christ. This secret the Christian in Asia must try to share with all of his brothers; perhaps in this there is a contribution the Christian in our part of the world can make to development which is *his* truly to make, but not as from him, but from Christ who makes all things new, who gladdens the heart of our youthfulness. In a world where the soul of the elder children of the Christian faith—it seems— is so often shrouded over with a mantle of futility and hopelessness, of boredom or lack of nerve, perhaps the Asian is called to reveal to them anew the meaning of Christ for man, the *joy* of the message which they have forgotten, the bursting forth of God's love in the world, which for them begins to be dim memory only, but which for us is the reality of our hope.

This is surely a task of the servant church in Asia, to serve our peoples in their search to find themselves, to serve the growth of Asian man to the fullness of his stature in Christ. The church in Asia is called to be handmaid to that fulfillment of peoples in a truly human communion which, beyond needful economic and material sufficiency, is what development, finally, is all about.[10] This is the servant task which the Christian and the Christian churches of Asia can give themselves to, with a profound sense of hope: knowing that growth will be, if illumined by the Word of God, the emergence of Christ, the revealing of (to use a shopworn phrase) the Asian visage of Christ, and the growth of Asian man toward Christ, toward whom all men and all creation "groan" with the hope of coming to the glory of sons in the Son of God (cf. Romans 8).

C

Antoine de Saint-Exupéry's book *Wind, Sand and Stars* ends with his account of a railway trip when he decided to walk through the train through all its length, making his way through the third-class carriages crowded with hundreds of Polish workmen sent home from their jobs in France. He tells of stepping over sprawling bodies, peering into compartments, seeing men, women, and children stirring uneasily in their sleep, hearing obscure moans and raucous snoring, seeing a whole nation, all humps and hollows and dirt, returning (he says) to its native poverty.

And he thinks of all the human beauty, all the human promise and quality that poverty and dirt and dehumanizing labor had destroyed in these people, of the little houses and tiny garden plots they had been torn from, of the loves and hopes which had been allowed to wither and die in their hearts. He looks at a derelict of a man, head shaven, hunched over in sluggish sleep, and a shabby woman, grown prematurely old with work and weariness, asleep beside him.

I may at this point be permitted to quote him at length:

> Between the man and the woman a child had hollowed himself out a place and fallen asleep. He turned in his slumber, and in the dim lamplight I saw his face. What an adorable face! A golden fruit had been born of these two peasants, . . . a miracle of delight and grace.
>
> I bent over the smooth brow, over those mildly pouting lips, and I said to myself: This is a musician's face. This is the child Mozart. This is a life full of beautiful promise. Little princes in legends are not different from this. Protected, sheltered, cultivated, what could not this child become?
>
> When by mutation a new rose is born in a garden, all the gardeners rejoice. They isolate the rose, tend it, foster it. But there is no gardener for men. This little Mozart will be shaped like the rest by the common stamping machine. This little Mozart will love shoddy music in the stench of night dives. This little Mozart is condemned.
>
> I went back to my sleeping car. I said to myself: Their fate causes these people no suffering. It is not an impulse to charity that has upset me like this. I am not weeping over an eternally open wound. Those who carry the wound do not feel it. It is the human race and not the individual that is wounded here, is outraged here. I do not believe in pity. What torments me tonight is the gardener's point of view. What torments me is not this poverty to which after all a man can accustom himself as easily as to sloth. . . . What torments me is not the humps nor hollows nor the ugliness. It is the sight, a little bit in all these men, of Mozart murdered.

And he concludes:

> Only the Spirit, if it breathes upon the clay, can create man.[11]

May I suggest that perhaps this anecdote recalls for us something of the motivation for our commitment to development? Nearly all of us present here come from nations which, in any lining up of the rich and the poor peoples, belong to the column of the poor. We have our acres of slums, our rows of shanties set up in swamps of filth, our masses of unemployed and underemployed, our urchins sleeping on sidewalks each night, scavenging for food in garbage heaps, our beggars, our uncared-for sick, our emigrating professionals (the draining of our best energies), our hopeless and often despairing young. It is these images we are asked to keep before us: call up the living memories of individual children, men, women, the sick, the leprous, the aged we have seen, so that we remain aware in our hearts of what we are talking about, and not of economic facts and statistical figures *only* (not of gross national product *only*), . . . so that we do not end up with another sea of words which we ourselves will not return to later, but be with our whole beings summoned to deeds we must do in the pursuit of the gospel.

May I suggest that we look upon our peoples, in their poverty, in their hunger, in their need for literacy, for education, for opportunity, for liberty, as the little child in Saint-Exupéry's pages: the child in whom Mozart lies sleeping, Mozart and Chuang-tzu, Yoshida-shoin and Rizal and Gandhi, a hundred geniuses whose creativity is meant to enrich the world . . . and, silent in that slumber, music which will never perhaps be sung to gladden the hearts of men, poetry which will never lift up their souls, color, the sweep of columns and arches, pages of immortal thought, which could enrich the heritage of all men, which could bring light and joy, wonderment and courage, to ages still to come. In our undernourished, poorly clothed, badly educated peoples, their hidden greatness, the gifts they can lay at the tables of their fellowmen, their contributions to history—all these lie dormant, never to be called forth perhaps because poverty imprisons their humanity and stunts its possibilities perpetually. In each of our poor, in each of our peoples, there is a little, not of Mozart only, but (if we are to believe the Scriptures) of Christ himself, stillborn, murdered, because they have been kept in the most terrible of bondages, that which holds them from becoming all they were meant to be.

Let it be a torment then to us: not so much perhaps the dirt and the poverty, the squalor and the ugliness. But the torment of the gardener: the sight, a little bit in all our brothers, of Christ not come to fruition, of the dead, the stillborn Christ.

D

One last word which, strangely enough, even in assemblies such as this one, sometimes takes courage to say. And it is this: for the Christian there must be, in all this concern for development, a constant reference, a constant return to the person of Jesus Christ—the Christ in whom and for whom man and his world were made, the same Christ as the Jesus of the Gospels, the carpenter's son and the Son of God who came to serve man and to lay down his life for man.[12]

The Christian is one who has, in his life, come to know the person of Jesus Christ and his gospel, and has been given (not as a privilege but as a humbling task) some experience of the reality of the living Christ. And henceforth he meets his brother in a love and a concern that finds its foundation and energy within that faith and that experience. I must confess I do not understand the mentality (more, I do not understand the thrust behind the mentality) that wishes to make the person of Jesus Christ and the life and gospel he gives us as something finally unnecessary and irrelevant or at most implicit in the mind and heart, in the personal belief and life *of the Christian* in the world. For me, the Christian's own self-giving to the labor and the concerns of the development and liberation of man depends for its authenticity and enduringness on his faith and commitment to God in Jesus Christ. Love for the brother will finally not be brave words only, but genuine self-gift in the measure that it is rooted in the surpassing knowledge and love of Jesus Christ and in obedience to his Spirit. This is, I believe, the message of Paul and John as I read them, and no secular reading of the gospel—if it remains a reading of the gospel and not its surrogate—will, finally, change the reality of this.

The task of development is finally the liberation of the full imprint of Christ in man, in every man, in all of mankind. This is the vision of faith. And this task will not be conceived and carried out on local and international planning boards only, but in the purpose, dedication, and courage of individual men and women for whom "preaching the good news to the poor, the proclaiming of the release of captives, the recovery of sight to the blind, the setting at liberty of those who are oppressed"—people for whom all these things are not formulae and phrases merely, but deeds and the task of life itself. Such was the pattern of the life of Jesus; such was the shape of the self-giving of the Christians we call saints; and it is our faith that this is the norm for the life of the disciple till the end of time.

II. THE CHURCH ON THE SIDE OF THE POOR

It is commonplace now to say that to speak of development from the standpoint of emerging peoples is to speak of revolution.[13] For many Christians revolution is seen as a Christian imperative. What is called for is that the Christian move from words to deeds. The great abyss the churches have not been able to cross, we are told, is this gulf between speeches given and lives placed where words are already beginning to turn stale.

A

A Christian leader, already well known as a spokesman for the under-developed world, speaking on the theme, "misery is violence," has described the threefold violence which crushes the underdeveloped part of mankind.[14]

First there is, he has said, *the violence of "herodian" oppressors,* the phenomenon of internal colonialism: the wealth of a small privileged group is maintained without reference to, and more often than not at the expense of the misery of millions of their countrymen. Pope Paul VI has spoken of social and economic development in the underdeveloped nations "practically by-passing the great majority of the people, in most cases abandoning them to a level below human dignity, and, at times, exploiting them." In my own country, some twelve percent of our families have to divide less than 1½ percent of the nation's income, while the upper 4 percent of the people receive more than 25 percent of the nation's total income. Land distribution, although bad, does not (as far as I know) match Brazil's 6 percent of proprietors owning 95 percent of the acreage. Still, conditions like these, as Dom Helder Câmara (whom I am citing here) has said, amount to a state of genuine violence.

Second, there is *the violence imposed by the developed world on the underdeveloped world:* there is the international monetary and trade system devised by the rich nations to suit their own needs and in many cases to exploit the poor nations: "the rich countries refuse to allow the poor nations to own and use whatever material resources they possess —for their own interests, and in their own way." Capitalism so often and on so large a scale subordinates human beings to profits and makes use of international politics and cultural imperialism for its own purposes. On the other hand, socialist superpowers nurture supermilitarism too, promote wars, count the individual and his freedom for naught.[15]

In the face of this second violence, our times have seen the awakening, in the new nations, of what Pope Paul VI has called "an enormous restlessness." Peoples in the developing regions have come to the realization of their need and their right "to move from a modest and often miserable standard of living to a higher, richer, worthier and more human level."[16]

[All this] leads them, [Paul VI continues] to compare their condition of life with those of developed countries, and confronting their situation of inferiority, . . . they resent the very well-being which has been brought about in their midst and which is enjoyed only by the few—whether foreigners or native-born—to their almost exclusive advantage. . . . Tears and anger more often than not mark the psychology of these young nations. They suffer from a new fever, a fever which was at first unnoticed but is now felt as unbearable: an awareness of the economic and social imbalance which separates them from, and humiliates them when set side by side with more prosperous nations.

The third form of *violence* is that *exercised by governments which support the two forms of violence* which have just been described; in the name of law and good order, often using the Christian name as shield, they collaborate in the perpetuation of present structures of oppression and injustice in their own countries.

And thus we have Christians (as we have said) who speak of the necessity of revolution. The contrast is made between *reformism* which accepts the given structures and merely desires to change their workings for the better, *evolutionism* (developmentism) which seeks by planned improvement of the technology and economics of nations gradually to narrow the gap between the front-runners and the rest of the world, and *revolution,* which seeks to subvert the present *dis-*order which obtains, "to transform the foundations of these systems," radically and rapidly to create new structures which will be geared toward building up a freer, more just humanity. And, it is urged, we as Christians in the Third World must opt for, must be in the vanguard of the revolution: the only issue is the choice of means—the peaceful use of power or its violent employ; the sheathed weapon or the naked edge.[17]

Confronted with views like this, which no thoughtful Christian can in conscience dismiss out of hand; confronted with the fact that even now committed Christians in some nations are jailed and tortured for taking positions which in all conscience they believe derive from the gospel, the question must be raised in all seriousness. We must ourselves raise it here at our conference: must the Christian, must the church, opt for revolution?[18] Must the Christian churches in Asia align themselves unequivocally with the poor and the victims of social injustice, with poor men, and the poor nations as well—against unjust structures which impede justice and impede development? Since development meets insurmountable barriers in Dom Helder Câmara's "three forms of violence" in the underdeveloped world, and if development is the primary task of the church in our midst today—must the church in Asia not take its stand once and for all with the poor?[19]

B

Perhaps in order to answer this question we must first ask ourselves another: in the Scripture teaching on the rich and the poor, on the mighty and the powerless, on whose side does God place himself? And we are told, are we not, that nothing is more clear in the sacred writings than this: that God places himself on the side of the weak, of the poor, of those without influence or power, that God comes again and again to be their protector, their advocate, their defender—he who proves himself their Father.[20]

The poor who are the victims of man's injustice, whose frightful misery Job describes (Job 24:2–12), are defended by the prophets of Israel. Amos blushes with shame over the crimes of Israel (Amos 2:6ff.; 4:1ff.; 5:11ff.); other prophets (e.g., Ezek. 22:29) denounce the violence and robbery which stain the conscience of the nation: the crimes perpetrated against the poor, frauds in trading which victimize them (e.g., Hos. 12:8; Amos 8:4ff.), land-grabbing (e.g., Isa. 5:8; Micah 2:2), enslavement of the little ones (e.g., Jer. 34:8–22; cf. Neh. 5:1–13), the abuse of power, and the perversion of justice itself.

Yahweh promises justice to the oppressed; he warns the rich of the misfortunes which are to visit them (Isa. 5:8–10; 10:1–4; Hos. 12: 8–9).

The "cry of the poor," the voice of the afflicted, the persecuted, the heavily burdened, pierces the very ears of Yahweh (Job 34:28); the downtrodden express their hopes for a better and fuller tomorrow when the situation will be reversed (Ps. 54:7–9 [5–7]; 69:23–30 [22–29], but they look for their help from Yahweh, who is their strength in weakness and who will stand for them. Their enemies are thus God's enemies (Ps. 9:14–19 [13–18]; 18:28). Their very need and distress is itself a title to Yahweh's care and love (Ps. 10:14; Isa. 66:1–2).

Thus it will be one of the tasks of the Messiah on his coming to defend the rights of the wretched and the poor (Ps. 72:2ff., 12ff.; 106; 112; Isa. 11:4; 49:13). A sign of his coming is the blessing of the poor with good things: the good things of the earth, prosperity, and the fullest human well-being (Matt. 11:2–6; Luke 1:46–55; 4:17–21 [cf. Isa. 61:1]; 6:20–26).

The poor are the heirs of the Kingdom (Matt. 5:3; Luke 6:20–26).

Thus Mary, in whom the mind and heart of God's poor, the *'anawim*, finds expression and is summed up, rejoices in her canticle in the threefold upheaval that has been foretold of the messianic era.[21]

> The little ones receive mercy; the proud are scattered in their conceit;
>
> The mighty are put down from thrones and the lowly are raised up in their stead;
>
> The rich are sent away with empty hands, but the hungry are filled with good things. (Luke 1:46–55)

Lastly, Christ himself came as one of the poor: he is born in poverty, as the Lucan narrative on Bethlehem tells us; he grows up in the obscurity, laboriousness, and lowliness of Nazareth; as an itinerant preacher he "has nowhere to lay his head" (Luke 2:6f.; Matt. 8:18–20; John 19:23; II Cor. 8:9). He has a predilection for the poor and he is to be recognized in the poor—it is in the poor we encounter him; it is with the poor he identifies himself.[22] "I was hungry and you gave me food; I was naked ᴧand you clothed me; as you did it to one of the least of these my brethren, you did it to me."

If these indications are correct, God must be said to be on the side of the poor. The meaning of the poor in these texts is of course not limited to the economically deprived, or to the *poor of Yahweh,* "the pious souls, humble and trusting in God, the 'anawim of whom the Old Testament so frequently speaks." Père Benoît equates them with "everyone who is unfortunate or unhappy in the eyes of men, the sick, the crippled, the ugly, whether in body or in soul or in mind, the despised, the rejected, the disreputable, and, of course, sinners.[23] For all these, Jesus has a pronounced predilection. He seeks them out. He commits himself to their company. He pursues them so as to save them both physically and morally." May we not say, the poor are the *underdeveloped*—persons in need, and by extension, people, nations in need and caught in the grip of exploitation, violence, dependency?

And thus the question must be asked: If God is on the side of the poor, where should the church, where should Christians, stand? If Christ identifies himself with the powerless and deprived, with whom should the church take its place?[24]

In recent years it has been said again and again that the church must side with the poor. It has been argued that within the Third World especially the very preaching of the gospel—if it is to be credible at all —demands that the church take this stand. And yet of course the objection is raised: the church is the church of all and for all, rich and poor, those at ease and those deprived by life. The church cannot be on the side of one group of men ranged against another side.

But there are answers which are being given too, which point in another direction. These answers state the traditional position, but inflect it to one side.

It seems to me that an absolute requirement of the gospel, a matter of being faithful to Christ—no matter how wrongly this fidelity may be interpreted— is that the Church, as long as she is able to speak out, as long as her voice is not stifled, should demand changes in the inhuman social structures that are holding up the full development of our people, and that are keeping them in conditions which are sub-human and unworthy of the children of God.[25]

We are well aware of the unfortunate and at times inhuman conditions in which many of our brethren still live. We wish to espouse their cause, to feel their impatience for the more equitable distribution of material goods; we shall freely, without fear or favor, denounce unjust economic differences, proclaim the human and Christian dignity of the lowly, defend their personal and collective rights, and with ever greater decisiveness support the rightful aspirations of the world of the working-man.[26]

But there is also a more clearly defined stance that says the church and the Christian must take sides:

We need to redefine the meaning of solidarity in the present situation. On the basis of the common vocation of all men who are truly equal and motivated by universal love, we must redefine relations between persons, groups of men, and between nations. We must face the present situation where nations and classes confront each other in conflict. There is a possibility of changing this without breaking the continuity of the status quo and without taking one's stand on the side of the victims of oppression and injustice; through *this solidarity with the oppressed and victimized,* we shall manifest our own solidarity with those who perpetrate oppression—by freeing them from their role of oppressor.[27]

Finally, I suggest that we can say with Jürgen Moltmann, that "the goal of Christian universalism can be realized precisely through the *dialectic* of siding with the humanity of the humiliated and oppressed." It is not with a side-in-conflict that the church takes its stand, but rather with *humanity,* with the purpose of the liberation of humanity, of those whose poverty and powerlessness call for advocacy and defense, for promotion and growth. And Moltmann speaks well of "the *dialectic* of siding with the humanity of the humiliated and oppressed." For to stand on the side of the poor is *not* to take a stance of enmity or hate against those who possess wealth and power among individuals, or human groupings, or nations, but rather to take issue with attitudes of selfishness and the structures which institutionalize egoisms, against the politics and trade systems which exploit the poor, against the abuse of power over the lives and livelihood of men; it is to take up, as the Andean Conference on Justice and Peace tells us, the cause of ultimate solidarity with the humanity of those in power against their own misuse of that power, to struggle for the redemption of man from his own injustice and inhumanity, for the reconciliation of brothers.

It has been well said that in the harshly real world we live in, Christians and the churches will not bring about reconciliation and peace by posing as a suprahistorical "meeting place for negotiation and peace," as a "neutral table for conversation and arbitration."[28] Sermons of transcendent and atemporal wisdom receive little hearing (if any) from men bent on pursuing utterly immediate ends, from parties locked in conflict. *"Sub specie aeternitatis,"* to cite Moltmann again, all worldly conflicts become relative and insignificant. To reconcile sides, finally, paradoxically enough, one must dialectically take sides, to achieve the purposes of justice and peace.[29]

C

So it is that we return to the theme of *the church as servant:* the church of the poor at the service of the poor. The theology of the servanthood of the church, after the pattern of the Ebed Yahweh, is much spoken of these days in all Christian communities. The Second Vatican Council, for instance, made it the burden of its very first pronouncement, its message to mankind. The bishops there gathered spoke of Christ's love "impelling us to serve our brothers patterning ourselves after the example of the Divine Teacher, who came not to be served but to serve. Hence the church, too, was not born to dominate but to serve. He laid down his life for us, and we ought to lay down our lives for our brothers."[30] And again:

> We carry in our hearts the hardships, the bodily and mental distress, the sorrows, longings, and hopes of all the peoples entrusted to us. . . . Let our concern swiftly focus first of all on those who are especially lowly, poor, and weak. Like Christ, we would have pity on the multitude weighed down with hunger, misery, and lack of knowledge. We want to fix a steady gaze on those who still lack the opportune help to achieve a way of life worthy of human beings.[31]

Cardinal Lercaro, one of the prophetic voices at the Council, spoke in this vein:

> We (the bishops at the Council) shall not meet the truest and deepest demands of our times, we shall not answer the hope of unity shared by all Christians, if we do no more than make the preaching of the Gospel to the poor one of the many themes of the Council. In fact it is not a theme; it is in some measure *the* theme of our Council. If it is true to say that the aim of this Council is to bring the Church into closer conformity with the truth of the gospel and to fit her better to meet the problems of our day, we can say that the central theme of this Council is the Church precisely in so far as she is the Church of the poor.[32]

In assuming the role of the servant church at the service of the poor, she is to make sure, first of all, that she is ready to face the kenotic self-emptying to take up the dedication to and solidarity with the poor that this involves. Certainly her institutional life cannot be an island of affluence in the midst of a sea of misery all around her; she must share in some real way in the deprivation and weakness of the poor.[33] In Asia she lives in the midst of as great and terrible a poverty as is found anywhere on the face of the earth, in the midst of the immense and harrowing need of millions who have only the barest means to sustain life. Surely in these regions above all it is demanded that her servant role emerge with new clarity at a time when wealth and poverty exist side by side in such stark contrast; surely it is demanded that she lay aside the trappings of great wealth and vain pomp, and not be identified with those who put their trust "in chariots and fine horses" and power in the councils of the mighty. "Poverty is a matter of life and death for the church (in Asia)," it has been said. "Poverty is the sense of effective detachment from material possessions and the actual elimination of luxuries is a weapon of special potency in Asia. . . . Christian leaders . . . must lead lives which both are, and appear to be, closer to the masses than they are at present.[34] In some real way she must share at least by way of renunciation something of the deprivation and powerlessness of the poor.

Without this solidarity her words would mean little. Without this solidarity and what it engenders, the opening of the heart to the suffering of the world, credibility remains hard to buy. Without this solidarity, the church in Asia cannot do what this hour in history asks of her: to renew herself, to transform herself to become the prophetic community which can effectively proclaim the gospel to the poor peoples of the developing world.[35] Without this solidarity she cannot take the committed stance against the various forms of injustice and exploitation that the work for the development of peoples will inevitably call for.

And so in the end we come back to the truth that the first revolution that is being asked of Christians, if they are to play an authentically Christian role in the various revolutions which must take place if the peoples of Asia are to come to fuller development, is the basic one of *conversion to the gospel:* they must be converted to what, in the light of Christ crucified and risen, they must in the first place be. The church is asked to follow Christ in poverty and servanthood; she is asked to serve by deeds of self-giving along with the whole frontier of development. No task need be foreign to Christians in this work, no matter how new and unaccustomed. But the words of the sixty-first chapter of Isaiah and those of the twenty-fifth chapter of Matthew remain, despite the new largeness, the immensity of the work of development, despite labors which are continent-wide and which span the whole world, tasks as complex as the giant computers and intricate statistical calculations—despite all these, the Scripture texts remain the charter for the Christian:

> He has sent me to bring the good news to the poor,
> to bind up the hearts that are broken,
> to proclaim liberty to captives,
> freedom to those in prison, . . .
> to comfort all those who mourn. (Isaiah 61:1–2)

> For I was hungry and you gave me food,
> I was thirsty and you gave me drink;
> I was a stranger and you made me welcome,
> naked and you clothed me,
> sick and you visited me,
> in prison and you came to see me. (Matt. 25:35–36)

"The new criterion of theology and of faith," Jürgen Moltmann has written, "is to be found in praxis." And Johannes Metz has said that the men of our time will not listen to the church if all she has to give them today is more *theoria,* even (as in *Populorum Progressio*) the theoria of *this-worldly* action. She must share in the *praxis,* she must take part in the work, she must "dirty her hands," she must commit herself to collaborating with men of goodwill in building the new earth for men. The servanthood of the church must be genuine; "it must bring the hoped-for future into practical contact with the poverty and misery of the present. This is necessary not only on the basis of the modern historical world; it is also the demand of Jesus himself."[36]

The announcement of the coming of the kingdom must be seen in the crucial points of human development: in the poverty and misery of men, in human hunger and need.

> The Christian certainty of hope becomes practical in the transformation of the present. In the expectation of divine transformation we transform ourselves and the conditions around us into the likeness of the new creation. This is a possibility—the very possibility from which Christian faith lives. This possibility is realized in repentance, in conversion, in new birth to living hope and in new life. . . . A messianic stream of renewal runs through history from the Christ of God who died in this world and was raised into the coming new world of God's righteousness. In him there are, and always were found, not only the inner repentance and liberation of the heart but also the reformations, renaissances, and revolutions of external conditions. . . . Christian hope dare not evacuate the present by dreaming about the future; . . . it must rather draw the hoped-for future already into the misery of the present and use it in practical initiatives for overcoming this misery. Through criticism and

protest, on the one hand, and creative imagination and action, on the other, we can avail ourselves of freedom for the future.[37]

When we gather together as Christians to confront the massive problems of development, the various forms of violence we cannot cope with, let alone overcome, we may perhaps be tempted to despair, to the thought that all we can do is discuss, talk, write pronouncements, and in the end leave things as they are: let misery remain as it has been, and injustice, and poverty and underdevelopment. But we remind ourselves that the faith of the Christian must always, somehow, draw on its reserves of hope. That itself is part of the struggle. For it is in times of despair that we must remember Paul's words, that it is "to shame the wise that God chose what is foolish by human reckoning, and to shame what is strong that he chose what is weak by human reckoning; . . . (God has chosen) those who are nothing at all to show up those who are everything" (I Cor. 1:27–29).

As Christians in Asia we are small in numbers and without much influence in the councils of nations. But as the Lord's arm is not shortened, our hope, and the courage born of it, even if constantly broken, is just as constantly renewed.

NOTES

1. Cf. Hans Küng, *Justification* (London: Burns & Oates, 1964), p. 130. Küng is here engaged in dialogue with Karl Barth's thought, to indicate lines of convergence with Catholic theology.

2. Cf. *inter alia* Robert Butterworth, "Christ and Creation," in *The Way, Supplement: The Shape of Theology* (London, 1967), pp. 15–23; and Michael Richards, "Towards a Theology of Development," *The Clergy Review* (July 1969), pp. 510–518.

3. *Vid.* the splendid work of A. Feuillet, *Le Christ, Sagesse de Dieu d'après les épîtres pauliniennes* (Paris: Gabada, 1966), especially the sixth chapter, on Col. 1:15–20, pp. 163–273. Yves Congar's preface, itself well worth careful reflection on this matter, says that "an entire theology of terrestrial realities finds its foundation here, and Feuillet indicates how such a theology should be Christological. It should go beyond the untenable separation between the so-called profane world and a supernatural domain which would not be involved in our day-to-day life. The cosmic role of Christ and, in its wake, that of the church or the messianic people, demands that we get beyond such a point of view; the bonds which obtain between the cosmos and man require the same thing. In this whole matter an extrinsicist viewpoint is unacceptable. Christ and, after him, the church are the bearers of the absolute future of the world: it is gratuitous and supernatural by the very fact that it is absolute, but it is the future of the world.

That toward which history is tending, unity and wholeness, is given to the world
and will be given to the world from on high, but that gift does fulfill and will
fulfill the longing which is at work in all things: *creatura exspectat* (Rom. 8:19)."
In Feuillet, op cit., pp. 1–12. The thought of Teilhard de Chardin on this theme
is well known, and it will suffice to note here the work by George Moloney, *The
Cosmic Christ: From Paul to Teilhard* (Sheed & Ward, 1968). A profound book
with much the same burden is Émile Mersch's *Le Christ, l'homme et l'univers,*
Museum Lessianum, Section théologique, LVII (Desclée de Brouwer, 1962). (It
is worth noting that Mersch seems to have arrived at his ideas without any
contact with the work of Teilhard.)

4. Cf. Yves Congar, *Jesus Christ* (Herder & Herder, 1966), p. 19 and passim;
also Hans Urs von Balthasar's rich but difficult work, *A Theology of History*
(Sheed & Ward, 1963), and the more recent *Man in History: A Theological Study*
(Sheed & Ward, 1968).

5. We could gather together a splendid florilegium of texts from Vatican II
speaking of the Christian's task in building up the world. *Gaudium et Spes* alone
yields some key sections (22, 32, 34, 39, 43, 45). Cf. also *Lumen Gentium,* 48,
and the decree on the apostolate of the laity, *Apostolicam Actuositatem.*

6. *Vid.* Harvey G. Cox, "Barbie Doll and the Specter of Cultural Imperialism" in *Christianity and Crisis,* April 27, 1970, pp. 81–82. Also Michel Peuchmard, O.P., "Let Us Be," in *New Blackfriars,* L (1968–69), pp. 136–143.

7. " 'Let us be. Leave us to find our own ways.' This sums up what Latin
Americans expect of us now. The time of domination and assistance is over. Such
a demand is very congenial to the catholicity of the Church. Yet the structures
that correspond to this spirit need to be built up. What is at stake is the life of
the Church: living together in diversity." Peuchmard's article, cited above, ends
with these words. And Harvey Cox (loc. cit.): "What Latin Americans need from
us more than anything else is not our aid, or our missionaries, or our Barbie dolls.
They need us to get off their backs and out of their heads. They need the right
to define who they are and where they want to go without our cajoling or
coercion."

In this context, see Richard Shaull, "Towards a Theology of Human Liberation," in *New Blackfriars,* XLIX (1967–68), pp. 509–517; as well as Gustavo
Gutiérrez, "Notes for a Theology of Liberation," in *Theological Studies,* XXXI
(1970), pp. 243–261; and Rubem Alves, *The Theology of Human Hope* (Corpus
Books, 1971).

8. Cf. the Second Vatican Council's decrees *Lumen Gentium,* 13; *Ad Gentes,*
22; and the references given under the word "catholicity" in the index of the
Abbott-Gallagher paperback *The Documents of Vatican II* (Guild Press, 1966).
I have briefly outlined some elements of this theme on p. 9 of the proceedings
of the East Asian Jesuit Secretariat Conference (EAJSC) sponsored by *Jesuit
Missions,* Hong Kong, 1968 (copyright by Jesuit Missions, New York).
See also, among other works, *Liberté des jeunes églises* (Louvain, Semaine de
Missiologie, 1968). Cf. E. Loffeld, "Nature propre et consistance de l'église
locale," in the volume just cited, pp. 122–143.

Of special interest are Pope Paul VI's remarks on September 28, 1968, to a delegation of African statesmen, and the speeches and parts of addresses on the theme of the "Africanization of the Church" which he gave during his visit to Ruanda.

9. Cf. the Jesuit Missions conference proceedings indicated in the preceding footnote, p. 71.

"Christianity in Asia is a 'young' faith, and Asia itself is young. Reading publications from Europe and North America which exhibit what one theologian calls a massive 'loss of nerve' among Christians in the First World, one wonders, with the Jesuit Father General, Pedro Arrupe, if the history of Christianity is ready to open a new chapter, in Asia and Africa, where the good tidings of the faith will be received as *good tidings* by the young peoples of the world." I quote these lines from a term paper submitted by one of my students. He concludes: "Have Europe and America grown too old, too cynical, too tired, to be gripped by the newness of the faith?" I might refer the reader also to *Time* magazine, Jan. 12, 1970, where the story, "Another Base," appears on page 46, as follows:

"At the turn of the century, most Christians were either Europeans, Russians or North Americans. By the year 2000, however, nearly 60% of Christendom's 1.9 billion souls will be living in the so-called Third World—Africa, Asia, Oceania and Latin America. As never before, Christianity is on the move—southward—and on the way to becoming predominantly a religion of nonwhites.

"So predicts Dr. David B. Barrett, author of *Schism and Renewal in Africa* (1968) and secretary of an ecumenical research team based in Nairobi. Christianity's growth in Africa is the most dramatic aspect of the geographic and ethnic shift. By the end of the 20th century, the number of African Christians of all faiths will have grown from 4,000,000 in 1900 (3% of the continent's population) to 351 million (46%). In the process, Christianity in Africa will have surpassed its rival Islam by 25 million adherents. The remarkable growth is attributable to normal population increase and a high incidence of conversion: one of every three African Christians is a first-generation convert.

"For sheer size and rapidity of growth, this must be one of the most spectacular stories," says Theodore L. Tucker, executive director of the Africa Department of the National Council of Churches. Three hundred million African Christians "might well give Christianity a permanent non-Western base." With Christianity in mild decline in the developed world (a projected 65% of its populace in 2000, as opposed to 77% in 1900), the day may well come when African and South American missionaries are sent to the far north for the purpose, in Melville's phrase, of christianizing Christendom."

10. See, among the many titles we might cite, Paul Caspersz, "The Role of the Church in Asia," and "Ceylon and the Search for an Asianized Church," in *New Blackfriars,* Jan. 1970, pp. 17–29 and 288–296.

11. Antoine de Saint-Exupéry, *Wind, Sand and Stars* (Harcourt, Brace & World, Harbrace Paperback, 1967), pp. 239–243.

12. Henri de Lubac, "The Church in the Present Crisis," in *Clergy Monthly* (Ranchi, India), May 1970.

13. See the brief introduction in *Herder Correspondence,* Aug. 1968, "The Theology of Revolution," pp. 227–233. See also Harvey Cox (ed.), *The Church Amid Revolution* (Association Press, 1967).

14. Dom Helder Câmara, in his conference "Violence and Misery," *Herder Correspondence,* June 1969, pp. 177–179, and *New Blackfriars,* L (1968–69), pp. 491–496. See also his book *The Church and Colonialism* (London: Sheed & Ward, 1968). On Dom Helder's own work, read José de Broucker, *Dom Helder Câmara* (Paris: Fayard, 1968); *Informations catholiques internationales,* May 15, 1968, pp. 4–7; and M. de Certeau, *Études* (Paris), July 1970, pp. 104–113.

15. The literature on the question of economic imperialism is abundant. By way of sampling, see Peter J. Riga, "American Foreign Policy, Some Moral Considerations," in *World Justice* (Louvain University), XI (1969–70), Dec. 1969, pp. 211–225; and the Pelican paperback *The Dialectics of Liberation,* ed. by David Cooper (London, 1969), especially the essays by John Gerassi, Paul Sweezy, and Herbert Marcuse, pp. 72–109 and 175–192.

Jeremias Montemayor, in his Tokyo AECD paper, indicates some of the lines of thinking on economic aid ("moral reparations") from the former colonizing nations.

16. Pope Paul VI, on the first anniversary of *Populorum Progressio,* March 27, 1968. (See an English version in *L'Osservatore Romano,* April 4, 1968.)

17. On the theology of liberation, see the references given in Note 7, above. See also Gustavo Pérez Ramírez, "Paques en Amerique latine: liberation," in *Verbum Caro: Communio,* 1970, pp. 18–27. Father Juan Luis Segundo, of the Centro Pedro Fabro in Montevideo, Uruguay, and his associates at the center have written on the theology of liberation from the Latin American perspective. See Segundo's articles in *Perspectivas de Diálogo,* the monthly published at Montevideo, Uruguay.

18. José de Broucker, "Has the Church Opted for Revolution?" in *New Blackfriars,* XLIX (1967–68), pp. 540–543.

19. Joao da Veiga Coutinho, "The Church and the Third World," *Cross Currents,* XVIII (1968), pp. 435–449. Reprinted in *Impact* (Manila), Jan. 1970, pp. 4–10.

Cardinal Bea Studies, Vol. I, *Mission and Development Ecumenical Conversations* (Quezon City: Cardinal Bea Institute, 1970), devotes an entire symposium to this remarkable article (edited by Pedro S. de Achutegui).

20. The reader is asked to go over the entries on "Poverty" in any recent biblical dictionary or dictionary of biblical theology for indications of the evidence on this point. See for instance X. Leon-Dufour's *Dictionary of Biblical Theology* (London: G. Chapman, 1969), s.v. "Poor," pp. 386–388.

21. *Vid.* Herman Hendricx, "Poverty, Riches and Equal Distribution of Goods," in *Impact,* May 1970, pp. 17–20, and June 1970, pp. 20–24.

22. Yves Congar, "God Reveals Himself in Poverty," in his book *Jesus Christ,* tr. by Luke O'Neil (Herder & Herder, 1966), pp. 66–85, a beautiful and inspiring essay. See also the same author's *Power and Poverty in the Church* (Helicon Press, 1964). (*Philippine Studies,* July 1965, pp. 725–733.)

23. Cited by Congar, in the chapter cited above, pp. 69–70. Benoît, *L'Évêque dans l'Église du Christ* (Paris: Desclée de Brouwer, 1963), p. 360.

24. See the rather "strong" article, "L'Église écartelée," by B. Dumas, O.P., in *Parole et Mission* (Paris), LI (July 20, 1970), pp. 293–301, and the comment by the Scripture scholar, Dominique Barthélemy, O.P., pp. 301–303. Cf. also: 16 Bishops of the Third World, "Gospel and Revolution," *New Blackfriars*, XLIX (1967–68), pp. 140–184.

25. Dom Helder Câmara, at the "Poverty Is Violence" meeting in London, April 13, 1969. See Note 14, above.

26. XII Plenary Assembly of the Spanish Episcopal Conference, 1970; *L'Osservatore Romano*, Aug. 13, 1970. Comunicado de la conferencia episcopal española, al término de su XII Asamblea Plenaria, July 11, 1970, as published in *Ecclesia*, No. 1500, July 18, 1970—a valuable document. In connection with the same Plenary Assembly, see the inaugural address of Archbishop Morcillo González, on "The Church and the Poor."

The address given by Pope Paul VI on "The Church of the Poor" at the general audience on June 24, 1970, deserves careful reading: *L'Osservatore Romano* (Italian daily edition), June 25, 1970. Cf. *Documentation catholique*, July 19, 1970, pp. 657–658.

Also, speaking on the same theme, P. Henri de Riedmatten, O.P., at Geneva, International Labor Conference, June 17, 1970 (*Documentation catholique*, July 19, 1970, pp. 683–685), and the Cardinal Secretary of State, in the name of Pope Paul VI, to the 57th Semaine Sociale of France: *L'Osservatore Romano*, July 2, 1970) Christians must be in the front ranks of those who struggle to vanquish poverty in society. Cardinal Villot's letter is something of an essay at a systematic study of the theme.

27. Conclusions of the First Andean Regional Conference of the National Commissions of Justice and Peace of the Catholic Hierarchies, May 12, 1970.

28. Jürgen Moltmann, *Religion, Revolution and the Future* (Charles Scribner's Sons, 1969), pp. 129ff.

29. Ibid.

30. In the Abbott-Gallagher edition, *The Documents of Vatican II*, pp. 3–7.

31. Ibid., p. 5.

32. Cited in Congar, *Power and Poverty in the Church*, p. 149.

33. Avery Dulles, *The Dimensions of the Church*, Woodstock Papers (Newman Press, 1967), p. 63.

34. Paul Caspersz, "The Role of the Church in Asia," *New Blackfriars*, LI (1969–70).

35. Cf. Coutinho (in the article cited in Note 7, above), last section of the essay.

36. Moltmann, *Religion, Revolution and the Future*, p. 139.

37. Ibid., p. 140.

Twenty-two

Theological Insights
for a Secular Anthropology
M. M. Thomas

[The book from which this essay is taken, titled in part "The Secular Meaning of Christ," is a study of representative Indian patterns of secular ideology, and serves as a sequel to Dr. Thomas' earlier work, *The Acknowledged Christ of the Indian Renaissance,* in which he dealt with the thought of India's great religious humanists. In this essay we have the most explicit statement of Thomas' thought on the relation between Christian faith and ideology, according to which he is able to critically evaluate the ideologies behind all political systems in India, from liberal nationalism and democratic socialism to Marxism-Leninism. On the one hand, he can criticize liberal nationalists for not being conscious of the sinfulness of man or his need for divine forgiveness. On the other hand, he can criticize the ideology of Communism for regarding human selfhood merely as the reflection of social relations in disregard of the spiritual dimension of human life. Here he examines four basic elements of the Christian understanding of man in society which are relevant to "a realistic ideology of social humanism," and translates them for us into meaningful secular terms.—Ed.]

The basic thesis I wish to affirm here is this. Every theology has an anthropological content inherent in it or derivable from it; and every anthropology is based on theological presuppositions either explicitly or implicitly. By theology I mean the intellectual articulation of man's faith in God or in a structure of meaning and sacredness which is seen as his ultimate destiny. And by anthropology I mean, in its broad sense, the understanding of the nature of man and his relation to nature, social culture, and history. Feuerbach and, following him, Karl Marx have spoken of theology as in itself anthropology, the illusory consciousness of an alienated human existence. Bultmann speaks of theology as essentially a mode of real self-understanding, an overcoming of self-alienation. What one may assert without the danger of being contradicted is that

The Epilogue of his book *Secular Ideologies of India and the Secular Meaning of Christ* (Bangalore: Christian Institute for the Study of Religion and Society, 1976). Reprinted by permission.

theology and anthropology are integral to one another. They are so because man as finite spirit is involved in the temporal processes of life and at the same time transcends it in his sense of an eternal destiny whichever way that sense is interpreted. The relation between Christian theology and Christian anthropology has been best expressed by Paul Lehmann by his dictum, "All theology is anthropology as a reflex of Christology."

Indeed, the Bible does not deal directly or systematically with the anthropological question. It is concerned primarily with God, but God in relation to mankind. And in speaking of God's purpose for human existence and the words and deeds of God in human history to forward that purpose, the Bible has a great deal to say about the secular realm of man, society, history, and nature. The God of the Bible is the God of history. He is "the God of Abraham, Isaac, and Jacob, not the God of the philosophers," as Pascal has said. Therefore, in the biblical approach to the saving knowledge of God, the central emphasis is on doing the will of God or responding to the purpose of God in the historical realm, and not on philosophical vision or mystic union. Salvation is of man as historical being, and it invests history and human freedom and action in history with ultimate spiritual significance. Nature itself is seen as the Creation of God providing the background for history as salvation and sharing in it. The God of Moses is the God of exodus and law. He delivers his people from slavery, and the prophet Amos discerns the hand of God in the liberation of all peoples from bondage. God gives law and demands justice in all social relations. This prophetic interpretation of God sees man as placed under a moral and spiritual imperative of realizing freedom and righteousness in societies and between societies. Salvation involves social liberation. God's word and deed in Jesus Christ stands as the fulfillment of those in the Law and the Prophets. God was in Christ reconciling the world unto himself, overcoming man's contrariness to God; and through the cross he has broken down all walls of partition among mankind, and united them into a unity in Christ. Salvation includes community and unity among mankind. God has raised Jesus from among the dead as the guarantee of the final victory of God and man over all evil in individuals, society, and the cosmos, and over death. Through his Spirit, God has brought into being the church, the community of those who believe in Christ to be a witness to the renewal of all things in Christ; to cooperate with him in it and to be a foretaste of it in its life. In the End, God will transform the kingdoms of this world into the Kingdom of God and his Christ.

The Bible thus is the story of the mighty works of God in history— a theology. No doubt, it rules out all forms of Secular Humanism which closes itself at the secular and becomes secularistic not only as opposed to the Christian gospel but also as devoid of a comprehensive understanding of the reality of man and therefore liable to become dehumanizing in the long run. Positively however, a Secular Humanism which affirms humanization of nature, creativity of man in purposive history, liberation from social bondage, and realization of love in human relation as the promise and potentiality of mankind in every historical situation and which struggles to realize them within the limits and possibilities of the situation is integral to the faith and hope of the Christian gospel.

Let us look more closely at some elements of the Christian theological understanding of man which are most relevant to a realistic secular ideology of Social Humanism.

First, *the reality of man as created in the image of God.* The first biblical story of Creation says: "Then God said, Let us make man in our image, after our likeness; and let them have dominion over (all) . . . the earth. So God created man in his own image, in the image of God he created him; male and female he created them" (Gen. 1:26-27). In secular language it is an affirmation that man is a spiritual person called to fulfill himself by establishing mastery over nature and by entering into dialogue and communion with other persons in society. Man is finite spiritual freedom. He is no doubt evolved from nature and is subject to its mechanical and organic necessities, but in his sense of selfhood or personhood, unlike the subhuman beings, he knows that he is so subject, but also that he can transform nature and subject it to his purposes. He is also a person among many persons in society, and at this level he knows that he is called to recognize in reverence the mystery of other persons and become himself within a social communion of persons. Thus selfhood in man appears with his knowledge of objective natural necessity and of the otherness of other persons on the one hand, and the sense of spiritual destiny on the other. The sense of destiny is in a sense man's awareness at spiritual depth that he is not yet himself but that he has to transcend himself to become himself through exercise of creativity and responsibility. An orientation to the Future or/and the Beyond is thus inherent in it as an imperative. This imperative is the call of the Infinite Spirit, of the ultimate values of Truth, Goodness, and Beauty on man's finite spirit, and is sustained by it.

Therefore the reality of man, human society, and human history cannot be interpreted in purely naturalistic or purely spiritual terms. Humanism is not naturalism at a higher stage, or a closed social organism, or spirituality at a lower stage. Man is becoming creatively open to the future, with objectives of dynamic nature, subjective self-understanding of persons and societies and the reality of a transcendent Providence, all playing their roles in their interrelation. An interpretation of the dialectic of history has to take all these elements into account to be essentially human or adequately true.

The vision of man created as the crown of creation, with glory only a little less than God's own and destined to dominion over the creatures inspires a sense of mystery which is seen not only in the writer of Genesis, but also in the psalmist (Psalm 8) and the writer of the Epistle to the Hebrews (Hebrews 2). From such a sense of the mystery of man's personhood has arisen the modern demand that societies and states should recognize the fundamental rights of the human person for freedom, for self-determination, and for the pursuit of truth, goodness, and beauty, and the right to follow the path of service to God, as dictated by his own reason and conscience, in this freedom. From it also arise the ideological movements to transform closed static societies which restrain human creativity, enslaving man to nature and to blind traditions of the past, into open dynamic societies oriented to the future.

Secondly, *the reality of man as a fallen creature.* Though the Bible declares the creaturely finiteness of man as in itself "good" (Gen. 1:31) it sees him as involved in a constant spiritual rebellion against the Creator and his own situation of finiteness and relations of dependence. He wants to be absolute and in the center of the universe like God (Gen. 3:5). The result is total alienation from God, neighbor, nature, and oneself. St. Paul gives another description of the sin of man. He says: "Although they knew God they did not honor him as God or give thanks to him, but they became futile in their thinking and their senseless minds were darkened. . . . (They) exchanged the glory of the immortal God for images resembling mortal man or birds or animals or reptiles" (Rom. 1:21–23). Instead of accepting life as a gift of grace in thankfulness, man rebels and involves himself in perversity of consciousness and spirit leading him to worship of idols created by him. In secular language one might speak of the fall as the innate tendency of individuals and groups for self-love and self-centeredness leading to search for power over others. Since this is doing violence to the reality of the self and its relation to God and neighbor, it results in self-alienation in the spirit of man. This he seeks to overcome by creating means of self-justification, that is, idolatrous religions to justify himself before God, pharisaic righteousness of legal morality to buttress the self against an accusing conscience and impossible utopias to hide his power and interests exploiting his neighbor in society. Luther's attack on justification by the works of religion and morality, Karl Marx's discovery of false consciousness and ideologies to hide class interests, Nietzsche's discovery of the powerless seeking self-aggrandizement through morality, and Freud's doctrine of the conscious region of the mind acting as smokescreen for the real egoistic impulses of man—all these are evidence of the endless and frustrating struggle of man for self-justification. The fact that he wants to hide his self-love not only from others but also from himself indicates that at depth man is aware that his true destiny does not lie along that path. The awareness of a destiny which is constantly betrayed and the impossibility of self-efforts to fulfill that destiny are characteristic of the spiritual condition created by man's rejection of God.

By locating the self-alienation of man through self-centeredness in the spirit of man, Christian understanding sees it as affecting the totality of human existence (body, mind, conscience, and soul as well as individuality and sociality) and the total sweep of human history (past, present, and future). At this point it differs from other concepts which locate the source of human alienation in some one part of man or one historical social system and therefore easily removable. For instance, those who think the material body is the source of alienation hope to overcome it by spirituality and asceticism; those who consider ignorance of the mind the cause of evil seek to remedy it through education; and those who see in capitalism the seeds of self-love expect to redeem human nature through socialism. And so on. All these have elements of truth in them, especially in dealing with particular evils, but what is common to them all is the rejection of the universality of self-love and the affirmation of the capacity of man and history for self-redemption. Christian faith rejects it as the product of a superficial interpretation of human reality, especially the anxieties and insecurities of the finite self which has not found the security of the love of God. But the Christian understanding of the universality of sin does not mean its equality everywhere, making relative choices irrelevant. What it points to is the fact that every good of man has the potentiality of self-righteousness in it, that every creativity of man has the spirit of destructivity inherent in it, that while man's reason and conscience reflect the imperative of truth and goodness they are also conditioned by the false purposes of the self which they serve. The symbolism of Anti-Christ becoming most active just before the coming of Christ declares that the higher reaches of human goodness, creativity, rationality, and morality are most infected by the subtle spiritual anxieties of self-idolatry and self-righteousness.

It is this insight that gives strength to the dictum of Lord Acton that power corrupts and absolute power corrupts absolutely. From this arises the imperative to avoid monopoly of political, economic, or social power in any one person or party, for it is easy to find ideological justification for exploitation and oppression. Therefore to minimize corruption, power should be decentralized, all people directly sharing in it. Where that is not possible its corruption should be minimized by making it responsible to the people whose welfare is affected by it and by inbuilt opposition and legal safeguards. In fact when a nation or class or party holds monopoly of power, the same insight justifies power politics, nonviolent and peaceful where possible, violent where necessary, to realize a measure of democracy and justice in the power structure.

Thirdly, *the reality of the crucified and risen Jesus Christ* as the true man and as the source of renewal of human nature and through it of all things.

It is the Christian belief that in a human existence totally tainted by the contrariness of man's spirit of self-centeredness, God incarnated, or rather inhominized himself into history, assumed our sinful humanity, and through his incarnation, life, and death redeemed it of its sin. Jesus Christ crucified and risen is therefore both the prototype of true manhood in history and the source of ultimate humanization of human nature and mankind.

Indeed, this is the starting point of all Christian understanding of man. Even the understanding of man as created in the image of God and as a fallen creature finds its confirmation only in the light of Jesus Christ. He is the image of the invisible God (Col. 1:15) and his life of sonship to God the Father and of brotherliness to all mankind gives us the picture of human personhood and its destiny in love of God and neighbor. For the writer of the Epistle to the Hebrews, it is Jesus, risen and crowned with glory and honor, who is the first fulfillment of the glorious destiny promised in Psalm 8 that all things will be put under the feet of man. It is in the crucifixion of Jesus the Divine Incarnate—by Pax Romana, Hebrew religion and law, Jewish nationalism, and the populism—that human nature and all the highest human achievements in religion, morality, and state are revealed in the final analysis as enmity to God and misdirection of the true destiny of man.

The cross of Jesus is also the answer to the human problem of justification of human existence. Responding in faith to the free divine forgiveness and acceptance offered by the Crucified, man is released from the necessity to seek security and justification by his own spirituality and moral or social idealism. But this release from anxiety from the search for means of self-justification is a release for self-giving love of God and neighbor, which the cross itself reveals as the destiny of man.

Centrality of the divine forgiveness releases men and women from the idolatry of communalism of religion, race, nation, class, sex, and caste or even ideology which, in alienated conditions, provided spiritual and social security. For in the new humanity in Christ "which is being renewed in knowledge after the image of its maker," the distinction of nature, history, culture, and religion are not absolutized but transcended in the awareness of solidarity with all mankind and common participation in the new humanity in Christ. "Here there cannot be Greek and Jew, circumcised and uncircumcised, barbarian, Scythian, slave, free man, but Christ is all, and in all." Through Jesus Christ, a new communion of the Spirit, based on mutual forgiveness and gratitude to the divine forgiveness received in Christ, building up tissues of love, comes into being among the communities of the world, producing the spiritual ferment of their renewal and humanization (Col. 3:11–17). The church of Christ confessing Jesus as Lord is the structured nucleus of this communion.

In secular anthropological terms, this faith in human salvation through God in Christ means the recognition of the ultimacy of the pattern of Jesus' humanity for existence, that a life of mutual self-giving love is the criterion and goal of mature manhood and human community. It is also necessary to recognize that this goal transcends human organization and planning, ideology and politics; it is the sphere of voluntary spiritual responses of faith. But organization, planning, ideology, and politics have their positive function of creating the conditions of political freedom and social justice which make such spiritual responses of faith and love easier. More especially, Jesus himself has declared that societies will be judged ultimately by the criterion whether they are structured to express concern for "the least" in society, that is, the poor, the powerless, and the oppressed. "As you did it to one of the least of these my brethren, you did it to me" (Matt. 25:40). For a sinful world with its limits, it is the sign of the Kingdom of love. Without justice in the power structure of society, love becomes demoralizing charity. But as Nicolas Berdyaev has said, ideologies and politics do become dehumanizing when they elevate themselves into total schemes of human salvation and claim to be means of bringing about not only justice but also love and communion; for when it does this ideologies and politics are absolutized into holy crusades with the seed of self-righteousness expressing itself in ruthlessness. This is indeed the story of Stalinism and a great many other revolutions of justice turned into new oppressions, and devouring their owr children. Justification by grace through faith not by works is a theological doctrine which has great relevance to the secular ideologies and political movements of liberation in our time, and needs to be translated into secular insights for incorporation in political and social philosophies. And in a world where many hitherto oppressed nations, races, and classes are becoming awake to the exploitation they have suffered for ages, the idea that mutual forgiveness is the ultimate foundation of community and unity should mold even the necessary power struggles which they wage, lest their hate convert them into oppressors in their turn.

The liberation which Jesus Christ offers to mankind includes the affirmation of his Lordship over all natural and cosmic powers, in fact the whole universe. The New Testament and after it the creeds of the church speak of "all things" in heaven and on earth as being created through Christ and for the purpose revealed in him, and as brought into harmony with that purpose through the humanity liberated by Christ. "In him all things were created, in heaven and on earth, visible and invisible, whether thrones or dominions or principalities or authorities —all things were created through him and for him. He is before all things, and in him all things hold together. . . . In him all the fulness of God was pleased to dwell, and through him to reconcile to himself all things, whether on earth or in heaven, making peace by the blood of his cross" (Col. 1:16–20). The same epistle sees Jesus' crucifixion, which brings forgiveness to sinners, as having "disarmed the principalities and powers and made a public example of them triumphing over them in him" (2:15). Man alienated from God has traditionally divinized the powers of nature and the cosmos, worshiped "the elemental spirits of the universe" and enslaved himself to them. In so doing, he has perverted himself and them. Christ, in liberating man from spirits and gods, has also secularized nature and cosmos, and thereby made it possible for mankind to master it through science and technology. By technology here we mean the whole complex of material and social engineering, and of techniques of management and control—all of which are directed to the exploration and mastery of nature and natural forces in society and history. But modern man alienated from God and given to false purposes of the self and societies, constructs such technology as can be utilized as means of self-glorification, as instruments of economic exploitation of peoples, political imperialism, and war; he has also divinized technological dynamism to such an extent that he sees persons as fodder for the machine and allows it to destroy the ecological and organic bases of human living, for the present and future generations. The point is that the misdirection of technology cannot be interpreted in isolation from the framework of the "subjective spiritual" and the "objective social" conditions and purposes within which man relates himself to nature in the creation and utilization of technology; and any reorientation of it to the quality of human life requires redemption at the spiritual and revolution at the social levels of life. It is this truth that may be suggested in St. Paul's statement that the creation waits with eager longing for the revealing of the sons of God so that it may be liberated from "futility" and "bondage to decay" (Rom. 8:19–21). It goes to the credit of Karl

Marx that he has seen the importance of the context of self-alienation and social relations for the technological exploitation of nature; but his tendency to see the human selfhood merely as the reflection of social relations has prevented him from seeing the spiritual dimension of man's technological creations, where the gospel of salvation in Christ has deep relevance. Indeed, in the service of the Eucharist, in which the church celebrates salvation, the material world in the form of bread and wine finds its consecration in the context of the fellowship of believers offering themselves to God in the self-offering of Jesus Christ.

Fourthly, *the reality of man and society in the light of the consummation of their Absolute future in the Kingdom of God.* The Christian hope is based on the power of the Spirit who raised Jesus from the dead, as the firstfruits of the New Creation, and who is powerfully at work in all societies and all creation renewing them. It is hope in the future of man incorporated in the future of the risen Jesus Christ, and is expressed as the second coming of Jesus. As St. Paul puts it: "We await a Savior, the Lord Jesus Christ, who will change our lowly body to be like his glorious body, by the power which enables him even to subject all things to himself" (Phil. 3:20–21). Note that the meaning of man's whole historical existence in the body in relation to society and nature is here taken up in the Kingdom, through its death and resurrection. Indeed, the Revelation speaks of the consummation in terms of "a new heaven and a new earth" (Rev. 21:1). The secular meaning of these eschatological affirmations of theology for anthropology lies in the affirmation in history of a Reality, a Providence, a Presence which transcends the resources of nature and the purposes of man, which ultimately determines their Future, and which is available in every Present to humanize nature, man, and society—even when, or precisely when, objective social conditions and subjective human wills give no hope. It is a Human Hope which can comprehend within itself and grapple with tragedy as the outcome of the historical process as a whole, and of every historical situation. Eschatology is not just teleology which speaks of a determinism within the historical process making a Utopia the inevitable result at the end. Nor is eschatology speaking about an End which is imposed on a meaningless historical process; the kingdoms of this world are the raw material for the Kingdom of God. The historical process is affirmed through its transformation which is as radical as the one which happened quietly in the inhominization of God in Jesus in the history of the world, or as what happened with greater trauma in the resurrection through death of the historical humanity of Jesus. Such an eschatological hope alone can give natural necessity, human determinism, and transcendent providence each its due place in the interpretation of the historical process as a whole and the human reality in any historical situation. Living from an Absolute Future which is ever "at hand," men and women are sustained in historical action for specific historical utopian goals, without paralyzing despair, even when they can see only failure or at best temporary or imperfect achievement resulting from their action. Their hope is in a spiritual power which brings into being that which is not, and uses the weak to confound the strong. Says St. Paul: "Therefore, my beloved brethren, be steadfast, immovable, always abounding in the work of the Lord, knowing that in the Lord your labor is not in vain" (I Cor. 15:58). The meaning of every historical action directed to love and justice in history and every fragmentary realization of truth, goodness, and beauty in life is protected, redeemed, and fulfilled in the End. How, we do not know. But our guarantee is the risen Jesus Christ.

Twenty-three

Orientations for
an Asian Theology
Sebastian Kappen, S.J.

[One of the papers presented to the Asian Conference of Third World Theologians meeting in Wennappuwa, Sri Lanka, January 1979. Fr. Kappen, who is one of the younger Catholic theologians of India and who works with the Centre for Social Reconstruction in Madras, defines theology as "primordial encounter with God." By this he means that authentic theology is not abstract but concrete, for we encounter the living God at the level of human life or we do not encounter him at all. The "thematization" of theology must therefore embrace all the dimensions of life including the existential, the social, the ethical, and the historical. This process of thematization, if it is authentic, cannot end in dogmatic formulations, for this would amount to a denial of the living God. It becomes instead a "power in praxis that heals the human situation." There is no other way God can appear to us. Given Kappen's definition of theology, its purpose must be to "render explicit the dimensions of meaning implicitly contained in the original God-encounter." For Asian theologians this means that it is in our people's "struggles to fashion a more just and humane society that we have to meet a living God." This is an earnest effort to construct an Asian theology of liberation.—Ed.]

The aim of this paper is neither to summarize nor to evaluate Asian Christian theology, past or present, but to suggest, tentatively, the direction theologizing should take in the future. Any such venture already presupposes a conception of theology. In the present case, the presupposition itself is the result of a protracted process of grappling with the problem of God and the human being in the Asian context, especially in the context of religious pluralism, Marxism, and the sociopolitical situation. Therefore, an elucidation of what I mean by theology will itself provide the framework for deriving guidelines for the future. It will also provide the frame of reference for a critique of past and present theolo-

From *Asia's Struggle for Full Humanity,* edited by Virginia Fabella, M.M. Copyright © 1980, Orbis Books, Maryknoll, N.Y. 10545. Reprinted by permission.

gies. Admittedly, my views are largely shaped by the Indian experience. Whether and how far they apply to other Asian countries, it is up to others from those countries to decide. The fundamental notion that constitutes both the point of departure and the point of arrival of this paper is that theology is a critical reflection on our primordial encounter with God. Let me explain in detail what this means.

GOD-ENCOUNTER: THE MATRIX OF THEOLOGY

It is on purpose I have used the word "encounter" in preference to "experience." Experience is liable to be understood in a purely subjectivist sense, as though God were a mere projection of the human mind. Encounter, on the other hand, involves a coming face to face with an "other," in this case, with the ultimate "Other," with the ground and goal of humanity and history. This "Other" is neither personal nor impersonal but transpersonal. In any genuine God-encounter, the absolute Other is experienced as the inmost *within* of the subject who encounters, be it individual or community. Encounter in this sense is not a function of any of the human faculties like sensation, intelligence, or will. It takes place at the inmost being of man, where feeling, knowing, willing, and loving have their common root. It is there that man is invaded and inhabited by the Absolute, where the Transcendent becomes the Immanent, where the inbreaking of the divine becomes an indwelling and an inspiriting. To meet God in this manner is to be taken hold of by God, to be uprooted and swept off one's feet in such a manner that one no more controls oneself; it is, at the same time, to experience the relativization of everything else, whether it be job, security, fame, wealth, or even life itself. Such relativization is, in fact, the only guarantee that one has encountered the Absolute.

But where does encounter with God take place? It cannot be on the level of religious symbols—whether word symbols (myths, legends, creeds, scriptures), act symbols (cult, prayer, religious dance, ceremonies), thing symbols (temples, altar, consecrated food, sacred utensils, sacred places), or person symbols (priests, religious teachers, consecrated virgins). These are, at best, forms in which an original God-encounter expressed itself and, as such, are derivative in character. No form is adequate to the content; no symbol is capable of expressing the richness of the original experience, which is ineffable and unfathomable. More, forms and symbols can even distort what they are meant to convey and thus become alienated and alienating. Finally, even the original God-encounter, which these symbols represent and are meant to communicate, is itself historically conditioned and need not necessarily be relevant to the contemporary human being. It follows then that the primary locus of God-encounter is to be sought not within but outside and beyond religion in its symbolic, institutionalized forms.

And this privileged locus can be nothing other than practical life, at once individual and social, whose texture is made up of all that people do and of all that is done to them—dating and mating, sowing and reaping, producing and consuming, buying and selling, planning and organizing. This is the world of praxis, meaning the historical process whereby people transform themselves in transforming their environment of things, persons, and structures (economic, social, political, and cultural). Praxis comprises not merely action but also passion: *passion-from* as openness to the mystery of life and *passion-for* as striving for values, ideals, and goals. It is the world of praxis that mediates the presence and the inbreaking of the divine. For us, Asian theologians, this means that it is in the action and passion of our people, in their condition of bondage to systems of exploitation and domination, in their struggles to fashion a more just and humane society that we have to meet the living God.

How does this God confront us today? God comes to us and to all people of goodwill in the form of an unconditional challenge to shake off our shackles and to fashion a new home for the human family, a new society "in which the free development of each will be the condition for the free development of all." In truth, there is no other way the divine can appear to us. For what is God but the absolute negation of all evil and the absolute affirmation of all that is good, true, and beautiful? Not in the sense that we form a notion of him by negating all limitations and imperfections, but in the sense that he is himself the act of negating, just as light is the act of dispelling darkness. To encounter God therefore is to become the negating and affirming that God really is; it is to become both a wielder of the sword and a herald of peace. Through him who has encountered God, the divine "No" to exploitation, injustice, and misery and the divine "Yes" to whatever furthers the fullness of humanity reverberate in history and radiate to the ends of the earth. In other words, his response itself mediates the presence of God in the world. If so, theologians should by no means confine themselves to their own personal encounter with God. They should remain open to the God who reveals God in the response of others around them, to whichever caste, religion, or community the others may belong. More importantly, they should realize that it is not so much in the establishment as in those social forces and trends which strive to break the fetters which the establishment imposes that the working of the divine in history reveals itself unmistakably and unambiguously. Anyone who ignores or dissociates himself or herself from these energies of the new age to come has no right to theologize.

Theological reflection is genuine only when it forms a moment in the total human response to the challenge of God embedded in history. It is but one phase of a movement which originates from and returns to the world of praxis. But in any living process any one moment includes all the others. So, too, theologizing should encompass not only God but also humans who encounter God and the encounter itself; it should direct itself both to the divine challenge and to the human response. Keeping this in mind, let us elucidate further the concrete task of theological reflection.

Let me state first what theological reflection is not. It is not an attempt to flee from the concrete world of praxis to the world of sterile abstractions. It is, rather, a process of concretion, of greater and greater immersion in reality, in the reality of God's challenge enfleshed in history. An analogy might prove useful here. Looking down from a plane as it flies at a high altitude one sees the entire landscape below but not the various objects. But as the plane glides to a landing, the same objects begin to appear more and more distinctly, revealing their proper contours and colors. So it is with the course of theological reflection. Reflection leads one to perceive clearly what was already perceived, though confusedly, in the primordial encounter with God. Hence, it is more like contemplation than like discursive reasoning. And yet it is not mere contemplation; it is also a process of *becoming* what one contemplates and thereby attaining to a richer and fuller mode of *being*. For the same reason it can in no way be termed an "inscape" into the inwardness of one's self where one is alone with oneself. Such a self in isolation is but a fiction of the mind. For one's deepest being is a being-with: with things, with other people, and with the absolute Other. Centered in oneself, one is also centered in one's kind and in God. In his other inmost being one is open to the mystery of existence, a hearer of words, a hearer of the Word. Theological reflection must therefore take place in a spirit of communion with all that is, and of compassion for all who belong to the human family.

THEOLOGY AS THEMATIZATION

The main thrust of reflection must be directed to rendering explicit (thematizing) the dimensions of meaning implicitly contained in the original God-encounter. The dimensions of meaning to be thematized are many. Here I can do no more than enumerate the more important ones. To begin with, there is the existential dimension. The experience of being taken hold of by the Absolute is what throws light on the deeper problems of existence such as people's being-unto-death, the ambivalence of their freedom, their bondage to sin and guilt, and finally, the ultimacy of their hope. The divine that invades the human is also power—power that enables him or her to conquer the forces of death and decay, to cast off all that smothers freedom, and to overcome the inner breach between the Is and the Ought. However, the manner in which these existential challenges are perceived and responded to will vary from place to place because of the uneven development of capitalism and variations in the persistence of traditional attitudes and values. The problem is all the more complicated since traditional and capitalist forms of existential alienation coexist in the same people, in the same group, and even in the same person.

Another important dimension which needs to be thematized is the social. The divine challenge, the human response, and the something new which that response always creates—all the three have a social significance. The divine challenge is more often than not enfleshed in a social situation, say, of exploitation or domination. Take, for instance, the oppression of landless laborers in a particular place. All who are attuned to the living God will see in this situation a challenge to organize the laborers against the forces of oppression. The collective resistance that results is equally revelative of God, insofar as it makes the divine "No" to evil operative in history. Finally, if as a result of organized struggle there is greater equality and justice in that area, that too has a theological meaning. For the splendor of God can be seen only as reflected on the faces of humans—the divine being nothing but the depth-dimension of the love that binds the many into one.

Human beings being-with-their-kind is always mediated by things, whether given or produced by labor. Conversely, their relation to things is mediated by their fellow humans. Hence the material world is something like the extension in time and space of human social existence. But in all societies dominated by the institution of private property—and Asian societies are no exception to this—nature and the product of labor act as a principle of division, and even as an instrument of exploitation and domination. From being expressions of creativity, products tend to smother every authentic manifestation of the human. Such being the case, an adequate response to it should include also a commitment to the socialization of property so that both nature and the products of labor become vehicles of human togetherness. For the world to radiate and manifest the glory of human beings and God it is equally necessary that the production of the useful is at the same time the creation of the beautiful because the beautiful is that point of convergence where human transcendence unto (reaching out to) the divine and God's immanence (indwelling) in the world meet and fuse into one single incandescence. That is why the theology of the future will have to be also an aesthetics. Only then shall we recapture something of that reverence which the ancient seers of Asia felt for the earth and its fruits, for labor and its products. Only then shall nature cease to be something that is violated and ravished by human lust for profit and power. This means that the goal of Asian development will have to be qualitatively different from the Western brand of gadget civilization.

Finally, the theologian must focus also the historical dimension of God-encounter. History is not merely the stage on which the drama of the human being's meeting with the Maker is enacted. It is essentially constituted by divine challenge and human response. What is history but the transcendence of God become the self-transcendence of men and women through project and praxis? It is the unconditional call of the divine that beckons us to break loose from the ever rotating wheel of cyclic time and march forward to the horizon of human-divine fullness, despite reverses and regressions. The ultimate human project, too, is transcendent. That is why it invariably takes the form of myth. For absolute transcendence can be expressed more adequately through myth than through concepts. As examples one may cite the myth of the kingdom of God in Christianity and that of the classless society of Marxism. Transcendence reveals itself also in the unto-deathness of praxis that aims at translating the project into reality. History is made only by those who are prepared to risk death so that others may have life, life in full measure and overflowing.

The existential, social, cosmic, and historical dimensions of our primordial God-encounter are essentially intertwined, one implying and flowing into the other. This underlying unity is only implicit in the original experience and must in its turn be thematized. It is failure to do so that explains the fragmentation of Western theology into the dogmatic, the mystical, the spiritual, and so on. The Asian mind, with its native genius for the unity of all, is better equipped to avoid this pitfall.

The structured unity of meanings we arrive at should not be set up as an eternal and immutable dogma valid for all time. All dogmas point to the pathetic attempt of human beings to reify the living God by housing him in fixed conceptual molds. Their emergence is understandable in the ages gone by, when men lived in a relatively stable universe in which the consciousness of historical time was all but rudimentary, thanks to the low development of productive forces. But today God is encountered not so much as one *who IS* but as one *who comes.* And God's coming coincides with human beings becoming, which is history.

That is why every knowledge of God must be subjected to critical revision in the light of subsequent historical experience.

THEOLOGIZING AS PROPHECY

If theological reflection is but a moment in the total response of the human being to the divine challenge as revealed in history, it is clear that it cannot stop at the stage of thematization. The theologian cannot remain neutral before the call of God as though he or she were a mere looker-on. He is personally involved in what he is contemplating; he stands challenged by the same call from the beyond which he is trying to fathom. To refuse to respond to it is to deny the living God. One cannot deny God and at the same time claim to theologize. On the other hand, to respond to him is to proclaim the challenge one has accepted of working for the total freedom of humankind. And what is this but to prophesy? Thus every theologian is also a prophet, one who challenges people to march forward to their ultimate destiny. But the prophet is impelled from within not only to proclaim the new age of freedom but also to make present the future he announces. Thus through prophecy theological reflection becomes world-transforming praxis; knowledge becomes power that changes the face of the earth. But theology becomes power only if it is appropriated by the oppressed masses whose interest primarily is to change the world.

The Asian theology of the future, or any genuine theology for that matter, will have to be of the downtrodden and the unwanted of the earth. So too the theologians of tomorrow will have to be people who have made a historic option in favor of the disprivileged classes. Only then will theology slough off its esoteric character, its elitist jargon, and its exclusivist, sectarian features. Herein is to be sought also the criterion for the validity of theology. Only that theological reflection is true which grips the masses and thereby becomes a power that changes the world. All theologies of powerlessness stand self-condemned and must be discarded once and for all. Where theology becomes power, the resulting praxis will prepare the ground for ever more profound encounters with God, for to eradicate justice and oppression is to clear up an open space where the divine can appear before the human; it is to prepare the way of the Lord.

THEOLOGY AS CRITICISM

We encounter God not in a vacuum but as men and women placed in specific relations of production and structures of power, and as bearers

of a particular culture. We go to meet the living God with minds and
hearts shaped by ideas, values, beliefs, attitudes, assumptions, myths,
and symbols handed down to us from past generations. All these factors
determine the way we are attuned to the total mystery of human existence and therefore also to God. The specific attuning we have received,
the conditioning we have inherited, may be for good or for bad; for good
if it renders us perceptive to the various dimensions of meaning in our
God-encounter, for bad if it obscures or falsifies them. The aim of criticism is to identify the latter so that by eliminating them we dispose
ourselves the better for an adequate grasp of what the living God demands of us today. In this sense criticism is a preparation for theological
reflection. Seen from another angle, it is also a constituent of theological
reflection. We seldom, if ever, meet the naked God. He appears before
us clad in the garb we ourselves have put on him. Criticism removes the
veils hiding his face just as it removes the blinkers from our own eyes.

I shall discuss three important biases which may blur, distort, or
frustrate our encounter with the living God. They have to do, respectively, with money, power, and what I would call the Anti-God.

1. The Renunciation of Money

Money is more than a mere means to thesaurization. Being the universal equivalent of all commodities it confers on men control over production, circulation, and consumption. In the money form are expressed all
the evils of an economy based on private property, competition, and
exploitation. It presupposes as well as creates the division of society into
the propertied and the propertyless, into employers and workers, into
consumers and producers. As the reification of all social relations it
expresses as well the alienation of the human inherent in capitalism.
More than anything else it distorts our perception of reality, not exclud-
ing our primordial experience of God.

Where the theologian—or any believer for that matter—either belongs or owes allegiance to the moneyed classes, he is likely to use God
to legitimize his class interests and thereby reduce him to the position
of an accomplice in the exploitation of the poor. In the process, theology
is degraded to the level of an ideology, and the divine to the level of a
commodity. Money, the universal equivalent of all commodities, can
from now on be exchanged also for things divine. The rich can buy the
favor of God by providing donations to religious institutions and feasts
and by having religious services held for the benefit of the living and the
dead. They can buy also theological expertise and even theologians. Thus
we see the amusing phenomenon of the glitter of gold passing for the

brilliance of theological reflection, and of theologians who have sold their soul to mammon. If money can be exchanged for divine favors, the reverse also is possible. Those who claim the right to mediate the favor (grace) of God can convert it into money. In consequence, the higher the position one occupies in the religious hierarchy, the greater is his command over money, over production, circulation, and consumption. Similarly, those who have "accumulated" knowledge of God can now indulge in the accumulation of capital or at least in thesaurization The end result is that money is divinized and the divine monetized. Correspondingly, the believer develops a religious attitude to money and a mercenary attitude to God. But all exchange is on the basis of equivalence. If so, God and money must have a common essence which is nothing but human labor, mental or manual. It follows then that the God who is exchanged for money is not the living God but a human product.

This is not merely a possible but a real danger to Asian theology, if the situation of the Indian churches can be taken as typical of the whole of Asia. The individual theologian may not have much money, nor may he indulge in conspicuous consumption. But he theologizes within the framework of churches which might be owning immense property, movable and immovable, whose economic interests coincide with those of the privileged classes. So too, the system of values operative in church institutions and organizations is in the main capitalist—one of private interest, competition, individualism, and consumerism. No wonder that the theologies currently taught in seminaries are largely theologies of legitimization of the status quo. They serve to legitimate not only exploitation within the country but also the interests of economic imperialism, for the obvious reason that the financial nerve center of the Asian churches often lies in Western countries.

In order to develop a theology that is faithful to the living God, the Asian theologian has to opt out of the institutional church or at any rate dissociate himself from its practice, if not also from its theory. He has to make a historic option in favor of the poor and the oppressed; in other words, he has to declass himself. Like the rich young man of the Gospel he too is called upon to sell what he has and give it to the poor.

2. Renunciation of Power

Power is understood here as the possibility some have to impose their options—ends and means—on others. As such, it is in principle opposed to God. For God is encountered as an unconditional demand to break all fetters and march forward to the reign of total freedom. He who exercises power or is in league with the wielders of power will either fail to encounter the living God or use him to sanction the existing structures of domination. This is usually a subconscious process and need not involve bad faith. It can, and often does, coexist with good intentions. A classic instance of this may be found in Paul's advice to Christians: "Let every person be subject to the governing authorities. For there is no authority except from God, and those that exist have been instituted by God" (Rom. 13:1). This God, too, is of man's making and therefore can be exchanged for power which is no less a human product. In consequence, the wielders of secular power are vested with religious authority, and religious authority with secular power. God becomes kingified and kings deified. In either case the human being is reduced to slave.

Here too we are not describing a possible deviation that may affect religious practice and thinking. It describes more or less the actual course taken by religions, especially by Christianity. It is well known that in medieval times there were magistrates who enjoyed episcopal powers, and bishops vested with magistrates' powers. Coming to our own times, the Indian churches have been using God to legitimize whatever regime happened to be in power. Very much to the point is the support given by the institutional church to the dictatorial rule of Indira Gandhi. True, bishops are no longer in a position to exercise direct political power, except in the case of the bishop of Rome. This, however, is more than compensated by the possibilities of exercising power within the Christian establishment itself. The structure of power embodied in these institutions is largely feudal, characterized by personal dependence and patronage. In the case of the Catholic Church it is also centralized and monarchical. The possibilities of domination are further enhanced by the inflow of foreign money. Such being the case, it is understandable that God is pressed into service to reinforce and consecrate ecclesial power structures. That is why the emergence of a theology of the living God will be possible in Asia only when theologians have the courage to renounce all power and, like Jesus, identify themselves with the powerless and the downtrodden of today.

3. Renouncing the Anti-God

The process we have described whereby the human being uses God to legitimize his own interests of exploitation and domination already explains the birth of the Anti-God. But there are other factors too, which more directly contribute to his emergence, of which the chief are cult, dogma, and law.

Cult may be authentic or inauthentic. Cult is authentic when it is part of man's response to the demand of God as revealed in history. It will then inevitably lead to creative, liberating praxis. Cult in this sense belongs essentially to the domain of prophetic—symbolic action, and never leaves the terrain of human self-transcendence in history. Cult becomes inauthentic, alienated and alienating, when it is detached from the dialectic of divine challenge and human response, and is set up as something absolute. Where this happens, cult is transposed from historical time to cyclic time in which nothing new ever happens. False cult is the result of our attempts to have a God whom we can manipulate and dispose of as we please. The God of cult is a silent, passive God who is bound to make himself available where and when the human being chooses. In this sense, cult may be seen as a way of reifying the divine, which has for its counterpart the divinization of things (the altar, the consecrated bread). Made in the image of alienated man, this God is neutral to the rich and the poor, and dispenses his favors to the exploiter and the exploited. He is very much alive in Asian churches and his rule is reinforced by ever new and spurious cults imported from the West. He has his array of theologians, too, vowed to defend and extend his Kingdom.

The Anti-God also breeds and is bred by dogma. Dogma too dehistoricizes God and fixes him into eternal and immutable concepts. The reification cult accomplishes at the level of symbolic action, dogma accomplishes through conceptualization. It, too, is the result of human striving to be the measure of the Creator. The same tendency is noticeable in the development of religious law. If dogma is the law of our thinking about God, law is the dogma concerning human action in response to God. Through law what people perceived as the will of God in earlier ages is absolutized as valid for all ages. Thus it too dehistoricizes the demands of God. Both deflect the human attention from the challenge of the living God in the here and now of history. Both curtail human freedom: the first curtails freedom of thought; the second freedom of action. Of the two, the law is the greater source of unfreedom, because what passes for the law of God is, more often than not, the sum of norms formulated by the privileged classes for the furtherance of their own interests. Besides, the religious law that is operative in most Asian churches smacks of ecclesiastical imperialism as it has been imported from the West and imposed on us as normative for our thinking and acting. Fortunately, both dogma and the law are on the way out and the voice of the living God is beginning to be heard at least in certain Christian circles.

As far as Asian Christianity is concerned, the Anti-God of money, power, cult, dogma, and law is a domiciled foreigner. However, it should not be forgotten that he draws nourishment also from certain indigenous secular and religious traditions: from the dichotomy of matter and spirit advocated by certain systems of philosophy, from the individualism of religious quest especially in Hinduism, from the tendency to understand salvation as liberation from history rather than as freedom in history, from the traditional stress on contemplation in contrast to action, from precapitalist structures of exploitation and domination, and finally from developing capitalism. At the same time, the Anti-God destroys all that is valid in our religious traditions and thereby renders futile our search for identity. In order to develop an Asian theology, we must put on the agenda the liquidation of the Anti-God and the destruction of such theologies as are centered upon him.

JESUS AND ASIAN THEOLOGY

The Christian theologizes between memory and hope—between the memory of Jesus and hope in the Kingdom to come. If in our reflections we have focused the God of hope, we did so out of reverence for the memory of Jesus. In fact, his entire life and teaching go to prove the validity of the approach to theology we have been advocating so far. To substantiate this, nothing less than a critical survey of the Synoptic Gospels is needed. Since that is not possible here, I shall confine myself to making a few general observations.

Jesus lived from one unique experience; his own primordial encounter took place on the banks of Jordan when significantly he identified himself with the common run of mankind by choosing to be baptized for the remission of sins. From then on he was a man possessed, taken hold of by the spirit (power) of God, by that spirit which was to lead him to the desert, to the villages and towns of Palestine, to confrontation with the powers that were, and finally to death on the cross. Every word he uttered, every deed of his, was in response to the challenge of the living God he encountered.

The God of Jesus is to be encountered in the domain not of cult but of history. He is *one who comes* to usher in a new age, in which there will not be any division of society into the rich and the poor (Matt. 5:3), in which the dispossessed will regain possession of the earth (v. 5), in which man's hunger for justice will be satisfied (v. 6), in which class conflict will be replaced by brotherhood and the sword by peace (v. 9). Equally, it is in history that man *goes* to meet God. The good Samaritan met him in responding to a human need (Luke 10:29–37); Zacchaeus in redressing the injustice he had done to his fellowman (Luke 19:1–10); the rich young man was told that he should sell what he had and give it to the poor if he wished to have a share in the life of the new age to come (Mark 10:17–22). Jesus' teaching on this point reflects his own experience of God. It was in the heart of the world that he met his God—at weddings, at festal meals, by the lakeside where fishermen cast and hauled their nets, by the wayside wells where womenfolk came to fetch water, at gatherings of people, in the company of outcasts, in the fellowship of his disciples, in the togetherness of friendship, and in the innocence of children, and, above all, in contesting the forces of oppression.

Jesus was no theologian in the sense that he wrote treatises on God. But there is no doubt that he did reflect on his own encounter with God and sought to grasp its implications for himself and for all people. I have elsewhere tried to bring out the existential, social, cosmic, and historical meaning of Jesus' teaching on God (*Jesus and Freedom;* Orbis Books, 1978). Here I shall only comment on his language. He did not speak in abstract, desiccated concepts. Neither did he employ an esoteric language as do most theologians today. Instead he spoke in images, symbols, pictures, and parables. This is not to be attributed solely to the historical conditioning of a more primitive age. It shows rather that his thinking vibrated in unison with the life of his people. He was one with them and naturally spoke their idiom. Besides, he was too involved in the unspeakable mystery of the God he encountered to be able to speak of him in the manner in which a scientist would speak of test-tube babies. He would not dissect God with the surgical knife of cold reason. For him, knowing was also loving, speaking was also prophesying. It is in similar fashion that the Buddha spoke, that the ancient seers of India spoke of Brahman and the Atman. Asian theology will come to its own only when it will have made a complete break with the rationalism of Western theology and evolves a new manner of discourse about God drawn from the life of God and his people. We have to develop a new theological language which would express the fusion of thinking and loving, seeing and prophesying, vision and commitment.

To Jesus, reflecting and speaking were but aspects of his total response to the Father. And that response he himself summed up as one of preaching the good news to the poor, proclaiming release for prisoners, giving sight to the blind, setting free the oppressed, and restoring land to the landless (Luke 4:18–19). His word was power, resonant with the divine force that re-creates the world. No wonder that, at his words, the paralytic took up his bed and walked away, the blind saw, the deaf heard, and the dead rose from death. The same force may be seen also in his fierce denunciation of the scribes and the Pharisees whom he called a brood of vipers and whited sepulchers (Matt. 23:13–33), in his severe strictures on the Sadducean priesthood for their converting the Temple into a den of thieves (Mark 11:17), and in his defiant appellation of Herod as a fox (Luke 13:32). If such words of force have been long since muted in the churches, it is because theologizing has been divorced from encounter with God, and faith from practice. Where reflection starts not from one's own meeting with God but from the interpretations raised to the nth degree of the God-encounter which other people are supposed to have had, it will naturally end up in sterile speculation which changes neither the world nor the thinker himself. The springtime of Asian Christian theology will burst forth only when we refuse to theologize by proxy, that is, when we refuse to be mere relaying stations for ideas fabricated elsewhere and muster enough courage to face the naked God and creatively respond to his challenge to create a social order of justice and freedom.

Like the prophets of old, Jesus too instituted a severe criticism of wealth, power, and the Anti-God, a criticism which was at once a consequence of and prerequisite for his own encounter with the living God. He rejected the cult of money as incompatible with faith in God and required of his followers that they give up wealth (Mark 10:21; Matt. 6:24). In doing so, he also repudiated the prevalent notion that wealth was a sign of divine favor, a notion manifestly born of an attempt to use God to legitimize social relations of exploitation. No less severe was his criticism of power and of those who "made their subjects feel the weight of their authority" (Mark 10:42). He envisaged a society in which power will give way to service. For him the spirit of God was a subverter of all power, one who pulled down the mighty from their thrones, overthrew oppressors, and demolished prisons (Luke 4:18). True to this conviction he identified himself with the powerless: the simple, the uneducated, the little ones, and the socially despised.

An equally fundamental concern of Jesus was the liquidation of the Anti-God. He would have nothing to do with a cult that does not change the world. For him worship that coexists with "unlove" is an empty gesture (Matt. 5:23, 24; Mark 12:32–33). Furthermore, he denied the distinction between the pure and the impure, between the sacred and the profane, which is the very basis of all religions (Mark 7:15). Of course he prayed; but his prayer was directly geared to meeting the immediate challenges that faced him in the critical phases of his life. It was rooted in history and not transposed to the realm of cyclic time. Nor was what came to be called the Eucharist originally a cultic act. It had its basis in the meals he had with the outcasts of society, the publicans and the sinners, which anticipated the New Humanity of the future, the festal meal of the end-time, when "many will come from east and west and sit at table with Abraham, Isaac, and Jacob in the kingdom of heaven"

(Matt. 8:11). It may, therefore, more appropriately be called a prophetic action. It was only subsequently that it was interpreted in cultic terms. Similarly, even a cursory reading of the Gospels will show that Jesus was opposed to reifying God into dogmas and laws. He had no hesitation in radically reinterpreting the Law and the Prophets. He even went to the extent of abrogating parts of the written law (Matt. 5; 10:1–11). More significantly still, he subordinated the law to the well-being of human beings and thereby rendered it relative and provisional (Mark 2:27). In short, his teaching is an emphatic repudiation of the Anti-God of cult, dogma, and law.

With no official cult, no set creed, and no legal code, what Jesus initiated can in no sense be called a religion among other religions. If anything, it was a prophetic movement reaching out to the ultimate horizon of the fullness of man and God in the age to come. Unfortunately, this movement, in passing through the mold of Greco-Roman thinking and culture and under the impact of pagan religions, was transformed into a dogmatic, cultic, law-ridden religion. Hope in the God *who is to come* was replaced by the cult of Jesus, the *already-come;* the Kingdom of God was replaced by the churches. Disciples became Christians; pilgrims became settlers. What is worse, Christianity came to terms with money and power, and assumed the role of being a provider of legitimization to exploiters and oppressors. Though in recent years the official teachings of the churches have shown welcome signs of a return to the radical message of Jesus, it is not matched by any corresponding change in practice.

It follows from our reflections thus far that we have to return to the Jesus of the Gospels and make our own his vision of God and humanity. However, Jesus is not to be thought of merely as an example to be followed in our quest of God. He is also one in whom we encounter God. And this is just what marks us out from followers of other faiths. These others too meet God in the realities of life. But, unlike them, we have met God *also* in the words and deeds of Jesus. However, these two modes of encountering the divine—in Jesus and in the world of today—do not run on parallel lines. They condition and illumine each other. The relationship between them is one of unity in tension: of unity because it is the same God whom we meet in either case; of tension because it is under historical conditions so different from ours that God revealed his face to Jesus. The difference in respect of the historical context implies also that fidelity to the contemporary challenge of God may require that we go beyond the concrete forms in which Jesus himself responded to the Father.

We may not look to the West for a prophetic theology which does justice to God's self-revelation both in Jesus and in the world of today. In countries where Christians are the majority it is easy for them to nurse the illusion that the entire destiny of mankind depends on them, that the church is the center of the universe. And where the church is made the center, hope in the Kingdom of God is rendered peripheral. This danger is much less in Asia, where Christians form but a small minority. Any exclusive claim we as Christians may entertain falls to the ground when we realize that we are no better than the followers of other faiths in respect of morality or concern for human values. This makes it easier for us to recapture the Jesuan vision of the Kingdom of God which includes all—irrespective of caste or creed—who seek the well-being of their neighbor. However, even in Asia it is a vain hope that the Christian establishment will give the lead in relevant theologizing, since it is very much under the rule of the Anti-God. A relevant theology is more likely to emerge from those groups of dissenting Christians who in loyalty to Jesus have thrown themselves into the life of the people and their struggles for justice. It is heartening to note that more and more of such groups are being formed, at least in India. They are able to forget all denominational differences and meet on the common basis of discipleship under Jesus and commitment to the Kingdom. They, in truth, anticipate the Jesus community of the future which will transcend all sectarianism. Understandably, these groups have no difficulty in joining hands with people of other religions or even with Marxists. The Christ of dogma divides; Jesus of the Gospels unites. Which proves once again that what we need is a theology not centered upon the church but open to the new humanity of theandric fullness, in which Jesus hoped and for which he died.

Twenty-four

Doing Theology in Asia Today:
A Korean Perspective
Yong Bock Kim

[Dr. Kim sees a trend toward "historicalization" in Asian theology today— that is, toward theological reflection in conscious relation to the historical conditions of the Asian peoples. In this context a new theme for theological reflection appears in the concept of "the people in Asia," understood as the oppressed, the poor, and the exploited. Taking South Korea as a case in point, Kim traces the development of a "people's theology" in the disciplines of biblical studies, church history, and reflective theology, which attempts to relate the gospel meaningfully to the struggles and aspirations of the people. The scope of "people's theology" is general history; its stance is on the side of the people; and "it seeks to be free and concrete beyond philosophical and ideological frameworks."—Ed.]

To this day theological thinking in Asia remains "Western" in its basic shape and message. This is because Christian communities are still islands of religion, more continuous with the Western Christian cultures than with the national or local communities of Asian people. However, there has been a progressive approximation of theology to the historical conditions of the Asian peoples. Evidence of this historicalization is not abundant but it is very significant for our reflection on doing theology in Asia today.

There are three salient experiences in the history of the Asian Christian community that give us an important basis for our theological endeavor.

The first step was Western missionaries' study of the history of Asian peoples, their culture and religions. This process has gone on since the arrival of the Western missionaries, as a preparation for their missionary enterprise. However, the heritages of the Asian peoples were regarded as discontinuous with the gospel, from the Western Christian point of

From *WSCF Journal* (World Student Christian Federation), I, 3 (1979), pp. 1-3. Reprinted by permission of the World Student Christian Federation.

view, and therefore they did not have any positive place in theological reflection. Paganization of the gospel and syncretism of theology were much feared, in favor of the westernized gospel. In spite of such "theological containment" practiced against Asian heritages, the "native" Christian life was inevitably mingled with the religions and cultures of the peoples in Asia. This resulted in a gap between the formal doctrine and theology of the "missionary" churches and the actual religious life of Christians in Asia. In spite of the unconscious, informal indigenization of the actual Christian life in Asia, the formal theological thinking and doctrines remained Western, by and large.

The next step toward religiocultural contextualization was demanded by the national aspirations of the colonized peoples of Asia, under Western and other colonial powers. The question for theology in Asia during the colonial period was the relationship between the Christian gospel and the national aspirations of Asian peoples for liberation from their colonial domination. The historical context of Asia for theology was defined politically, not merely religioculturally. Here again, the fact that the theology of the churches in Asia was Western created difficulties in clarifying the implications of the Christian gospel in relation to the colonial situation, particularly when the colonial power was Western. The theology of Western missionary churches restricted the gospel to the nonpolitical, and therefore nonhistorical, realm. However, the actual Christian life of Asian churches, consciously and unconsciously, was bound to be politicized one way or another, although official churches in Asia remained procolonial or "neutral" politically, or pronationalist. The most significant thrust was Christian participation in the anticolonial and national liberation struggles. A good example is found in the participation of Korean Christians in the March First Independence Movement (1919) against Japanese colonialism. The heritages of Asian Christians' struggle against colonial domination in Asia are deeply intertwined with the secular heritages of Asian national liberation, and this provides an important historical point of reference for Asian theology today. One task of Asian church history is to clarify this experience.

In postcolonial Asia, as a third step, there was a resurgence of new nationalism together with renewed affirmation of national cultures. In this context the Christian community responded positively to the questions of nation-building, and indigenization as a theological concern rose among some Asian theologians. However, it was soon discovered that true national liberation and true national community-building needed a far more profound social revolution and cultural transformation than any of the national elite groups in Asia ever realized.

Any genuine and therefore human development of Asian peoples demanded this social and cultural transformation to overcome the traditional and colonial structures of power that oppressed and exploited the Asian peoples or alienated them from the center of history. This constitutes the historical context of Asian Christian witness in a broad sense.

It is in this context that a new theme for theological reflection appears, that is, "the people in Asia." Although there is debate as to the term "the people," it is clear that an important segment of the Asian theological community takes this theme with utmost seriousness. There are those who regard the term "people" in a socialist perspective; and there are others who view the "people" as a broader political concept: the oppressed, the poor, and those exploited by the powerful. This distinction is not mutually exclusive, and yet these represent two different strands of theological concern on the theme.

"People's participation," "people as the subject of history," and "people's democracy"—these are used without precise definition, and different national contexts reflect variations.

For the sake of convenience, let us illustrate the case of the Korean theology of *Minjung* (people). In the "school of *Minjung* theology," *Minjung* is understood as a political concept. *Minjung* are the ruled, dominated by the powers that be. In history, the condition of the *Minjung* is determined by the total structure of the ruling power and by the *Minjung*'s struggle to be masters of their own destiny. The *Minjung*'s history is clarified by their social biography (story of the people) and their socioeconomic history. Naturally, *Minjung* theology approaches the reality of the people in this framework of their social biography and socioeconomic history.

Traditionally, theology has often used the framework of the dominant philosophy or ideology that is akin to the ruling power rather than the story of the people.

In this perspective there are several resources that are important for *Minjung* theology.

1. The biblical resources are interpreted to clarify God's dealing with the *Minjung.* Korean Old Testament scholar In Syek (Paul) Sye, S.J. *(The Cry of God: The Liberation of the Poor),* made an important contribution to *Minjung* theology by clarifying the legal codes (Covenant code, Deuteronomic code, etc.) as advocating the rights of the poor people in the light of their socioeconomic historical background. Professor Sye argues that the prophets are the spokesmen for the poor and the psalms are the glad songs of the poor people.

Prof. Ahn Byung Mu began an important process of New Testament interpretation starting with the Gospel of Mark, where he finds the real context of Jesus' message in Jesus' relationship with the *ochlos (Min-*

jung). Professor Ahn uses extensive socioeconomic historical materials
to discover Jesus' message to the people *(Minjung).* It is one of his
contentions that the writer of the Gospel of Mark protests the Pauline
kerygmatization of Jesus' message and recovers the historical message of
Jesus to the *ochlos.*

Efforts in biblical studies in the school of *Minjung* theology have yet
to bear much fruit, but the beginnings are so fruitful that real contributions are expected in the years to come.

2. A second point of reference for *Minjung* theology is reinterpreta-
tion of church history in the perspective of the *Minjung.* The early
churches and missionary churches in Asia were nonestablished in their
societies (they were religious minorities), and the medieval churches
since Constantine the Great (A.D. 313) and the Reformation churches
were churches of established Christendom. Histories of these churches
should be read upside down, that is, from the people's point of view, to
discover "heterodoxical" and nonestablished traditions that correspond
to the aspirations of the people in each era.

Prof. Suh Nam Dong takes the traditions of Joachim of Floris,
Thomas Münzer, and others as important points of historical reference
for *Minjung* theology. I have been developing a thesis that the social
foundations of the *Minjung* church can never be the establishment of the
ruling power ("Social Foundations of the *Minjung* Church," to be published soon by the Korean Student Christian Federation).

3. The most striking aspect of *Minjung* theology is that the *"Minjung*
theologians" in Korea are taking up the traditions of the *Minjung* struggle for liberation. They are taking not only the revolts and rebellions of
the people seriously, but especially the literary and artistic expressions
of the *Minjung's* struggle and aspirations. The literary works of poet
Kim Chi Ha and other writers have been a great inspiration here. *"Han*
of *Minjung"* (righteous indignation of the people under oppression) has
emerged as one of the most important moments of the social biography
of the *Minjung,* and has excited reflection in Korean theological circles.

Moreover, Prof. Hyun Young Hak has been working on theological
reflections on the Korean traditional Mask Dance of the people. He finds
in the scenarios, styles, and languages of the *Talchum* (Mask Dance) the
dynamics of social transcendence among the oppressed people.

The above are only a few examples that indicate the emerging shape
of *Minjung* theology. The most important point is that it is an attempt
to relate the gospel message to the struggle and aspirations of Asian
peoples in their present historical conditions. Its scope is general history;
its stance is on the side of the people (with no apologies); and it seeks
to be free and concrete beyond philosophical and ideological frame-

works. The people are the most concrete subjects of history.

Minjung theology seeks dialogues with African, Asian, and Latin American theological developments as well as with traditional Western theological communities to enhance the fruitfulness of theological reflection in our own historical context.

To name only a few, theological developments in black Africa, especially in southern Africa and the early developments of the Kimbangu Church, are of great interest to us. Liberation theology, though with some reservations, has inspired us here. Black theology in North America has made an impact on the Korean scene.

As we seek these ecumenical exchanges and dialogue, our main agendas for dialogue are with our secular counterparts, traditions of antifeudal peoples' movements (Taiping Movement in China, Tonghak Movement in Korea), traditions of national struggles for liberation and independence, and ideologies and religions that are deeply and concretely related to the continuously interweaving social biographies of Asian peoples.

Minjung theology must develop further before its shape is clearly known; but it is an attempt to be faithful theologically to the gospel in the lives of Asian peoples today. We would appreciate the reader's interest and encouragement KSCF will be publishing a volume on *Minjung* theology this year. It is hoped that its English translation will be available soon.

PART SEVEN

Theological Statements
of Asian Churches
and Other Christian Groups

Twenty-five

Theological Declaration by Christian Ministers in the Republic of Korea, 1973

[It is well known that Christians have taken a leading role in the protest against martial law in South Korea with its accompanying political oppression. Although President Chung Hee Park has since been killed by a member of his own Intelligence Agency, and the law which banned political dissent has been lifted, the situation does not seem to have changed substantially. In May 1973, one year following the declaration of martial law, a group of Christian ministers in South Korea issued an underground statement declaring the faith that undergirded their struggle for the restoration of democracy. The Theological Declaration has been widely circulated through various religious news services and is here reprinted from *Documents on the Struggle for Democracy in Korea,* edited by the Japan Emergency Christian Conference on Korean Problems, and published in 1975 through the National Christian Council of Japan.—Ed.]

We make this declaration in the name of the Christian community in South Korea. However, under the present circumstances, in which one man controls all the powers of the three branches of government and uses military arms and the intelligence network to oppress the people, we hesitate to reveal those who signed this document. We must fight and struggle in the underground until our victory is achieved.

The historical situation of the Korean people has been very grave since last October. President Park's consolidation of power has had certain demonic consequences for the life of the Korean nation and people.

The Christian community, as an integral part of the Korean people, now stands up and speaks out on the present situation, compelled by the divine mandates of the Messianic Kingdom.

Since World War II, our people have gone through trials and suffer-

From *Documents on the Struggle for Democracy in Korea,* edited and copyright by the Japan Emergency Christian Conference on Korean Problems (Tokyo: National Christian Council, 1975), pp. 37–43. Reprinted by permission.

ings, of social chaos, economic deprivation, and especially the tragic Korean War and the resulting political dictatorships. It has been an ardent aspiration of our people that a new and humane community might be restored to their lives. However, the hopes of the people for such a restoration of humane community has been cruelly crushed by President Park in his absolutization of dictatorship and ruthless political repression. This is done in the name of the so-called October Revitalization, a set of false promises which is only the sinister plan of some evil men.

We Christians are compelled to speak out and take accompanying actions on the following grounds:

1. We are under God's command that we should be faithful to his Word in concrete historical situations. It is not a sense of triumphant victory that moves us today; rather it is a sense of confession of our sins before God; and yet we are commanded by God to speak the truth and act in the present situation in Korea.

2. The people in Korea are looking up to Christians and urging us to take action in the present grim situation. It is not because we deserve to represent them. We have often fallen short of their deeper expectations, and yet we are urged and encouraged to move on this course of action, not because we envision ourselves as the representatives of our people, but because we are moved by their agony to call upon God for their deliverance from evil days.

3. We stand in a historical tradition of such struggles for liberation as the independence movement by Christians against Japanese colonialism. We realize that our Christian community has often lacked the courage to take a decisive stand, and that the theological outlook of the official bodies of our Christian churches has been too pietistic to take up revolutionary roles. However, we do not feel disheartened by the weakness of some of our brothers; rather we are determined to seek our theological convictions from the historical traditions of our church.

The firm foundation of our words and deeds is our faith in God the Lord of history, in Jesus the proclaimer of the Messianic Kingdom, and in the Spirit who moves vigorously among the people. We believe that God is the ultimate vindicator of the oppressed, the weak, and the poor; he judges the evil forces in history. We believe that Jesus the Messiah proclaimed the coming of the Messianic Kingdom, to be subversive to the evil powers, and that his Messianic Kingdom will be the haven of the dispossessed, the rejected, and the downtrodden. We also believe that the Spirit is working for the new creation of history and cosmos, as well as for the regeneration and sanctification of individual man.

In this grave historical situation, we as a Christian community believe:

(1) that we are commanded by God to be representatives before God the Judge and Lord of History, to pray that the suffering and oppressed people may be set free.

(2) that we are commanded by our Lord Jesus Christ to live among the oppressed, the poor, and the despised as he did in Judea; and that we are summoned to stand up and speak the truth to the powers that be, as he did before Pontius Pilate of the Roman Empire.

(3) that we are compelled by the Spirit to participate in his transforming power and movement for the creation of a new society and history, as well as for the transformation of our character; and that this Spirit is the Spirit of Messianic Kingdom who commands us to struggle for sociopolitical transformation in this world.

Therefore, we express our theological convictions on the following issues:

1. The present dictatorship in Korea is destroying rule by law and persuasion; it now rules by force and threat alone. Community is being turned into jungle. Our position is that no one is above the law except God; worldly power is entrusted by God to civil authority to keep justice and order in human society. If anyone poses himself above the law and betrays the divine mandate for justice, he is in rebellion against God. Oriental tradition, too, understands that good rule is carried out through the moral persuasion and virtue of the ruler. One may conquer people by the sword; but they cannot be ruled by the sword.

2. The present regime in the Republic of Korea is destroying freedom of conscience and freedom of religious belief. There is freedom neither of expression nor of silence. There is interference by the regime in Christian churches' worship, prayer, gatherings, content of sermons, and teaching of the Bible.

   The Christian church and other religious bodies must be the defenders of conscience for the people; for destruction of conscience is a most demonic act. In defending the freedom of religious belief against interference by the regime in Korea, Christian churches are also defending freedom of conscience for all people.

3. The dictatorship in Korea is using systematic deception, manipulation, and indoctrination to control the people. The mass media have been turned into the regime's propaganda machine to tell the people half-truths and outright lies, and to control and manipulate information to deceive the people.

   We believe that Christians are witnesses to truth, always struggling to break any system of deception and manipulation, for to tell the truth is the ultimate power that sets men free for God's Messianic Kingdom.

4. The dictatorship in Korea uses sinister and inhuman and at the same time ruthlessly efficient means to destroy political opponents, intellectual critics, and innocent people. The use of the Korean Central Intelligence Agency (CIA) for this purpose is somewhat similar to the evil ways of the Nazi Gestapo or the KGB of the Stalin era. People are physically and mentally tortured, intimidated, and threatened, and sometimes even disappear completely. Such treatments are indeed diabolical acts against humanity.

We believe that God has created humans in body and soul. Body as well as soul will be resurrected at the day of judgment of the Messianic Kingdom. We believe especially in the sanctity of the human body; therefore any violation of it is equal to killing a man. It is a murderous act.

5. The present dictatorship is responsible for the economic system in Korea, in which the powerful dominate the poor. The people, poor urban workers and rural peasants, are victims of severe exploitation and social and economic injustice. So-called "economic development" in Korea turned out to be the conspiracy of a few rulers against the poor people, and a curse to our environment.

We as Christians must struggle to destroy this system of extreme dehumanization and injustice; for we are witnesses to the ongoing movement of the Messianic Kingdom in history, in which the poor will be enriched, the oppressed will be vindicated, and peace will be enjoyed by the people.

6. The present regimes in the South and North are using the unification talks only to preserve their own power; and they are betraying the true aspirations of the people for the unification of their land. We believe as Christians that the people deeply yearn for authentic community on the basis of true reconciliation. Without transcendence beyond the past experiences of bitter conflict and differences in ideological and politicoeconomic systems, and without transformation of our historical conditions of oppression, true unification cannot be realized.

A CALL FOR ACTION AND SUPPORT

1. *To the people in Korea:* Withdraw any form of recognition of the laws, orders, policies, and other political processes of dictatorship

that have been wrought since October 17, 1972. Build various forms of solidarity among the people to struggle for the restoration of democracy in South Korea.

2. *To the Christians in Korea:* As preparation for the above struggle, we Christians should renew our churches by deepening our theological thinking, by our clear stance and solidarity with the oppressed and poor, by the relevant proclamation of the gospel of the Messianic Kingdom, and by praying for our nation; and we should prepare ourselves for martyrdom, if necessary, as our forefathers did.

3. *To the Christians of the world:* Most of all we need your prayers and solidarity, and we ask you to express our common bond through actions of encouragement and support.

CONCLUSION

Jesus the Messiah, our Lord, lived and dwelt among the oppressed, poverty-stricken, and sick in Judea. He boldly stood in confrontation with Pontius Pilate, a representative of the Roman Empire, and he was crucified in the course of his witness to the truth. He has risen from the dead to release the power of transformation which sets the people free.

We resolve that we will follow the footsteps of our Lord, living among our oppressed and poor people, standing against political oppression, and participating in the transformation of history, for this is the only way to the Messianic Kingdom.

Twenty-six

Credo of the
Wednesday Forum (Philippines)

[In 1973—one year after the declaration of martial law—the Wednesday Forum was begun by a Protestant minister, Cirilo Rigos, and one of his lay members, former Senator Jovito Salonga. It developed into an ecumenical dialogue on human rights issues and had considerable influence. Among invited speakers were both supporters of the government and its critics. Its main objective was to provide a mature Christian perspective for responsible political participation. The Credo showed that the struggle for development and for human rights had become an ecumenical concern for the churches in the Philippines. The theological basis of the Forum was embodied in its Credo.—Ed.]

We believe that over and above all things, over and above all loyalties, is the primacy of God's sovereignty.

We believe that God is concerned not only with the spiritual but with things that are material to man—food and clothing and shelter, his government, his institutions, and his society. To confine God to purely spiritual things is to separate him from the world he made, the very same world for which Jesus Christ, our Lord and Master, gave his life.

We believe in the inherent worth and dignity of every human being, created in God's own image, and because of this he is entitled to the respect and concern of his fellowmen and his Government. Every man is so sacred and important in the eyes of his Maker he should not be used as a tool of any system, group, or institution. The powers of Government should be used to benefit man, not to abuse or betray him.

We believe in the need for the development of the whole person. Total human development presupposes and requires a wide and equitable distribution of basic values—wealth, power, knowledge, respect, and well-

From *CCA News* (Christian Conference of Asia), XII, 2 (Feb. 15, 1977). Reprinted by permission of the Christian Conference of Asia.

being. Concentration of any of these in the hands of a few is a fertile source of injustice.

We believe in the validity of the Great Commandment—love of God and love of fellowmen.

We believe that the Great Commandment can be fulfilled only if society is just and free. Wherever there is injustice or oppression, there is need for redemption not only from the evils that produce them but from the structures that make them possible.

We believe that the Christian churches—their leaders and members, the pastors and the laity, the entire priesthood of believers—have a prophetic ministry to perform.

We believe that this prophetic ministry, so aptly explained in the Scriptures, means:

that we should be concerned with the just relationship between man and society, including the institutions and structures erected to serve his needs;

that the churches must deal with specific problems, not with platitudes and pieties, if they are to be faithful to their task. They cannot pretend to be blind and dumb in the face of poverty, exploitation, and injustice. By their silence they become involved in the very injustices they fail to speak and do something about.

that as ministers we must lead in seeking the truth, for it is only the truth that shall make us free. Having the available facts, we should exert all efforts to get the most informed analysis and interpretation.

that we should have the courage to proclaim the truth and the fortitude to defend it. The Christian gospel reminds us that a few people who know what they believe and are not afraid to express it can change the world.

that we should seek solutions and make concrete suggestions, in the light of basic human values. Reconciliation should be encouraged as long as it does not involve the sacrifice of truth and justice.

that we shall respect the laws, but in the event of conflict, prefer to obey God rather than man. We desire order, but only when it is balanced with the human aspiration for freedom, equality, and dignity.

Twenty-seven

A Declaration on Human Rights by the Presbyterian Church in Taiwan

[The Presbyterian Church in Taiwan is one of the confessing churches in Asia today. This Declaration was authorized by the General Assembly Executive Committee meeting at Taichung in July 1977. The text was written by pastors and lay people from all over the island in the full knowledge of the possible consequences of their actions. The final version was unanimously approved by a Specially Designated Committee of the Executive Committee in August of the same year. Concerned that the 17 million Taiwanese who have been born on the island shall have the right to decide the future of Taiwan, the Declaration boldly urges the present government to "face reality and to take effective measures whereby Taiwan may become a new and independent country." Underlying this demand is the theological affirmation that "Jesus Christ is Lord of all mankind" and that "human rights and a land in which each of us has a stake are gifts bestowed by God."—Ed.]

To the President of the United States, to all countries concerned, and to Christian churches throughout the world:

Our church confesses that Jesus Christ is Lord of all mankind and believes that human rights and a land in which each one of us has a stake are gifts bestowed by God. Therefore we make this declaration, set in the context of the present crisis threatening the 17 million people of Taiwan.

Ever since President Carter's inauguration as President of the United States he has consistently adopted "Human Rights" as a principle of his diplomacy. This is an epoch-making event in the history of foreign policy.

We therefore request President Carter to continue to uphold the principles of human rights while pursuing the "normalization of relationships with Communist China" and to insist on guaranteeing the security, independence, and freedom of the people of Taiwan.

From a mimeographed circular.

As we face the possibility of an invasion by Communist China we hold firmly to our faith and to the principles underlying the United Nations Declaration of Human Rights. We insist that the future of Taiwan shall be determined by the 17 million people who live there. We appeal to the countries concerned—especially to the people and the government of the United States of America—and to Christian churches throughout the world to take effective steps to support our cause.

In order to achieve our goal of independence and freedom for the people of Taiwan in this critical international situation, we urge our government to face reality and to take effective measures whereby Taiwan may become a new and independent country

We beseech God that Taiwan and all the rest of the world may become a place where "Mercy and truth will meet together; and righteousness shall look down from heaven." (Psalm 85, verses 10 and 11, Today's English Version and King James Version.)

16th August 1977

Twenty-eight

Confession of Faith
of the Presbyterian Church
in Taiwan

[Prepared in May 1979 and to be discussed by the General Assembly in 1981, this Confession, like the Declaration on Human Rights (No. 27, above) affirms that the "homeland" is a gift of God. But it goes on to declare that "Christ frees people and delivers the oppressed." This last phrase has special meaning for the Taiwanese, being a translation of the term *chhut-thaau-thi'n,* which signifies the hope that one day the people will emerge out of their situation of darkness, oppression, and suffering to see the sky and breathe the sweet air of springtime. The Presbyterian Church in Taiwan uses this term to express the grace and salvation of Jesus Christ for those who have long suffered from sin. These Taiwanese Christians are struggling to understand their suffering and hope in terms of the passion, death, and resurrection of Christ.—Ed.]

We believe in the one true God, creator and ruler of humankind and all things. He is the King and Judge and Lord of history and the world. He was born a man, Jesus Christ, who became our brother and is the Savior of humanity. Through Christ's suffering, death, and resurrection, he revealed his love and justice, reconciling us to himself. His Spirit is among us, enabling us to be Christ's witnesses to all peoples until he comes again.

We believe the Old and New Testaments are the Holy Scriptures, the revelation of God and the record of his salvation. They are the rule of faith and life.

We believe the church is the Covenant Community of God, ecumenical, rooted in this land, fulfilling the will of God through worship, fellowship, education, proclamation, and service.

We believe in repentance by the grace of God, in the forgiveness of sins, and in giving glory to God through a life of devotion, love, and dedication.

From a mimeographed circular.

We believe God gives the human person dignity, ability, responsibility, and a homeland, so that he/she may participate in God's creation and manage the world together with him. Therefore the human person shapes his/her social, political, and economic systems, is creative in the arts and sciences, and seeks after the one true God. But the human person has sinned, misusing these gifts and thus destroying his/her relationship with God, his/her fellow beings, and all things. His/her only salvation lies in complete trust in Jesus. Christ frees people and delivers the oppressed *(chhut-thaau-thi'n)*. He makes the human person a new being and is making the world to become his Kingdom. Amen.

Twenty-nine

Joint Catholic-Protestant Statement on Christian Presence Among Muslim Filipinos

[In July 1978 a group of concerned Roman Catholics and Protestants came together in Marawi City, Mindanao, Philippines, to draw up a statement of reconciliation with Filipino Muslims. It was an epochal event viewed against the background of centuries of deep-seated misunderstanding, prejudice, hatred, and oppression of Muslims by Christians. The statement is in two parts—the first addressed to their Muslim brothers, the second to their fellow Christians. They ask forgiveness for their share of the blame for the tragic past, and they seek a "dialogue of life" with their Muslim neighbors. They further call upon all Christians in the Philippines to treat the Islamic religion and culture of Filipino Muslims with respect, to repudiate any form of witness or mission which is coercive in character, and to join with Muslims as allies in meeting the social, economic, and political challenges of nation-building.—Ed.]

At the invitation of the Prelature of Marawi and Dansalan College, we are a gathering of twenty-six Christians from the Roman Catholic and several Protestant Churches who are concerned about and involved in the "why" of the Christian presence in the midst of Muslim Filipinos. We do not speak as official representatives of our denominations, but we do speak as Christians who feel a call from God to live as disciples of the Lord Jesus by a life of faith and hope among our Muslim brothers. We seek with them a solution to the prejudice, hatred, and oppression which have for so long marked the relations between Christians and Muslims in this land.

PART ONE (ADDRESSED TO MUSLIMS)

We ask of you, our Muslim brothers, that our presence among you will be welcomed. We are humbled by much that has marked our past

From *Occasional Bulletin of Missionary Research,* III, 1 (January 1979), p. 31. Reprinted by permission.

history and we ask your forgiveness for our large share of the blame for the tragic past. Now we wish to come with nothing but ourselves—stripped of pretensions and with no ready-made answers to the problems that hinder a fruitful relationship.

We seek a dialogue of life with you. With God's help we sincerely desire to achieve a more comprehensive viewpoint of his plan that includes all of us as brothers. In any genuine dialogue we realize the vulnerability that we place ourselves in—a vulnerability in regard to many ideas about ourselves and you. This dialogue must lead us to abandon entrenched positions and preconceived ideas.

We, like you, wish to come to a greater appreciation of our own religious tradition and to find a greater security in it, yet we believe that we have much to learn, and hope that through opening ourselves to the riches of your tradition we can return to our own enriched.

We see this dialogue of life as including participation and engagement in the struggle against oppression in all its forms in solidarity with you. When any person is oppressed we too are in bondage.

The full flowering of this dialogue of life between our peoples cannot be completed until all persons are truly free to live according to their traditions and conscience.

We believe that God, the Creator, is at work in history. In his providence we share in creating a more just world order—one in which both Muslims and Christians can live truly human lives in solidarity with each other. Despite the incredible difficulties that are the product of sin, we have a hope that cannot be quenched because it is sustained by God the Fashioner and Finisher of history.

May God, the Merciful and Compassionate, bless our efforts and strengthen us to engage in this task, this dialogue of life through which we pray all may be healed and made whole.

PART TWO (ADDRESSED TO CHRISTIANS)

To you, our fellow Christians, we wish to point out that the history of this region where we are at work—Mindanao and Sulu—and the prevailing atmosphere in Christian-Muslim relations here, press us to weigh carefully the implications of our presence among our Muslim brothers. From a Christian perspective a dialogue of life implies at least the following:

Christians need to take seriously and treat respectfully the Islamic religion and culture of Filipino Muslims. We need to understand and celebrate the fact that the Philippines is a multifaceted and plural society religiously and culturally rich in its diversity.

Christians repudiate any form of witness or mission which is coercive in character or which deliberately attempts to exploit conditions of poverty, disease, or disaster so as to lure Muslims away from their faith and into the Christian religion.

Christians must repudiate the role of arrogant proselytizers. The "crusading mentality" and all methods of mass evangelism are offensive and threatening to our Muslim brothers. We should be among Muslims as friends and fellow citizens, not as rivals, but as Christians attempting to witness to our faith and to the best in our religion.

Christians join Muslims as allies in meeting the social, economic, and political challenges of nation-building, including the struggle against oppression in all its forms. We must be sensitive to the rights of Muslims to a just share in the natural resources of the whole country and especially of their traditional homeland.

Christians ought to listen attentively to the Muslims' own articulation of their grievances and encourage serious consideration of the suggestions they themselves offer as solutions to their problems.

Christians should insist that government officials at all levels deal with Muslim citizens tactfully and justly.

Christians should insist that the educational system and the media, both public and private, foster positive and respectful attitudes toward Muslim Filipino history, religion, and culture.

Christians ought to regard any injury done to Muslims as an injury done to ourselves and feel that any conditions of injustice or oppression brought about by Christians in relation to Muslims morally diminishes the whole Christian population of the nation.

Christians of different churches will express solidarity in the dialogue of life among Muslims. "Going it alone" may be necessary at times but it is not desirable.

Bibliographies and Journals
on Asian Theology

BIBLIOGRAPHIES

Anderson, Gerald H. (ed.). *Christianity in Southeast Asia: A Bibliographical Guide.* New York: Missionary Research Library, 1966.

Anderson, G. H.; Apilado, M. C.; and Elwood, D. J. (eds.). "A Selected Bibliography in Western Languages," appended to *Asian Voices in Christian Theology,* ed. by G. H. Anderson (Orbis Books, 1976).

"Annotated List of Periodicals Concerned with the Vocation, Role and Function of Christianity in Africa, Asia and Latin America," *Exchange* (Leiden), No. 1 (1972), pp. 1–24.

Baago, Kaj (ed.). *Library of Indian Christian Theology: A Bibliography.* Madras: CLS, 1969. Includes most of what Indians have produced in Christian theology, but omits some important Western contributions to the indigenization of Indian Christian theology.

Balchand, Asandas. *The Salvific Value of Non-Christian Religions According to Asian Christian Theologians Writing in Asian-published Theological Journals, 1965–70.* Manila: East Asian Pastoral Institute, 1973. Reprinted in *Teaching All Nations* (Manila), X, 1 and 2 (1973), pp. 10–37, 115–152.

Callewaert, Winand M. "The Hindu-Christian Dialogue: A Bibliography," *Journal of Dharma* (Bangalore), IV, 2 (April–June 1979), pp. 186–211.

Chao, Jonathan Tien-en. "Chinese Theological Development: A Selected Bibliography," *Reformed Bulletin of Missions* (Philadelphia), III, 5 (1968). Reprinted in *Occasional Bulletin of Missionary Research,* XX, 6 (July–Aug. 1969), pp. 1–14.

Elwood, Douglas J. (ed.). "A Selected Bibliography in Western Languages, Classified and Annotated," appended to *What Asian Christians Are Thinking,* ed. by D. J. Elwood (Manila: New Day Publishers, 1978).

Henkel, Willi. "Theologische Zeitschriften in Afrika, Asien und Australien," *Neue Zeitschrift für Missionswissenschaft,* XXVIII, 2 (1972), pp. 139–143.

Kumazawa, Yoshinobu, and Amagai, Yukimaro. "Selected Bibliography of Christology in Japan," *Northeast Asia Journal of Theology,* No. 2 (1969), pp. 117–134. Sources listed are in Japanese only.

Rye, Tongshik (ed.). *A Bibliography on Family and Religion in Korea* (1945–1970). Tokyo: Centre for East Asian Cultural Studies, 1972. Emphasizes the 1960's. Includes a six-page section on "Christianity" which contains many articles on theological themes and issues.

Spindler, Marc R. "Indian Christian Periodicals: The Daily Life of Indian Theology," *Exchange*, No. 20 (1978), pp. 1–53. Includes a historical review since 1947, with analyses of eight major periodicals, a list of Indian Catholic periodicals, and a bibliographical guide to Indian periodical literature.

Thomson, Alan. "Theological Publications in Indonesia: A Bibliography," *Southeast Asia Journal of Theology*, XV, 1 (1973), pp. 113–116. Sources listed are in Indonesian only.

Yanagita, Tomonobu. *Japan Christian Literature Review*. Sendai: Seisho Tosho Kankokai, 1958. Supplement, 1960.

JOURNALS

Al-Mushir (The Counselor). Theological Journal of the Christian Study Centre, 126-B Murree Road, Rawalpindi, Pakistan. Quarterly.

Asia Theological News. Asia Theological Association, P.O. Box 73-119 Shihlin Chung Cheng, Taipei, Taiwan, ROC 111. Bimonthly.

Bangalore Theological Forum. United Theological College, 17 Miller's Road, Bangalore 560 006, India. Semiannually.

Bulletin of Christian Institutes of Islamic Studies. Henry Martyn Institute, P.O. Box 153, Hyderabad, A. P., India. A continuation of *Al-Basheer*. Quarterly.

Bulletin of Satyodaya Centre for Social Research and Encounter. Paul Caspersz, S.J., Editor, Kandy, Sri Lanka. Monthly.

Ching Feng. Quarterly Notes on Christianity and Chinese Religion and Culture. Christian Study Centre on Chinese Religion and Culture, Tao Fong Shan, Shatin, New Territories, Hong Kong. Quarterly.

Dialogue. Ecumenical Institute for Study and Dialogue, 490/5 Havelock Road, Colombo 6, Sri Lanka. Three issues annually.

East Asian Pastoral Review. East Asian Pastoral Institute, P.O. Box 1815, Manila, Philippines. Continuation of *Teaching All Nations* and *Good Tidings*, combined. Quarterly.

Evangelical Thrust. Published by the Philippine Council of Evangelical Churches, Manila. Monthly.

Exchange. Bulletin of Third World Christian Literature. Interuniversity Institute for Missiological and Ecumenical Research, Boerhaavelaan 43, Leiden, Netherlands. Three issues annually.

Indian Church History Review. The Church History Association of India, Wesley Press, P.O. Box 37, Mysore City, India. Semiannually.

Indian Journal of Theology. Bishop's College, 224 Acharya Jagadish Bose Road, Calcutta 700 017, India. Quarterly.

Indian Missiological Review. Sacred Heart Theological College, Shillong, 793 008, India. Quarterly.

Indian Theological Studies. St. Peter's Seminary, Malleswaram West P.O., Bangalore 560 055, India. A continuation of *Indian Ecclesiastical Studies.* Quarterly.

Japan Christian Quarterly. Christian Literature Society (Kyo Bun Kwan), 4-5-1 Ginza, Chuo-ku, Tokyo, Japan. Quarterly.

Japan Missionary Bulletin. Oriens Institute for Religious Research, 28-5 Marsubara 2 chome, Setagayaku, Tokyo, Japan. Eleven issues annually.

Japanese Religions. NCC Center for the Study of Japanese Religions, c/o Kyoto Diocese of Japan Episcopal Church, 602, Karasuma-Shimotachiuri, Kamikyo-ku, Kyoto, Japan. Seminannually.

Jeevadhara. Theology Centre, Kottayam, 686 017, Kerala, India. Bimonthly.

Journal of Dharma. An International Quarterly of World Religions. Dharma Research Association, Centre for the Study of World Religions, Dharmaram College, Bangalore 560 029, India. Quarterly.

Korean Religions. Institute for Ecumenical and Inter-Religious Studies, International P.O. Box 3251, Seoul, Korea. Occasionally.

Logos. A Journal of Christian Thinking in Asia. Aquinas University College, Colombo 8, Sri Lanka. Quarterly.

National Christian Council Review. Wesley Press, P.O. Box 37, Mysore City, India. Monthly.

Northeast Asia Journal of Theology. Northeast Asia Association of Theological Schools, c/o Japan Lutheran Theological College, 3-10-20, Osawa, Mitakashi, Tokyo 181, Japan. Semiannually.

Philippine Priests' Forum. P.O. Box SM-419, Sta. Mesa, Manila, Philippines. Quarterly.

Philippine Studies. Ateneo de Manila University, P.O. Box 154, Manila, Philippines. Quarterly.

Philippiniana Sacra. University of Santo Tomas, P.O. Box 2806, Manila, Philippines. Quarterly.

Religion and Society. Christian Institute for the Study of Religion and Society, 17 Miller's Road, P.O. Box 4600, Bangalore 560 046, India. Quarterly.

Religious and Social Issues. Bulletin of the Christian Institute for the Study of Religion and Society. Ashram, Chunnakam, Sri Lanka. Semiannually.

Silliman Journal. Silliman Iniversity, Dumaguete City, Philippines. Quarterly.

Southeast Asia Journal of Theology. Association of Theological Schools in Southeast Asia, P.O. Box 841, Manila, Philippines. Semiannually.

Taiwan Journal of Theology. Taiwan Theological College, 20 Lane 2, Sec. 2, Yang Tel Ta Road, Shihlin, Taipei, Taiwan.

Theology and the Church. Tainan Theological College, 115 Tung Men Road, Tainan, Taiwan. Quarterly.

TRACI/ETS Journal. Journal of the Evangelical Theological Society and the Theological Research and Communication Institute, E-537, Greater Kailash 11, New Delhi 110 148, India. Three issues annually.

Vidyajyoti. Journal of Theological Reflection. Institute of Religious Studies, 23 Raj Niwas Marg, Delhi 110 154, India. A continuation of *Clergy Monthly.* Monthly.

Voices of the Third World. Published by the Ecumenical Association of Third World Theologians, 475 Riverside Drive, New York, N.Y. 10115. Semiannually.

Word and Worship. National Biblical, Catechetical and Liturgical Centre, Post Bag No. 577, Bangalore 560 005, India. Monthly.

Index